THE CIVILIZATION OF THE AMERICAN INDIAN SERIES
(*Complete List on Page 368*)

The Arapahoes, Our People

THE ARAPAHOES,
OUR PEOPLE

By *Virginia Cole Trenholm*

UNIVERSITY OF OKLAHOMA PRESS
Norman

By Virginia Cole Trenholm

Footprints on the Frontier (Douglas, Wyoming, 1945)
Wyoming Pageant (Casper, Wyoming, 1946) (with Maurine
   Carley)
The Shoshonis: Sentinels of the Rockies (Norman, 1964) (with
   Maurine Carley)
The Arapahoes, Our People (Norman, 1970)

International Standard Book Number: 0–8061–0908–4

Library of Congress Catalog Card Number: 76–108799

Copyright 1970 by the University of Oklahoma Press, Publishing
Division of the University. Composed and printed at Norman, Oklahoma, U.S.A., by the University of Oklahoma Press. First edition.

Preface

INVITATION SONG

My people, come and join us
On this road that we're traveling.
It is good, and it is a happy place
Where our Father is.

—May Whiteshirt James

AFTER SINGING her composition in the soft tongue of the Arapahoes, May James began to pray. As I sat listening—there at Swapping Back Mission, deep in Arapaho country near Geary, Oklahoma—the expression *Our People* (*Inuñaina*) began to penetrate my consciousness. Over and over I had heard it, but never had it been more forcibly impressed upon me than when my fullblood Arapaho friend prayed for my safe return to Wyoming so that I might write the history of her people. As the only outsider, I was not one of their number, but I was so impressed by their cordiality, their depth of feeling, and their love of music that I could not consider myself alien.

As we were returning to Geary, May asked, "What will you name your book?" Frankly, I did not know, for at that stage I had only a working title, *The Arapahoes*, which was certainly unimaginative for Indians with such a rich heritage. While I hesitated, I could feel her eagerness. She had given much in the way of time and patience, and she was entitled to an answer. Suddenly a thought occurred to me. Besides giving me her song and her prayer, May had given me a title. "I believe," I told her, "I'll call it *The Arapahoes, Our People*. She smiled in satisfaction.

vii

On my return I found awaiting me a perceptive letter from a friend who had worked among the Northern Arapahoes at Wind River and who was in a position to advise. She warned of a general lack of historical perspective, which has contributed to the Arapaho mystery that has deepened with the years. "Fact and legend," she said, "are inextricable in many intelligent Arapaho minds." She illustrated this by saying that an Arapaho told her in all seriousness that members of the large Friday family are all descendants of the famous Friday—"you know, the one who was Robinson Crusoe's assistant." She went on to explain another problem: the subordination of fact to pride. Old-timers talk of the past in very personal terms, with no over-all view. Each emphasizes the wonderful contributions of his own grandfather, and "history" is distorted according to whose grandchild has talked to the historian.

Her analysis is understandable in view of the absence of a clear-cut record of events, such as the Kiowa Calendar. The Arapahoes have had to depend on the conflicting tales of their elders for their legendary history. In order to bring persons and events into proper focus, it is therefore necessary to follow some sort of historical outline, at the risk of sacrificing the Indian point of view. Prehistory is conjecture, but documentary accounts are not always infallible. Untrustworthy as they sometimes may be, we must depend upon them for our source material. Through the eyes of the trader, the traveler, the settler, the soldier, and the Indian agent, we have a series of pictures which reveal Our People, not as they are today, but as they were when the journals were written.

No more typical Plains Indians can be found than the Arapahoes, who were among the earliest arrivals on the Northern Plains. Our People have the distinction of occupying the Northern, Central, and Southern Plains simultaneously. Unlike their allies, the bands on the Central and Southern Plains were generally friendly toward the white man, but they fought fiercely when forced into open warfare upon two occasions, the Battle of Tongue River and the Bates Battle, both of which were waged by them alone and were defensive in character. In depredations and Indian warfare, they were conformists, taking their place at the side of their long-standing allies, the Cheyennes and Sioux. Their history is not one of battles, but of a people living in turbulent times.

The Northern Arapaho elders, jealous in their guardianship of the secrets of the past, gently but convincingly let it be known that the white man should not "go too far" in his attempt to learn that which does not concern him. Can one blame them for their caution? With characteristic good humor, one of the council members commented one day when he picked up a sprig of parsley on his plate: "Ugh! White man take all we got—even take our carrot and leave us the top."

A Southern Cheyenne woman, praying at the Northern Arapaho Sun Dance at Ethete, Wyoming, in 1966, said in essence, "We have so little left!" Her remark applies more to the Southern bands than to the Northern, for the Cheyennes and Arapahoes of Oklahoma have lost their ceremonials as well as their reservation. Since the important Dorsey, Mooney, and Kroeber cultural studies were published around the turn of the century, at a time when the government was suppressing the old ways, some of the elders have attributed their loss to the publicity surrounding these studies. Naturally they are reluctant to talk and are ever apprehensive of being quoted.

While studying Arapaho child life, Sister Inez Hilger found, as I did, that the elders do not wish to speak of their religion. "We do not think it should be talked about so carelessly" is their way of saying they think it is too sacred to be discussed. They object particularly to being questioned about Flat-Pipe or about the Rabbit-Lodge, where the preliminary ceremony takes place before the actual three-day ritual of the Sun Dance begins. We respect their reticence and hope their ceremonial secrets may be kept inviolate.

When the Wind River Arapahoes realized that I was not there to pry into the secrets of their age-old order, the Sun Dance, or write derisively about the Peyote Cult, they showed me every consideration. I am grateful to Adam Shakespeare, keeper of the Flat-Pipe, and Benny Goggles, keeper of the sacred Wheel and chairman of the Sun Dance Committee. I gave my copy of John G. Carter's "The Northern Arapaho Flat Pipe and the Ceremony of Covering the Pipe" to Shakespeare, who did not have one. Later I questioned him about Carter, who is the only white man ever permitted by the Arapahoes to speak and write about the sacred ceremony. While he agreed with what Carter had to say, he opposed my attending a ceremony, "since it has already been recorded." Besides, he and other elders feared the risk of permitting me, a non-Arapaho, to see the sacred object. They were afraid "for" me as well as "for" themselves, as certain misfortunes had followed the previous showing of the Pipe to a white man. Like James Mooney, who was also refused, I had hoped that friendships might pave the way, but I had to abide by the elders' decision.

Others besides Adam Shakespeare and Benny Goggles who contributed significantly to this study were Nickerson Shakespeare, a highly respected elder; Mike Goggles, who, though old and blind, was remarkably clear; Jake Whiteplume, another respected elder; Scott Dewey, at the time chairman of the council; William Shakespeare, who has assisted in several linguistic studies; Gabriel Warren, who exhorts the Sun Dancers when they become tired; Ben Friday, Sr., great-grandson of Chief Friday; Arnold Headley, a council member who is doing a fine job of recording tribal symbols and interviewing some of the very old Indians, whose tales he is tape-recording in Arapaho; and Peyote Men Ralph G. Hopper, Tom C. Hair, Nickerson Quiver, Tom Shakespeare, and Abraham Spotted Elk. Through the efforts of Ralph Hopper, I was permitted to attend a cult meeting during which I was able to observe the Arapaho Way in which the ritual was conducted. The Kiowa and Comanche ways are also used at Wind River.

The Northern Arapaho women who proved most helpful in this endeavor were Nellie Scott, who has served on the tribal council more than twenty-five years; Minnie Antelope, who at the time of her death was the oldest member of her tribe; Elizabeth Little Owl Friday, granddaughter-in-law of Chief Friday; Cecelia

Friday, her daughter; Amy Willow, granddaughter of Chief Medicine Man; and Mrs. Arnold Headley, her daughter. Many others contributed in various ways.

On my first trip to the Cheyenne-Arapaho country of Oklahoma, I was met by Eugene Woolworth, a council member who the following year was made chief at a powwow at Colony, Oklahoma. Our meeting was prearranged at the agency in Concho. Woolworth led the way to Geary, where I was welcomed by Mr. and Mrs. R. L. McElhaney. Mrs. McElhaney (Iolita, a fullblood Kiowa), with the help of several Arapaho friends, had graciously prepared a dinner in my honor. Next to me at the table sat May Whiteshirt James, who became my scout, companion, and warm friend in the days ahead and on my second trip in the fall. While we drove around the countryside locating members of the tribe, May, who is reticent in a crowd, tried to acquaint me with the language and customs of her people.

Other Arapahoes in Oklahoma who proved helpful were Gus Yellow Hair of Geary, great-grandson of Chief Little Raven, his wife, Mary, and his mother, Mrs. Old Bear, a granddaughter of the Chief; James V. Fire of Watonga, a grandson of Chief Sharp Nose of the Northern Arapahoes; and Theodore Pratte of Geary, who, with Yellow Hair, is still able to recount tribal legends told by Ute, the last great narrator. Pratte and Yellow Hair took care of him in his declining days.

The late Morgan Otis, then of Lawton, Oklahoma, a Kiowa-Apache descendant of a member of Custer's Seventh Cavalry, furnished a tape recorder and arranged my first long interview with Jesse Rowlodge, son of Chief Row-of-Lodges, whom we found at that time at Colony. Rowlodge, who has helped in several ethnological studies, went over my notes on Arapaho culture with me and amplified some of the material.

In Oklahoma, where integration and acculturation are pronounced, the Arapahoes are more curious about their history than are their fellow tribesmen at Wind River. When I held open interviews with some of the elders at the Baptist mission at Geary, about thirty members of the tribe turned out on consecutive nights to hear what was said and to take part in round-table discussions, with some coming from as far away as Oklahoma City.

A generation ago, children were pinched so that they would stay awake and listen to the long, tiresome stories recounted by the elders. Today, in this fast-moving atomic age, they depend upon schools instead of tribal narrators for their knowledge. Milo Petska, who worked among the youth at Wind River several years, believes that the young people on the Wyoming reservation are at the crossroads, as he put it, ready to learn of the role their tribe has played in the history of events. He even suggests the possibility of teaching tribal history in the reservation schools. Perhaps this volume will help in accomplishing this objective.

I have sought to tell the story of Our People by relating them and their way of life to the world about them. Their single path following the buffalo has branched into many roads leading in many directions; the Bison Path People of yesterday have become Our People of today. Throughout, they have miraculously retained their identity.

It would be impossible to name all of those who helped during the time I was engaged in research for this project, but there are some to whom I am especially indebted. Regina Flannery, professor of Anthropology, Catholic University of America, and John C. Ewers, Department of Anthropology, Bureau of American Ethnology, Smithsonian Institution, gave wise counsel and pointed the way to source material which contributed toward a solution of the Atsina–Gros Ventre–Arapaho puzzle.

Sister Inez Hilger of Tokyo, Japan; Professor Donald Berthrong, University of Oklahoma; Professor D. B. Shimkin, University of Illinois; and Miss Genevieve Seger of Geary, Oklahoma, offered suggestions and encouragement. Ruth Underhill, professor of Anthropology, University of Denver; Miss Alice Marriott and Miss Carol Rachlin of the Southwest Research Associates, Oklahoma City; and Professor Omer C. Stewart of the University of Colorado, kindly furnished materials not otherwise available.

For their patience and unselfish assistance while I was working in their departments, I want to thank Mrs. Leone Harrington, Missouri Historical Society, St. Louis; Robert Kvasnicka, Indian Office Records Division, National Archives, Washington, D.C.; Mrs. Rella Looney, Indian Archives Division, Oklahoma Historical Society, Oklahoma City; Mrs. Alice Timmons and Jack Haley, University of Oklahoma Library, Norman; Mrs. Laura Ekstrom, Colorado Historical Society Library, Denver; Mrs. Katherine Halverson, Wyoming State Archives and Historical Department, Cheyenne; Mrs. Gwen Rice, Wyoming State Library, Cheyenne; and Gene Gressley, director, Western Research Center, University of Wyoming, Laramie.

I would like further to acknowledge the help given me by the Denver Public Library; the Colorado Division of State Archives and Public Records, Denver: the University of Colorado Libraries, Boulder; the Kansas State Historical Library, Topeka; the Bethel College History Department, North Newton, Kansas; and the Pioneer Museum, Colorado Springs, Colorado.

I wish to express my gratitude to Neal E. Miller, director of the Wyoming State Archives and Historical Department, for procuring National Archives microfilm pertaining to the Arapahoes, and to Mrs. Viola McNealy, of his department, for making the original map showing the location of their reservations.

For their many kindnesses, I wish also to thank Agent Paul Vance, of the Cheyenne and Arapaho Agency, Concho, Oklahoma; Agent Clyde W. Hobbs, of the Wind River Indian Agency, Fort Washakie; the Rev. and Mrs. Fred Smyithe, St. Michael's (Episcopal) Mission; Father Jerome Zumach, St. Stephen's (Catholic) Mission; and Mr. and Mrs. Burrell Nickeson, who live near Ethete, Wyoming, and whose long friendship with their Arapaho neighbors aided in my own acceptance by members of the tribe.

Virginia Cole Trenholm

Cheyenne, Wyoming
July 9, 1970

Contents

Illustrations

xvii

Illustrations

Map

The Arapahoes, Our People

CHAPTER ONE

Bison Path People

Dᴜʀɪɴɢ ᴡɪɴᴛᴇʀ sᴛᴏʀʏᴛᴇʟʟɪɴɢ time, Arapaho tribal narrators still recount tales of bygone days when war was considered an act of valor and the prairies were black with buffalo, but rarely do they speak of the woodland people with whom their forefathers mingled before coming to the plains. Time has severed the link between the Arapahoes and the related tribes to the east, the Algonquians who lived in dome-shaped wigwams and traveled the still waters in birchbark canoes. Yet they were of the same linguistic family, sharing their traditions and recognizing a superior power, Manibus (Manito), more generally known to the Arapahoes as Man-Above. Whether in the woodlands or on the plains, they were contemplative and devout, with a depth of feeling uncommon even among Indians who are inherently religious.

Only select tribesmen are privileged to tell the official version of the creation myth, and those permitted to listen must undergo a three-day fast in order to hear it in its entirety.[1] From fragmentary accounts we find that in the long ago there was nothing but water, on which an Arapaho and his sacred Flat-Pipe (*Seicha*) were floating. He was crying in loneliness and distress until several ducks flew to his rescue. Flat-Pipe (Earthmaker or the Creator) commanded the ducks to dive to the bottom of the water and bring up dry land, but all attempts failed. Finally a turtle succeeded in obtaining from the depths the clay with which *Seicha* made the world and every living creature.

[1] George A. Dorsey and Alfred L. Kroeber, *Traditions of the Arapaho*, 1–7; William Philo Clark, *The Indian Sign Language*, 42–43. Many versions of the Arapaho creation have been published. For one given by Sherman Coolidge (E-tus-che-wa-ah), see Robert C. Morris, "Wyoming Indians," Wyoming Historical Society *Collections*, I (1897), 82–93.

In the process he first made the Arapahoes, then the other Indians. Afterwards he fashioned the white man "beyond the waters." Finally the original man, who was also a god, gave the sacred Pipe to his kinsmen, the chosen people. Since his head and his heart were good, he urged the surrounding tribes to live in peace. The Indians who were not among his people were destitute when they came to him, but he gave them "prairie gifts" and skin lodges. The legend further states that the Arapahoes never let their hearts get tired of giving; then all of the other tribes loved them. On the contrary, they were confronted by hostiles before the arrival of the white man, or the European as they prefer to call him, and their migration to the plains may have resulted from enemy pressure.

The Arapahoes are a handsome people, their fullblood men tall, gaunt, and muscular, usually about five feet, eight inches to six feet in height, the women shorter by about six inches. They are lighter complexioned than their Shoshonean adversaries—the Shoshonis, Utes, and Comanches—and although they sometimes tend to add flesh as they grow older, they are seldom obese. Because of their prominent Roman nose, they were known to the Osages as Big Nose People.

In historic times they have had many names, perhaps the earliest known being the old Algonquian designation *Bison Path People* (Buffalo Indians), or *Kananavich*, variously spelled.[2] Of the five known divisions, only two are extant, the Gros Ventres (Hitounena) and the Arapaho proper (Hinanaeina). The latter are made up of the Northern and Southern bands, whose dialects are so similar that there is little perceptible difference. Tentatively separated in the 1830's and more permanently divided during the reservation period, they have nevertheless maintained a close relationship. In late years, since the invention of the automobile, mo-

[2] For other names, see James Mooney, "Arapaho," in Frederick Webb Hodge (ed.), *Handbook of American Indians North of Mexico*, Bureau of American Ethnology (cited hereafter as BAE) *Bulletin* 30, I, 72; Alfred L. Kroeber, "Arapaho Dialects," *Publications in American Archaeology and Ethnology*, XII, 3 (1916), 73–74; Hugh L. Scott, "The Early History and Names of the Arapaho," *American Anthropologist* (cited hereafter as *AA*), N.S., IX (1907), 558.

bility has increased, and it is common for the Northerners to enjoy prolonged visits with their kinsmen to the south during the winter, while the Southerners go north in the summer to take part in ceremonial observances.

Flat-Pipe, which is in the possession of the Northern bands, has tended to preserve unity among the Arapaho proper. On the other hand, the Gros Ventres, with their own tribal fetish, have become independent culturally. There has been little intercourse between the two major divisions of the Arapaho nation in recent years. The Gros Ventres, as we shall see, were significant for a time on the Northern Plains, but as the Arapaho proper emerged to assume an independent role, the former faded from the historic scene.

Remnants of three obsolete tribes, whose history is too vague for reconstruction but whose dialects have lingered sufficiently for linguistic studies, are still to be found among the Arapaho proper. In translated form, they are the Woodlodge People, the Rock People, and the South People (not to be confused with the Southern Arapahoes). The Woodlodge People (Basawaunina) were by far the most important, for to them is attributed the Flat-Pipe. A related people who joined the Gros Ventres on the Canadian Plains before the arrival of the first white men, their descendants are still distinguishable in the ranks of the Northern Arapahoes. It is a genealogical requirement that the keeper of Flat-Pipe be able to trace his descent through this line.

The sign of the Arapaho, which is made by tapping the breast with the tips of the fingers several times, is interpreted by the Blackfeet and Crows as meaning "Tattooed Breasts" (Tattooed People), since it was the custom to tattoo three symbols on the breast: one to the right, one to the left, and one between. This was done by scratching the skin with yucca needles, then rubbing wood ashes into the wound to make an indelible bluish symbol. The Northern bands, who consider themselves the mother tribe inasmuch as they have the Flat-Pipe, tap their left breast only—to indicate "Good Hearts" or "Mother People." The Southerners, who refer to the Northern bands as Sagebrush Men, explain their own sign, made by placing the right forefinger alongside the nose, as pointing to their parting row, which represents the path to the sun. It caused them to be called, erroneously, Rubbed Nose Indians.

Richard F. Burton, an early traveler and writer, was contemptuous of those whom he encountered in 1862 on his way to Salt Lake. He made this derogatory statement regarding the sign last mentioned: "The Arapahos, or Dirty Noses, rub the right side of that organ with the forefinger; some call this bad tribe the Smellers, and make their sign to consist of seizing the nose with the thumb and forefinger."[3] Burton, with his superficial knowledge of aboriginal culture, was so repulsed that he painted a most unsympathetic (as well as unrealistic) picture of the tribe. He had not been with them long enough to judge, yet he seems to have had a wide following, for his impressions are reflected in accounts by contemporaries who did not bother to credit their source.

Linguists who have made repeated studies of the Arapaho language have shown that Burton was also in error when he said these Indians had such a scanty vocabulary, "pronounced in a quasi-unintelligible way," that they could hardly converse with one another in the dark. Furthermore, he affirmed that in order to make a stranger understand them, they had always "to repair to the campfire for pow-wow." He was unaware of the importance of "the smoke." No council was complete without its formality, for the smoke from the campfire, as well as from the pipe, conveyed their prayers to Man-Above and helped seal the most solemn agreement. The campfire was thus the nucleus of the council chamber.

In disposition the Arapahoes are far from the stoic Indians of the plains. They have a keen sense of humor and are great practical jokers. Even in time of frustration or adversity they can manage to laugh. Then, too, they are highly imaginative, and their tales revolving around their cultural heroes have made a definite

---

[3] Richard F. Burton, *The City of Saints*, 136. John G. Bourke, in "Mackenzie's Last Fight with the Cheyennes," *Recruiting News*, 213, says he was "not ignorant enough to give the slightest credit to the sensational story set afloat by Burton."

contribution to the literature of the West. Their cycle stories, the most popular of which relate the escapades of Found-in-Grass and Blood-Clot-Boy, have been told the length of the plains, from the Gros Ventres in Canada to the Southern Arapahoes in western Oklahoma.[4]

Found-in-Grass is important because he is believed to have caused the buffalo to come forth from a hole in the ground. And yet the Arapahoes attribute their culture to three "hard thinking" but unnamed heroes. The first, after days of fasting and prayer, had a vision in which he saw a way of driving buffalo over cliffs to slaughter. In another vision he learned how to corral wild horses by running them into enclosures. After being broken, the horses relieved women and dogs from the drudgery of transporting heavy burdens. Since the Indians had no tools with which to butcher, our hero cut a narrow piece of bone from the shoulder blade of the buffalo, using a sharpened flintstone, then fashioned it into the first knife. Soon everyone knew how to make the sharp-bladed instrument.

The second inventor made the arrow point from a shortrib, then fashioned a bow. Armed with his new weapon, he stationed himself along a buffalo trail. When one of the animals approached, he shot it in a vital spot and it fell dead. After killing three others—four in all, the magic number representing the four cardinal points—he told his people of his discovery. From then on it was no longer necessary to drive animals over bluffs to kill them. Left Hand, a Southern Arapaho head chief, told the story somewhat differently. He claimed that the "very oldest people" used a last rib of a buffalo for a bow and rushes for arrows, with leaves from the elm tree for the heads. The shape of these leaves was afterwards copied in flint, he affirmed.[5]

[4] Alfred L. Kroeber, *The Arapaho*, American Museum of Natural History (cited hereafter as AMNH) *Bulletin 18*, Vol. XIII, Pt. 1 (1902), 22–23. For additional cycle stories of Found-in-Grass and Blood-Clot-Boy, see Alfred L. Kroeber, "Gros Ventre Myths and Tales," AMNH *Anthropological Papers* (cited hereafter as *AP*), I (1907), 82–139. See also John M. Cooper, *The Gros Ventres of Montana, II*, Catholic University of America *Anthropological Series* (1956), 462–87; Dorsey and Kroeber, *Traditions of the Arapaho*, 298–309, 341, 388.

[5] Scott, "Early History," *loc. cit.*, 559.

The third important contributor to Arapaho culture was one who also fasted and prayed several days. In the vision that came to him, he discovered that when struck, certain rocks would cause a spark. After he had demonstrated this wonder to his fellow tribesmen, they found it far better than using a fire drill. Thus Our People explain in general the origin of their culture, one that is typical of the plains.

Of their own origin they are vague. Little Raven, chief before Left Hand, stated in the 1880's that the Arapahoes were an agricultural people before crossing the Missouri.[6] "Before we went hunting so much we lived on what we raised from the ground," he said. "The Arikarees stole the corn and the art of raising it from us." Their history suggests that this might have been an inaccurate recollection of the days when the Arapahoes obtained corn in trade with the Arikaras on the Upper Missouri. Left Hand made no mention of an agricultural life before coming to the plains, but he believed that his people originated beyond the Missouri River. The Gros Ventres, on the other hand, admit to being as one with the Arapahoes in early times, but they say they came from the south, although they do not specify where.

Specialists on the Plains Indians in the fields of ethnology and anthropology express two divergent opinions concerning the origin of the Arapaho nation. For the sake of clarity, let us call one the Mooney Theory, the other the Ancient Occupancy Theory. James Mooney, whose studies are basic with regard to the American Indian, writes:

> According to the tradition of the Arapaho they were once a sedentary agricultural people, living far to the n. e. of their more recent habitat, apparently about the Red r. valley of n. Minnesota. From this point they moved s. w. across the Missouri apparently about the same time that the Cheyennes moved out from Minnesota, although the date of the formation of the permanent alliance between the two tribes is uncertain.[7]

[6] Clark, *The Indian Sign Language*, 13–14.
[7] Mooney, "Arapaho," *loc. cit.*, 72–74. See also John R. Swanton, *The Indian Tribes of North America*, 384–86; Edward S. Curtis, *The North American Indians*, VI, 137–60.

Elsewhere Mooney attributes the tradition to William Philo Clark, the sign-language expert, who made this statement: "Very reliable tradition located this tribe in western Minnesota several hundred years ago, meeting the Cheyennes as they—the Cheyennes—came out on the prairie and for many years moving and camping with or near them so that for all practical purposes they were one people, and the history of one relates very closely to the history of the other."[8]

While it is conceded that the Arapahoes may have lived in the northern Minnesota area before migrating to the plains, material evidence, documentary or otherwise, is lacking to show where they were located or that their route was southwestward. Records show that the Cheyennes were late arrivals, their entrance to the plains taking place in historic times, but no mention is found therein of the Arapahoes. Although the tradition accepted by both Clark and Mooney is historically unsound, Mooney's theory is so readily accessible that there prevails the popular idea that the Arapahoes moved southwestward onto the plains from Minnesota at about the same time as the Cheyennes. On the other hand, there is reason to believe that they were on the Northern Plains generations before the Cheyennes left Minnesota.

From the linguistic angle, Truman Michelson, an able ethnologist, attempted to disprove the Mooney Theory as early as 1912.[9] He divided the Algonquians into four primary groups: the Blackfeet, the Arapahoes, the Cheyennes, and the Eastern-Central groups, comprising all other dialects in the linguistic family. The first three are Plains Indians, the fourth Timber or Woodland Indians. Michelson's comparative study shows that the languages of the Arapahoes and Blackfeet are so distinct from the Eastern-Central Algonquians that neither could have been a recent offshoot from the main stock in the woodland region. Alfred L. Kroeber,

[8] James Mooney, "The Cheyenne Indians," American Anthropological Association *Memoirs*, I (1905–1907), 372; Clark, *The Indian Sign Language*, 39.

[9] Truman Michelson, "Preliminary Report on the Linguistic Classification of Algonquian Tribes," BAE, *Twenty-eighth Annual Report* (1906–1907), 221–90; Scott, "Early History," *loc. cit.*, 545. See also Waldo Wedel, *Prehistoric Man on the Great Plains*, 242; John C. Ewers, *The Blackfeet*, 6.

a leading authority on the Arapahoes (who were the subject of some of his most valuable studies), gave hearty endorsement to Michelson's findings, for he was convinced that the Arapahoes had been separated from the Eastern-Central Algonquians for more than a thousand years.

Soldier-scholar Hugh L. Scott, who was likewise an early exponent of the more plausible Ancient Occupancy Theory, was unable, after careful checking, to discover among the Arapahoes a tradition placing them farther east than the Missouri River. In the scant references to the Cheyennes east of that stream, he could find no mention whatever of the Arapahoes. The explanation is logical. They were not there, for their westward migration had taken place long before. If not a thousand years, it was so remote that they lacked any knowledge of a previous culture.

It is conjectural, but possible, that all of the Arapahoes, while living a semisedentary life before entering the plains, were together in a parent tribe whose name we may never know. The Algonquian designation (Bison Path People) was obviously given to them after their migration. We cannot be sure why they left their habitat to the east, but there were probably several contributory causes. Besides possible pressure from hostile groups, they may have faced the problem of overpopulation, or perhaps they were attracted by the idea of a nomadic life on the plains. It is not even known whether the migration was spontaneous, prolonged, or made intermittently by various bands.

From the archaeological standpoint, a significant attempt has been made, in a series of theoretical maps, to trace the migration of the "Arapaho-Atsina" (Gros Ventres) in prehistoric times.[10] The maps place the tribe astride the Red River of Minnesota, just south of the present Canadian boundary, in A.D. 1100–1300, in the same location in 1400, and slightly to the west in 1600. The first split is indicated before 1700, by which time the westward movement is believed to have expanded via Devil's Lake, across the Couteau du Missouri, to the area around the mouth of the Little

[10] Gordon Hewes, "Early Tribal Migrations in the Northern Great Plains," *Plains Archaeological Conference News Letter*, I, 4 (July 15, 1948).

Missouri River. By 1720–30, the same authority suggests that the Atsinas, after a second split, had moved northeast into Saskatchewan, nearly to the site of Saskatoon, with the Arapahoes possibly moving southward in the middle of the eighteenth century. The approximate date of the first split (before 1700) is consistent with information given to Pierre-Jean de Smet, the Jesuit priest, who was told in 1846 that the division took place 150 years earlier, that is, about 1695. The priest said the Indians gave as the reason a difference between the chiefs.[11]

From the ethnological point of view, there is a composite map, also theoretical, placing the northwesternmost branch of the Algonquians—the Arapahoes and the Blackfeet—on the Northern Plains in 1650.[12] The other three Algonquian-speaking Plains tribes (Cheyennes, Plains Ojibwas, and Plains Crees) were later arrivals. This map shows the Algonquian area extending as an arch in Canada from the northern Minnesota line to northern Montana.

For the most part, the above-mentioned maps agree with the assumption that the Arapahoes were ancient occupants of the Northern Plains, perhaps as early as, if not earlier than, the Blackfeet. Their westward migration occurred so long ago that we are unable to establish their whereabouts upon arrival. Inasmuch as the trek must have been arduous for Indians on foot, we are convinced that once they were on the plains, the Arapahoes did not move great distances before acquiring horses, though in the many years of their residence they undoubtedly penetrated deep into the area.

The Bison Path People were so closely related that no tribal divisions were discernible until the latter part of the eighteenth century. It is doubtful that the earlier separation was either clear cut or complete. The Indians, gregarious by nature, were famous for prolonged alliances with the fractious Blackfeet and later the Cheyennes and Sioux. Would their ties not have been stronger

[11] Pierre-Jean de Smet, *History of Western Missions and Missionaries*, 254, 265 n.

[12] Charles O. Paullin, *Atlas of the Historical Geography of the United States*, Pl. 33, Fig. 81.

with their own people? Judging by the close relationship between the Northern and Southern Arapahoes, who have not been permanently separated by the intervening miles, we propose that the history of the Bison Path People be considered that of a single tribe until documentary evidence proves otherwise.

Kroeber, while recognizing the Arapahoes as ancient occupants of the Northern Plains, believed as late as 1939 that the plains did not have one of the well-developed and characterized cultures of North America until after the acquisition of the horse. "Previous to that," he maintains, "there was no important plains culture, the chief phases in the area being marginal to richer cultures outside."[13] Within the last few years there have come to light facts to suggest that the prehistoric pedestrian on the Northern Plains had a distinct culture and that the horse did not play as important a role as has been thought.[14]

The Bison Path People, as pedestrians or foot Indians, found it necessary to stalk the herds for survival. As their cultural legend claims, their chief method of killing buffalo was to drive them over cliffs. This process, involving ingenious methods, required the combined effort of the entire family. Even though the buffalo and its byproducts provided their basic needs, Our People did not live by meat alone. The Northern Plains provided ample vegetables and wild fruits in season. Foods, as well as herbs for medicinal purposes, were dried and stored away for winter. Transportation was limited to the dog-drawn travois and to the strong backs of women and girls, who served as beasts of burden in moving from one camp to another.

We know so little about the prehistoric Arapahoes that we are unable to point out fundamental differences between their way

[13] Alfred L. Kroeber, *Cultural and Natural Areas of Native North America*, 76.

[14] William Mulloy, "A Preliminary Historical Outline for the Northwestern Plains," *University of Wyoming Publications in Science*, XXIX (July, 1958), 6, 16–21. Present-day authorities seem to think undue emphasis may have been placed on the horse by such scholars as Clark Wissler ("The Influence of the Horse in the Development of Plains Culture," *AA*, n.s., XVI, 1 [1914] 1–25) and Walter Prescott Webb ("The Spread and Use of the Horse Among the Plains Indians," *The Great Plains*, 52–68).

of life and that of the other Northern Plains Indians, if indeed there were differences. All we know is that during the many years of their residence on the Northern Plains they lost all trace of a previous culture with the exception of their religion, for their concept of the Supreme Being is aboriginal.[15] Since no description is given of His appearance and He is not introduced into their folklore in human form, He seems to have been above and beyond their conception of cult beings, even above Earthmaker, the sun, and the moon. The span of years is great between 1613, when Samuel de Champlain, who had joined the Hurons and Algonquians against the Iroquois, visited the Manito of the Cataract (on the upper waters of the Ottawa), and 1846, when adventurer George F. Ruxton visited Manito (Manitou Springs, Colorado).[16] Nevertheless, the Indians showed through their offerings at the latter that they were still strong in their native belief.

The ancient communal rites were undoubtedly different from the present Sun Dance in ritualistic form, but the Indians, while worshiping Manito (Man-Above), recognized the life-giving rays of the sun in their prayers to such an extent that they were considered sun worshipers by the first explorers. Even before the emergence of the Medicine Lodge (or Offerings-Lodge as the Arapahoes call it), the old Algonquian idea of sacrificial gifts to Manito was present. The origin of the Medicine Lodge ceremony (the Sun Dance), with its characteristic center pole, is obscure, but the Arapahoes, having deep religious convictions, were logical leaders in its perfection and distribution. They may even have introduced it among the Cheyennes, as one authority suggests, though the credit is usually given to the Sutaios, whom they absorbed.[17]

As a full-fledged tribal ceremony, the Sun Dance may be as recent as the late 1790's or 1800.[18] With the acquisition of the horse, the migratory Arapahoes, who had customarily visited the cataracts,

[15] Cooper, "Religion and Ritual," *The Gros Ventres of Montana*, II, 1–9.
[16] Francis Parkman, *The Struggle for a Continent*, 109; George F. Ruxton, *Ruxton of the Rockies*, 237.
[17] Leslie Spier, "The Sun Dance of the Plains Indians," AMNH *AP*, Vol. XVI, Pt. 7, 491; Donald J. Berthrong, *The Southern Cheyennes*, 62.
[18] Ruth M. Underhill, *Red Man's Religion*, 142.

sulfurous springs, or other phenomenal works of nature to make their sacrificial offerings to Man-Above, ranged great distances from the general areas in which these were found. Consequently, their Offerings-Lodge took on the form of a house of worship, one which could be erected wherever the tribe wished. Throughout the high plains, materials for the center pole and brush shelter could be found in abundance.

The early separation of the Northern bands from the main division of the Bison Path People took place soon after the first white man came to the Northern Plains. Henry Kelsey, a runaway slave from York Factory, a Hudson's Bay Company post, stayed for a time (in 1691) among the Crees and Assiniboines, who mentioned "a nation that knew not ye use of Canoes and were resolved to go to wars."[19] The reference is too vague for positive identification, but there is a possibility that he was alluding to the Bison Path People.

When the northernmost bands moved into the Saskatchewan area, sometime before 1720, they entered the limelight. History came early to that part of the Northern Plains, where they served as a frontier tribe in their relations with the Canadian fur traders. Theirs was a buffer state between the Blackfeet and their mutual enemies, the allied Crees and Assiniboines, for which the Bison Path People suffered accordingly.

Just when they became allied with the Blackfeet, who called them Atsinas (Entrails People), we are not sure, but a well-preserved Blackfoot legend, attributed to Big Brave of that tribe, indicates that the Atsinas sought sanctuary in the Blackfoot country because of the Assiniboines, who were about to exterminate them.[20] According to his story, they came from the "far down-river country," which might not have been as remote as it seemed to the foot Indians. Big Brave was vague and unsure of his facts—as he revealed when he disclaimed any knowledge of pottery

[19] Henry Kelsey, *The Kelsey Papers*, 13; Arthur Morton, *A History of the Canadian West*, 113.

[20] Big Brave's account was first published in the *Great Falls Tribune*, May 19, 1940, and later appeared as a chapter in James Willard Schultz, *Blackfeet and Buffalo*, 271–81.

making or dishes. "We do not know that our long-ago people made them," he admitted. "We are poor minded; we lose, we forget our past. You whites, how wise you are. You write about the things that you do, and see, and the knowledge of it is always with you." Even so, his story indicates that the alliance between the Gros Ventres and Blackfeet may date back to their original encounter on the plains.

When the first white contacts were made, many of the Atsinas were speaking the Blackfoot language. This so confused the fur traders that they classified them as Blackfeet rather than as a separate nation, an error that was later perpetrated by no less an authority than Thomas Fitzpatrick, the fur trader who became the first resident Indian agent for the Cheyennes and Arapahoes. He stated more accurately that the Arapahoes were Gros Ventres.

Although, to the delight of folklore collectors, Our People have handed down countless legends and myths, their lack of traditional history is disappointing. Like Big Brave, they have forgotten details of the past, and they cannot agree upon such important matters as the cause or the time of the tribal divisions which separate them. The Gros Ventres say the first separation resulted from a quarrel between the head chiefs over the division of a buffalo carcass.[21] This may be true, but doubt is cast upon it because it is the same reason the Hidatsas (Minetares or Gros Ventres of the Missouri) give for separating from the Absarokas (Crows).

Left Hand, whom we previously quoted as saying that the Arapahoes originated north of the Missouri, further stated that the Gros Ventres and Arapahoes became separated by "the breaking up of the ice."[22] He added: "That is the way we left some of our people there." His reference is to the second and only split the Arapahoes recall. The Northerners and Southerners still refer to the Gros Ventres as Our People. In the statement just quoted, Left Hand alludes to a well-known legend which is also discredited because it is told by other Plains tribes. Although its historical significance may be questioned, it should not be ignored, for it is

21 Curtis, *The North American Indians*, V, 103.
22 Clark, *The Indian Sign Language*, 39.

the generally accepted Arapaho explanation for the division at the time of the crossing of the Missouri.

According to the legend, at some unknown time a plague brought terror into the hearts of the people. Fearing that all might die if they remained in the vicinity of the bad spirit, they fled southward until they crossed a sizable stream. There a great tragedy occurred. One-third had crossed, another third was in the act of crossing, and the others were still to the north. As the Indians walked over the ice, which had been weakened by spring thaws, they saw a horn protruding. A child begged his grandmother to cut it off for him. In the Southern Arapaho version, as it is told today, it was a young woman, not a child, who wanted the horn for an awl. As the chopping began, a great monster arose, crushing the ice and drowning all of the people who were crossing. Those who were already on the opposite side (the Arapaho proper) continued southward; those who were not (the Gros Ventres) fled northward. In telling this same tale, a Gros Ventre indicated the event occurred not at the time of the early separation (in the 1600's) but much later, probably a century later.[23]

Tribal divisions were not uncommon in early historic times. We know that other separations took place among the Bison Path People, but we have no record or legend telling where or when they occurred. Undoubtedly the factors which brought about the known divisions were more basic than legendary quarrels or mythical disasters. They may have been fundamentally economic, for there were certain limitations in the Indian economy. As the maximum population that could be managed by a buffalo-hunting tribe was reached, internal frictions arose. In their competitive Plains Indian culture, the Arapahoes, like other tribes, would follow competing leaders who favored a division of the tribe. As the history of the Bison Path People unfolds, we shall observe that there is a certain amount of truth in both legends of separation given here.

[23] Curtis, *The North American Indians*, V, 103.
[24] Alexander Henry used the term *Slave Indians* to include the Blackfeet, Bloods, and Piegans.

In prehistoric times, the Bison Path People were among a number of Plains tribes known to their enemies by the Cree term *Archithinue*, variously spelled in early records.[24] As a general term meaning "stranger" or "alien," as well as "enemy," it was applied to both the Bison Path People and their friends and foes.

To the British at Hudson Bay, the Indians of the Northern Plains, with the exception of the Crees and Assiniboines who served as their guides, were all "Strangers." In 1743, James Isham, one of the early traders, expressed a desire to have the "Earchthinue" come to the bay with their furs. He had seen a "Slave" who had given him an account of the land of her people. She had led him to believe they lived in a country with "a fine Navigable River that op'ns into the sea, and with great plenty of the best and finest fur's, which is their Chiefest Commodity's."[25]

The Bison Path People, who came into history as Strangers, were given still another general designation by the French-Canadians: *Gens de Vache* (Cow or Buffalo People). Unfortunately, the Vérendryes, the most famous of the explorers who repeatedly but unsuccessfully attempted to find a route to the Western Sea, were not that discriminating. Their records of Indians they encountered are so vague that few can be identified.[26] Nevertheless, one is impressed by the way in which the *Gens du Serpents* (the northernmost bands of the Snakes or Shoshonis) were terrifying the countryside, for, according to Little Raven, it was in a daring raid on one of their camps that the Arapahoes obtained their first horses.[27]

Legardeur de Saint-Pierre, the Vérendryes' successor, was the last of the French explorers to attempt to find an outlet to the sea. While wintering at Fort de La Rayne on the Assiniboine River in 1751, he meditated upon the state of affairs in the area.[28] He feared

[25] James Isham, *James Isham's Observations on Hudson's Bay*, 113. Judging by the context, the word should not have been capitalized, since the woman was probably a captive from a Columbia River tribe.

[26] Chevalier de La Vérendrye, "Journal of the Voyage Made by Chevalier de La Vérendrye with One of His Brothers in Search of the Western Sea," in "Margry Papers," *Oregon Historical Quarterly*, XXVI, 2 (June, 1925), 116–27.

[27] Clark, *The Indian Sign Language*, 40.

[28] Jacque Le Legardeur de Saint-Pierre, "Memoire ou Journal du Voyage," in *Margry Papers*, VI, 640.

the hostiles—the Blackfeet, Sarsis, and Gros Ventres—might prevent the accomplishment of his plans. This is the first direct mention we can find of the historic name *Gros Ventre*, which was to identify a tribal division as well as the nation to which it belonged. Although the identity of the Indians mentioned by Saint-Pierre is clear, the French caused endless confusion by applying the same name—that is, Gros Ventre—to the unrelated Hidatsas (Minetares), who were of Siouan Crow stock. Historians have tried to simplify matters by labeling one the Gros Ventres of the Prairie (sometimes Plains) and the other the Gros Ventres of the Missouri. Anthropologists prefer to call the former, the Gros Ventres of our study, the Atsinas or Montana Gros Ventres, since they were eventually located with the Assiniboines on the Fort Belknap Reservation in northern Montana.[29]

Officials of the Hudson's Bay Company attempted to counteract French influence by sending their representative, Anthony Hendry, to the Gros Ventre–Blackfoot country in 1754.[30] Even though Hendry did not identify the Indians he met, we are convinced they were Gros Ventres, for that tribe would have been in the direct line of his journey. He failed in his mission; the chief was indifferent to his proposal that the Indians shift their trade to his company from the French. The idea did not sound feasible because Hudson Bay was "far off, and they could not paddle," a statement reminiscent of Kelsey's "nation that knew not ye use of Canoes."

The Indians who evinced no interest in Hendry's proposal seemed well satisfied with existing conditions. Were they not living a life of affluence, with plenty of buffalo? Perhaps they could have caught two hundred beaver a day instead of ten, as Hendry observed, but had he understood their logic, he would have known that they did not need that many. Besides, they preferred to buffalo, for, unlike the Crees, they were by nature

[29] The two-volume study *The Gros Ventres of Montana* (Catholic University of America) is the most comprehensive account since Kroeber's.

[30] Anthony Hendry, "The Journal of Anthony Hendry, 1754–55," Royal Society of Canada *Proceedings and Transactions* (cited hereafter as RSC *PT*), Series 3, No. 1 (1907), 307–54.

hunters, not trappers. They were now equestrian tribesmen whose
dexterity in handling their mounts aroused Hendry's admiration.
Admittedly, he was no horseman, but he delighted in the opportunity to take part in a buffalo hunt.

As early as 1760, some of the Bison Path People, possessing
the horse, may have gone south as far as the Black Hills to join
the Kiowas in fighting their common enemy, the Snakes. We can
but guess that the earliest migrants were the South People, or
South Men, the now extinct tribe which migrated into the Southern Plains at such an early date that one authority surmised they
may have been known to the Spaniards, who came north from
Santa Fé, as Quartelejo Apaches.[31] They were found along the
Arkansas in eastern Colorado and may possibly have been included, erroneously, among the various Padouca (Apache) groups
on early maps. They may also have given rise to the idea proposed
by one historian that the Arapahoes originated in the South.

In 1763 the French gave up their possessions in Canada, but
a number of Montreal traders, with Assiniboine helpers, continued
to control the fur business. In the spring of 1772 the British
again made a bid for the rich trade they hoped to conduct with
the Blackfeet and Gros Ventres. This time they sent Mathew
Cocking, second in command at York Factory, to investigate the
Saskatchewan country.[32] Six months later, he encountered the
Bison Path People. This time there is no question about whom he
meant, for he identified them as "Water-fall Indians," or Fall
Indians, their British name. At the time of Cocking's visit, they
were attempting to impound buffalo. Three years earlier, Hendry
had found "equestrian natives," but Cocking watched as they
drove the animals into enclosures. It should be noted that horses
at this time were far from numerous, and even after they were,
the old method of hunting buffalo was often employed, especially

---

[31] Alfred B. Thomas, "Spanish Expeditions into Colorado," *Colorado Magazine*, I, 7 (November, 1924), 289; N. H. Winchell, *The Aborigines of Minnesota*,
76n.

[32] Mathew Cocking, "Journal of Mathew Cocking from York Factory to
the Blackfoot Country, 1772–73," RSC *PT*, Series 2, Vol. II, Sec. 2 (1908), 103–12.

when the supply of horses had been reduced by raids from enemy tribes.

The pound Cocking describes was circular, "fenced round with trees laid one upon another, at the foot of an Hill about 7 feet high & an hundred yards in Circumference: the entrance on the Hill-side where the Animals can go over; but where it cannot return: From this entrance small sticks are laid on each side like a fence, in form of an angle extending from the Pound; then to about 1½ mile distant Buffalo dung or old roots are laid in Heaps, in the same direction as the fence; These are to frighten the Beasts from deviating from either side."

Cocking spoke well of the *Archithinue*, for he was impressed by their sprightly horses and pack animals that aided the women in transporting their luggage, though the Indians apparently did not have them in sufficient numbers to permit a plains-type surround of a buffalo herd. Cocking also noted that the people were cleaner in food and clothing than his Cree and Assiniboine guides. The equestrian Indians on the Northern Plains at this time included the Blackfeet and Sarsis, as well as the Gros Ventres. All were indebted to their common enemy, the Shoshonis, who brought the first horses to the area. These were obtained from their kinsmen, the Comanches, to the south. Neither the Crees nor the Assiniboines had been sufficiently armed by the traders to start raiding for horses; thus the Gros Ventres and their allies were enjoying a temporary superiority. After spending two weeks with the Indians at the pound, Cocking found they met with little success. Perhaps they were having trouble enough supplying their needs without entering the unknown, for he was unable to induce any of them to accompany him to York Factory.

Cocking made two significant observations regarding their culture. First, he found that the natives were raising small plots of tobacco, which the Arapahoes tell us came to them supernaturally. It was not grown extensively enough to be considered an agricultural product, nor did the Indians continue to raise it after they acquired a taste for the white man's tobacco. Second, he found the natives cooking in earthen vessels of their own manufacture. The Gros Ventres, who with their allies were at war with the Shoshonis, showed the trader their primitive armor, a quilted sleeveless jacket, six folds thick, worn by their warriors.

Unable to toll the natives to Hudson Bay or to compete with the free-lancers from Montreal, the British were forced to move into the Saskatchewan country. In the autumn of 1780, they completed Buckingham House, their first trading post in Gros Ventre–Blackfoot country. Trade might have flourished had it not been for "the great plague" that took an untold number of lives the following year. Blackfoot tradition states that the Piegans, the southern division of the nation, made an attack upon a deserted Shoshoni village where all who remained were sick and dying.[33] Besides taking everything they could carry in the way of lodge skins and other possessions, the Piegans carried back to their people the "bad medicine" (smallpox), which claimed countless lives among the allied tribes as well as among the enemy.

War ceased for a time, then broke out again. While the Gros Ventres were helping the Piegans chase their enemies (the Shoshonis, Flatheads, and Kutenais) beyond the mountains from whence they came, a rival fur-trading firm was entering the field: the North West Company, organized by independent traders at Montreal in 1779. Competition was keen between the two when the North West Company built Rocky Mountain House at the mouth of Clearwater, a tributary of the Saskatchewan.

By 1786, David Thompson and his band of forty-six employees of the Hudson's Bay Company had ascended the Saskatchewan and erected Manchester House, which the Gros Ventres later destroyed. Thompson and Alexander Henry of the North West Company provide through their journals a great deal of valuable information regarding the Gros Ventres, who in that day were a people with many names. No tribal division is noted, but they are called Fall Indians of the Saskatchewan, *Gens de Vache*, Atsinas, Buffalo Indians, Big Belly Indians of the South Saskatchewan, and Gros Ventres of the Falls, Plains, or Prairies.

[33] David Thompson, *David Thompson's Narrative of His Explorations in Western America*, 336–38, and *Journals of David Thompson*, 205 n.

After the British arrived in their midst, they were usually referred to as the Fall Indians, a British term that has been credited to Edward Umfreville in his study of the Hudson's Bay Company (1790).[34] They were so called, he reports, because they inhabited a country on the southern branch of the Saskatchewan "where the rapids are frequent." Judging from their language, he was inclined to believe they were a tribe that had detached itself from some distant nation not yet known. The nation to which he refers was unquestionably the Bison Path People. He says: "In this people another instance occurs of the impropriety with which the Canadian-French name the Indians. They call them *gros ventres*; and that without reason, as they are as comely and as well made as any tribe whatever; and are very far from being remarkable for their corpulency." Umfreville had interpreters for the other languages (Blackfoot, Cree, and Assiniboine), but no one had yet gained sufficient knowledge of the Gros Ventre tongue to make himself understood. The Blackfoot language, his medium of conversation, was both agreeable and readily acquired.

Alexander Mackenzie of the North West Company, while exploring the Saskatchewan area in 1789, noted for the first time two divisions of the Gros Ventre nation.[35] He found the "Fall or Big-bellied Indians," numbering about six hundred warriors, next to the Blackfeet and extending to the confluence of the north and south branches of the Saskatchewan. He also observed a second division inhabiting the plains from the north bend of the Missouri River to the south bend of the Assiniboine, to the number of seven hundred men. He added further that some of the Fall Indians came to the Blackfeet to exchange dressed buffalo robes and bad wolf skins for articles of no great value. It is possible that there may have been a sacred pipe in each division in Mackenzie's time, just as there are two in the Arapaho nation today.

There is every reason to believe that the bands on the Assiniboine included the Arapahoes, who were still a part of the Gros

[34] Edward Umfreville, *The Present State of Hudson's Bay*, 197.
[35] Alexander Mackenzie, *Voyages from Montreal on the River St. Lawrence through the Continent of North America to the Frozen and Pacific Oceans*, I, cx, cxi.

Ventre nation as late as 1790. Although Indian lore is sometimes misleading, this may explain the difference in the legends of separation as given by the Gros Ventres and the Arapahoes. If the Arapahoes were in the main division, which did not actually separate until the crossing of the Missouri, the Fall Indians, or Atsinas of the Saskatchewan, may have been a splinter group. This would account for the Arapahoes' knowledge of but one division.

The French chronicler Jean Baptiste Trudeau and his confederate, François Marie Perrin du Lac, while trading on the Upper Missouri, mentioned the Kananavich, whom they found to be allies of the Cheyennes but of a different language.[36] Thus we find Our People of many names coming into notice along the Missouri by this name rather than as Atsinas, Fall Indians, or Gros Ventres. The French were seemingly unaware that these were some of the same Indians whom they had called *Gens de Vache* or *Gros Ventres* and that they had but recently detached themselves from the main group. An explanation for this may lie in the facts that the Arapahoes had few dealings with the Missouri River village people.

During the summer of 1795, Trudeau, then on the Platte, saw and spoke to many chiefs and leading men of the "Tocaninanbiche" tribe about long marches beyond the mountains. They had not taken part in the "mighty excursion" of the Cheyennes two years before, but they had heard about it and were able to point out the Cheyenne chieftain who was its leader. It is possible that the Arapahoes arrived after the Cheyennes had set out upon their excursion, which would mean that the time of their arrival south of the Missouri was between 1793 and 1795.

Trudeau tells us that the Cheyennes were so lacking in knowledge of the pale-faced stranger that they considered him a deity

[36] Jean Baptiste Trudeau, "Trudeau's Description," *Mississippi Valley Historical Review* (cited hereafter as *MVHR*), VIII, 1–2 (1921), 167. See also his "Journal of Jean Baptiste Trudeau among the Arikara Indians in 179ᵣ," *Missouri Historical Society Collections* (cited hereafter as *MHSC*), IV (1912–13), 31, and "Trudeau's Journal," *South Dakota Historical Collections* (cited hereafter as *SDHSC*), VII (1914), 453.

to whom they sacrificed dressed skins by throwing them into the river. The Bison Path People may have reacted similarly when they saw the first white men on the Canadian Plains, if we are to judge by their mythology. Their somewhat ambiguous mythical character, Spider-Above, which corresponds to Coyote, the Shoshoni trickster, suggests the mysteries of the white man as well as of Man-Above, whose unusual powers are beyond their comprehension. A Southern Arapaho, though failing to make the distinction between Man-Above and Spider-Above, explains the latter by saying:

> A spider does very mysterious things. He spins a web from his mouth in a mysterious way. Furthermore, he may suspend himself by a thread that comes from his mouth, and then climb up on it again. Hence the spider is a symbol of mysterious performances. One can't understand them. Neither can we understand the Supreme Being. The Supreme Being, however, is not a spider.[37]

Even though Perrin du Lac speaks of the Sioux, Cheyennes, and "Tocananabich" as if they were already a federation whose cultural traits were similar, they could not have been associated any length of time.[38] He attributes the Sun Dance "exclusively" to these three tribes, and yet he adds "other neighboring tribes," which indicates that it might already have become a plains concept.

An authority on the American Indian says the Cheyennes, Arapahoes, Blackfeet, and Gros Ventres must have come into contact with the Mandans and Hidatsas fairly early in their career, for "their whole ceremonial and most of their social life was manifestly derived from them."[39] It is difficult to reconcile this with the fact that the Arapahoes had little direct contact with the village people. Since certain Mandan behavior patterns are observ-

---

[37] Sister M. Inez Hilger, *Arapaho Child Life and Its Cultural Background*, *BAE, Bulletin 148*, 144. This was repeated by Jesse Rowlodge in a personal interview at Concho, Oklahoma, in 1965. Spider-Above, it would seem, is symbolic of anything—Man-Above, the Spider, the white man—that is anything beyond comprehension.

[38] M. François Perrin du Lac, *Travels Through the Two Louisianas and among the Savage Nations of the Missouri*, 62–82.

[39] Paul Radin, *The Story of the American Indian*, 294–95.

able among the Arapahoes, it is possible these may have become accepted after the latter crossed the Missouri. Examples are found in the Sun Dance—the Medicine Lodge (Offerings-Lodge) and the practice of self-torture and ceremonial wife surrender. The influence of the village people must have been strong to introduce such elements into the Arapaho ceremonial system.

Charles LeRaye, who found Our People with the Cheyennes on the headwaters of the Cheyenne River, gives the first insight into the relations between the Cheyennes and the Teton Sioux.[40] LeRaye reported that an uncertain peace had been reached between the Cheyennes and Sioux, but it was threatened by a mutual fear of treachery.

In 1884, Little Raven said that when his father was a child, the tribe was at war with the Sioux. At his death in 1855, he was sixty years old. This would suggest that the Arapahoes were at war with the Sioux from the time they (the Arapahoes) crossed the Missouri. Little Raven said further that the Cheyennes first made peace, then the Arapahoes. Their alliance with the Sioux lasted until reservation days. In maintaining a balance of power in this relationship, the Cheyennes and Arapahoes became almost inseparable, but they held their own camp circles and kept their separate Sun Dance rites, thereby remaining independent both socially and politically.

The journals of Trudeau and LeRaye are historically important. They not only solve the mystery of when the crossing of the Missouri took place, but they also show that it occurred about the time the Cheyennes were driven from their villages on the Missouri. Looking back to the "very reliable tradition" mentioned by William Philo Clark, it is obvious that the southwestward migration of the Gros Ventres (including the Arapahoes) coincides roughly with the Cheyenne entry into the plains, but what the tradition did not tell was that the Gros Ventres had been on the Northern Plains many generations before the historic crossing.

The Cheyennes and representatives of three unnamed tribes

[40] Charles LeRaye, "The Journal of Charles LeRaye," *SDHC*, IV (1908), 165; Clark, *The Indian Sign Language*, 39–40.

(one no doubt the Kananavich) were trading with the Arikaras in the spring of 1802, but it was not until two years later that a wandering trader visited an Arapaho camp.[41] Some of the Tattooed People were still trading at Chesterfield House, at the confluence of the Red Deer and Bow rivers. In 1801, The Feather, a Blackfoot chief, drew a map for Peter Fidler of the Hudson's Bay Company locating the various tribes on the Northern Plains.[42] It shows the Tattooed People (Arapahoes) with eighty tents near the mountains, considerably to the south of the Missouri, with the Blackfeet to the north of the river. In his scale of miles, The Feather shows the approximate distance a young man could walk in thirty-three days and indicates that it was so great that never a Blackfoot and only "a chance" Fall Indian had gone as far south as the "Rib Indians" (Bannocks). Although The Feather used the Blackfoot term for the Arapahoes, he referred to the Gros Ventres by their British name, Fall Indians, rather than as Atsinas, as we might expect.

Fidler (1801) feared that Chesterfield House might suffer the same fate at the hands of the Fall Indians as the two other trading posts, Manchester and South Branch, which were destroyed by them in 1793 and 1794, respectively. Among the hostile tribes in the area were the Fall, the Tattooed, the Blackfoot, and the Blood, who were then having trouble among themselves. Vigilance was necessary to prevent the traders from losing their scalps to the Fall Indians, who had threatened to lift them.

D. W. Harmon of Alexandrea, a North West Company post on the Assiniboine River, reported difficulty with the "Rapid Indians" the same year Fidler's map was made at Chesterfield House.[43] He stated these Indians were forming a war party to come against the Crees and Assiniboines, and he did not blame

41 Pierre-Antoine Tabeau, *Tabeau's Narrative of Loisel's Expedition to the Upper Missouri* (cited hereafter as *Tabeau's Narrative*), 87.

42 The Peter Fidler Map, drawn with the help of The Feather, is in *The American Heritage Book of Indians*, 324–25. Fidler's reference to Chesterfield House is in "Chesterfield House Journals," London, Hudson's Bay Company Archives, B. 34/A/3 and B. 39/A/2.

43 D. W. Harmon, *A Journal of Voyages and Travels in the Interior of North America*, 51, 55, 78, 119–20.

them. He realized that if they came, they would attack the whites as well as the natives, for they were infuriated over the trader's furnishing guns to their enemies. The latter, not waiting for the Gros Ventres to attack, went in search of them, defeated them through the use of superior weapons, and returned with a number of women and children as slaves.

The Fall Indians were desperately trying to hold their ground, but the odds were against them. Their kinsmen, who had stood by them in warfare with their enemies in years past, had forsaken them. Even their old friends the Blackfeet were uncertain allies, for as Harmon points out, eighty lodges had joined a like number of Assiniboines to wage war against them. Instead, they became embroiled in an argument over a horse and fought a day-long battle among themselves.

Alexander Henry of the North West Company, who had every opportunity to gain first-hand information regarding the Gros Ventres, tells of their desperation—of their plundering the two forts and murdering the servants of the Hudson's Bay Company, at the same time being repulsed in similar attacks upon near-by North West posts.[44] He abhorred their cruelty in 1802 when they murdered a party of Iroquois and whites on the Bow River. It "was horrid—cutting the bodies open, tearing out the still quivering hearts, and devouring them with the ferocity of tigers in the presence of our people whose fate it was to winter in that quarter."

While the Fall Indians were still waging their war of survival in the Saskatchewan area, the "Big Bellies of the Fort de Prairie" (as François Larocque called the main division of the Gros Ventre nation in 1805) were encamped on the Big Horn River, where they were attempting to make peace with the Crows.[45] On speaking terms at the moment, they were conversing by means of signs. Larocque described twelve lodges of the once powerful Shoshonis

[44] Alexander Henry and David Thompson, *New Light on the Early History of the Great Northwest*, II, 718–22, 733–35.
[45] François Antoine Larocque, "Journal of François Antoine Larocque from the Assiniboine River to the Yellowstone," in *Sources of Northwest History*, XX, 20.

living among the Crows on the Yellowstone as a remnant of their tribe, which had been destroyed. They may have constituted all who remained after warfare and smallpox had played havoc with their numbers on the Canadian Plains. Just why they did not repair to their habitat across the mountains we cannot guess, unless they may have married into the Crow nation.

Lewis and Clark, on their "tour of discovery" following the Louisiana Purchase, did not contact the Bison Path People, but on their way eastward they had a brush with straggling Indians who led them to believe they were Gros Ventres, though Thompson later identified them as Blackfeet.[46] The allied Indians were not to forget that Lewis fatally wounded one of their number during the melee. This was but the beginning of a series of incidents which caused the Piegans and their Gros Ventre allies to close the upper reaches of the Missouri to white infiltration. The Kananavich bands, who had already learned to distrust the white man, were still closely affiliated with the Gros Ventres, from whom they had recently separated.

While trading among the Arikaras, Pierre-Antoine Tabeau had an opportunity to study the "Caninanbich" when some of them accompanied the Cheyennes to the Missouri to trade. He found that, under the tutelage of the Cheyennes, they were becoming astute traders. Had it not been for their advice, Tabeau believed they might have left to his discretion the price of the "trifles" he bought.[47] He complained of the Cheyennes' "half knowledge of the value of merchandise" and added that their vainglory had been a detriment to his trade with the Kananavich and others who had obstinately deferred to their judgment. He was frank in saying that had it not been for the interference of the Cheyennes, he would have "made better use" of the nations.

The Arikaras had previously accompanied the Cheyennes to the foot of the Black Hills, where they met eight other friendly nations, including the Caninanbiches and the "Squihitanes," who

[46] Meriwether Lewis and William Clark, *Original Journals of the Lewis and Clark Expedition* (cited hereafter as *Lewis and Clark Journals*), II, 80–249; Thompson, *David Thompson's Narrative*, 375; Ewers, *The Blackfeet*, 46–48.
[47] *Tabeau's Narrative*, 34, 153–55.

were not identified beyond their speaking the same language. They may have been the mysterious Rock People or Rock Men, an obsolete tribe said to have lived with them "in the long ago," but the present-day Arapahoes can give no information concerning their history.

Even though Lewis and Clark did not contact Our People, they acquired information that sheds further light on Arapaho history.[48] The two explorers found that the *Gens de Vache* (the main branch of the Gros Ventres), whom they mistakenly considered of the "Me-na-tare" family, were at the mouth of the Yellowstone River, where they were waging a defensive war against the Sioux and Assiniboines. They comprised five hundred lodges, thirteen hundred warriors, and five thousand people. They did not cultivate the soil, but lived by hunting, their range being "on the S. E. fork of the Yellow Rock [Yellowstone] River, called Big Horn River, and on the heads of the Loup."

The explorers believed, incorrectly, that the little-known Fall Indians, whom they called "Gens de Rapid," belonged to the Minetares. They had 260 tents, 660 warriors, and were said to rove between the Missouri and the Bad River Fork of the Saskatchewan. The "Kanenavish" numbered 150 tents, 400 warriors, and 1,500 people and were on the head of the Padouca Fork of the Platte River and the South Fork of the Cheyenne River. As the explorers point out, the Indians had no idea of exclusive right to the soil, nor was it possible to describe their limits because they were frequently displaced in warfare with their neighbors. One can see that the once strong Gros Ventre nation was beginning to disintegrate, with a large segment, the Kananavich, migrating southward.

The Assiniboines and Crees, not content with pushing the main division across the Missouri, were now joined by the Sioux in a relentless drive against the Gros Ventres at the mouth of the Big Horn. During their warfare, there ensued a battle in which the Gros Ventres lost their Flat-Pipe to the Assiniboines, who eventually returned it and made a peace that was never broken.

[48] *Lewis and Clark Journals*, VI, 101–103.

The Arapaho proper pride themselves on never having lost their sacred tribal fetish.

The census figures given by Lewis and Clark, though roughly estimated, are revealing in that the main branch of the Gros Ventres that crossed the Missouri left a little less than one-third of their number in the north, as the Gros Ventre legend signifies. On the other hand, the explorers account for a generous two-thirds. We also note in comparing the explorer's figures with those of Mackenzie that the main division, or rather the larger division, had supplemented its numbers at the expense of the northernmost bands. This could further explain their desperation.

In 1806, Henry also located the "Buffalo Indians" at the sources of the Platte and Cheyenne rivers.[49] He says some called them the "Caneninavish tribe" and that they comprised five hundred tents, again showing a flexibility in numbers. Henry reported that the Cheyennes were wintering in the Black Hills and southward but returning to the Missouri in the spring to trade. Though we find infrequent mention of the Arapahoes joining their excursions to the villages, the Cheyennes maintained the Missouri River contacts, which were to the advantage of the Arapahoes, who, while living their free and easy plains life, traded horses and buffalo robes for the British trade goods brought to them by the Cheyenne intermediaries.

H. M. Brackenridge, who gives a table of the Indians of Louisiana, mentions the "Kan-ne-na-wish" as a "wandering people" on the headwaters of the Yellowstone River. He attributes to them fifteen hundred warriors and five thousand souls. His reference appears to be to the main branch of the Gros Ventres, but he shows by the use of the name the close relationship between the Gros Ventres on the Yellowstone and the Kananavich, whom Trudeau placed on the headwaters of the Cheyenne River.

Lewis and Clark recorded yet another name for Our People: the "Blue Bead Indians." Supposedly, this name was given to the Arapahoes because of their fondness for New Mexican turquoise,

---

[49] Henry and Thompson, *New Light*, 384; Henry M. Brackenridge, *Views of Louisiana*, 85.

which was a prized item of trade among the Plains Indians even in prehistoric times. On the other hand, it may have originated in the north, since Clark shows on his map (1808–10) "Blue Bead Mountain" and "Blue Bead River" in the Big Horn district, leading one to believe that it was here that the Indians obtained volcanic glass for beads and pipes. If the beads were of stone, they could have come from the Blue Bead Quarry near present-day Cody, Wyoming. All efforts to locate Arapaho blue beads either in museums or among the Indians have failed.

Diligent research has been unable to bring to light a date for the name *Arapaho* earlier than 1810, when John Bradbury, the English naturalist, spoke of the robbing by the "Arapahays" of Joseph Miller, an Astorian, or employee of John Jacob Astor.[50] The following year, he mentioned the Indians as "Arapahoes" when he was increasing his collection at an Arikara village. He casually tells us that while he was there, some Cheyennes arrived to inform the Arikaras of a proposed visit of their tribe.

> One of the Indians [Bradbury states] was covered with a buffalo robe, curiously ornamented with figures worked with split quills, stained red and yellow, intercised with much taste, and the border of the robe entirely hung round with the hoofs of young fawns, which at every movement made a noise much resembling that of the rattlesnake when that animal is irritated. I understood that this robe had been purchased from the Arapahoes, or Big Bead [Blue Bead] Indians, a remote tribe, who frequent the Rocky Mountains. I wished much to purchase the robe and offered him such articles in exchange as I thought most likely to induce him to part with it; but he refused. The following day it was purchased by Mr. McClellan, who gave it to me, for silver ornaments and other articles, which amounted to about ten dollars.

The many names by which Our People were known in their

[50] John Bradbury, *Travels in the Interior of America,* 124, 139. No source material can be found to refute the statement (LeRoy Hafen to Clark Wissler, April 16, 1930, copy in Colorado State Historical Society Library) that "Bradbury's use of the term Arapaho, 1810, appears to be about the earliest. Before that time the name was a puzzle."

early tribal history are often perplexing, though they serve as a key to the Arapaho mystery. Like a jigsaw puzzle, the pieces gradually fall into place and a definite picture emerges. The time and circumstances under which the name *Arapaho* came to light give credence to the explanation that it may have been derived from the Pawnee word *tirapihu* or *larapihu,* meaning "buyer" or "trader." In 1885, William Philo Clark tried unsuccessfully to ascertain the origin, but the Indians could give him no reason for it, nor was he able to find a similar word used by any of the surrounding tribes. Later, Hugh L. Scott logically proposed the name *A-ra-pa-hoe* as a Siouan Crow term meaning "lots of tattooes," or "Tattooed People," the Blackfoot name for the Arapahoes.[51]

Obviously, the word did not originate among Our People, for they do not refer to themselves by that name, nor do they have an *r* sound in their language. Significantly, when the name became known in history, it was applied—as the term *Gros Ventre* had been —to the nation as a whole, as well as to an important tribal division. In this case, history reverses itself, for the Arapahoes were no longer of the Gros Ventre nation; the Gros Ventres were to be known thereafter as of the Arapaho nation.

[51] Mooney, "Arapaho," *loc. cit.,* 72; Clark, *The Indian Sign Language,* 556; Scott, "Early History," *loc. cit.,* 556.

CHAPTER TWO

On the Headwaters

By the end of the eighteenth century, the Arapahoes were wandering freely from the Cheyenne River on the north into eastern Colorado and from the Rockies into the Black Hills. Mountain Indians, the Cheyennes called them, but they were more exactly headwater-plains Indians, for they spent long winter months camped in sheltered nooks along clear-water streams on the Eastern Slope of the Rockies. From there they would venture far into the Central Plains on their buffalo hunts—sometimes as far as western Nebraska and Kansas. They led a wild life, untouched by European civilization.

The Arapahoes say that when they first encountered the Cheyennes in the Black Hills, they believed them to be an enemy tribe and sought to exterminate them. Then, recognizing "some sort of kinship," they accepted them as friends and from then on were at peace. Both were of the Algonquian linguistic family, but they had to resort to signs to make themselves understood. The close association that developed was mutually beneficial, for the Cheyennes needed the Arapahoes as allies in their warfare with the Crows as much as the Arapahoes needed the Cheyennes as intermediaries in trade relations on the Missouri.

Well equipped with horses through purchase or raids, Our People fought creditably against the Crows north of the Platte and with the Utes and Shoshonis in the mountains and to the west. They believed that Man-Above created the Rockies as a barrier to separate them from the Shoshonis and Utes. After their migration to the south, they were thrown into closer contact with the latter, with whom they were almost constantly at war. Our People could easily defeat them on the plains, for the Utes were mountain Indians, unskilled in fighting horseback; but in the mountains, the enemy had the advantage. To the east were the Pawnees, who comprised a formidable foe, but on the south the Arapahoes had more or less amicable relations, before 1825, with both the Comanches and Kiowas, who preceded them in their migration from north of the Platte.

As equestrian nomads, Our People remained relatively unnoticed by traders until Manuel Lisa, one of the most fearless of the early fur men, entered the field. He was not concerned with an outlet to the Western Sea, but like the French, he, too, had a dream. He had learned through one of the wandering Plains tribes that somewhere near the source of the Missouri was a stream that flowed south through Spanish Territory and on to the Gulf of California.[1] This, we now know, was the Green River, or Upper Colorado, better known to the Indians as the Sisk-ka-dee (Prairie Hen), to which all trails were to lead during the rendezvous period.

By locating the stream, Lisa hoped to form a link between the fur trade of Santa Fé and his own on the Upper Missouri. His inspiration came from Jean Baptiste Champlain, who returned in the summer of 1811 from a trading expedition to the Arapahoes on the headwaters of the Platte. They told him the Spaniards came each year to trade with them but did not specify how far north the white man came, nor did they mention that the contacts were probably with the South People, whose habitat was doubtless as far away as the Arkansas River. The Arapahoes showed evidence of their dealings with the Spaniards, for in their camp were items they had received directly or indirectly from that source. Furthermore, they were well aware that it took about thirty days for a trip from the Cheyenne River southward to make the necessary contacts.

Hoping to encounter some of his countrymen from Santa Fé, Lisa equipped Champlain and his party with goods suitable

---

[1] Richard E. Oglesby, *Manuel Lisa and the Opening of the Missouri Fur Trade*, 5; Henry E. Bolton, "New Light on Manuel Lisa and the Spanish Trade," *Southwest Historical Quarterly* (cited hereafter as *SWHQ*), XVII (1913), 61-64.

for Spanish trade and sent them from Fort Mandan (North Dakota) to the Platte. Just where they encountered the Arapahoes has not been ascertained. David H. Coyner says in a fictitious account entitled *The Lost Trappers* that they went far to the south, perhaps to the "Spanish River" (the Arkansas).[2] Historians agree that they may have gone as far as the Comanche country.

Undaunted even though he had not heard from Champlain, Lisa dispatched Charles Sanguinet, who was already familiar with the Arapahoes, to the same area the following year. With Sanguinet he sent a letter "to the Spaniards of New Mexico" in which he said he had sent twenty-three hunters to the Arapaho nation. The year before, they had come to Fort Mandan, where he had equipped them for their return journey. They were, he explained, the ones who informed him that the Spaniards of Mexico were coming each year to trade with the Arapahoes.[3]

Sanguinet's mission was primarily one of diplomacy, designed to establish friendly trade relations. Lisa admitted in his letter that he had received no news from Champlain and his party, but he was sending his trusted servants, Sanguinet and two *engagés*, to let them know where to come out with their peltry. At length, in December, a message reached Lisa from Sanguinet, who stated that upon his arrival among the "Arepaos" he had learned that the Blackfeet had killed three of his men, including Champlain. The others had scattered and their beaver cache had been plundered. Lisa was later to learn the details of the disaster from Ezekiel Williams, the lone survivor, who was charged by the press with the murder of Champlain.

Williams attempted to vindicate himself in a letter written from Boonslick (Missouri) in August, 1816, following the charge, which was published in the *Western Intelligencer*.[4] He said Lisa had promised to keep his fort and maintain friendly relations with the Indians in order that the party's return would not be cut off. The twenty members of the group were all on foot except for

[2] David H. Coyner traces their ramblings in *The Lost Trappers*.
[3] Bolton, "New Light," *loc. cit.*, 65–66.
[4] Ezekiel Williams' letter, reprinted from the *Missouri Gazette*, is in "Adventures in Colorado," *MHSC*, IV, 2 (1913), 202–206.

two men in Champlain's employ. Journeying southward about forty-five days, they struck a stream which they later discovered to be the Arkansas. There, trapping and hunting through the winter, they remained unmolested. In the spring, Indians, whom they did not identify, began harassing them.

In June the trappers assembled at the headwaters of a stream, later found to be the Platte, and agreed they should scatter in order to survive. Half the party crossed the Rocky Mountains, perhaps to Green River. The others, including Champlain and Williams, went south along the mountains. Proceeding to the Arkansas, they encountered Indians who informed them that Lisa's fort on the Missouri had been destroyed and that the whites and Indians were killing each other. This disturbing news made their return to the Upper Missouri impossible, so the hard-pressed trappers again divided, with four of the company going south to find the Spanish settlements. They were not heard of again.

The remaining six, including Champlain, Williams, and four employees, set out to hunt in a cove in the mountains near the Arapahoes' winter camp. Although they were careful to remain but a few miles apart, three of their number were found slain a few weeks later. The survivors, knowing that the only course left to them was to place themselves in the protective custody of the Indians, sought sanctuary among the "Arapahow" nation, where they found the horses and equipment of their comrades who had just been killed. Trappers and traders later learned that baseline trails were more hazardous than those out on the level plains, where there was less chance of ambush.

Champlain and a companion decided to stay with the Indians until a white man might happen along to verify the report that Lisa's fort had been destroyed. They would then know what to do. Williams set out alone, following the river in an attempt to reach St. Louis and report the plight of his friends. When he returned to the Arapahoes the following summer, he called a council of the chiefs, but all they would tell him about his companions was that they eventually left the camp with their horses and furs. When last seen, they were headed in the direction of the

Crows, who later reported they had seen two white men dead in their village. These the Arapahoes presumed to be Champlain and his companion. Although they disclaimed any part in the trappers' deaths, they readily confessed that they killed the three men in the cove before the others took protection among them.

That the Arapahoes could be found almost anywhere along the Eastern Slope, near the headwaters of the Platte, is borne out by the diaries of the Astorians. On his overland journey to the mouth of the Columbia River (Astoria, Oregon) in September, 1811, Wilson Price Hunt found the Cheyennes just east of the Black Hills, which on early maps extended westward to the Laramie Range, including the hills in the Fort Laramie area. The Cheyennes were trading horses with the Arikaras at the time, probably animals that had been brought north by the Arapahoes, whom Hunt called "Arropolus" and placed along the Platte River.

In the Big Horn area he encountered eight Indian men with three families whom he believed to be Flatheads and Snakes.[5] They said they were on their way to the home of the Arapahoes. Had they comprised a war party, this would have been understandable, but it is unlikely that straggling families of Flatheads and Shoshonis would be going into the camp of their bitter enemy. Since they appropriated a gun that had been carelessly left in camp, they were in all probability Gros Ventres on their way to visit the Arapahoes, or Arapahoes returning from a visit with their kinsmen.

When Robert Stuart and his small band of eastbound Astorians were in the vicinity of present-day Grandview, Idaho, the following year, they encountered the unfortunate Joseph Miller and his three companions—Hoback, Reznor, and Robinson.[6] Stuart provides more details of their unhappy experience with the Arapahoes, perhaps, as has been suggested, in the Medicine Bow area of Wyoming. Miller and his companions had found sixty lodges of "Arapahays, an outlaw'd band of Arapahoes," who robbed them of several horses and most of their clothing. In the spring,

[5] Wilson Price Hunt, "Diary," in Philip A. Rollins (ed.), *The Discovery of the Oregon Trail* (cited hereafter as *Oregon Trail*), 85; Washington Irving, *Astoria*, 323–29.
[6] Robert Stuart, "Narrative," in Rollins, *Oregon Trail*, 161.

they were again overtaken by "the same rascals" and robbed of the rest of their horses and almost everything else they owned. When Stuart met them, they were almost naked and without a single horse to carry their meager possessions.

In their wanderings they discovered the Arapahays, whom they credited with a population of about 350; the Arapahoes, with 2,700; and the "Black Arms" (Utes) with 3,000. The Arapahoes and Utes were at odds, but both professed friendship for the whites. Especially was this true of the latter, whose territories were said to extend to the neighborhood of the Spaniards. The mention of the Arapahays as a separate band is understandable since a popular —or sometimes unpopular—chief might assemble groups of his friends and relatives and strike out to form a band of his own. The name has not survived, but it apparently referred to a band, or bands, of Arapahoes temporarily separated from the main group.

While Robert Stuart and his small party tarried among the friendly Shoshonis on their way east, they learned certain details of Champlain's party. News had a way of traveling, even in enemy camps. The Snakes told how the Arapahoes fell in with Champlain and his companions while they were trapping beaver some distance down "the Spanish River" and how the Arapahoes murdered them in the night and took possession of all they owned. Since both Green River and the Arkansas were known as the Spanish River, it is somewhat confusing. If Green River is meant—and it probably was, since it was in Shoshoni country while the Arkansas was far to the south—the men killed may have been those who separated from Champlain's party in the first place.

When Stuart told the Shoshonis that the white man would soon take vengeance upon the Arapahoes, they were elated and offered their services. Stuart apparently thought the Indians were referring to Green River, for he observed that there is "a kind of wild tobacco which grows spontaneously in the plains adjacent to the Spanish River (Green River) Mountains, the leaves are smaller than those of ours, and it is much more agreeable, not being nearly so violent in its effects."

On reaching the Platte, the Astorians mistook it for the

Cheyenne River. Here, in a secluded spot, they erected a shelter and laid in an ample supply of meat (eighteen buffalo) for the remainder of the winter. They believed themselves secure from roving Indians because of their location and the cold and "boisterous" weather. It was December, 1812, and there was about a foot of snow on the ground, but this did not deter the hardy Arapahoes, who heard the firing when the white men killed two deer and came to investigate.

In the vicinity of the hut, the Indians gave a yelp that brought the Astorians to their feet. Seizing their arms, they rushed out to find twenty-three warriors as surprised as they. The Indians, advancing in a friendly manner, indicated that they were a war party against the Crows, who sometime earlier had stolen many of their horses and some of their women. They claimed the enemy winter camp was a six-day march ("six sleeps") to the north, somewhere on Powder River.

The war party had come from winter camp on the South Platte, sixteen sleeps from the Astorians. Stuart had no complaint to make of the behavior of his guests, for they were more decent than one might expect of a war party. As night approached, they threw up temporary breastworks of logs for their own protection, while the chief and subchief accepted an invitation to sleep inside the hut. First one, then another of the Astorians remained on guard throughout the night, for the Shoshoni account of Champlain's fate was not to be forgotten.

The next morning, the braves, after appeasing their voracious appetites and receiving the best of the meat that was in store, departed in good spirits. They had, Stuart affirmed, begged a good deal for ammunition, but after being convincingly refused, they had laughed and given up their entreaties. The Astorians were sure that such good behavior was but a blind to throw them off guard so the Indians could return with reinforcements and destroy them. With the Crow encampment so near and the motives of the Arapahoes in doubt, the first white men to follow the course of what was later to be known as the Oregon Trail were not in an enviable position.

There was no alternative but to abandon their "Chateau of Indolence" and make their way down the river, which they had by now decided must be the Niobrara. Little realizing how far they were from civilization, they hoped to make their next cantonment on the banks of the Missouri. The Indians had left them with the faithful pack horse they had received in trade from the Shoshonis after being relieved of their own horses by the Crows. Stuart did not consider that the Arapahoes had left the nag as an act of kindness, for it would have been more hindrance than help to a war party.

Some historians seem to be of the opinion that the Arapahoes divided into the Northern and Southern bands with the crossing of the Missouri.[7] The editor of the Hunt and Stuart journals says:

> The Arapahoes, in their migration, reached ultimately the upper stretches of the Missouri River, whence a portion of them (the later so-called Northern Arapahoes) veered to the headwaters of the Yellowstone River, while the rest of them (the later so-called Southern Arapahoes) made their way to the valley of the South Platte in northeastern Colorado.

Technically, a division took place, as it has been pointed out, but no Arapaho bands are known to have dwelt in the Montana Gros Ventre country. The Indians encountered by the Astorians were not Southern Arapahoes, but the Arapaho proper or bands thereof. As will be seen, the Northern and Southern divisions of the Arapaho proper were not formed until about twenty years after the Astorians came through their territory.

After Williams' successful recovery of his cache, A. P. Chouteau and Julius de Mun, both of St. Louis, set out in 1815 with a large party of trappers for the Upper Arkansas.[8] There they encountered Caleb Greenwood, who was to spend many years as a trapper and trader among the Arapahoes and Cheyennes.

---

[7] Rollins, *Oregon Trail*, 333–34 (editor's note); Hiram M. Chittenden, *History of the American Fur Trade of the Far West*, II, 878.

[8] T. M. Marshall (ed.), "The Journals of Jules de Mun," *MHSC*, V, 2, 3 (1928), 167–208, 311–326; Chouteau Collection, Missouri Historical Society (cited hereafter as MHS).

Chouteau and De Mun were among the first white men to operate successfully on the headwaters of the Arkansas and Platte in Arapaho country.

Various tribes of particular areas, friendly or not, would gather periodically for the purpose of trade even before European goods were introduced. One of the favorite sites was on Horse Creek, a tributary of the Platte. It was here in 1813 that the Comanches, who some years before had roved the Central Plains together with their kinsmen, the Shoshonis, came for the purpose of trading Spanish horses for whatever items the Cheyennes had to barter.[9] Among the tribes assembled were the Arapahoes, who also had horses for the highly competitive Indian market. Before the bargaining got well under way, a Sioux bludgeoned a Kiowa with his tomahawk. This seemed to be the signal for general action, for the Sioux then attacked the Kiowas and finally drove friend and foe alike into the foothills to the west.

Another grand encampment was held three years later—this time on Cherry Creek (in the Denver vicinity)—but the Kiowas and Comanches did not attend. The nature of the old trade councils had changed, for besides the Cheyennes, with their goods from the Missouri River, there were forty-five employees of Chouteau and De Mun who were prepared to deal directly with the Indians. Horses brought from the south by the Arapahoes and Kiowas were exchanged for trade goods. The two tribes were said to "wander in the extensive plains of the Arkansas and Red river [and to] have always great numbers of horses, which they rear with much less difficulty than the Shiennes, whose country is cold and barren."

In 1820 the Arapahoes and Pawnees waged an unusual war, unusual in that it was the first time a white man, Edwin James, was present to report the details.[10] Since he was a guest in the lodge of the chief, whose brother was slain, James shows prejudice in favor of the Pawnees. Even so, his account proves of interest. The battle

[9] George E. Hyde, *The Pawnee Indians*, 106; Edwin James, *Account of an Expedition from Pittsburgh to the Rocky Mountains*, XV, 282; XVII, 156–60.
[10] *Annual Report of the Secretary of War*, 1820, "Indian Affairs," 250; *American State Papers*, II, 45; James, *Account of an Expedition*, XVII, 157–60.

was fought by ninety-three Pawnee warriors, on foot and poorly armed, against a large body of well-armed "Arapaho Indians of the Rocky Mountains."

The attackers obviously had the advantage, but they did not rout the Pawnees without loss to themselves. James states that the battle started about ten o'clock and soon raged with great fury.

> Every muscle was called into action in our little band (the Pawnees), who hung firmly together, discharging their arrows and occasionally a fusee at the enemy with the steadiest aim. The dead and wounded were falling in every direction in both parties. The enemy were so numerous that numbers of their braves, armed only with a shield, having rejected their offensive weapons, hovered in front of their companions, intent only upon the acquisition of the renown dearest to the heart of the warrior, that of first striking the body of a fallen enemy. Many of them however were killed, even by their own people, as they rushed along and intercepted the flight of the arrow or bullet from its destined mark. The combatants were at very close quarters, and the arrow had its full effect. They were for some time intermingled, and contended with their war-clubs and knives. The partizan, who had been wounded severely early in the action, and had received several more wounds during its continuance, now was struck by an arrow, which buried itself to the feathers in his body.

When the Pawnee chief's brother fell, he exhorted his braves to use their knives after their arrows were expended. This they did as they fought their way to the creek, where the Arapahoes left them to return to exult over the slain. The only principal warrior left in the badly defeated band of Pawnees declared that he was ashamed that he had survived. Although badly wounded, he ran back toward the enemy and was seen no more.

When James reached an encampment of the Arkansas River Indians, he learned that a band of Cheyenne "seceders" had left their nation on the Cheyenne River and had placed themselves under the protection of Bear Tooth, chief of the Arapahoes. During the close relationship between the Arapahoes and Cheyennes, one or the other might sometimes have a principal chief whose influence was recognized by both tribes, but Bear Tooth was more than the leader of the two allies, the Arapahoes and the Cheyennes who had recently joined them. A man born to command, he was a dictator over all Indians on the Arkansas River. "His orders were uniformly characterized by discretion and propriety, and were regarded by his subjects as inviolable laws," James says of him. At the time of his visit, the chief was in a large intertribal encampment with the principal body of the nations he ruled. He was reported to be very favorably disposed toward the white man, which was fortunate for the Long Expedition, to which James belonged. Its members learned that Bear Tooth had given protection in his own lodge to a miserable American who had escaped from the horrors of a Spanish prison. From the prisoner, Bear Tooth had acquired a few English words and an abiding faith in the white man.

On his westward trek, Stephen H. Long was impressed by the absence of red men after he left the Pawnees on the Republican River. He found the chief evidence of their occupancy, their beads, at Manito, for the nomads had gone nineteen sleeps below on a war excursion against the Spaniards of Mexico on Red River. Previously, the Arapahoes, Kiowas, and Cheyennes had carried on a limited trade with the Spaniards, with whom they exchanged dressed buffalo hides for such commodities as blankets, wheat, maize, and flour. This had been brought to a halt by their warfare. The intertribal conclave described by James was more likely a strategy meeting of the allies than a trade fair, though it may have been both.

John Bell, official journalist for Long, told of encountering a war party from Bear Tooth's band.[11] The warriors had planned an attack on the Pawnees but withdrew after discovering the enemy's excessive numbers. They asked that the explorers report their friendly manner to their chief, for they knew it would please him. With the Arapahoes engaged in war on two fronts, it was fortunate for the white men that an unknown prisoner had won the heart of the great Bear Tooth.

11 John R. Bell, *The Journal of Captain John R. Bell*, 202.

43

Jacob Fowler, a former Kentucky landowner who went west to recoup his fortune, arrived with a party of traders on the Arkansas in the fall of 1821.[12] Although he does not name the chief, it could have been none other than Bear Tooth whom he saw for the first time about sundown November 23. A tall Indian, running into camp, called out, "Me Arapaho chief! White man mine!" Shaking hands as hurriedly as possible, he asked for the white chief and was directed to the lodge of Captain Hugh Glenn, who was in charge of the party. The excited Indian rushed inside but was back in an instant.

Thumping his breast—the sign for Arapaho, which the traders failed to recognize—he kept saying, "White man mine. Arapaho plenty!" as he pointed to the direction from which he came. The exuberant Bear Tooth had in his retinue more than his own, for again there were representatives of the other Arkansas River tribes he controlled. Fowler observed that the Arapahoes were the most "sivvel to the white man's habits" of any of the tribes, but communication with them was a problem because Bear Tooth's vocabulary was exhausted with the few English words of greeting. Captain Glenn had only one interpreter for the many languages spoken along the Arkansas, and there is reason to believe that he was unable to cope with the Arapaho.

Fowler, who built a three-room log house on Fountain River (in Colorado), in 1822, observed that the Indians were "sartainly" ignorant of the ways of the white man and that they did not promise much in the way of trade. Except for twenty beaver pelts, they had nothing to offer but horses. Not only did the country seem to include few fur-bearing animals, the early habits of the people tended to preclude their becoming trappers. Even so, Fowler opened up from Pueblo to Taos a trail that became an important trade route.

Before his arrival, the Arapahoes and the Crows had fought a battle in which the former lost fifteen men, the latter nine. The wounded included a young warrior who two years earlier had not only been shot through the body but who had also been

12 Jacob Fowler, *The Journal of Jacob Fowler*, 54–55, 59, 65, 85.

44

scalped. A more recent injury (a gunshot wound in the foot) had not healed, but he and his father were the first to rush forth on horseback when an alarm was spread that the enemy was near. Fowler was impressed by such bravery.

Besides being friendly in every respect, the Arapahoes were ready to go to the defense of the whites. When word came that the Ietans were preparing an attack, the chief ordered some of his warriors to turn them back. Then the remaining Arapahoes began circling the white men's lodge. By nightfall, they had set up about 250 protective tipis, which they considered ample.

Jealousy and friction were inevitable in the large encampment of savage tribes. One instance caused great anxiety among the traders, who were aroused early one morning by the sound of two Indians striking each other. One of the antagonists, who proved to be the Kiowa chief's son, came running toward the white man's lodge. He was then chased around it by an Arapaho, a brother of the chief, who overtook the Kiowa, and although he felled him with a blow, several women were able to revive him. The traders feared the consequences, but the difficulty was soon resolved when the Kiowas returned the medicine bag the chief's son had stolen. In accepting it, the Arapahoes considered the incident closed.

Bear Tooth gave the traders a dog feast on Christmas Day—an honor because dog meat has always been considered by Our People as "a dish fit for the chief." He placed the fat meat before his guests, and they ate heartily without knowing at the time what it was. This was the "great feast" before parting, for the traders were determined to leave three days later. Bear Tooth, telling them they were in danger of having their horses stolen, begged them to stay with him one more moon. In spite of his sorrow, the white men, after presenting him with a medal, departed. The chief was so overcome with grief that he threw himself on the bed and wept.

On January 4 the traders saw him again when he and two of his brothers brought to their camp a mule which had been lost and for which the Indians were rewarded. Noticing a horse that the white men thought might have strayed from the Crows, one of the brothers claimed it as his own. The traders agreed it could have been his and turned it over to him, but he demanded extra presents from the man who had cut off its tail. This accomplished, there was a long smoke, after which the Indians, affectionately embracing their white friends once more, departed.

In spite of all the loving-kindness Bear Tooth expended upon his new friends, who may even have owed their lives to him, they did him the disservice of giving the Crows powder and lead and four knives when they met them a few days later. This was inconsequential compared to what the Indians took. The Crow chief, discovering some of their thievery, saw that the items were returned, but other articles were taken and the Indians were gone before the loss was discovered. After the Crows had completed a bout with the Arapahoes in which they killed five and lost three of their own, they returned and tried to drive off the traders' horses. Failing in this, they again made friendly overtures. This time they took everything loose, from blankets to a big iron kettle.

About the same time Fowler was having his experience with the Arapahoes on the Arkansas, a French fur man named Jacques La Ramie disappeared while trapping on a tributary of the Platte.[13] He had gone trustingly into Arapaho country, where he set his traps and selected his location for a winter shelter. When spring came and he did not return, his friends became alarmed and set out to find him. According to James Bridger, who claimed to have been with the search party, the men went up the Laramie River and its tributaries. Near the mouth of Sybille Creek they found an unfinished cabin and near by a broken beaver trap. Bridger said the Arapahoes admitted to him two years later that they had killed La Ramie and put his body in the ice under a beaver dam, although no trace of it was ever found. The mystery of the trapper so captivated the imagination that his name became a symbol of the fur trade in Wyoming. It has been given—as

[13] John Hunton, *John Hunton's Diary*, II, 120; *Fort Laramie Scout*, January 28, 1926; Hunton Papers and Correspondence, Wyoming State Archives and Historical Department, Cheyenne.

THE GROS VENTRE CHIEF MEXKEMAHUASTAN ("Iron that Moves").
The original painting, by Carl Bodmer, is in the Joslyn Art Museum.

Courtesy Bureau of American Ethnology

Above, A CAMP OF THE GROS VENTRES on the Upper Missouri. The original painting, by Carl Bodmer, is in the Joslyn Art Museum. *Below, Little Raven's Tent*, a lithograph by Vincent Brooks Day and Son.

Above, AN ARAPAHO MOTHER with her two warrior sons. *Below*, HA-NIS-KRAH ("He Sees through a Fog"), an Arapaho chief, wearing grizzly bear robe; his wife Hoo; and a celebrated warrior known as The Great Jumper. Both drawings, by George Catlin, are in the collection of Paul Mellon.

Courtesy Whitney Art Gallery, Cody, Wyoming

MEDICINE MAN, Northern Arapaho chief, and family preparing a feast of dog meat.

Courtesy Bureau of American Ethnology

CHIEF LITTLE RAVEN, his daughter, and two sons sit with William
Bent (*center*) at Fort Dodge.

Courtesy University of Oklahoma Library Manuscript Division

INDIANS IN COUNCIL with Colonel Wynkoop. The Arapahoes were represented by Little Raven, Big Mouth, Little Colt, Yellow Bear, Little Big Mouth, Standing Elk, Skunk, Foolboy, and Little Mountain. The lithograph is by Vincent Brooks Day and Son.

Courtesy Missouri Historical Society

"THE SEVEN WISE MEN OF THE GREAT FATHER" (Samuel Tappan, William Harney, William T. Sherman, John B. Sanborn, C. C. Augur, Alfred Terry, and Nathaniel G. Taylor) in council with the Arapahoes and Cheyennes at Fort Laramie.

SHARP NOSE, Northern Arapaho chief, wearing fine hairpipe breast-plate and choker.

Courtesy Bureau of American Ethnology

Laramie—to a mountain, a fort, a town, a city, and a county, as well as to the river on which he is believed to have met his death.

The year 1821 was important in the history of the Southwest because of Mexican independence and the establishment of the Santa Fé Trail. William Becknell of Missouri proved that it was practical to go by wagon train from Independence to Santa Fé.[14] He was followed by two important expeditions, one led by Thomas James and the other by Captain Hugh Glenn and Jacob Fowler. The great trail they helped to blaze made a beaten track through the country of the Arkansas River tribes. North and northwest of it could be found many bands of Arapahoes and Cheyennes, since a considerable part of the route touched their range. Even Bear Tooth, with his affection for the white man, found it hard to restrain his people from preying upon travelers on this inviting trail.

As early as 1806, Henry had spoken of the Buffalo Indians, the "Caneninavish," as a very numerous nation (five hundred tents) inhabiting "the sources of two large rivers, one of which empties into the Missouri River below the Pawnee village."[15] This he correctly believed to be the "Riviere Platte." The other, which he said ran to the south, "empties of course, into the Gulf of Mexico." Perhaps he was confused and meant only that the Indians inhabited the North and South forks of the Platte. Then again, he may have been referring to the Arapahoes on the headwaters of the Platte and the South People on the Arkansas. If so, Henry placed Our People—at least the South Men—on the Arkansas earlier than either Long or Agent Fitzpatrick, who refuted the claim of the Cheyennes to the Arkansas River in his annual report of 1847.[16] They had selected a place to settle along the river to

14 William Becknell, "Journal," in A. B. Hulbert (ed.), *Southwest on the Turquois Trail*, 56–68; see also *Missouri Historical Review* (cited hereafter as *MHR*), IV, 2 (January, 1910), 64–68; Thomas James, *Three Years Among the Indians and Mexicans*, 170; Fowler, *Journal*, 170.

15 Henry and Thompson, *New Light*, I, 383–84.

16 Fitzpatrick to Superintendent of Indian Affairs, Upper Platte Agency, October, 1847, Indian Office Records (cited hereafter as IOR), National Archives (cited hereafter as NA).

about fifty miles above Bent's Fort (near present Las Animas, Colorado).

> If [Fitzpatrick said] the right of preemption stands good, the Aripahoes have much the best right, as they occupied this country long before the Cheyennes ever saw it. Twenty years ago the Aripahoes were in possession of this country and north to the South Fork of the Platte and beyond, without any tribe to dispute their claim. The Cheyennes at that time were living on the south side of the Missouri river, between the Cheyenne and White rivers, and along the Black Hills.

Missouri trapper William Heddist was one of fifteen men who left Taos in April, 1824, to trap on the headwaters of the Upper Colorado (Green River).[17] The party eventually divided, and nine of the men continued to the head; the others, including Heddist, remained along the way. Fortunately for them, they were joined by another group, under the leadership of Antoine Robidoux, only two days before a war party of Indians attacked. All of the trappers were robbed and one man was killed. Heddist called the Indians Aripehos, but elsewhere they are referred to as Comanches or Shoshonis. There is a strong possibility they may have been Gros Ventres moving south for a visit with the Arapahoes. Also at this time, about thirty lodges of Arikaras broke away from their tribe to join the Arapahoes and Cheyennes along the Platte, but they were not well received.[18] Dogs, the Arapaho chief called them, and he disclaimed any responsibility for their conduct.

General W. H. Ashley, returning to the mountains in 1824, spent eleven days with the Loup Pawnees, whose usual wintering place was at the fork of the Platte.[19] While he was with these Indians, he discovered they were not on good terms with the Arapahoes and Kiowas but were anxious to cultivate friendly

[17] LeRoy R. Hafen and Ann W. Hafen, "The Old Spanish Trail," in *Far West and the Rockies*, I, 94.

[18] *St. Louis Enquirer*, July 19, 1824.

[19] Harrison C. Dale (ed.), *The Ashley-Smith Explorations and the Discovery of a Central Route to the Pacific*, 59-64, 126.

relations. Only two years before, Thomas James, who spent a number of years among the Indians, had encountered two thousand Pawnees who told him they had made peace with the Arapahoes and Comanches and were on their way to pay them a visit.[20] This was too long a time for the two tribes to remain at peace.

The Pawnees sent five men with Ashley to meet with the enemy and propose another treaty. At length the Pawnees, sensing that the Arapaho camp might be near by, tied bundles of wood on their backs and departed. But this was not the last Ashley was to hear of their peace efforts. Sometime around the first of February, his party was overtaken by three Arapahoes who said they had been visited by the Pawnee delegates, whom they received with friendship. After being told of Ashley's journey up the Platte, they set out with sixty or seventy other warriors from their encampment on the Arkansas to join him. The snow was so deep that they alone had proceeded after their second day's encampment.

After giving them presents, Ashley advised them to be at peace with the other tribes, especially the Pawnees, because it would be to the advantage of both. After thanking the white men for the gifts, the braves departed. We have no way of knowing whether or not they were among the warriors who later attacked one of Ashley's detachments in the Green River area.[21] Following the battle, in which one of the trappers was killed, the leader (James Clyman) joined Fitzpatrick, who was then in the Uinta Mountains of Colorado.

In 1828, Charles and William Bent and their partner, Ceran St. Vrain, established a small trading post at what is now Pueblo, Colorado. Their first mishap was an attack by the "Arapaos" on Sylvester Pratt's trapping party.[22] The details are lacking, but it was reported that Ceran's leg was broken. Then came an epidemic of smallpox, which brought disaster to the venture. Ceran, however, continued to trap as far as Green River, where he spent the

20 James, *Three Years Among the Indians and Mexicans*, 171.
21 James S. Clyman, *James Clyman, American Frontiersman*, 44.
22 Mooney, "The Cheyenne Indians," *loc. cit.*, 376.

most "vigrus" winter yet experienced. He planned to take his
furs to Missouri, but without ammunition, he was compelled to
give up and sell all he had to pay his hired men.

When Bent's Fort was built on the Arkansas some years later,
the junior partner (William) made a bid for the Cheyenne trade.
As a consequence, a large body of the nation left the Black Hills
and cast their lot in the area already claimed by the Arapahoes.
This major move, occurring in the early 1830's, created a division
of the Cheyennes, who before that time had come to the Southern
Plains chiefly to trade or to make war on the Kiowas, the last of
whom they had pushed from the Black Hills.

The division of the Arapahoes is not as obvious, for there had
been roving bands claiming their territory from the headwaters of
the North Platte to the Arkansas for many years. But the establishment of Bent's Fort and other posts along the two major streams
and their tributaries tended to draw certain bands to the area to
trade. Intermarriage between the whites and Indians cemented
relations, for the traders acquired not only the damsels of their
choice, but also their wives' extended families.

In later years the bands on the North Platte were to be known
generally as the Northern Cheyennes and Arapahoes, those on the
Arkansas the Southern. Bands of both Northern and Southern
Arapahoes frequented the South Platte, and Cherry Creek and its
environs became their heartland. Travelers on the Santa Fé Trail
met with harassment by Indians along the route, necessitating, in
the spring of 1829, the sending of troops from Fort Leavenworth
(Kansas) for their protection. Much of the trouble was attributed
to the Arapahoes. About 350 of them and their Kiowa and Comanche allies attacked the soldiers. There may have been some Gros
Ventres in the attacking force, for they were among the Arapahoes by now in considerable numbers.[23] The Arkansas River
tribes were still living in harmony, although relations were beginning to be strained. Horse stealing had been a part of their way
of life, but the difficulty between the tribes was becoming more

[23] *American State Papers,* IV, 277.

serious: they were starting to lift scalps belonging to members of previously friendly tribes.

When attacks along the trail proved more rewarding and less dangerous than intertribal warfare, the Arapahoes discovered that it was better to compromise than lose one of their men.[24] They would seldom risk the life of a warrior unless for revenge or in open warfare. Furthermore, they were quick in appraising a situation, and they did not hesitate to press their advantage when they found the white man lacking in numbers or arms.

Twelve traders encamped on the Cimarron River in 1828 were visited by a few seemingly friendly Arapahoes. When they observed the defenseless state of the white men, they withdrew, only to return with their number increased to thirty, all afoot and carrying rawhide ropes. They demanded horses, and the traders, afraid to deny them, gave them one apiece. Mounting their gift horses, they demanded two apiece. In desperation, one of the white men shouted, "Well, catch them!" At that the Indians sprang into action. Swinging their lariats and yelling, they dashed toward the herd and ran off all five hundred horses and mules belonging to the traders.

[24] Josiah Gregg, *Commerce of the Prairies* (Vols. XIX–XX in Reuben G. Thwaites [ed.], *Early Western Travels*), XIX, 177–81, and *Commerce of the Prairies*, ed. by Max L. Moorhead, 52–57. Although Ashley had little first-hand information, he believed the Arapahoes and Kiowas were principally to blame. See Dale L. Morgan, *The West of William H. Ashley*, 191. Chouteau (Chouteau Collection, MHS) also blamed the Arapahoes for some of the depredations attributed to the Pawnees.

CHAPTER THREE

$\mathcal{A}$ *Way of Life*

W<small>HILE CLAIMING</small> Colorado as their heartland, the Arapahoes reached the peak of their power and enjoyed their native culture to the fullest. Before the geographical separation, there were four bands: the Long Leg (Antelope), the Greasy Face, the Quick-to-Anger, and the Beaver.[1] Membership, though largely determined by birth, was as flexible as the names, for there was nothing to prevent anyone from going to live with friends and relatives in another band.

Each band had its favorite winter resort, from which the Indians, on the advent of spring, would sally forth on hunting excursions or for purposes of war, only to meet again at some specified place for their midsummer ceremonials. Each had its own chief and headmen, with the principal chief of the tribe being the leader of the band which had already gained prestige by having produced the previous dignitary. As a rule, he was an Antelope, so named because his group was constantly on the move. Nicknames by which the bands were recognized were temporal and indicative of the disposition of the leader, an incident worthy of note, the appearance of the members, or, in later years, their location. Although the office of the head chief was not hereditary, a son might distinguish himself to the extent that he could succeed his father. When the most exalted—though far from the most wealthy

---

[1] Band names vary with informants. See James Mooney, *The Ghost Dance Religion and the Sioux Outbreak of 1890*, BAE, *Fourteenth Annual Report*, Pt. 2, 956–59; Scott, "Early History," *loc. cit.*, 545–60; Kroeber, *The Arapaho*, 7–8; Henry Elkin, "The Northern Arapaho of Wyoming," in Ralph Linton (ed.), *Acculturation in Seven American Indian Tribes*, 207–55; Hilger, *Arapaho Child Life*, 187–89. The names of the bands above are those given by Sage (*ibid.*, 188). For Sage's autobiography, see A. F. C. Greene, "The Arapaho Indians" (Wyoming State Archives and Historical Department), 32–40.

—member of the tribe died, the bravest, most generous, and most popular leader from the Antelope band was chosen to take his place.

In 1897, Left Hand referred to the two bands among the Northerners as the Antelope and Spunky Men, and gave the names of the two among the Southerners as the Ugly Face (the band to which he belonged) and the Funny Men. He said the Ugly Face band was so named because many of the people were badly pock-marked from smallpox, while he gave as the reason for the name *Funny Men* that they were smaller in stature. They looked "funny" because of their size. Scott interpreted this to indicate an incorporation of other people into the tribe. F. V. Hayden also implied this in his 1862 study when he stated that he found the Southern Arapahoes referring to themselves by the obscure name *Na-wuth-i-ni-han*, which suggests "a mixture of different kinds of people of different bands."[2]

The chief-producing unit, the one referred to here as the Antelope, was later known (in reservation days) among the Northerners as the Forks-of-the-River band, whose area was in the vicinity of "Lower Arapaho" (Arapaho, Wyoming). The members there are predominantly Catholic, with Black Coal, their chief, being one of the first converts. Sherman Sage, a Northern Arapaho spokesman, was obviously referring to Black Coal's successor (Sharp Nose, of another band) when he said:

> By the time we separated into two groups, the Northern group and the Southern group, the whites had come among the Indians and our organization was pretty well disrupted. A chief was no longer chosen by our people because he belonged to a certain band. He was chosen because he had proved to be a leader of our people in our dealings with the whites.[3]

Some of the descendants of the Forks-of-the-River band still

---

[2] F. V. Hayden, "Contributions to the Ethnology and Philology of the Indian Tribes of the Upper Missouri Valley," *American Philological Society Transactions*, N.S., XII (1862), 321; Scott, "Early History," *loc. cit.*, 552.

[3] Mooney, *The Ghost Dance Religion*, 956; Kroeber, *The Arapaho*, 8.

maintain that Black Coal was the last real head chief of the Northern Arapahoes. Nevertheless, Sharp Nose, who was associated with the Ethete area, likewise served his people well, though it is possible that the white man may have been at least indirectly responsible for his selection.

Mooney mentions a third band, which he calls the Greasy Face, at Wind River under Spotted Horse. This may have been a small portion of the original band, recognized by this name. If so, it lost its identity in the Forks-of-the-River band under Black Coal or the Bad Pipes or Spunky Men under Sharp Nose. The older Indians do not recall a third band at Wind River. Sage, who claimed the Southerners had no bands, must have meant that they did not retain their original identity.

When the Indians assembled for ceremonial purposes, they formed a Camp Circle, exemplifying meticulous organization and responsibility.[4] Each band comprised a segment of the circle, which opened to the east. All important activities took place in a large tipi erected within the enclosure to house the keeper and Flat-Pipe, which was so sacred that it could not be carried horseback. The keeper, who was heavily guarded while the tribe was on the move, was forced to walk while he or his wife carried the precious bundle. Besides the Pipe, it included a petrified ear of corn and the turtle that was said to have brought up the clay in the creation myth. The Pipe was so holy that its name was mentioned with awe and reverence. Christianized Indians today consider it the Ark of the Covenant, or "Chariot of God," for the "shadow" (the soul) of the person who looks upon it is transported "home"—that is, to the place where souls go after death.[5]

Mooney, who was denied the privilege of seeing the "sacred medicine" in 1892, had been encouraged by the elders until he

[4] A semblance of the old Camp Circle is found in the vast circle of tipis on the Sun Dance ground at Wind River. A definite attempt to revive it was made in 1935. "It wasn't perfect, but it was the best we could do," Sage is quoted as saying. Hilger, *Arapaho Child Life*, 192–93.

[5] John G. Carter, "The Northern Arapaho Flat Pipe and the Ceremony of Covering the Pipe," BAE *Bulletin 119*, 69–101. For a correlation between the Flat-Pipe of the Gros Ventres and that of the Arapahoes, compare Carter's study with Cooper's *The Gros Ventres of Montana, II*, 33–129.

arrived at the Indian camp in the Wind River Mountains.[6] Weasel
Bear, a Basawaunina who later showed the Pipe to the reservation
missionary, the Reverend John Roberts, because of a special kindness, announced that a white man was among the Arapahoes to learn
"their sacred things, but these belong to the religion of the Indians,
and a white man has no business to ask about them." While studying the Arapaho culture in 1900, Kroeber saw only the bundle
hanging from its tripod in the Sun Dance Lodge as we see it today.[7]

Even though the bundle is reverently carried into the Offerings-Lodge and out again at the end of the ritual, it is at no time
revealed. Our People have a legend that long ago Flat-Pipe was
smoked on the Northern Plains, but because of the wickedness of
the tribesmen it became sealed. The only occasion upon which
it is revealed is during the Covering the Pipe Ceremony, which
has been conducted only once by a white man, John G. Carter,
an attorney, now deceased.[8]

Robert Friday, son of Chief Friday, directed Carter's every
move. Certain requirements had to be met, but first of all he had
to gain the confidence and help of "certain Arapahoes." No more
co-operative person could have been found than Friday. After
procuring the necessary gifts and agreeing to "do it their way,"
Carter entered into the spirit of the occasion. Every detail was
carried out and recorded to perfection, with the proper ritual.
Each gesture was slow and significant, and the prayers were either
silent or barely audible. There was no singing or dancing at any
time. Answers are vague with regard to why Carter was so
honored, but the fact remains that the Indians consider him the
only one who has ever had the right to "talk about" Flat-Pipe.

Next in importance to the Pipe is the sacred Wheel (*Hehotti*),
which is considered second only to Flat-Pipe.[9] About eighteen

[6] Mooney, *The Ghost Dance Religion*, 961–62.

[7] Adam Shakespeare, Keeper of the Pipe, traces his Basawaunina lineage
through his mother. His three predecessors were Fred Wallowing Bull, Oscar
White, and Collie Jutson.

[8] Carter, "The Northern Arapaho Flat-Pipe," 69–101; Kroeber, *The Arapaho*, 279–308.

[9] A Covering the Wheel Ceremony is also observed at Wind River. The
sacred Wheel of the Southern Arapahoes—that is, the last one used—is believed

inches in diameter, it is made of a circular piece of wood, with one end tapered like the tail of a serpent, the other fashioned into its head. Designs similar to those found on gaming wheels are incised on four opposite sides—two in the form of a cross (morning star) and the other two, the mythical Thunderbird. Like all Plains tribes, the Arapahoes believed that thunder and lightning were produced by Thunderbird, whose flapping wings caused the sound of thunder and whose flashing eyes sent forth lightning.[10] Dwelling in its nest were many smaller birds whose talons reached down and struck their victims. Four sets of eagle tail feathers—48 in all—are attached to the Wheel by means of buckskin thongs. The eagle feathers comprise the most sacred part of the Wheel, for that bird has always been prized for medicine purposes.

The outer rim of the sacred wheel is black and the inside red—the symbolic colors of the Sun Dance. The serpent is considered a harmless water snake, representing the oceans that surround the earth, while the four designs probably represent the Four Old Men, the four directions. The Wheel, like Flat-Pipe, has a keeper whose duty it is to protect it from all harm.[11] He may "wrap it" from time to time in accordance with a vow someone has made to "wrap the Wheel," a detailed ceremony similar to that of Covering the Pipe. In fact, it took the place of that ceremony among the Southern bands, who had no Flat-Pipe. The antiquity of the Wheel is unknown, but it is affirmed that the one belonging to the Southern tribe was broken in a windstorm about 1896 and had to be "renewed." It was inherited by Singing After, who is said to have made exorbitant charges for its use.[12] The Indians

---

to have fallen into the hands of a curio hunter and to have been lost in a fire that destroyed his establishment in Oklahoma City. Information supplied by Rowlodge and Yellow Hair, 1965.

[10] George A. Dorsey, *The Arapaho Sun Dance*, 12–21; Mooney, The Ghost Dance Religion, 967. Benny Goggles, the keeper of the sacred Wheel at Wind River, is also a medicine man.

[11] Robert H. Lowie, "Plains Indians Age Societies," AMNH *AP*, Vol. XI, Pt. 13, 919; Truman Michelson, "Narrative of an Arapaho Woman," *AA*, N.S., XXXV, 4 (1933), 596.

[12] Cheyenne and Arapaho Agency Correspondence, Indian Archives Division, Oklahoma Historical Society (cited hereafter as OHS).

requested that they be allowed to have another made. The Bureau of Indian Affairs had no objection, so they called upon a Northern Arapaho to make the last one used.

The unsung heroes of the migratory tribe may have been the Coyote Men, whose duty it was to take up stations on the nearest and highest hills to keep watch and give warning in case of the approach of an enemy.[13] There was no ceremony for these sentries, but they performed an important service. Pledged to celibacy for the duration of their office, they usually numbered about six or eight braves who took great pride in the performance of their duties. They distinguished themselves by wearing white buffalo robes and painting their faces with white clay. Each carried a "coyote gun" or club decorated with feathers and other ornaments. Upon his resignation, a Coyote Man could choose his successor and deliver to him his staff of authority. The rugged guardsman, who built no shelter but depended upon the protection of his buffalo robe, seldom returned from the hills, even to sleep, for it was there that he received his inspiration.

In the highly organized Arapaho society, marriage was institutional.[14] No normal Indians remained single, except for the Coyote Men during their term of office. Marriage took two forms: the family sanctioned and the romantic. The man desiring to have a girl for his wife would negotiate through one of his female relatives, and the girl would be represented by an older brother or, if she had no brother, by an uncle. After his approval had been given to the match, he would discuss matters with her parents, and there might be an exchange of gifts between the two families before the girl was even consulted. In fact, she had little to say in the matter. She could reject the offer, it is true, but she almost invariably followed the wishes of her male relatives, regardless of how she felt.

Occasionally a girl might be so fond of a suitor that she would elope with him in spite of her brother's disapproval. This was the romantic and less honorable form of marriage. But she was not

13 Kroeber, *The Arapaho*, 279–308.
14 Hilger, *Arapaho Child Life*, 193–216.

necessarily a family outcast, since she could redeem herself by bringing peace offerings or by inducing her husband to present a horse to the offended parents. Then all would be forgiven. Cousins were called "brothers" and "sisters" and marriage was forbidden among relatives, however remote.[15]

As a rule, in the family-type marriage, the girl's parents would provide her tipi. After the couple had entered their new dwelling, there would be a feast, accompanied by prayer and words of advice. But when the feast was over, the in-law taboos had to be recognized.[16] A man and his mother-in-law could speak to each other only if he presented her with a horse. Similar restrictions applied to the father and his daughter-in-law, except that not even a horse could be given. Brothers and sisters were not permitted to sit near each other or speak after puberty, a taboo which may have been engendered by the desire to keep blood relatives of different sexes apart. If they found it necessary to communicate, they would have someone relay the message. A woman of any age was not supposed to look at her brother, "a sign of respect."

Polygamy was practiced freely, but there was no polyandry. If the brother had a sister of marriageable age who was admired by his brother-in-law, he might give her to him, even though he already had one or more wives. If the wives were sisters, one tipi was considered sufficient, but if they were unrelated, there was ordinarily one tipi for each. Upon the death of a husband, his brother was obligated to marry the widow.

Some husbands were kind, but wife beating was not frowned upon. Powder Face, a notable warrior of the Southern Arapahoes, exemplified an affectionate husband.[17] He would sit in front of his tipi and lovingly stroke his wife's tresses, regardless of who might see. On the other hand, a jealous husband could abuse his wife by cutting off her nose or by slashing her cheeks if she were found guilty of misconduct. And yet the offended husband could

[15] Kroeber, *The Arapaho*; Michelson, "Narrative of an Arapaho Woman," *loc. cit.*, 596–610.
[16] Kroeber, *The Arapaho*, 10; Truman Michelson, "Some Arapaho Kinship Terms and Social Usages," *AA*, N.S., XXXVI (1834), 137–39.
[17] Hubert E. Collins, *Warpath and Cattle Trail*, 193–94.

readily be appeased by a "pipe of settlement" or by the gift of a horse from his wife's paramour. It was not unusual for a husband to make an outright gift of his wife to another man. Since children were usually reared by grandparents anyway, there was no problem of a broken home.

Certain taboos were observed relative to various stages of life, though the Arapahoes did not have menstrual huts, puberty rites, or coming-of-age ceremonies. William Philo Clark attributed to the Gros Ventres a "Manhood Dance," but no corresponding ceremony can be found among the Arapaho proper.[18] During their menstrual period, women were not permitted to enter a sick room or take part in any ceremonial practices, a law that was supposed to be imparted from mother to daughter. A married woman would refrain from wearing the clothing of a pregnant woman because she feared she might "catch" pregnancy.[19] She was even reluctant to discuss childbirth because she might cause a relative to become "that way." Medicine men and women could produce fertility and sterility, the former through the administration of a potion of boiled roots and the latter by fumigation using a smudge of herbs. The secret of these medicines was not divulged by those having the power to administer them.

Babies were born in the family tipi or, if the tribe were migrating, in the open. Although the father was not even present for the ordeal, he was the parent to be congratulated. For the most part, babies were loved and tenderly cared for, and yet families were usually limited. While abortions seem to have been unknown, the practice of limiting a family by nursing an infant four or more years was prevalent.

Both men and women observed certain food taboos, one of the most necessary being the abstinence from eating "twins"— the tenderloin, or the two rows of meat lying next to the backbone of the buffalo. Boys as well as girls were admonished to refrain from eating such "undesirable" portions of the butchered animal from childhood through child-bearing age. If they violated this

[18] Clark, *The Indian Sign Language*, 198.
[19] Hilger, *Arapaho Child Life*, 4, 12–14, 217.

taboo, twins would be born to them. This also held true with twin seeds or twin nuts, which were to be avoided. A pregnant woman further refrained from eating rabbit, lest her child have a harelip, and she would not drink hot tea or hot water, for it would cause difficulty during childbirth.

A nursing mother would likewise refrain from drinking hot substances, hot coffee in particular, for fear it might "cook" the milk.[20] She would protect her breasts carefully from the heat of the fire or the sun for the same reason. There are those still living who remember that the colostrum in the mother's first milk was considered unwholesome and such milk was not given to an infant. In order that her milk might be "good," the mother would have a baby raccoon nurse first.

The umbilical cords of both boy and girl babies were put away to dry.[21] These the mothers preserved in beaded amulets stuffed with sweetgrass. The small bags were shaped to represent the long-lived lizard, as a rule, to help the child reach maturity. The amulet might be tied to the cradleboard or braided in the hair and later attached to the clothing in the case of a girl. The mother usually kept her son's among her treasures, but it was never thrown away. For baby powder, she used dried buffalo manure to diaper her infant before strapping him on the cradleboard. It was considered more absorbent and less chafing than cow or horse manure.

A cradle—a separate one for each child—was made jointly by several women under the direction of one of the Seven Old Women.[22] As the women worked, they prayed that the cradle might be well made and that the baby who would occupy it might have a long life. This ceremony took place before the child was born to assure his having a haven of comfort and a feeling of security. A typical Arapaho cradle was ornamented with quill-work, even after beads became the vogue of other tribes, princi-

[20] Kroeber, *The Arapaho*, 16; Hilger, *Arapaho Child Life*, 44–46.
[21] Hilger, *Arapaho Child Life*, 22–24; Kroeber, *The Arapaho*, 54–58.
[22] For a detailed description of an Arapaho cradle, see "A Northern Arapaho Quilled Cradle," *Material Culture Notes*, Denver Art Museum, 53–60. See also Kroeber, *The Arapaho*, 16.

pally because the women thought quills, colored with various vegetable dyes, were prettier. The cradleboard was a practical device, for the mother could attach it to her back, hang it on the pommel of her saddle or on a tree limb, or stand it to one side so that she would be free to use her hands in her arduous tasks.

Mrs. D. B. Dyer, who came to the Cheyenne and Arapaho Reservation in 1883 as the bride of the Indian agent at Darlington, Oklahoma, had an opportunity to study the Indian way of life before it had been changed materially by the white man.[23] She was intrigued by the babies she found strapped to their cradleboards and by the older infants she could see "peeping over the mother's shoulder as they were held in place by her bright-colored shawl, where the child rode securely and apparently without the slightest inconvenience." Mrs. Dyer never failed to unwrap their heads to admire "their little round dark faces, clear bright eyes, and their heavy, thick, black hair, and then examine, in wonder, the infinitesimal beaded bags of medicine braided in their tiny scalp-locks, and the different kinds and shapes of hocus-pocus, put in and around the little precious creatures to keep away bad angels."

When the child was ready to learn to talk, the mother would feed him the boiled meat and eggs of a meadow lark, which could, according to legend, speak the Arapaho tongue.[24] She might also further his speech by rubbing the bill of the bird between his lips. About this time or soon after, the infant's ears were supposed to be pierced. This was done ceremonially when the father could afford to pay a respected elder his due for performing the service, which was usually worth a horse. If this were not done before the next Sun Dance, the children would be taken to the Offerings-Lodge, where the medicine man would go through the motion of piercing their ears. A grandfather would later finish the process with a porcupine quill or sometimes a knife. If the baby cried, this was considered good, for it showed that he had endured pain,

[23] Mrs. D. B. Dyer, *Fort Reno or Picturesque Cheyenne and Arapaho Army Life before the Opening of Oklahoma*, 65.
[24] For words to the Meadow Lark Song, see Kroeber, *The Arapaho*, 317–18. Hilger says (*Arapaho Child Life*, 42 n.) the song is considered evil and the child is not allowed to sing it.

and he was consequently prepared to face the hardships of life. Later, in reservation days, when school children were forced to cut their hair, they would also be brought to the Offerings-Lodge, where this disagreeable but necessary task could be performed by a medicine man.

The mystery of death, as well as of birth, involved the supernatural, and the Arapahoes in general believed that the spirit of the deceased went to the land of the rising sun on a plain far away, beyond and below the mountains.[25] A warrior killed in battle did not have to travel over this long trail; rather, he was privileged to go along the "comfortable road," the Milky Way. Left Hand, however, believed that the dead went upward and perhaps later turned into owls. He is quoted as saying: "Sometimes when there is a sick person in a lodge and a whirlwind (a "dust devil") strikes the lodge, the sick person dies and his spirit goes out of his body with the whirlwind. When we see a whirlwind coming down the road . . . we get out of the way—that is a dead man's spirit. If I do not get out of the way it will take my life."[26]

Our People, who believed in reincarnation, thought an old person might return to live again in the form of a wrinkled, emaciated baby. This did not mean that reincarnation in human form came to all. Even those subject to rebirth lost their identity, for they were not recognizable, except that they caused certain babies to be old looking.

When death occurred, the grieving members of the family would often tear off a sleeve and gash themselves on the arms and legs or even on the forehead.[27] Then they would unbraid their hair and bob it proportionately to the esteem in which they held the deceased. The corpse was placed in state so that all might see it. One horse was given to anyone furnishing fine clothing for the

[25] Clark, *The Indian Sign Language*, 41; Mooney, *The Ghost Dance Religion*, 983; H. R. Voth, "Funeral Customs Among the Cheyenne and Arapaho Indians," *Folklorist*, I (1893); Kroeber, *The Arapaho*, 11; Hilger, *Arapaho Child Life*, 160–68.

[26] Scott, "Early History," *loc. cit.*, 559.

[27] Kroeber, *The Arapaho*, 16–17.

burial and another to the gravedigger for his service. The grave, somewhere in the hills, had to be deep enough to prevent wild animals from digging up the body. To safeguard it further, thorny brush was placed atop the grave. Hair cut from grieving relatives was wrapped and buried with the dead.

At the grave, the man's best horse was shot and left lying. The mane and tail of the horse on which the body was taken to its burial were cut off and the hair was strewn on top of the grave. Weapons were sometimes buried with the body, though this was not the general rule. After the funeral, which took place the same day if the person died before sundown or the next day if after, the family would give away the tipi in which the death had occurred. If it happened to be in a brush shelter instead of a skin lodge, the temporary dwelling was destroyed.

The survivors would burn cedar leaves at least four nights to keep the spirit away, for it was thought that it would tarry that length of time. The mystic number four is also found in the belief that the Indian knew four days ahead of time when death was to occur. Unlike the Shoshonis, who were afraid of mentioning the name of the deceased for fear of calling back the spirit in the form of a ghost, the Arapahoes spoke the name of the departed freely, and if he happened to be a man of distinction, his name was often perpetuated by being given to someone else. Like other Plains Indians, Our People feared the dark, and as a consequence, fighting would cease at nightfall, to be resumed at daybreak. They were also afraid of ghosts, especially "ghost arrows," which might be shot mysteriously into their bodies and which, although invisible, could cause great pain. Relief came only when a medicine man had sucked these out of the flesh.

Since there were no rules governing the distribution of property, the survivors were without rights, and little generosity was shown the widow or orphans. Usually the brothers and sisters of the deceased confiscated the property, even though the family might try to prevent their doing so. Sometimes dissatisfied survivors would kill the horses and attempt to destroy other property that had been confiscated. Only occasionally was a grown son or daughter allowed to keep what we would consider a natural inheritance.

Mourning sometimes lasted from one to three years, and it was not uncommon for a woman to cut off a finger at the first joint as an expression of grief or as a vow to cause her to live.[28] While in mourning, the Indians wore old clothes, showed little interest in amusements, and left unbraided and uncombed their hair after it was cut at the time of bereavement. Although the mourners frequently visited the grave, there was no ritual connected with their visits—that is, they did not place furniture or food on it, nor did they build a fire near by as some tribes were wont to do.

When the mourning period was at an end, the bereaved would invite some of the old men and women to their tipi to share food with them. There an elder would paint their faces and hair red.[29] The Paint Ceremony was spoken of as a cleansing rite, and it usually took place in the morning so that those whose lives were to be renewed could be further purified by spending the day in the sunshine. After this, the period of grief was over, and the survivors could braid their hair again and return to a normal life.

There seems to have been no punishment for a murderer beyond his being shunned by other members of the tribe, who insisted that his food would taste bitter thereafter.[30] The usual practice was for him to reinstate himself with the family of the person he had killed by presenting a horse. If it were accepted, his offense was pardoned.

Even though Our People are mystified by the origin of the tribal name, they have always placed great significance in individual names. Most members of the tribe had three or four during their lifetime, names that were either "new" or "used."[31] A new

[28] Michelson, "Narrative of an Arapaho Woman," *loc, cit.,* 604–605.

[29] The Northern Arapaho Paint Ceremony is held publicly. The one the author witnessed took place at night, just before the second annual powwow at Ethete (1966). The keeper of the Pipe offered a silent prayer over the participants and a woman helper painted their cheeks red.

[30] Kroeber, *The Arapaho,* 17.

[31] Hilger, *Arapaho Child Life,* 58–67, 105.

name might represent an incident that had occurred before a child's birth, or it might involve animals, freaks of nature, or war experiences worthy of being remembered. A used name could be one belonging to a distinguished elder whose name might assure the longevity of the child.

The various names applied to an individual were usually given consecutively, and it was not uncommon for someone to ask another for his name. If he were willing to give a horse in exchange, the request was not denied, and a name of his choice was officially bestowed upon him at the next meeting of his age society. The one deprived would take another and announce his choice at a meeting of his society. Handsome Scabby Bull of the Southern Arapahoes was at one time known as Sitting Bull, but when the Northern Arapaho Sitting Bull gained distinction in the Ghost Dance Cult after coming to Oklahoma, Scabby Bull relinquished the name in his favor.

The occurrence of the same name more than once in a single tribe, as well as in neighboring tribes, has resulted in confusion. There were three Sitting Bulls of importance in intertribal plains history, one Arapaho and two Sioux, and there were three Roman Noses, one Arapaho (Medicine Man) and two Cheyennes. There were many Left Hands among the Arapahoes and Cheyennes. Not only was Left Hand, chief of the Southern Arapahoes, erroneously reported killed at Sand Creek, but the worthy chief was later said to have been one of the two Arapaho prisoners sent with more than seventy other Plains Indian prisoners to Fort Marion, Florida, in 1875. The first was a false report, the second a case of mistaken identity, for the Left Hand who was taken to Fort Marion was a Cheyenne. A perusal of census records and allotment sheets, an excellent source for Arapaho nomenclature, shows what names were like when they were meaningful and it took a horse and a meeting of an age society to change them.

Food was plentiful before the white man overran the plains, and the Arapaho, either with or without the horse, was a proficient hunter. Big game consisted for the most part of buffalo, deer, and elk, which furnished hides for lodgings and clothing besides supplying the chief diet.[32] In winter, hunters might work singly or in pairs as they tracked their quarry, or they might clothe themselves in wolf skins and stalk their prey. Their old technique of driving buffalo over cliffs continued to be practiced to some extent where the terrain was favorable as long as they could be found. One of the major buffalo runs used by the Platte River Indians may be seen near Interstate Highway 25 on the bluffs near Chimney Rock in the Chugwater, Wyoming, area. When the early pioneers arrived, wagonloads of buffalo bones could still be found at the base of the bluffs.

Women of the tribe gathered and stored wild fruits and vegetables for winter use, for chokecherries, squawberries, wild haws, and currants grew in profusion along the headwater streams. They prepared pemmican with dried meat, pounded fine and mixed, as a rule, with melted fat, marrow, and a paste from wild chokecherries, crushed pits and all. Sometimes this was placed in skin casings, at others it was dried in cakes resembling sausage patties, but dark in color from the chokecherry stain.[33]

The family dwelling, or skin lodge, of the Plains tribes varied in the number and size of poles.[34] The Arapahoes, Cheyennes, and Gros Ventres used a three-pole foundation, while the Shoshonis, Comanches, Blackfeet, Crows, and Utes used four. The former was considered more wind resistant. Authorities pronounced the Crow tipi more elegant in shape but inferior to the Arapaho in painted decorations. An outlet was left at the top for the smoke to escape, and the lodgeskin flaps were attached to two poles outside the general framework. The opening at the top could be closed in bad weather by moving the poles.

The tipi, its entrance facing the rising sun, had the prevailing west winds at its back. The opening was shielded by a skin curtain with a stick at the bottom and top. After a person entered, the curtain would drop back into place. The Arapahoes had an ingenious bed on a frame a few inches off the ground, with a

[32] For a discussion of Arapaho foods and their preparation, see *ibid.*, 175–79. See also Robert H. Lowie, *Indians of the High Plains*, 13–14.

[33] Lowie, *Indians of the High Plains*, 30–32.

[34] Clark, *The Indian Sign Language*, 39.

66

backrest at the head and foot. Ceremonial objects were placed at the rear inside the tipi; a fireplace and kettle for cooking occupied the center. Horn spoons, bowls, and weapons of war were likewise in evidence.

The dress of Our People followed the usual Plains Indian custom, with moccasins the distinguishing garb.[35] The soles were of tough rawhide, the rest deerskin or other soft leather. The front, or tongue, was short, but the upper part of the moccasin was long enough to turn over at the top, with the leather cuff extending about the beadline.

Styles in hairdress changed, and the dignitaries eventually discarded the bun over the forehead. For a time, the warriors parted their hair on each side and left it standing in the middle "to make them look fierce."[36] Later they changed their style to braids or masses tied together over the ears, with a scalplock in the middle of the back of the head. Women wore their hair loose before adopting the style of parting and braiding it on both sides. Young women painted streaks down their faces and on their cheeks, forehead, and nose to signify war, but old women painted a spot on each cheekbone, one on the forehead, one between the eyes, and a line from the mouth down to the chin to indicate peace. Faces might be painted for ceremonial purposes or merely for decoration, but paint on the face was generally symbolic of happiness, since mourners refrained from its use.

As we have mentioned, ceremonial smoking was highly important, since no stranger was greeted, no friend or relative entertained, no war party organized without a smoke. The pipe might be of red catlinite, such as other Plains tribes used, or it might be no more than the legbone of an antelope. It was of no set length or design, but to a people given to ceremonials, it was indispensable. The bands in the mountain areas to the north smoked a mixture of kinnikinnick and pulverized tobacco, while those on the Southern Plains used crushed sumac leaves. Before tobacco was obtained in trade with the whites, members of both Northern

[35] BAE *Bulletin 148*, Pl. 14.
[36] Kroeber, *The Arapaho*, 21–30.

and Southern bands smoked whatever they could find. According to one of the Southerners, they often used grape and oak leaves, which they dipped in meat soup and wrapped to keep them fresh.

Politically, economically, and socially, the Arapahoes were well organized and satisfactorily adjusted before the arrival of the white man. Harmonious relationships in the extended families within the bands helped to maintain functional units. Communal responsibility was practiced to a high degree, and the unwritten laws of the tribe, which will be discussed in the next chapter, were respected and obeyed. And yet they in no way prevented the individual from living to the fullest his life of freedom.

CHAPTER FOUR

"All the Lodges"

THE ARAPAHOES group their tribal ceremonies, except the
rites connected with Flat-Pipe and the Wheel and the shamanistic
practices and small-scale celebrations involving the main events
in family life, under the general head *Bayaawu*, or "All the
Lodges." First and most important, they include the Sun Dance;
second, the age societies for men; third, the Buffalo Lodge, the
only organization known to have been devised exclusively for
women.

According to an account attributed to Tall Bull, a Southern
Arapaho, All the Lodges originated from a vision involving a
man and his wife who were, at the time, camping at the side of a
river.[1] One morning when he went in search of food, he saw in
the light of the rising sun a buffalo cow. He made an attempt to
head her off, but she eluded him. Finally catching up with her at
the water's edge, he "sat down to shoot."

Looking toward him reproachfully, she said: "Leave me
alone; don't shoot me. I want to tell you something that will be
for your benefit and the benefit of your people."

In consternation, the man laid his weapons on the ground
and listened as she spoke. "I have taken pity on you," she reminded
him, "although you tried to kill me. . . . There shall be lodges for
different societies among your people; in these my whole body
can be used for various purposes."

Then she explained the *Bayaawu*. Instead of killing the cow,
the man returned to his people and told them about his vision,
which was to become a law for them in the future. In this manner,
laws and codes were revealed and handed down through secret

[1] Kroeber, *The Arapaho*, 151–54.

rites from one generation to another. They were rigidly enforced by the more advanced age societies.

The Sun Dance took the form of a religious service and was highly important, though held but once a year, for it brought the various bands together and helped to maintain unity. It was a large-scale reunion, an occasion in which members of different bands could renew old acquaintances and exchange bits of information on all that had happened since they last met. This did not minimize the religious significance of the Sun Dance, but it added enjoyment to the event while the bands temporarily occupied their place in the Camp Circle.

Wrapping the Pipe or the Wheel might be done at any time, but the "pledger" who "put on" the Sun Dance had only one opportunity per year to carry out his vow. The ceremony, which began with the individual and his pledge, subsequently involved the priests, the directors, the dancers, the "grandfathers" and the musicians. The age societies, in pre-reservation days, were a vital part of the procedure, and each of the lodges had a special duty to perform.[2]

The most exhaustive study of the Sun Dance on record is that made among the Southern Arapahoes in 1901 and 1902 by George A. Dorsey, then curator of the Department of Anthropology at the Field Columbian Museum.[3] His work is valuable because he was able to record the details of the ritual as they were carried out by the old order. Even though it concerned the now extinct Southern Arapaho Sun Dance, it is of special interest today because it is the guidebook used by the Northern Arapahoes for their ritual. Dorsey's account is preferred to Kroeber's because it is more complete, even to colored pictures showing the paints

[2] Since the age societies are no longer in existence, duties which were once automatically assumed by them are now handled by the chairman of the Sun Dance Committee. Interview with Benny Goggles, chairman, Ethete, Wyoming, 1965.

[3] Dorsey, *The Arapaho Sun Dance.* The Sun Dance reviewed briefly above was held in Indian Territory (Oklahoma) in 1902. The one witnessed by Dorsey the previous year was hurried and some of the details were omitted because of bad weather.

used. As one might expect, there is a marked similarity between
the two rituals.

Dorsey describes the Southern Arapahoes as joyous in their
Camp Circle, made up of the bands which were at that late date
scarcely functional. Their ritual, the same as it had been for
generations, had a completeness and spontaneity which he found
lacking in other performances. Whether he happened along when
the dance was momentarily sanctioned by the government, which
had done everything but outlaw it, or whether he had a hand in
staging it so that he could write about it is an argument that has
not been settled. Correspondence in the Cheyenne and Arapaho
Agency files at the Oklahoma Historical Society indicates that
there were those who labeled the spectacle a fraud.[4]

The formation of the Camp Circle was the forerunner of the
eight-day ceremony. The event itself began with a prayer by the
high priest, who impersonated the sun. This took place in the
lodge of the head of the age society to which the pledger belonged.
The priest, painted red even to his sheet, then stopped at three
different stations within the circle to address himself to Man-
Above, Old-Woman Night, and the advanced age societies. Then
he prayed for peace and happiness for all. After pronouncing the
name of the one who had vowed the dance, he instructed some of
the members of his age society to find a complete buffalo hide and
make a frame for it in the form of the animal, since live buffalo
(by 1900) were no longer available.[5]

The erection of the Rabbit-Lodge was the first order of
business. The name of the tipi was derived from a myth in which
a male and female rabbit conducted the rites in the Offerings-
Lodge, and the men helping with the ritual were known as Rabbit
Men or Rabbit People. After the sacred Wheel was taken into the

[4] Cheyenne and Arapaho Agency Correspondence, Indian Archives Division, OHS. John H. Seger, for whom Seger Colony (Colony, Oklahoma) is named,
was the most outspoken in his opposition. When efforts were being made by the
government to suppress the Sun Dance, it was continued under other names.
See also Sun Dance File, OHS.

[5] Today all addresses and announcements are handled by means of a loud-
speaker.

Rabbit-Lodge, a secret ceremony was conducted by important tribal members.

As the rites continued into the second day, the Lodge-Maker's robe was prepared, the ceremonial straight pipe was filled, and a piece of rawhide was cut for the center pole. During the time these activities were taking place and the Sun Dance songs were being rehearsed, duties were being performed by other members of the tribe elsewhere, the most significant being the "killing" of the buffalo. An old warrior, who was granted this privilege, mounted his horse and, with gun in hand, charged the stationary creature on a wooden frame, going through the act of buffalo hunting before finally shooting it. Other important functions included the search for timbers for the great lodge and the preparation of the lariat to hold the willows to the center pole. Late in the afternoon, three Rabbit Men left their tipi and went in search of a desirable location for the Sweat-Lodge.

Its construction took place on the third day, when willow canes were planted securely at one end and bent to form a dome-shaped enclosure, which was covered with robes.[6] A buffalo skull was placed in front of the lodge so that it looked toward the entrance. On top of it was temporarily placed the Wheel, with the feathers hanging down upon the skull. When all was in readiness, the Wheel was taken inside and the ceremonial sweat began. Other important events of the day included the bringing in of the cedar tree, a part of the main ceremony in the Offerings-Lodge, and the Lodge-Maker's public appeal for presents to help defray the expense of the ceremony.

Excitement ran high on the fourth day as the war societies staged a lively sham battle, which took place when the center pole was being "captured." The victorious society had the privilege of dragging it to the middle of the Camp Circle, where it was placed with the other poles needed in the construction of the Offerings-Lodge. Before the day was out, the center pole, with its offerings—a buffalo robe, a bundle of willows, a ceremonial

[6] In the Northern Arapaho ritual, the sweat follows the dance—that is, on the eighth day. It is a concluding purification rite for the participants.

digging stick, and the less practical but more ornate moon shells and eagle tail feathers—securely fastened in the fork, was raised to its proper position. The other poles and beams were quickly assembled and the construction of the great lodge was complete. Ceremonial articles, including the Wheel, skull, straight pipe, rattle, badger pack, and paint bags, were then placed within the lodge on a temporary altar.

After the evening meal, the Lodge-Maker and others required to fast throughout the remainder of the ceremony entered the enclosure and the Offerings-Lodge was prayerfully dedicated. Following the singing of several Sun Dance songs, the rawhide was incensed, and the Offering-to-the-Moon rite was observed. Lodge-Maker's wife was Mother Earth for the duration of the eight-day event, and her body was painted red—the earth and Indian color. According to Arapaho mythology, through the marriage of Moon to Mother Earth, a son, Lone Star (the North Star) was born. At the conclusion of the rite, the grandfather and the Lodge-Maker's wife left briefly but returned for the ceremonial smoke. Dorsey discusses this part of the service as having taken place in 1901 and 1902, but it was one of the "undesirable features" which were suppressed when the Sun Dance was revived at Wind River about thirty years ago.[7] Another was self-torture. A dancer would fasten a buffalo skull to a thong laced through the muscles in his back and drag it until the weight pulled the thong through the flesh. This was a carryover of the old system of attaching the dancer's body to the center pole by means of a thong, which would eventually sever the muscles of the chest. One of the elders explained this as suffering for the sins of the tribe.

For the first part of the dance, the participants were covered from head to foot with white body paint. Dressed in kilts, they had "breath feathers" in their scalplocks and eagle-bone whistles in their mouths when the ritual in the lodge began. The first period of dancing was directed reverently to Man-Above, to whom they

[7] The Sun Dance was not revived among the Arapahoes of Oklahoma. A reason given by one of the elders is that all who knew how to put it on properly had died.

73

addressed their silent prayers as they danced and blew their whistles. The dancing and drum beating continued, with brief intermissions, throughout the night.[8]

On the fifth day, the dancers formed a line facing toward the center of the lodge just before sunrise. When the singing and the beating of the drum began, they faced east and whistled and danced until the sun appeared above the horizon. Following this, they relaxed until the altar was completed. At this time they received their second paint, some yellow and others pink. When the priests marked off a consecrated spot, members of one of the age societies brought the necessary articles.

As a preliminary step in the construction of the altar, a trench about twelve inches wide, eighteen inches long east and west, and three inches deep was dug. The priests had already outlined the spot where the old sod was to be removed and the altar made. Two clumps of fresh sod with just the right texture were brought in and prayed over. They had been trimmed in such a way that they were round, with one (the "father") larger than the other (the "mother"). The two sods were thickly studded with rabbit brush, the emblem of fruit or fertility, and were placed to the west as the background for the altar. Beyond them were seven half-grown trees that had been transplanted for the occasion. One was a small cedar (a gift from Man-Above), which provides incense from its twigs; another a willow, which signifies long life and cleanliness; and the other five cottonwoods, which represent the five fingers and toes.

Fourteen small sticks—seven painted black and seven red, each about eighteen inches long—were sharpened at one end and placed in neat rows along the two outer sides of the trench, and seven curved cottonwood sticks, sharpened at both ends, were inserted in parallel rows within the pit. At the west end of the

[8] The Arapahoes, unlike the Shoshonis, do not dance to and from the center pole. They remain in one position as they blow their whistles, flex their knees, and fix their gaze on a spot above their heads on the center pole. All minor details are arranged by the grandfathers, who are a necessary but expensive part of the service. One estimate places the cost of a Northern Arapaho Sun Dance to a participant at about $300. This in itself eliminates the irresponsible.

trench was the buffalo skull, now painted with dots, and at the base of each row of upright sticks was a billet painted the same color. Everything to the north of the middle was red, everything to the south black, even to the color of the dots on the skull. When the altar was finished, the Wheel was placed at the west end with the head of the serpent looking east.

After this important work had been completed, time was taken to distribute gifts from Lodge-Maker to those who assisted with the various rites. Then the dancers, following the ceremonial washing of their bodies with wet sage, were painted again; they danced at intervals throughout the night.

Following the ritual to the rising sun, the morning of the sixth day, the dance continued as before, with periodic intermissions. A necessary part of the morning service each day in the Offerings-Lodge was the bringing of quantities of food, by the families of the dancers, for the grandfathers (or godfathers, as we would call them), who were to be honored by the participants the rest of their lives. After the pipe had been blessed by the high priests, the dancers and their grandfathers took part in the ceremonial smoke.

On the seventh day, the food offering, the smoke, and the paint ceremony were repeated in the morning before the dancing was resumed for the day. In the afternoon came the ceremony of the Wheel, perhaps the most difficult ordeal during the eight-day service because by now the Lodge-Maker and the dancers were at the point of exhaustion. Encouragement came from shouting women, who hoped to prevent a dancer from falling at this crucial time.[9] During the rite, Lodge-Maker, stirred by emotion, held up the Wheel toward the center pole from time to time as he prayed silently and begged Man-Above to look down upon him.

His grandfather finally took the Wheel with both hands and placed over his head with the feathers hanging down in front. This signified that Lodge-Maker had received "the Father's gift" for all of his people. Medicine water ("cherry water," as they call

[9] At the Northern Arapaho Sun Dance, this is done by an elder whose duty it is to exhort the dancers and keep up their spirits.

it at Wind River), made by secret formula, was then brought to the west of the lodge. Following the dance to the setting sun, the participants drank an emetic, then the holy water.

In the ceremony witnessed by Dorsey, the performers again danced to the sun in the purification rites on the morning of the eighth day.[10] Then the priests and dancers formed a semicircle, the priests toward the center. The straight pipe was passed down the line, with all smoking ceremonially. About ten o'clock the service ended, except for the sacrifice of clothing at the altar and at the center pole. While two of the priests rewrapped the sacred articles, women came forward and prayerfully made a sacrifice of their children's outgrown clothing. By noon, all sacrifices having been made, the offerings were left to the elements and the Indians returned to their respective locations.

Many changes had no doubt occurred in the old Sun Dance formula by the time Dorsey saw it, and many have been made since. The chief difference between the Northern and Southern Arapaho rituals is that the Flat-Pipe is included in the former. It is brought into the Offerings-Lodge at the beginning of the dance and removed with great solemnity before the conclusion. It has no direct function, however, except that the bundle is covered repeatedly while it hangs from its tripod to the south of the center pole.

The Arapaho ceremony at Wind River concludes with the appearance of the evening star at the end of the seventh day. Many years ago, when the Cheyennes and Arapahoes were camping side by side and holding their ceremonies at the same time, all of the participants died soon afterwards and the elders believed that they had done wrong by ending at sunset. Henceforth they would dance until the appearance of the evening star.

There are those who are prone to look upon the Sun Dance

10 After the purification rites in the Sweat-Lodge, the people go their way. The colorful scarves hanging from the overhead beams in the lodge are a reminder of the sacrificial gifts in the old Offerings-Lodge. The brush sides are taken away and the poles are sold—all but the center pole, which is too sacred to destroy. Upright poles marking the sites of former Sun Dances stand as stark reminders.

as a free show or pageant, but there is no question that it has always been and always will be a deeply religious experience in the lives of the Arapahoes, who do their best to discourage its becoming a tourist attraction. One year they did not even reveal the date to their agent until they had assembled from Oklahoma and elsewhere and the ceremony was already in progress.

The second division of the *Bayaawu* concerned the age societies, through which the unwritten laws of the tribe were transmitted.[11] Almost the entire population, from the pre-adolescent to the aged, belonged to one of the eight age-graded societies. Those who did not belong to one of the orders were held in disrespect and not permitted to take part in public affairs. Members of the principal groups were ranked according to the order to which they belonged. Those in the first six lodges (so called because of the enclosures in which their meetings were held), had special ceremonies, although neither a dance nor a secret ritual was attached to the first two, the youth groups. The name of the first lodge before the separation has not survived, but the one in the north was called the Blackbird, in the south the Fox or Kit-Fox. This order corresponds to the Boys Scouts of America, where the rudiments of camp life are learned. All youths, who joined at about the age of twelve, were allowed to proceed to the next order when they were about fifteen or sixteen years of age.[12] In both the north and south, they then became Stars or Star Falcons, whose sign consisted of three claw marks made by two fingers and a thumb.

There was no specified time for initiation into the next-higher order, but when Star Falcons were considered mature enough—probably at seventeen or eighteen—to appreciate the first of the men's organizations, they were permitted to join the Toma-

[11] Mooney, *The Ghost Dance Religion,* 986–87; Lowie, "Plains Indians Age Societies," *loc. cit.,* 919.

[12] Boys under twelve years of age could serve as pages for the various societies, and girls under fifteen could dance as "buffalo calves" in the Buffalo Dance, but they could not be members, according to Rowlodge. Interview, 1965. Hilger gives good accounts of the age societies as related to her by Rowlodge, Arnold Woolworth, Pete Lone Bear, and Jane Hungry Wolf. See Hilger, *Arapaho Child Life,* 117–23.

hawk Society, the same in both tribal divisions. Since meetings were not held regularly, a young man might be anywhere from twenty to twenty-five years old before being able to join.

The next of the societies was known as the *Betahanan*, which eludes exact translation, though it is sometimes referred to by the Southern Arapahoes as the Staff and by the Northern as the Spear. Men of this order (between twenty and thirty-five years of age) comprised the tribe's most powerful war society, for they were young and daring. Four of their leaders carried wooden clubs, notched along the edge, resembling a gun. It was their duty in time of battle to dash out ahead and strike the enemy with these weapons, then ride back to their places in the front lines. Needless to say, many did not return, but the honor was so coveted that there were always candidates for a vacancy. Their emblem was a buffalo wallow—half red and half black, in the center of their lodge.

When the Spear or Staff Society met, its members spent the first three days making and decorating their staffs of office. On the fourth day they danced as they held their weapons in a vertical position. The sponsor wore eagle feathers in his hair and various other ornaments which had been blessed. If anyone violated the tribal code or proved derelict in his duties by failing to attend a ceremony, a Spear Man might kill his dogs, destroy his tipi, or even shoot his ponies. This lodge held its last official meeting in Oklahoma in 1916.

The Lime-Crazy Society—Moths, the Southerners called them because they danced in and out of the fire—comprised the fifth order. The insignia consisted of a bow and a bundle of blunt arrows. The duties of the members, whose age ranged from about thirty to forty-five, were largely ceremonial, and when the Crazy Dance was performed, the crazy root was used to punish offenders and keep order. The Crazy Lodge met for the last time in Oklahoma in October, 1913. According to a Southern Arapaho who witnessed the dance, the participants would jump in and out of the fire. He was unable to explain how they kept from being burned unless they might have been given medicines to "immunize" them from the flames. They showed no signs of scars after their ordeal.

The sixth society was that of the Dog Men, the seasoned warriors, between forty-five and fifty-five years of age. They were fearless and strong. Besides having military duties, they had the honor of raising the center pole in the Offerings-Lodge. Since they were associated with the Sun Dance, the elders feel that they should not be discussed. Their paraphernalia consisted of deer-hoof rattles, sashes, and owl-feather headdresses, and they had certain food privileges. Their form of discipline was whipping, and their order was characterized by the ceremonial surrender of the wife, which was considered the supreme test of a man. If he managed to show no sign of jealousy, he was highly respected. Since this practice is contrary to the white man's moral code, it caused many early writers to consider the Arapaho women immoral. More recently, an anthropologist, speaking in their defense, said: "I am inclined to believe that their unfavorable reputation is due to the fact some institutional practices recorded by other writers and myself were observed and supposed to be of every day occurrence, whereas they are strictly circumscribed and do not justify the opinions expressed."[13] This same authority attributes the chastity rope to Arapaho as well as Cheyenne women.

On the battlefield, the Dog Men carried a rattle and wore a cape or buckskin strap around their necks. Those desiring to prove their prowess would shake their rattle and chant a war song until another warrior took the object from their hands. When forming an attack, they would peg themselves down by means of their capes or plant their lances in the ground and strap themselves securely to the stationary object. There they would remain during the heat of battle. They could order a retreat should it prove necessary, but under no circumstance could they release themselves. They were required to wait for another member of their society to perform this service. Should he become negligent in

---

[13] Michelson, "Narrative of an Arapaho Woman," *loc. cit.*, 596.

the confusion, the Dog Man thus secured was required to stay and, if necessary, die at his post.

Next came the Sweat Lodge or, as one of the Southern Arapahoes termed it, the Stoic Lodge.[14] Members were more honorary than active. They could accompany war parties and perform prayer services for their success, for whatever they asked of Man-Above was thought to be granted. The Stoic, who had passed through all of the previous degrees, had gained the power that comes to one who has fasted in the mountains.

The eighth and most honored lodge was that of the Water-Sprinkling-Old-Men, the seven high priests of the tribe. Each had a medicine bag, which was more tribal than personal, for it, too, might be covered. Gus Yellow Hair, great-grandson of Little Raven, and Theodore Pratt, who took care of old Ute, the last of the Water-Sprinkling-Old-Men, still relate the story of the medicine bags as told again and again by Ute in his declining years.[15] He was made chief at the last Sun Dance held by the Arapahoes in Oklahoma.

Ute's story concerns the supernatural way in which the medicine bags of the Seven Old Men came to the Arapahoes. There was a vision in which a man found himself in a cave. He saw the medicine arrows of the Cheyennes, but "they were too powerful." Instead, he took the seven medicine bags, which he gave to the seven most honored men in the tribe. That, in substance, is the story, which takes hours to tell, with its deliberation and embellishment.

The third division of the *Bayaawu* concerns the Buffalo Lodge.[16] In the original vision, there was an enclosure in which women were wearing wide belts and buffalo headdresses, moving small hoops, and blowing whistles. Old men, shaking their rattles and singing, sat at the back of the lodge. At the end of their fourth song, the women turned into a herd of buffalo cows and the men into bulls. Then they all vanished except one, a white

[14] Hilger, *Arapaho Child Life*, 121–22.
[15] Story told by Gus Yellow Hair, Geary, Oklahoma, 1966.
[16] Dorsey and Kroeber, *Traditions of the Arapaho*, 20–21, 49.

cow. She was a woman who was painted white and who wore white ornaments during the dance. The man to whom the original vision came spoke of it wonderingly because it came to him from Man-Above. After hearing the story, a woman with a sick relative vowed to give the dance as a form of prayer or supplication for his recovery, and so it began.

No men were present in the first part of the ceremony, except perhaps a few who contributed to the music. The entrance was closed while the women dancers removed their clothing, painted their bodies, and put on their ceremonial paraphernalia. In one part of the ceremony, they left the lodge in which the dance was being held and strung out, buffalo fashion, as they walked around the Camp Circle four times, from left to right, singing and shaking their rattles.

The action of the dancers throughout the long ceremony represented the buffalo lying down, standing, walking, going to water, and returning. Later, a hunter would go through the motion of killing one of the cows. When she appeared to die, he pretended to butcher her and take out the buffalo fat, which she had hidden beneath her belt. This symbolic dance lasted four days.

The Seven Old Women (Medicine Women), who received their power supernaturally, corresponded in a measure to the highest of the men's age societies, but they did not comprise a lodge. They had medicine bags in which they carried the tools of their trade, and they taught the arts and skills needed in making and decorating various articles. To them is owed a debt of gratitude for various fine museum pieces displaying embroidered symbols and for other fine handwork which they taught to the women of their tribe.

CHAPTER FIVE

White Man's Big Tipi

THE FUR trade, which flourished between 1824 and 1840 in the Central Rockies, was in full swing when Congress ordered a survey of the great industry in 1831. As a result, the Secretary of War issued a report in which he described the operation as "laborious and dangerous, full of exposures and privations, and leading to premature exhaustion and disability."[1] Furthermore, he found that few of those thus engaged reached an advanced age and fewer still preserved "an unbroken constitution." The labor was deemed "excessive, subsistence scanty, and life precarious," for the Indians were "ever liable to sudden and violent paroxysms of passion" in which they would spare no one.

By this time, Lisa's Missouri Fur Company (1807–20) was but a memory and General Ashley, after enjoying a brief but fruitful experience in the beaver country (1824–26), had turned his back on the Rockies. One of his men, Thomas Fitzpatrick, who was to figure prominently in Arapaho history, visited the mouth of the Laramie River three years after the renowned trapper Jacques La Ramie was killed by the Arapahoes. The Ashley interests had been sold to William L. Sublette, David E. Jackson, and Jedediah Smith (later killed by the Comanches). Then, in 1830, the business passed into the capable hands of Fitzpatrick, Milton G. Sublette, Henry Fraeb (killed by the Platte River Indians), James Bridger, and Jean Baptiste Gervais.

"Paroxysms of passion" are observable on the fur man's roster, but the Arapahoes, aside from several attacks on isolated parties, seemed not to resent the activities of the trappers, for the reason,

---

[1] *Sen. Exec. Doc.* No. 90, 22 Cong., 1 sess., 29; *Sen. Exec. Doc.*, 23 Cong., 2 sess., *Report of the Secretary of War.*

perhaps, that beaver were incidental to their livelihood. It is true that they received their medicine through various animals, but there is scant evidence in their legends, symbolism, or mythology to show any attachment for the small fur-bearing animal. And yet as the number of white invaders increased, their attitude changed. This may have been due in part to the arrival of their kinsmen, the more hostile Gros Ventres.

In 1829 the Pawnees were accused of a trader's murder that was later found to have been committed by the Arapahoes. This caused one fur man to conclude that the troublesome Pawnees might have been blamed unjustly for other acts committed by the Platte River Indians.[2] Open hostility was shown by the Arapahoes in the Black Hills in 1830 when they threatened the life of any white man who attempted to pass Chimney Rock.[3]

About this time, the Crows made an effort to reclaim their chieftain's son, who had been captured by the Cheyennes some time before.[4] After locating the main camp of the Cheyennes and Arapahoes at the mouth of a tributary of the Platte, the chief invited them and their Gros Ventre visitors to a feast, which the Cheyennes refused to attend. After the Crows had fed their guests, they sought their aid in effecting the release of the young Crow. The Cheyennes, learning the nature of their mission, consulted the captive, who had been so well treated that he had no desire to return to his people.

The Crows persisted even after the Cheyennes had sent word that he elected to remain in their tribe. Again the Crow chief feasted the Arapahoes and Gros Ventres, this time making it clear that he expected their aid in subduing the Cheyennes. One of the Gros Ventres reminded the chief that the Cheyennes and Arapahoes had been friends a long time, living and dying together. Furthermore, if any fighting took place, the Gros Ventres, as well

2 J. P. Cabanné to Pierre Chouteau, Jr., Near the Bluffs, April 19, 1831, Chouteau Collection, MHS.

3 Warren A. Ferris, "A Diary of the Wanderings on the Sources of the Rivers Missouri, Columbia, and Colorado, 1835," in Paul C. Phillips (ed.), *Life in the Rocky Mountains*, 29.

4 George B. Grinnell, *The Fighting Cheyennes*, 29–31. George Bent (George E. Hyde [ed.], *Life of George Bent*, 28–30) gives the date as 1827, Grinnell 1831.

as the Arapahoes, would fight with their allies. The chief, seeming to dismiss the matter, invited his guests to one last event in their honor, a farewell dance to take place the next day.

During the night, a spy slipped into the Arapaho camp to warn of the Crow chief's sinister plan. Coming under the guise of friendship, the chief proposed to spring upon the Arapahoes and Gros Ventres and destroy them. Meanwhile, in a daring show of horsemanship, two of his braves were prepared to dash into the Cheyenne camp, kidnap the chieftain's son, and make their get-away before the Cheyennes knew what was happening. All through the night scouts were sent out by the Arapahoes and Cheyennes, and both camps were heavily guarded.

Instead of holding the proposed dance, the warriors prepared for battle. At daylight they formed a battle line, but neither side made a direct charge. While they threatened each other, their braves met in single combat between the lines and were able to distinguish themselves. Finally, the Crow women broke camp and moved up the stream, which was thereafter to bear their name (Crow Creek), and the chief left his son to round out his life in the enemy tribe. Had the Crows encountered a party of trappers on their way home, they would have been in a proper mood to destroy them. The Cheyennes and Arapahoes, too, were geared for battle, so it was fortunate that no white man crossed their path until they had recovered from their "paroxysm of passion."

In 1831, George Nidiver and his party of traders had the uncomfortable experience of being caught between the Arapahoes and Pawnees on a journey up the Arkansas.[5] First they encountered a party of eighty poorly armed Pawnee warriors, only about half of whom were mounted. That night, in appreciation of the generous gifts of blankets, tobacco, knives, and powder given them by the white men, they pitched their camp in the same body of timber.[6]

Late afternoon the next day, Nidiver and a companion were

[5] E. F. Murray, "Mountain Man: George Nidiver," *Colorado Magazine*, X, 3 (May, 1933), 93–99.
[6] The Big Timbers, stretching for miles along the Arkansas, provided a favorite resort for the Cheyennes and Arapahoes. Their ponies fed on the sweet bark

on foot hunting buffalo when they saw Indians peering at them from a hollow. The white men took to their heels, a war party of Arapahoes in pursuit. Only two of the Indians were mounted, but the others were excellent runners, which meant that there was little chance for escape. The badly frightened white men headed for the nearest timber, a mile or so away. When they saw that the mounted Indians were about to overtake them, they turned to fire in their defense. But they noticed that the warriors had thrown down their weapons.

Dismounting, the Indians grabbed their captives and shook them soundly. Then they indicated that the whites were to sit down on the ground while they seated themselves in a circle around them. Lighting their pipe, they passed it among themselves as they apparently debated what they should do next. By signs the white men made them understand that they were from a large encampment not far away. This so impressed the Indians that they ordered the men to lead the way to the camp.

After they arrived, there was another smoke and further palaver; then the Indians made camp near Nidiver's party. Again the guards had to be vigilant, this time against a surprise attack by the Arapahoes. At midnight a prowling warrior opened fire on the guard. When the fire was returned, yells arose from all sides as the Pawnees made their presence known. Throughout the night and during the sporadic fighting with the Pawnees, the Arapaho camp remained quiet. It was not until a small cannon loaded with sixty bullets was discharged that the enemy was silenced. At daylight, the Arapahoes left, presumably to pursue the Pawnees. When the white men had a chance to determine their loss, they discovered that seven horses had been stolen and many more wounded.

That same year, the Arapahoes, Gros Ventres, and Blackfeet were assembled in great numbers on the Cimarron River when Josiah Gregg and his party of traders arrived. They had been warned by roving Sioux that they would encounter an immense

of the cottonwood, while the timber provided wood and shelter. Its eventual destruction contributed to Indian hostilities. See *Far West and the Rockies*, III, 162.

number of Indians, whom they mistakenly understood to be Blackfeet and Comanches.[7] On June 19, when the Gregg party descended into the Cimarron Valley, it was confronted by "an imposing array of death-dealing savages," a vanguard of the countless numbers who came over the opposite ridge directly toward them. Since this was the traders' first encounter with the natives, they were ill prepared, and yet they managed to make a hasty corral.

Meanwhile, "the more daring bolted off to encounter the enemy alone, while the timid and cautious took a stand with presented rifle behind the wagons." The Indians attempted to force their way into the enclosure, and fighting would have resulted had not some of the more prudent traders interposed. The Indians continued to make hostile demonstrations by rushing, with ready sprung bows, upon those who had gone in search of water, but their recklessness was checked by their own wise leaders.

With fife and drum, the whites drew up in line of battle and marched toward the hostiles, who were intrigued by the strange parade and sound of music. Gregg was not too sure that they did not consider it a "complimentary salute" rather than a show of strength. At any rate, they were undaunted when their principal chief, dressed in a long red coat, lighted his peace pipe and strode boldly toward the "warlike corps."

After accepting the peaceful overture and smoking with the chief, the commanding officer of the expedition directed him by signs to order his warriors to leave. Most of the Indians complied and joined a long column of women and children who were then emerging from behind a hill. Slowly descending toward the stream, they pitched their tipis, more than five hundred soon stretching through the valley. Gregg estimated the total number of Indians to be between two and three thousand, though others in his party thought there were no less than four thousand. The thought was

[7] Clark (*The Indian Sign Language*, 197) gives the number of Gros Ventres as 300–400 lodges. Dodge ("Expedition of Colonel Dodge," *American State Papers*, VI, 141) says that 700 lodges (3,500 Indians) came to the Arkansas. Clark's estimate sounds more plausible. Gregg, *Commerce of the Prairies*, XIX, 227–28, 231–32.

disquieting, since the traders' party did not number more than two hundred men. Even so, the whites had the advantage of better arms and the wagons, which could be used for defense.

The presence of women and children indicated that the Indians were on the move and not, at the time, bent on mischief. After the leaders of both factions had concluded their smoke and a big talk, the whites prepared to leave. Women and children, awed by their vehicles, watched their preparations. There was momentary concern that night, although the guard was doubled. The visitors proved to be a "band of squaws" accompanied by a few braves, who were dispatched without learning the nature of their errand. The next day, two braves kindly returned a horse that had strayed.

Around midnight there could be heard a thumping of drums and yelling that was construed by the nervous white men as a war song. The whole company was placed under arms, but when nothing developed, the men were finally permitted to retire. Just before daylight, someone sounded an alarm; instantly, everyone was up and armed. Several guns were made ready, but, to the embarrassment of all, the war party amounted to only eight or ten prowling braves, who were directed to stay away until morning, which they did.

The following day, the expedition had scarcely set out when the Indians began crowding around. By the time camp was pitched that evening, there were perhaps as many as one thousand "pertinacious creatures," males and females of all ages, overrunning the camp. That night, every means short of violence was used to drive them away, but without success. Consequently, the white men spent another restless night, with some of the Indians serenading and others going through the camp on a tour of inspection. Nothing of importance was lost except a pig of lead (between fifty and one hundred pounds) from one of the cannon carriages. This caused grave concern because some of the traders feared the Indians might mold it into bullets. After a night of suspense, there were those among the whites who were grateful to be alive.

The traders attempted to outdistance their guests the next morning by getting an earlier start, but the Indians were on the alert. By the time "the wagoners had geared their teams, the squaws had geared their dogs" and were hurrying behind. Most of the Indians dropped out during the morning, but the chiefs managed to catch up by noon to renew their "unratified treaty"— it had not been sealed with the necessary gifts. When the chief and his braves were presented with about fifty dollars' worth of presents, they left, apparently satisfied. Minor harassments continued for two or three days, but the last Indian finally disappeared.

The supposition on the part of most of the traders that there were many Comanches among these Indians could not have been true, for the Comanches and Arapahoes were on unfriendly terms at the time. Gregg believed they were principally, if not altogether, Gros Ventres and Blackfeet. They were perhaps the same "immense horde" of Indians who appeared hostile when encountered by William Sublette and his party on their way to Santa Fé.

Wolf Moccasin, who in 1884 gave Clark an account of the Gros Ventre visit to the Arapahoes, was characteristically vague. He said the former first joined his people on the headwaters of Powder River and, after remaining with them a few years, left when they were camped on the Platte.[8] A number of explanations can be found for the protracted visit. The Gros Ventres say the wife of their chief, Old Bald Eagle, ran away with her paramour. Runners located the couple among the Arapahoes, so the Chief, grieved and affronted, set out to find them. He was accompanied by a large number of his people, though perhaps not all of the tribe, as we have been led to believe.

Another logical explanation is that after the Gros Ventres destroyed Chesterfield House in 1826, they feared reprisals and fled southward.[9] After wintering on the headwaters of the Missouri, they then continued their journey until they reached the

[8] Clark, *The Indian Sign Language*, 41; Curtis, *The North American Indians,* V, 105–106.
[9] Regina Flannery, *The Gros Ventres of Montana I*, 12–13.

Arkansas the following spring. Various dates are given for the visit, but most authorities agree that it lasted about five years.[10]

Friday said at Fort Laramie in the winter of 1859–60 that the Gros Ventres finally left the Arapahoes because of a quarrel. He claimed the two tribes were camped together on the Cimarron when a disagreement arose over the trade they were carrying on with the Mexicans. The Gros Ventres wanted all, but the Arapahoes insisted that it should be divided equally, whereupon the Gros Ventre chief stabbed the chief of the Arapahoes. In retaliation, the male relatives of the Arapaho chief killed the chief of the Gros Ventres and a free-for-all resulted. Although peace was restored, the two tribes had reached a parting of the ways.

Before the Gros Ventres left, both tribes suffered devastating losses in a severe epidemic of smallpox, their number being reduced by half. The outbreak must have occurred after they encountered Gregg, for he made no mention of pockmarked Indians and there was little indication of diminished numbers. The Gros Ventres who survived were immunized and able to withstand the disastrous epidemic of 1837–38 on the Northern Plains, where they are reported to have lost fewer than two hundred, mostly infants.[11] The Blackfeet lost more than eighteen hundred and the Mandans, "the noblest of all Indians," who had boasted they had six hundred warriors, were reduced to about thirty souls.

The altercation between the chiefs and the ravages of smallpox may have hastened the departure of the Gros Ventres. However, there is evidence that the parting might have been peaceful, for we find that they were expected to return to the Platte and the Arkansas in September, 1835.[12] Their trip south, along the Eastern Slope, had been without major incident, but the return was so difficult that the large-scale visit was never repeated.

10 Dodge ("Expedition of Colonel Dodge," *loc. cit.*, 141) says the Gros Ventres went to the Arkansas in the summer of 1824 and returned home in 1832, indicating a stay of eight years, longer than most writers seem to think. Hayden ("Contributions to Ethnology and Philology," *loc. cit.*, 341) gives the erroneous dates of 1818–23. *Ibid.*, 322.

11 James M. Bradley, "Lieutenant Bradley's Journal," *Contributions to the History of Montana*, III (1900), 221, 226.

12 Dodge, "Expedition of Colonel Dodge," *loc. cit.*, 141.

In their effort to avoid the Crows, the Gros Ventres chose a route west of the mountains, where they were identified as Blackfeet by Fitzpatrick, who lost his horse and came near losing his life to them.[13] He was reduced to a skeleton and almost lifeless when he was discovered by his fellow trappers on Teton River. George Bent, who lived among the Southern Cheyennes and Arapahoes until his death, maintains that the eighteen or twenty young Blackfoot braves who accompanied the Gros Ventres south did not return to their homeland but stayed and married into the Southern bands. The last of their number died about 1880, he said. Although some authorities refer to these migrant bands as Blackfeet, we have Bent's word that they were mostly, if not all, Gros Ventres.

The northbound Indians had no idea that they would run into a strong force of white trappers, together with a contingent of Flathead and Nez Percé Indians, who were leaving the rendezvous, held that year at Pierre's Hole (Idaho). Making signs of peace and flourishing a British flag, the Indians accosted a party led by Milton G. Sublette, who sent a messenger back to the rendezvous to seek reinforcements. Without the knowledge of the white man, the Indians had already started building a fortress in the timber on the banks of the river. Once again the chief came forward with his pipe of peace. But this time a Flathead shot him (as directed), and one of the trappers grabbed his red blanket as he fell. The Gros Ventres then rushed to their fortress and held off the whites while the women finished its construction.

Two hours later, William Sublette and Robert Campbell, with about two hundred trappers and five hundred Flathead and Nez Percé Indians, came rushing to the scene.[14] Sublette led a

13 Zenas Leonard, *The Adventures of Zenas Leonard*, 35. For the story of Fitzpatrick's harrowing experience, purported to be told in his own words, see *ibid.*, 36–40.

14 Washington Irving, *The Adventures of Captain Bonneville*, 88–89. Eyewitness accounts differ. See Leonard, *Adventures*, 42–46; George Nidiver, *The Life and Adventures of George Nidiver*, 26–30; John B. Wyeth, *Oregon: A Short History of a Long Journey*, 63; Nathaniel J. Wyeth, *The Correspondence and Journals of Captain Nathaniel J. Wyeth*, 158–59.

direct attack in which he was wounded and two of his companions killed. Finally, he decided to rout the hostiles by setting fire to their makeshift fortress, which was covered with blankets. According to one account, a Flathead who had been able to communicate with the Gros Ventres told the trappers that about six hundred to eight hundred of their warriors would soon arrive. But the trappers misunderstood. They thought he was trying to tell them that the warriors were then attacking the rendezvous, so they withdrew.

After discovering their mistake, they returned, only to find that the Indians had fled. Gros Ventre casualties could not be determined, but in this famous battle between the Indians and the trappers, five whites, eight Flatheads, and ten Nez Percés were killed. Nine Gros Ventre dead were left, together with their possessions, in the fortress. Among the horses which the fleeing Indians abandoned was Fitzpatrick's valued steed.[15]

William Sublette had previously made application to trade with the Arkansas and Platte River Indians north of the Arkansas and east of the mountains.[16] His application, besides naming the Indians then occupying the Central and Southern Plains, also included "any other Indians that may come there to trade." The year before, Felix St. Vrain had complained that the licensed trader, then having to confine his activities to trading areas, was at a disadvantage. He suggested that the situation be remedied by granting the traders licenses to trade with the Indians by tribe, wherever they might be found.

Although liquor was generally frowned upon by the reputable traders, Sublette was granted permission by William Clark, then Superintendent of Indian Affairs, to take whiskey, not to exceed 450 gallons, for the special use of his boatmen while assisting in trade with the Indians. In addition to this privilege, Sublette was also allowed to take John Richard (Richeau or Reshaw, as he was later known in southeastern Wyoming) as

[15] Leonard, *Adventures*, 47.

[16] Sublette Papers, April 25, 1832, MHS; Ceran St. Vrain to William Clark, Rock Island, October 16, Bent–St. Vrain Papers, MHS.

one of his traders. Whiskey and Reshaw proved to be a bad combination.

A few days after the Battle of Pierre's Hole, five trappers started toward Fort Laramie.[17] The Gros Ventres killed four of them and wounded one so badly that he died a short time later. Before reaching their destination on the Upper Missouri, the Gros Ventres were again severely chastised, this time by the Crows, who killed sixty-seven and captured twice that many women and children.

It is reasonable to believe that perhaps half of the Gros Ventres remained in the north, for it would have been sheer folly for them to relinquish their claim to tribal lands with any expectation of returning. One authority suggests that those left in the north may even have improved their lot during the absence of their kinsmen.[18]

The explorer Maximilian observed that these people had been very poor, with few weapons, but had recovered somewhat and were, in 1833, able to supply their needs.[19] As mentioned earlier, the migrants, when first seen in the south, had dog-drawn travois, but when they were encountered by the trappers at Pierre's Hole, at least the vanguard had horses, so it would seem that they, too, had improved their lot, at least as far as horses were concerned.

Since the accounts which have come to light regarding the Gros Ventres who visited the Arapahoes are impersonal, we are impressed by Maximilian's description of those he met on the Northern Plains. Among the eight chieftains he encountered, he found several of "good open character," but he had nothing good to say of Mexkemahuastan (Iron-Which-Moves). Could the Chief's deplorable conduct the year before, when he had to be thrown out of Fort Union, have been attributed to the reverses he suffered when he returned to his homeland? We have no way of knowing that he was with the visiting delegation, but the

[17] Leonard, *Adventures*, 47,

[18] Flannery, *The Gros Ventres of Montana, I*, 16–17.

[19] Alexander Philip Maximilian, *Travels in the Interior of North America*, Vol. XXIII, Pt. 2, 75.

chances are that he was and that he might have had reason to be in a bad mood. When Maximilian met him, he had seemingly regained his composure and was well mannered, even to the point of posing for a portrait by Carl Bodmer, the artist with the expedition. Maximilian described the Chief: "He wore his hair in a thick knot on his forehead and had a deceitful, fawning countenance." Maximilian noted a disproportion of the sexes, which could also be attributed to the Gros Ventres' recent losses.

About this time, there was serious trouble with the Pawnees, who had recently annihilated a small war party of Cheyennes and had thrown the dismembered bodies into a creek. This so infuriated the Cheyennes that they induced the Arapahoes and a large force of Sioux to help them wipe out the mutual enemy. But when the allied forces neared the Pawnee camp, they were so surprised by the sudden appearance of the enemy riding directly toward them that they had no time to prepare their "great medicine," the three Medicine Arrows of the Cheyennes. As a consequence, these were captured in what was considered the greatest calamity ever to befall the Cheyennes. It seemed to be the end of the world, and the Cheyennes associate it in their memory with "the time the stars fell" (November, 1833).

The whereabouts of all of the Arapahoes on that historic night cannot be determined, but part of them were in the vicinity of Bent's Fort, drawn there by the wonders of Little White Man's Big Tipi (that is, William Bent's fort), then under construction.[20] To the imaginative Arapahoes—who could read a supernatural meaning in a cloud formation, a vortex of dust, or anything unusual, who were frightened half out of their wits by the sound of cannon fire—the event must have been one of terror. We can only conjecture their reaction when the sky suddenly become illuminated by a startling shower of meteors.

They were still talking about it in 1858 when Bear Head, leader of one of the principal bands, visited a prospector's camp on St. Vrain Creek in Colorado. "Do you remember when the

[20] Mooney, "The Cheyenne Indians," *loc. cit.*, 377; *Rocky Mountain News*, October 29, 1873.

93

stars fell?" he asked. A white man assured him that he did and gave the date. "That is right," Bear Head replied. "It was the first time we ever saw the white man in our country." Pointing to the comet then visible (in November, 1858), he asked: "Do you know what that star with a pointer means? ... That pointer points back to that fatal night when the stars fell, which signified that the paleface would fall upon us, as many as those falling stars, and destroy us; and the tears of our women would fall in numbers as those falling stars."

Early in 1834, William Sublette and Robert Campbell, en route to the Green River rendezvous, encamped at the mouth of the Laramie River. Here they erected a log-stockaded trading post, first known as Fort William on the Laramie, then Fort Laramie, or just Laramie. These two men, with a wealth of experience in the rich fur country of the Rockies, realized that beaver pelts had declined in both supply and demand and that the future trade market would depend primarily upon buffalo hides. Buffalo were so plentiful in the area that they could be hunted the year round. During the rendezvous period, the traders had depended mostly upon white trappers to procure their furs. Now the shift was to the Indian—the master hunter and craftsman—who would barter in tanned hides for whatever the white man had to offer. At last the traders had found an industry in which the red man excelled, but one which was to sound a death knell to Plains Indian culture.

An adequate warehouse for the bulky robes was mandatory, and it was a matter of prudence that it be constructed in the form of a walled fortress for the safe storage of trade goods and supplies. When the merchants had completed their awe-inspiring structure at the mouth of the Laramie, they were ready to court the tribes in the area. During the winter of 1834–35, French-Canadian John Sybille was sent to visit the Sioux, then in the Black Hills of South Dakota, to induce them to come to the post to trade. Bull Bear, an influential chief, accepted the invitation and came, one hundred lodges strong. Encouraged by his arrival, Lucien Fontenelle, one of the traders, predicted that the fort, located in the heart of the buffalo country, would prove advantageous.[21]

The white man's big tipi—Fort William on the Laramie—was impressive with its quadrangular stockade and blockhouses at diagonal corners. Alfred Jacob Miller, the first artist to arrive on the scene, not only painted the only extant picture of the old fort, but also gives a good written description.[22] Over the entrance, he tells us, there was a large blockhouse in which there was a cannon. The courtyard, about 150 feet square, was surrounded by small cabins, whose roofs reached to within three feet of the top of the palisades. The Indians encamped in great numbers near the post three or four times a year, when they brought peltries to be exchanged for dry goods, tobacco, beads, and alcohol. They had a mortal dread of the "big gun" which they had seen produce havoc with its loud "talk." They conceived it to be asleep, and they had a wholesome dread of its being awakened.

To this wholesome dread may be attibuted the fact that, in its long history, the fort was never directly attacked. The Platte River Indians, who accepted it as their trading center, recognized it as the most important post in the Central Rockies. It had but one important rival, Bent's Fort on the Arkansas, perhaps a year or so older, the date of its construction being in doubt.[23] The Arkansas River fort was destined to play a corresponding role in the history of the Southwest. Originally named for one of its founders, 25-year-old William Bent, it came to be known as Bent's Fort, the other two partners in the venture being William's older brother, Charles, and Ceran St. Vrain. William also had charge of Adobe Fort on the Canadian, where the Kiowas, Comanches, and Apaches came to trade.

Certain bands frequenting the area between the Platte and Arkansas rivers took their robes to Fort Convenience, a mysterious

[21] Lucien Fontenelle, to Pierre Chouteau, September 17, 1834, Chouteau Collection, MHS.
[22] Alfred Jacob Miller, *The West of Alfred Jacob Miller*, 40.
[23] For a complete account of Bent's Old and New Forts, see David Lavender, *Bent's Fort*, and Nolie Mumey, *Old Forts and Trading Posts of the West*.

and almost forgotten log cabin opposite the mouth of Clear Creek north of Denver.[24] The short-lived post was strategically located in the heartland of the Arapahoes, who were still considered hostile nomads because no treaty of amnesty had been signed with them, as had been the case with the Cheyennes.[25]

It is doubtful that much trading was done by the Arapahoes at this time; they were preoccupied by their continued warfare with the Pawnees.[26] In one attack the Arapahoes, together with some of their Cheyenne allies, annihilated a war party on what was later to be known as Pawnee Hill (north of Fort Lyon, Colorado). Another battle was fought at Pawnee Buttes (northwest of Fort Morgan, Colorado), with the same disastrous results to the Pawnees, who had come on foot to steal horses which they hoped to ride home victoriously. In a third recorded engagement, the Pawnees are credited with managing an escape by tying ropes together and climbing down the opposite side of the butte while their attackers were camped at its base.

Since the Arapahoes and Cheyennes seemed reluctant at first to go to the forts to trade, various methods were used to entice them. Reshaw is credited with introducing liquor among the Platte River Indians and causing so much turmoil that he could be traced by following the trail of dead Indians, killed in drunken brawls, he left in his wake. When the Southern bands did not take readily to the taste of whiskey, Captain John Gantt (Baldhead, the Indians called him) sweetened it in order to induce them to drink.[27] After they had acquired the habit, they would trade everything they owned to quench their thirst. Liquor was not unknown to the Arapahoes and Cheyennes before Gantt's time, but it was far less accessible. As early as 1820, Long made a significant observation regarding intoxicants, and he questioned the belief even then that

[24] LeRoy R. Hafen, "Mountain Man: Louis Vasquez," *Colorado Magazine*, X, 1, 14.
[25] General Henry Atkinson, "Treaty with the Cheyenne Indians at Teton River," July 6, 1825, 7 *U.S. Stat.*, 255–57.
[26] Hyde, *The Pawnee Indians*, 128.
[27] Moses Merrill, "Diary of Rev. Moses Merrill," Nebraska Historical Society *Collections*, IV (1892), 181.

the Indians possessed a strong natural desire for ardent spirits.[28] Their appetites were strong and ungovernable, he conceded, but they were unnatural, having been created through artificial means by the traders. Instances, he says, were not rare when Indians refused to accept liquor that had been offered to them. He observed:

> After a long abstinence from food, anything calculated to allay the cravings of the appetite is eagerly swallowed, and on such occasions nothing perhaps produces such an effect more speedily than spirituous liquors. Indians, while lounging about the trading establishment, are often destitute of food for a considerable time, and can obtain no other kind of refreshment from the trader but liquor, which is bestowed partly in exchange for commodities they may have to dispose of, and partly by way of encouraging them to return to him with the products of the next hunt. A small drought, on such occasions, produces intoxication, and the sudden transition from the state of gnawing hunger to that of unconcerned inebriety cannot fail to make them passionately fond of a beverage that can thus change their condition so much to their immediate satisfaction.

Because of language barriers, certain traders were sent to the tribes they knew best and whose language they could understand. Lucien Maxwell was in this way an ideal chief trader among the Southern Arapahoes. John S. Smith (Blackfoot John), who served in the same capacity with the Cheyennes, had also mastered the Arapaho language sufficiently to serve as interpreter at various times. When these and other traders went to an Indian camp, they took such items as mules, blankets, coffee, sugar, and tobacco. At the trading posts, everything from crackers to yard goods was bartered.

Legitimate traders preferred not to use liquor, but there were always unscrupulous peddlers who would slip into the Indian camps with their "Taos Lightning" and other intoxicants usually unfit for human consumption. Sometimes at the insistence of the Indians, liquor would be brought openly. In this event, the chief

---

[28] James, *Account of an Expedition*, XVII, 167–68.

would promise to be responsible for its handling. Kegs, the sizes of which depended upon the number of horses or robes to be bartered, would be brought to the door of the chief's lodge, where they would remain until the trader had completed his business and was safely on his way.

Sometime between 1830 and 1832, Gantt is credited with making the first peace treaty with the Arapahoes.[29] Kit Carson was with his party when this unofficial treaty was concluded. Until the time Gantt located his small trading post on the Upper Arkansas (near Pueblo, Colorado) and started dealing in whiskey, the Arapahoes had been relatively removed from intoxicants. They had actually caused little trouble beyond raiding expeditions, except for a time when the Gros Ventres were among them in great numbers. Ordinarily, they worked off their surplus energy by warring with their traditional enemies.

Intertribal warfare was by now threatening the frontier settlements, as well as travelers on the Santa Fé Trail. Chouteau, writing to the Secretary of War, was convinced that if peace could be restored, the tribes would return to hunting and the Arkansas River would become as valuable a trade route as the Mississippi and the Missouri.[30] In order to bring about a reconciliation of the Indians on both the Platte and the Arkansas, Colonel Henry Dodge was sent west by the Secretary of War in 1835.

Like Ashley, Dodge found the Pawnees at the Loup favoring peace with their old enemies, the Arapahoes and Cheyennes. With Gantt as guide, the expedition passed through neutral territory from the forks of the Platte to the mountains, where the various nations, including the "Arepahas" and the Cheyennes, would come to fight and to buffalo. Dodge then turned south through the finest buffalo range to be found (between the South Platte and the Arkansas rivers, from the Rocky Mountains into Western Kansas). The expedition finally encamped on the Arkansas, where three Arapahoes and a Blackfoot informed them that their people

---

29 Edwin L. Sabin, *Kit Carson Days*, II, 899.
30 A. P. Chouteau to Lewis Cass, November 12, 1831, Chouteau Collection, MHS; Dodge, "Expedition of Colonel Dodge," *loc. cit.*, 134.

—the Arapahoes, Gros Ventres, and Blackfeet—had assembled and were awaiting the white men's arrival.[31]

Dodge's Dragoons were surprised to find that the "Blackfeet" (Gros Ventres) spoke the same language as the Arapahoes, that they emigrated from the same country, and that they had the same manners and customs. There were 350 of them still among the Arapahoes. Their principal chiefs were Elk Tongue and Bear Tooth (not the same Chief Bear Tooth of the Arapahoes who had received the white men so warmly). As named by Dodge, the leading chiefs of the Arapahoes were Buffalo-Bull-that-Carries-a-Gun, Old Raven (Oc-che-ne), Strong Bow, Mad Bear, and Buffalo Belly.[32] About fifty Blackfeet (George Bent gives the number as eighteen) were then living with the Cheyennes, but they seem to have cast their lot with the Southern Arapahoes later.

The Arapaho proper numbered 360 lodges (1,800 men), or 3,600 souls, according to the records left by the expedition. They were described as being less warlike than the Cheyennes and "a small and more delicate looking race of Indians." This is the only reference we find to their being delicate or small in stature, but since they are not as tall as the Cheyennes, we conclude that this is a comparative statement. The report further states that the two tribes (the Arapahoes and Cheyennes) ranged between the Platte and the Arkansas and subsisted entirely upon buffalo. Since they had few guns and little ammunition, both nations still depended for the most part upon the bow and arrow for warfare and hunting. According to this same report, the Arapahoes formerly lived upon the Marias River, near the forks of the Missouri, but had long since emigrated to the place where Dodge found them. It may have been upon this river that the separation of the Arapahoes and the Montana Gros Ventres occurred.

On August 11, 1835, Colonel Dodge held a council with the Indians of the Arkansas. In his speech, translated by various interpreters, he praised the Arapahoes, Osages, and Comanches for

[31] Lemuel Ford, "Captain Ford's Journal of an Expedition to the Rocky Mountains," *MVHR*, XII, 4 (March, 1926), 564–65.
[32] Dodge, "Expedition of Colonel Dodge," *loc. cit.*, 140–44.

recently making peace and urged that the Cheyennes do likewise. After the Pawnee representative spoke, Little Moon of the Cheyennes said he wished the Pawnees would send each band of his tribe a Medicine Arrow. He referred to the Sacred Arrows and the like number of bands of his tribe, but the chronicler for the expedition interpreted his statement to mean that the exchange of arrows was the usual gesture of peace on the part of the Southern Plains tribes.

The lasting peace which Dodge hoped to bring about between the allied Arapahoes and Cheyennes and the Pawnees amounted to no more than a lull in their warfare, perhaps long enough to permit the Cheyennes to negotiate for the return of their Sacred Arrows. The reports of the expedition contain a few notes of importance to Arapaho as well as Cheyenne history. They state that soon after the Cheyennes were visited by General Henry Atkinson (in 1825, when he negotiated their first peace treaty), they came to the South Platte and entered into the "strictest terms of alliance, both offensive and defensive," with the Arapahoes and would doubtless in a few years become incorporated with that nation. This statement may have been prompted by statistics showing the Arapahoes then outnumbering the Cheyennes.

The Dragoons found business prospering. St. Vrain and William Bent were carrying on a lively trade in which buffalo robes were exchanged for such items as knives, kettles, and blankets. One of the officers of the expedition, impressed by the active trade being carried on with the "Chian, Rapahawes, and Grovents," observed that robes which the traders would purchase for as little as twenty-five cents' worth of goods would bring five or six dollars in St. Louis.[33]

In his wanderings (1830–35), W. A. Ferris found the "Arrappahoes" at war with the Utes, Crows, and Sioux but on friendly terms with the Snakes, Blackfeet, Gros Ventres, and Comanches, showing a shift in tribal relations. As a rule, the Arapahoes were on fair terms with the Sioux but at odds with the Utes and Snakes. Ferris makes no mention of their perennial enemies, the

[33] Ford, "Captain Ford's Journal," *loc. cit.*, 566–69.

Pawnees, or the friction with the Comanches, which was still unresolved, although they appeared to be momentarily at peace during Dodge's visit.[34]

Ferris was impressed by the Arapaho idea of hospitality. As we have observed, wanderers who found sanctuary with the tribe were well treated and no harm would befall them as long as they were in protective custody. Meanwhile, the hosts would place before their guests the best provisions they had in store and would even protect them at the risk of their own lives. Ferris was sure that some of the neighboring nations (the Shoshonean tribes—Utes, Shoshonis, and Comanches) detested them for no other reason than that they considered dog flesh a delicacy (*Sheridikas*, "Dog-Eaters," their Shoshonean enemies called them). He spoke well of their bravery and their integrity, which was put to a test by some of William H. Vanderburgh's men, who, while spending the winter of 1834–35 trapping near them, were well treated and lost nothing by theft. On parting, the chief instructed them to display a white flag next time they came to his country so that they would not be harmed.

When Robert Newell, who first went west with William Sublette in 1829, wintered among the "Arappahoes" two years later, the weather was so severe and the snow so deep that another trapping party lost most of its horses and had to depend on the frozen carcasses for food.[35] Nevertheless, Newell had a successful winter, but the Indians or the climate must have proved too much, for he resigned in the spring when he returned with his cargo to Bent's Fort and left the area.

By this time, two famous marriages had taken place. William Bent had acquired Owl Woman, daughter of Gray Thunder, keeper of the Cheyennes' Sacred Arrows, and Kit Carson had claimed Singing Wind (Waanibe), his Arapaho wife whom he called Alice. These marriages of policy in a broad sense included the women, their extended families, and the bands to which they belonged, as well as those commonly associated with them. In

[34] Ferris, "A Diary of the Wanderings," *loc. cit.,* 312–13.
[35] Robert Newell, *Robert Newell's Memoranda,* 35.

short, Bent and Carson formed a strong alliance with bands of both tribes. Although the Arapahoes had previously claimed the Southern Plains, the Cheyennes who came to Bent's Fort were soon recognized as a tribal division. The Arapahoes continued to come together as a single unit in one village when they so desired, but certain bands were inclined to stay in their own area—on the Platte or the Arkansas—after the two important trading posts were established.

The year cannot be determined, but it was probably in the mid-1830's that the Southern bands devised their own Sun Dance, with the sacred Wheel serving the same function as Flat-Pipe in their ceremonials, though they continued to revere the Pipe as their most sacred tribal fetish. This meant that the Southerners no longer had to travel great distances for their religious rites. The Wheel, as well as the medicine bags of the Seven Old Men, were periodically covered because of an illness or a personal vow.

Various reasons have been given for the formation of the Northern and Southern bands of the Arapahoes. One is that the white man split the buffalo herds with his trails and the bands divided accordingly. Another is that the Northern groups refused to join the war of 1864 against the whites, a date much too late for a division that can be documented a generation earlier. Contrary to this notion, the Northern groups did not refuse. A third, the Arapahoes' own version, is that some of the tribe preferred to go south because of the horse market. This may have caused the South People to migrate at the beginning of historic times, but the horse market was so well established by the 1830's that it is unlikely that it had much to do with the separation.

The first explanation, a split of the buffalo herds, unquestionably kept the bands apart, but the establishment of the white men's two forts, one on the Laramie and the other on the Arkansas, had far more to do with the separation than either buffalo or Spanish horses. To bridge the gap between the two posts (Fort Laramie and Bent's Fort), Fort St. Vrain was founded in 1835.

The Arapahoes whom artist Miller saw when he followed the

Platte were "finely formed" but warlike.[36] When they were out "scouring" the country, misfortune was sure to befall those whom they encountered. Miller was impressed by their horses, which "partook somewhat of the Arabian breed." There were no geldings—except those brought from the States—thus preserving all of their game spirit and the endurance of the stallions. War ponies were second in splendor only to the painted warriors who fearlessly and expertly handled them. Both had many a workout in untold battles with enemy tribes, where the warriors had a chance to exhibit their prowess in grand style in the late 1830's when they and their Cheyenne allies battled repeatedly with their traditional enemies, as well as with the Kiowas, Comanches, and Prairie Apaches, from whom they were separated by the width of the Arkansas River.[37]

The Battle of Wolf Creek was the last large-scale encounter between the Arkansas River tribes. According to George B. Grinnell, who received much of his information first hand from the Indians, trouble started in 1837 in the Cheyenne camp when Gray Thunder, then about sixty years old, refused to renew the Sacred Arrows.[38] These were substitutes, at least two of them, for the others were still in the hands of the Pawnees. The renewal was considered necessary before the warriors could depart, for a Cheyenne had killed a fellow tribesman. After a severe quirting, Gray Thunder finally conducted the necessary ceremony, but he warned that no good would come of the venture.

Meanwhile, the Arapahoes, who were then camped near the Cheyennes, were holding their Sun Dance. The man who had pledged the dance had fallen to the ground in exhaustion and had seen a vision. He told those about him that when the ceremony was over, they and the Cheyennes would make up a big party and go to war. Another man, who also had a vision, demanded an

---

[36] Miller, *The West of Alfred Jacob Miller*, 74.

[37] Rupert N. Richardson, *The Comanche Barrier to the South Plains Settlement*, 179; Grinnell, *The Fighting Cheyennes*, 32–41, 43–44; Mooney, *Calendar History of the Kiowa Indians* BAE, *Seventeenth Annual Report*, Pt. 1, 271–72.

[38] Grinnell, *The Fighting Cheyennes*, 70; Lavender, *Bent's Fort*, 162–63.

audience. He warned the Bow String soldiers (the Cheyenne warriors in attendance) not to go. In his vision, he had seen seven heads or scalps coming into the camp from all directions, and he was sure that they did not belong to the enemy.[39]

In spite of the ill omen in both camps, a war party of Bow String warriors, numbering about forty-five, set out on foot to locate the enemy. After spending most of their arrows on small game, they finally entrenched themselves on a southern tributary of the Washita near present-day Cheyenne, Oklahoma. Here, in a rock barricade, they awaited the arrival of the Kiowas, who were then coming along a trail toward them. The Kiowas, who had given the Bow Strings time to run out of ammunition, closed in on them and wiped them out, not even leaving one to carry home the news of the defeat.

A short time later, several of the Southern Arapahoes, who were with traders in the Kiowa camp, recognized the scalps of some of the Bow String warriors, then being displayed in a Scalp Dance. They lost no time reporting the news to the Cheyennes, who were thus obligated to avenge their injuries. A Camp Circle was formed and preparations were made for a large-scale attack, but before the warriors could leave, a heavy snow fell. Since the problem of survival was more timely than warfare, the attack had to be postponed until spring. By the time the buffalo returned, the Cheyennes still had not avenged their wrong.

The Arapahoes had left their winter quarters and were encamped on the Arkansas when their allies set up a large village just above them. After a council lodge had been erected, the Cheyennes invited the Arapahoes to a feast. Before going, one of the eccentric warriors (Flat War Club by name) made a strange demand. First he wanted to be carried, an honor the Cheyennes were glad to confer because of his unusual medicine stick. After he had eaten, he explained that he had yet another request. Since he was going on the warpath, from which he would not return, he wanted the privilege of making love to the warriors' wives. This request was also one which they could not deny, not only

[39] Mooney, "The Cheyenne Indians," *loc. cit.*, 271, 377n.

because of his medicine, but also because he was giving his body to the Cheyennes. At the end of his philandering, he sang his death song. One of the warriors then told the Arapahoes that the Cheyenne tribal leaders had come to the decision that they would not take prisoners. This was agreeable to the Arapahoes, who had been praised by Dodge for making peace with the Comanches.

The two tribes were camped on Beaver Creek, just south of the Sandhills, when their runners located some of the Kiowa and Comanche buffalo hunters to the south of them, near Wolf Creek. A Cheyenne who had been outlawed because he killed a fellow tribesman in a drunken brawl was the hero in the first encounter with the Kiowas. He ordered his followers to remain out of sight while he rode back and forth, signaling to an approaching Kiowa party of hunters that he had sighted buffalo. Unaware that he was not one of them, the Kiowas rode into a trap and were killed by the outlaw band. The subsequent attack upon the Kiowa-Comanche encampment was swift and ferocious, with many warriors killed on both sides.

By sundown, the warriors of both factions were apparently satisfied and withdrew. Some of the Cheyenne leaders urged that fighting cease and that the Arapahoes be sent among the enemy to sue for peace. As the Cheyennes and Arapahoes conferred, they saw mounted Kiowas ride up to a ridge, but they, too, must have had enough because they made no attempt to renew the battle.

Among the important guests at Bent's Fort in the summer of 1839 was Thomas Jefferson Farnham, an Oregon-bound lawyer who sought to arouse patriotic fervor for the possession of the disputed territory. To Farnham and other members of his "Peoria [Illinois] Party," we are indebted for a glimpse of the Arapahoes and their country in the late 1830's. Farnham found them south of the Snakes, conducting their summer hunt in New Park (Bull Pen), Old Park (on Grand River), and Bayou Salade (on the South Fork of the Platte).[40] Elsewhere he mentions being informed by three rugged trappers that the Arapahoes were

[40] Thomas J. Farnham, *Travels in the Great Western Prairies*, XVIII, 229, 266–67.

"fattening at the Bull Pen while the Snakes were starving on roots on the Great Bend River." The Arapahoes were so numerous, if we are to accept his figure (three thousand souls), that the Northern and Southern bands must have united in their hunting efforts in the three areas mentioned.

In enumerating the duties of the Arapaho man and his wife, Farnham found prestige and glory for the former, but little besides drudgery for the latter:

> His wife takes care of his horses, manufactures his saddles and bridles, and leash ropes and whips, his moccasins, leggins, and hunting shirts from leather and other materials prepared by her own hands; beats with a wooden adze his buffalo robes till they are soft and pleasant for his couch; tans hides for his tent covering, and drags from the distant hills the clean white-pine poles to support it; cooks his daily food and places it before him. And should sickness overtake him and death rap at the door of his lodge, his squaw watches kindly the last yearnings of the departing spirit. His sole duty, as her lord in life, and as a citizen of the Arrapahoe tribe is to ride the horse which she saddles and brings to his feet, kill the game which she dresses and cures; sit and slumber on the couch which she spreads; and fight the enemies of the tribe.

The Peoria Party, displaying such mottoes as "Oregon Dragoons" and "Oregon or the Grave," found three forts within ten miles on the South Platte: Lupton, Vasquez, and St. Vrain.[41] Robert Shortess, an Illinois farmer, was appalled by the drunken and debauched Indians near the forts and by the whites who were not much better. He termed this "a necessary consequence of the civilizing influence of commerce."[42] Thus far, liquor was the only influence that had made any appreciable difference in the Indian way of life.

---

[41] For the importance of these forts to Southwest history, see LeRoy R. Hafen, "Fort Lupton," *Colorado Magazine*, VI, 6 (November, 1929), 222–26; "Mountain Man: Louis Vasquez," *Colorado Magazine*, X, 1 (January, 1933), 14–21; and "Fort St. Vrain," *Colorado Magazine*, XXIV, 2 (October, 1952), 251–55.
[42] Robert Shortess, "The Peoria Party," in *Far West and the Rockies*, III, 104.

E. Willard Smith, an engineer whose trip west was a graduation present from his father, encountered his first Arapahoes at Fort Vasquez on the South Platte in September, 1839.[43] About dusk, a party of twenty-two, including a Cheyenne and a Blackfoot, visited his camp. They sat around several hours, resting and smoking with Vasquez. On leaving, they were given knives and tobacco. Later an Arapaho chief told Smith that somewhere on the headwaters of the Yellowstone was a petrified buffalo bull, worshiped by the Indians as great medicine. Perfectly preserved, it was said to stand in a lake on the shore of which tracks could be found in solid rock. No amount of bribing could tempt the Indian to divulge its location.

A similar story is told by a Southern Arapaho who maintains that the Gros Ventres used to tell again and again in sign language the story of a ruptured, petrified bull.[44] In describing him, they would cup their hands slightly to the right, as if the intestines were spilling into their fingers. This may explain why the Gros Ventres were known to the Blackfeet as Gut People (Atsinas) and later to the French-Canadians as Gros Ventres (Big Bellies).

The eventful days of the 1830's were not over when Father Pierre-Jean de Smet visited Fort Kearny (Nebraska), which he described as a military post "for the tranquility of the country and to provide for the safety of travelers crossing the desert to go to California, Oregon, and the Territories of Utah and Washington." De Smet found the environs anything but tranquil as he came near witnessing one of the many battles between the Arapahoes and Pawnees a short distance away. Almost forty strong, the former had managed to creep up on the Pawnees unnoticed in the darkness. In a surprise raid, when the Pawnees turned their horses out to graze the next morning, the Arapahoes, sounding their war cries, rushed into the herd and drove away several hundred horses at full gallop. Hearing the alarm, the Pawnees jumped on the horses then picketed in the camp and went in pursuit. The battle that ensued was described by the priest as being "more noisy than

[43] E. Willard Smith, "Journal," in *Far West and the Rockies*, III, 166, 179.
[44] Rowlodge Interview, Colony, Oklahoma, 1966.

bloody," with a reckless young Pawnee chief and one of the Arapahoes being the only ones killed, though many were wounded on
both sides.

In an attempt to stop the fray, De Smet rushed to the scene
with a general's aide-de-camp, but by the time he arrived, the
swift action was over and the Pawnees were the victors. After
they returned with their casualties and all of the stolen horses,
nothing was heard but "cries of sorrow, rage, and despair, with
threats and vociferations against their enemies."

De Smet's account shows that during intertribal wars, the
Pawnees, largely at the expense of the Arapahoes, had acquired
many horses and were better able to contend with the tribes on
the Southern Plains. Not only were the Pawnees contesting the
rights of the Cheyennes and Arapahoes, but also of the eastern
Indians, particularly the Delawares and Shawnees, who were beginning boldly to penetrate the Plains tribes' hunting grounds as
far west as the Rockies and as far south as Mexico.

CHAPTER SIX

The Great Medicine Road

FIVE YEARS after Colonel Dodge attempted to end the intertribal wars, the Southern Arapahoes and Cheyennes solved many of their own problems by holding a peace council with the Kiowas, Comanches, and Apaches. Perhaps Little Raven was more influential in bringing about this settlement than Dodge had been, since friendly relations between the Arapahoes and the Apaches had resulted from intermarriage, though the Arapahoes were still obligated to fight them because of their alliance with the Cheyennes.[1] In his desire for amicable relations, Little Raven prompted Bull, a lesser chief, to arrange a meeting between his Apache visitors and a war party of Cheyennes who had stopped with the Arapahoes temporarily on their way south to steal horses from the Comanches.

Bull offered the pipe to the Cheyennes, but they refused to smoke because they were not chiefs and had no authority to make peace. They agreed to carry the message back to their people and let them decide. Then, instead of going forward on their horse-stealing mission, they returned to the Cheyenne camp, on a tributary of the Republican River. After listening to the report given by Seven Bulls, the head chief decided in favor of peace. As part of their proposal, the Kiowas and Comanches had offered to return the scalps of the Bow String warriors to show their good faith.

When news of the important decision reached Bull, he told his Apache guests, and they returned to their people with the glad tidings. Shortly afterwards, representatives of the three enemy tribes (the Kiowas, Comanches, and Apaches) rode fearlessly into

[1] Grinnell, *The Fighting Cheyennes*, 63–69.

the center of the Cheyenne Camp Circle, dismounted, and seated themselves in a row. The Cheyenne chiefs, carrying their pipes, came forward and sat beside their guests. One of them offered the pipe to each of the dignitaries, who took his turn smoking. The Arapahoes had supposedly shown such evidence of friendliness that negotiations with the Cheyennes were all that remained necessary for a peaceful settlement of their difficulties.

When the delegates brought the scalps of the Bow String warriors, wrapped in a blanket, High Backed Wolf refused them on the grounds that they might open old wounds. The Cheyennes presented stacks of blankets as their gifts to the three tribes, whose representatives asked that no horses be given because they were well supplied. In fact, they had "made a road to give many horses" to the Arapahoes and Cheyennes and asked that a place of meeting be determined. It would have to be a wide area, for the Indians were many and there would be vast numbers of horses. The most logical treaty grounds proved to be the wide bottom lands on both sides of the Arkansas three miles east of Bent's Fort. Here the peace treaty, which was tentatively made between the leaders of the two factions in the Cheyenne camp, was to be ratified by a grand council.

The Arapahoes and Cheyennes were well established on the north side of the river when their former enemies arrived. Kit Carson was there to witness the Giving-Presents-to-One-Another-Across-the-River, as the Indians called their council. Among the Comanches were two male captives, one of whom was ransomed for six yards of red flannel, one pound of tobacco, and an ounce of beads, the other for a mule.[2]

Now that peace had been restored between the great tribes on the Arkansas, the Arapahoes and Cheyennes could turn their war efforts in other directions. They were now free to go on the warpath against the Kaws, the Delawares, and the Potawatomis.[3] The white men who thought friendly relations between the warring Arkansas River tribes would bring about safe trade relations

2 Lavender, *Bent's Fort*, 189.
3 *Salina* (Kansas) *Journal*, December 26, 1940.

No 129 COPYRIGHT 1900
CORNELIUS VANDERBILT & WIFE
(ARAPAHOE)
J. E. STIMSON
CHEYENNE, WYO.

MR. AND MRS. CORNELIUS VANDERBILT, Wind River Reservation.

Courtesy Wyoming State Archives and Historical Department

BEEF ISSUE DAY at Cantonment. Waiting at the holding pens.

Courtesy University of Oklahoma Library Manuscript Division

Beef issue day at Cantonment. Butchering after the issue.

Courtesy University of Oklahoma Library Manuscript Division

Above, NORTHERN ARAPAHO WOMEN BUTCHERING. *Below*, TANNING A DEER HIDE.

Courtesy Wyoming State Archives and Historical Department

Left, LEFT HAND, chief of the Southern Arapahoes. *Right*, LEFT HAND AND
HIS WIFE.

Courtesy University of Oklahoma Library   *Courtesy Gus and Mary Yellowhair*
Manuscript Division

CHIEF YELLOW BEAR, Southern Arapaho. Note the hawk bells on his leggings and the silver inlay on his pipe.

Courtesy University of Oklahoma Library Manuscript Division

CHIEF BIG MOUTH, Southern Arapaho. He was called the "talking chief."

Courtesy University of Oklahoma Library Manuscript Division

YELLOW HAIR AND HIS WIFE, Southern Arapahoes.

Courtesy Oklahoma Historical Society

were unrealistic. The following year, the Comanches attacked a caravan and killed and scalped Robert, the youngest of the Bent brothers.[4] The Arkansas River Indians, to whom warfare was a way of life, had made peace among themselves, but this did not include Americans, Mexicans, Utes, Pawnees, and other enemy nations. Scalps, especially of the traders, continued to be prized.

In the spring of 1840, De Smet traveled between the two forks of the Platte on his way to the Green River rendezvous. He described this favored land of the Arapahoes as "barren, rocky, and sandy, covered with scoria and other volcanic substances," with no fertile spots except on the rivers and creeks.[5] He was a three-day journey from the Black Hills (the secondary mountain system in eastern Wyoming and western South Dakota, which was even then known as the Black Hills) when he found himself in the midst of vast numbers of buffalo. His comment was: "If the earth is thankless and yields but little, Providence has provided in a different way for the subsistence of the Indians and travelers who traverse the regions."

In describing the land of the Arapahoes, De Smet drew heavily on the writings of Washington Irving, who in turn spoke through the experience of Captain B. L. E. Bonneville.[6] And yet the reader is left bewildered. How could this barren waste, infested with rattlesnakes "and other dangerous reptiles, which are met with at every step," support such countless numbers of Indians, buffalo, and wild horses as De Smet relates? The question was not fully answered until many years later when several bull-whackers were stranded on the Laramie Plains in an early winter storm and forced to turn their work oxen out to forage for themselves. Instead of perishing as expected, the animals were found to be in good flesh when they were rounded up in the spring. The white man had discovered something the Indians had known all along—that their country, believed to be a "barren waste," was not as barren as it looked. The short grass was rich in nutriment,

---

[4] Lavender, *Bent's Fort*, 189–90.

[5] Pierre-Jean De Smet, *Life, Letters, and Travels of Father Pierre-Jean De Smet*, I, 207, 210n.

[6] *Astoria*, 216–21.

so rich that it could sustain vast herds of buffalo before they were supplanted by the white man's cattle.

The beginning of the great migrations westward in 1841 was a turning point in the history of the Plains Indian. The Aztec prophecy had foretold: "When the white man shall come from toward the rising sun, the Indians' power and greatness must cease." The "night the stars fell," the Arapahoes were given another prophecy, and as they watched the white-topped wagons moving along the Great Medicine Road of the Whites, they were astounded. They were convinced that it was the white man's exodus from the east, for they could not conceive of there being more to come.

In the first band of homeseekers and missionaries to follow the course of the Platte, along what was to be known as the Oregon Trail, was John Bidwell, the principal historian of his emigrant party. He, too, was impressed by the Indians' cattle. He wrote:

> I have seen the plains black with them for several days' journey as far as the eye could reach. They seemed to be coming northward continually from the distant plains to the Platte to get water, and would plunge in and swim across by thousands—so numerous that they changed not only the color of the water, but its taste, until it was unfit to drink—but we had to use it. One night when we were encamped on the south fork of the Platte they came in such droves that we had to get up and fire guns and make what fires we could to keep them from running over us and trampling us into the dust. We were obliged to go out some distance from the camp to turn them. Captain Fitzpatrick told us that if we did not do this the buffaloes in front could not turn aside for the pressure of those behind. We could hear them thundering by all night long; the ground fairly trembled with vast approaching bands, and if they had not been diverted, wagons, animals and emigrants would have been trodden under their feet.[7]

De Smet was told by the Indians that wolves killed approximately one-third of each year's crop of buffalo calves. In strong bands, they would sometimes attack full-grown animals. Concen-

[7] John Bidwell, *Echoes of the Past in California*, 14–15.

trating upon a single cow or bull, they would force it to the ground and devour it.[8]

One of the first acts of violence on the part of the allied Platte River tribes took place at Battle Mountain.[9] In the ensuing fight, Henry Fraeb and four of his men were killed, along with perhaps twice that number of Indians. This left the Platte River tribes in a sullen mood, ready for vengeance at the first opportunity, though the Arapahoes did more encouraging than fighting, according to Jim Baker, an old Mountain Man. Perhaps they had learned a lesson in survival, since Rufus Sage found them to be a rare instance of increasing numbers.[10]

Meanwhile, an unnamed traveler on his way to Santa Fé (his name withheld by the *New York Weekly Tribune*, to which he contributed) paused with his party at Lower Cimarron Springs, where they were well received by a band of five hundred Arapaho warriors.[11] The white men pleased the Indians by camping on the battleground where the remains of their Pawnee victims still lay following a battle. Sage, who may have received his intelligence from the same unnamed source, says the Pawnee dead, half devoured by wolves, filled the air with "noisome stench." The following days, the whites visited the Arapaho camp, six miles distant, and had a chance to observe "savage life in a perfect state of nature." Among the women and children who stared at them, few had ever seen a white man. Sage was advised that the Pawnees had been defeated with great slaughter, their loss amounting to seventy-two of their bravest warriors and all of their horses. The white men gloated over the victory, for they considered the Pawnees a villainous set whose extermination was greatly to be desired.

The Mexicans by now constituted the Arapahoes' bitterest

---

8 De Smet, *Life, Letters, and Travels*, I, 207.

9 *Denver Tribune-Republican*, July 10, 1886; LeRoy R. Hafen, "Fraeb's Last Fight and How Battle Mountain Got Its Name," *Colorado Magazine*, VII, 3 (1930), 97–101.

10 Rufus Sage, "Rufus Sage: His Letters and Papers," in *Far West and the Rockies*, V, 214.

11 *New York Weekly Tribune*, November 13, 1841; Sage, "His Letters and Papers," *loc. cit.*, 137–38.

enemies as a natural hatred had built up over the years. George Nidiver and his party discovered this in 1831 when they were mistaken by Mexicans for Arapaho warriors.[12] He said they were deadly enemies and that although they might trade freely with each other, neither would spare the other when it had the advantage. When Nidiver neared the hut occupied by a young Mexican sheepherder and his aged father, the old man ran away in fright but the son recognized the strangers as white men and welcomed them. When the father had been assured they were not Arapahoes, he returned, killed a sheep and brought out milk and corn cakes for his guests. When the party, later returning to the Platte, discovered the presence of an Arapaho village, the Mexicans accompanying them were so frightened that it took little urging to hurry them by the encampment.

Before 1841 the Arapahoes had threatened to make war on the Mexicans if the latter did not return the Arapahoes whom they had enslaved. Charles Bent, who had met them on the "Animos" not far from Bent's Fort, had found them jubilant.[13] After being out against the Mexicans fifteen days, the warriors had eight scalps, ten horses, and two guns to show for their venture. Bent was convinced that war between the Arapahoes and Mexicans had begun, and he thought it would take little persuasion on the part of the Arapahoes to induce the Cheyennes and Sioux to join them. He did not mention the Comanches, but it is well known that they, too, had long been hostile toward the Mexicans and most of the Indians in the interior. Writing at this time, Josiah Gregg had not yet learned that peace had been established among the tribes on both sides of the Arkansas, for he mentions that the Comanches were particularly hostile toward the Arapahoes and Cheyennes.[14]

In the summer of 1842, Joseph Williams, an eccentric missionary, attempted to inaugurate religious acculturation among the "heathen French, Spanish, Indians, Half-breeds, and Americans" he met at Fort Laramie on his westward trek. He preached

[12] Nidiver, "Mountain Man: George Nidiver," *loc. cit.*, 93–99.
[13] Charles Bent, "The Charles Bent Papers," *New Mexico Historical Review*, XXX, 2 (April, 1955), 155.
[14] Gregg, *Commerce of the Prairies*, 437.

from Proverbs XIV:32. "The wicked is driven away in his wickedness; but the righteous hath hope in his death."[15] He said in satisfaction: "I felt the word, and I believe some of the people felt also. I spoke plainly and pointedly to them, and felt as though I would be clear of their blood in the day of eternity."

When John Charles Frémont, the Pathfinder, reached Fort Laramie in 1842, he was warned that eight hundred hostile lodges of the Platte River Indians had gone to Sweetwater, on the route he proposed to travel. Still smarting over their losses at Battle Mountain, they had declared their revenge against the trappers and the Snakes, some of the latter being at Fraeb's fort. Their excursion failed, for Frémont met the returning Oglalas, who said they had become embroiled in a bitter quarrel and disbanded, with the Arapahoes and Cheyennes going to the Laramie Plains to hunt.[16]

There, on July 18, Frémont witnessed a buffalo hunt by the Arapahoes and a few of their allies.[17] Although he does not say so, he must have watched the shifting scene through binoculars, for he was too far away to hear the report of guns or any sounds whatever and yet he could see plainly enough through clouds of dust to describe the action:

> We could see for a moment two or three buffalo dashing along, and close behind them an Indian with his long spear, or other weapon, and instantly again they disappeared. The apparent silence, and the dimly seen figures flitting by with such rapidity, gave it a kind of dreamy effect, and seemed more like a picture than a scene from real life. It had been a large herd, probably three or four hundred in number; but though I watched them closely, I did not see one emerge from the fatal cloud where the work of destruction was going on. After remaining here about an hour, we resumed our journey in the direction of the village. . . .

At the conclusion of the hunt, several of the Indians joined

[15] Joseph Williams, in *Far West and the Rockies*, III, pt. 3, 275.
[16] George E. Hyde, *Red Cloud's Folk*, 57.
[17] John C. Frémont, *Report of an Exploring Expedition to the Rocky Mountains*, 18–19.

Frémont's party, and one of the chiefs invited the white men to his lodge. The village was found to comprise 125 lodges, of which 20 were Cheyenne, pitched apart from the Arapaho. As Frémont rode along, he was impressed by the display of weapons of war. Burnished bright and spotlessly clean, they were affixed to tripods outside the tipis of the leading warriors. Said Frémont: "It reminded me of the days of feudal chivalry; and when I rode by I yielded to the passing impulse, and touched one of the spotless shields with the muzzle of my gun. I almost expected a grim warrior to start from the lodge and resent my challenge."

The chief spread out a robe for his guests. Then the women set before them a large wooden dish of buffalo meat. After the pipe had been passed around, the chief continued to smoke while the white men ate. Five or six other chiefs came in and took their seats in silence.

Fitzpatrick, guide for the expedition, followed in the wake of Frémont at a rate he could travel with the heavily loaded carts. He had with him twenty-five men, including Theodore Talbot, chronicler for the party.[18] On July 12, two days after catching their first glimpse of the Rockies, they met three Indians. They were said to be Blackfeet, but were probably Gros Ventres living with the Arapahoes. One proved to be an old friend of Fitzpatrick's who said that his encampment was on the South Fork of the Platte and that his people were trading with the Sioux. The rest had crossed over to the Arkansas, where the main body was soon to follow for a buffalo hunt. About fifty warriors, returning from a buffalo hunt of their own, brought a large supply of meat, which they shared. They were in great spirit, having lately been the victors in an affray with the Pawnees, and they had numerous fresh scalps to show for it. Talbot stated that at dusk some of the Indians mounted fine American or Spanish horses, some shaggy ponies, and others mules to return to camp. A few stayed to show their friendship.

The following day, a handsome young Indian came dashing

18 Theodore Talbot, *The Journals of Theodore Talbot*, 24–27.

up to Fitzpatrick, shook his hand, and expressed great pleasure in seeing him. Speaking the best of English, the Indian inquired about Fitzpatrick's health and plans. The latter's companions were surprised until he told them that in 1831 he had found the Indian, then a starving waif, on the prairie. He took him to St. Louis, where he placed him in school. Fitzpatrick had named him Friday because that was the day of week on which he was found.

The white men arrived at the Arapaho village about three o'clock in the afternoon and were welcomed by the two leading chiefs, Medicine Man and Cut Nose. This is the earliest direct mention we find of Medicine Man, whose name *Roman Nose* was given to him by the whites. In the brief time Talbot was among the Indians, he learned there were between sixty and seventy lodges of Gros Ventres, whom he believed to be "a species of Blackfeet," incorporated with the Arapahoes. They had delayed returning to the Northern Plains so long that they had finally decided to stay. Talbot observed that some of the Arapaho tipis had "dog homes" attached. These were made of wicker and covered with skins.

He found the camp one of "hustle and bustle," with small children playing, women working at various tasks, and men lounging, listlessly watching the commotion. Older boys, though they were guarding the horses, took part in gymnastics and war games. At sunset the horses were driven into the village and picketed near the tipis to avoid theft. One day there was unusual commotion, for someone had brought a keg of whiskey to camp. The effects were like laughing gas. Men started whooping, while dogs yelped and children scurried to and fro. Talbot made a strange observation:

> Most of the Indians are particularly fond of liquor and when it is growing scarce you will frequently see a man take a "sup" of liquor, hold it in his mouth a few minutes, then empty it into the mouth of his neighbor. When all is gone, they will even breathe on the less fortunate so that they can share the delightful fragrance.

The men drank freely, and one by one they fell to the ground.

117

Suddenly a brave in high spirits picked up Talbot and carried him some distance before setting him down.

In July, Cyprian Chouteau informed the government that Sybille and Adams were dealing in liquor.[19] In spite of the vigilance of Major Andrew Drips, whose duty it was to apprehend the guilty parties, Reshaw, traveling by night, managed to smuggle in a sizable cargo to be used by the traders on the Platte. Arriving at Pratte, Cabanné and Company (Fort Platte) on the North Fork of the Platte on August 15, 1843, he entered the fort first to see whether any government agents were present. Finding that all was clear, he and his helpers brought in fifteen well-laden pack horses and mules. When the gates were closed behind them, they unloaded their three hundred gallons of liquor, which they carried to the storeroom.

A report was circulated that alcohol was being traded at Fort John, a rival fort in the same vicinity on the Platte. The traders at both places had ample time to hide their stock before the inspector arrived ten days later. Cabanné vowed that he would not "suffer one drop to be traded but in self-defense," that is, unless the older company (Fort John) should force him in competition.[20] While the government was attempting to put a stop to the liquor traffic on the Platte, Mexican peddlers were causing so much trouble along the Arkansas that a company of Dragoons was stationed near Bent's Fort in an attempt to put a stop to it.

In 1843, Sage, crossing present southeastern Colorado on his way to Santa Fé, met several men with two pack mules laden, not with liquor, but with silver and gold. He did not indicate where the minerals were acquired, but he did say that gold had previously been found in the immediate vicinity of the Spanish Peaks (near Walsenburg, Colorado) and silver in the neighborhood of "De las Animas" (Purgatory).[21]

Some twenty years earlier, "while the Arapahoes were at

[19] John B. Sarpy to Major A. Drips, July 27, August 29, and September 7, 1843. Drips Papers, MHS.

[20] J. V. Hamilton to Major A. Drips, Fort John, October 17 and November 1, 1843, *ibid.*

[21] Sage, "His Letters and Papers," *loc. cit.*, 308, 334–37.

hostilities with the whites," a war party led by Whirlwind advanced against the Pawnees. The three warriors with guns soon expended their bullets on small game and were unable to find sufficient food. Discouraged, they held a council to discuss their problem. The question of return was debated, with the majority in favor of the affirmative. But Whirlwind prevailed upon them to proceed. While the discussion was taking place, someone observed on the ground several small pieces of a glittering yellow substance which proved to be soft and pliable. From these a supply of bullets was made and the warriors, revived in spirit, proceeded on their way. They met the Pawnees, whom they defeated, for every bullet discharged killed an enemy.[22]

On his way from the Platte to the Arkansas in 1844, Sage found a village of Arapahoes about three or four miles before reaching Cherry Creek. They numbered 525 lodges, or about 3,000 souls. Although they were similar in appearance to the Cheyennes and Sioux, he was able to distinguished them by the insignia of their nation: tattooed marks on their breasts. He declared they had maintained the strictest friendship since their treaty with the whites (Gantt's unofficial treaty) and had not been known to kill or wound anyone or commit other depredations. They seemed to take pride in bestowing their hospitality, but they would commonly expect a reward, which made them "exceedingly annoying as beggars."

He spoke disparagingly of their sense of morality. And yet he admitted that no effort had been made to improve them, though he regarded them as more susceptible to civilization than any of the other prairie tribes. He said: "They appear to be great admirers of the manners, customs, arts, and mode of living prevalent among the whites, and only lack the requisite instruction to become their successful imitators."

Sage gives insight into their character by recounting an experience in which a white man, a member of his party, found two horses, one a two-year-old colt, which they butchered and ate. When the Arapahoes appeared in search of the strays, the com-

[22] *Ibid.*, 231; A. Drips to H. Picotte, October 12, 1844, Drips Papers, MHS.

mandant decided to appeal to their "finer feelings." Consequently, he told them that they were near starvation when the Great Spirit, to whom they prayed, showed them the lost animals. By eating the flesh of the colt, they had blessed the Great Spirit. The owner of the animal pondered a moment. Then he extended his hand and exclaimed: "My heart is good. My white brother did well to receive the gift of the Good Spirit that the warriors might eat." This caused Sage to comment: "Where, let me ask, do we find in civilized countries an instance of noble generosity equal to that of the poor savage?" The unidentified Indian deserved one of the medals which had been given promiscuously. But these were now being frowned upon, and traders were forbidden to issue them under penalty of having their license to trade revoked.

When Joel Palmer and his emigrant band reached Fort Laramie in 1845, they found the trappers and hunters "half-Indian" in makeup, manners, and habits. Instead of bringing a superior culture to the red man, they were emulating his ways. They gave a bad impression of the white man in general by cheating, defrauding, and exchanging worthless trinkets for valuable pelts.[23]

Colonel Dodge had also deplored the "bare-faced" swindling of the unfortunate Indian. He said the articles of civilized manufacture, which were becoming more and more necessary, were sold to them at "hundreds percent" profit. The Indians could hold out for higher prices, but if they did not choose to accept the trader's price, they could keep their wares.[24]

Before Palmer's caravan proceeded westward unmolested, the white men feasted the Platte River Indians, who swarmed around them in great numbers. During their council, one of the Indians expressed himself as follows:

> A long while ago some white chiefs passed through this country, saying that they were the red man's friends, and that as the red man found them, so would he find all other palefaces. This country belongs to the red man, but his white brothers travel

[23] Joel Palmer, *Journal of Travels over the Rocky Mountains to the Mouth of the Columbia River*, 84.
[24] Richard I. Dodge, *Our Wild Indians*, 267.

through, shooting the game and scaring it away. Thus the Indian loses all that he depends upon for food. . . . Before the white man came the game was tame and easily caught with the bow and arrow. Now the white man has frightened it away and the red man must go to the mountains. The red man needs long guns.[25]

While trouble was brewing between the United States and Mexico over the annexation of Texas, the government sent three expeditions to safeguard the western territory. Frémont, with sixty well-armed men, was assigned to California; Lieutenant James W. Abert, with thirty-two men, was sent on a reconnaissance journey through the Indian country; and Colonel Stephen W. Kearny, with about 250 Dragoons, was ordered to march along the trail to South Pass in a brilliant display of armed might, the purpose being to show the Indians what they could expect in the way of punishment should they become unruly.[26]

The Arapahoes were at Fort Laramie in considerable numbers at the time of Kearny's stay and were the target of some of his remarks, for they had recently committed a number of murders in the area. If such acts of violence were repeated, Kearny threatened, he would turn loose his Dragoons and annihilate them. At nightfall, he added effectiveness to his words by firing a howitzer and sending a rocket into the air. The Arapahoes ran, screaming in terror. Fearful of this new magic, they fled to the mountains, where they remained quiet for a while. But just before historian Francis Parkman arrived, one of the braves, "in one of those inexplicable impulses which often possess Indians," murdered two white trappers.[27] Consternation reigned over the whole tribe because they expected the avenging Dragoons to descend upon them.

Wishing to atone for the rash act of one of their number, a large deputation of Arapahoes visited Fort Laramie. James Bor-

[25] Palmer, *Journal*, 50.
[26] Frémont, *Report*, 1842; J. W. Abert, "Report of Lieut. J. W. Abert of His Examination of New Mexico," *Sen. Exec. Doc.* No. 23, 30 Cong., 1 sess.; Kearny, "Report of a Summer Campaign to the Rocky Mountains," *House Exec. Doc.* No. 2, 29 Cong., 1 sess.
[27] Francis Parkman, *The Oregon Trail*, 243–45.

deaux, then in charge, refused their offer of several fine horses, thus causing the Indians to become more frightened than ever. As time passed and the Dragoons failed to appear, they imagined that Bordeaux was afraid to accept their gifts and that there would be no reprisals. Terror turned to insolence, and they expressed themselves as determined "to kill the first white dog" they could lay their hands on. The white men were but "cowards and old women"!

Parkman theorized that if a military officer had accepted the Arapahoes' offer to deliver up the murderer and had ordered him shot in the presence of the tribe, danger could have been averted. Although Parkman's study concerned the Sioux for the most part, he well understood the nature of the Indian. Parkman made several comparative statements. He found the Sioux inferior physically and mentally to the Crows and mentally to the Arapahoes, and he considered the Sioux the symbol of the American Indian, not because of superior qualities, but because of his resistance and aggressiveness.[28] The Sioux women were more promiscuous than the Cheyenne or Arapaho, for among them the right of the brother-in-law was unquestioned. He attributed to the Arapahoes, Sioux, and Crows an "Owns-Alone" rite, similar to an annual ceremony of the Mandans. It was also called a "squaw feast," when married men came forward to testify publicly to their wives' virtue and fidelity.[29]

While Parkman was in the Fort Laramie area, he found that Bull Bear and his warriors controlled the hunting grounds west of the fort, while Old Smoke controlled the Platte Forks range. It behooved the Arapahoes and Cheyennes to get along with these two despotic Sioux chiefs. The Northern Arapaho bands usually hunted in the area now dominated by Bull Bear, but they would also meet the Southern bands and hunt as they chose in the area claimed by Old Smoke. The Sioux still had not pushed the Crows permanently from the Powder River country.

Parkman found the Indians far more dangerous on the Santa

[28] Parkman, *The Journals of Francis Parkman*, 396.
[29] *Ibid.*, 47, 618n.

Fé Trail than on the Oregon. He was fortunate in that at the time
of his visit to an Arapaho camp on the Arkansas the Indians were
more concerned over the Texans and Mexicans than with his
party. Furthermore, Kearny had been through the same area a
few weeks before and had renewed his threat that he would exterminate the Arapahoes if they committed any more acts of violence.
The effects of his warning had not worn off.

With a show of courage, Parkman entered an Arapaho Camp
Circle. As he and his companions walked toward the chieftain's
lodge, hundreds of Indians flocked out of their tipis to look at
them and the many dogs throughout the village began baying.
The chief, who came forth and shook hands, was unnamed, but
he is described as a "mean-looking fellow, very tall, thin-visaged,
and sinewy, like the rest of the nation, and with scarcely a vestige
of clothing." The white men felt as if they were shut in "by a
dense wall of savage faces." In reconstructing the scene, Parkman
observed that some of the Indians crouched on the ground, others
sat behind them, and still others looked over their heads, while
many more stood behind, peering over each others' shoulders to
get a better view.

Although the chief ordered a woman to bring food, which
she placed in a wooden bowl before them, he did not offer the
whites a pipe, an indication that he was unfriendly. But when
Parkman began to open a bundle of presents—tobacco, knives,
vermilion, and other articles—a grin spread over every face. The
Indians' eyes began to glitter, and they eagerly stretched out their
arms to receive the gifts.

Like Frémont, Parkman was impressed by the Arapahoes'
pure-white shields, which were prized so highly that they were
handed down from father to son. He tried to purchase one with a
large piece of scarlet cloth, some tobacco, and a knife, but he was
unable to procure one of any value. When the Indians asked why
the white men wanted one, Parkman's interpreter told them in
sign language that the whites would use it to fight the Pawnees,
which immediately raised their standing in the Arapahoes' estimation. Parkman, who found the language difficult even for inter-

preters, said Lucien Maxwell, a trader who had been with them a number of years, often had to revert to sign language to make himself understood.[30]

Writing from Bent's Fort, one of Kearny's men spoke of the heterogeneous tongues and people of vastly different character assembled there. The six languages he found spoken were French, Spanish, German, English, Arapaho, and Comanche—a "perfect Bable of a place," he called it. Since he did not mention the Cheyennes, they were probably elsewhere at the time. Kearny, who was ill and could not bear being confined in the inner fort, was impressed by the Arapahoes, whom he called "a fine looking set of men, with mules to trade."[31]

Parkman had a literary counterpart in young Lewis H. Garrard, who tells a fascinating story of the Taos Trail (*Wah-to-yah*), where he had an opportunity to study the different tribes on the Arkansas in the mid–1840's. In company with Cheyenne interpreter John Smith, he came upon an Arapaho camp in the vicinity of Big Sandy Creek. Smith anticipated trouble and urged his companions to pull their wiping sticks from their guns. Perhaps he was aware that the Arapahoes did not like him. At any rate, it was his misfortune to confront Coho (The Lame), whom Garrard dubbed "the most infernal and meanest of the tribe." His band, as well, was considered the worst in the mountains.

The white men rode up, shook hands, and asked for Warra-toria, a friendlier chief. They did not locate him, but they went to the largest lodge, which proved to belong to Beardy, so called because he had a tuft of hair on his chin. According to Garrard, his features were coarse, inclining to sensuality. Although his appearance did not arouse the young man's admiration, he was hospitable, and after he had smoked with his guests, he urged them to stay. They excused themselves by stating that they must reach the Cheyenne camp by nightfall. Leaving hurriedly and looking back for charging Indians, Garrard rode headlong into a rush swamp and had to lead his horse. He and Smith met several other

[30] Parkman, *The Oregon Trail*, 328.
[31] S. W. Kearny, *Across the Plains to Bent's Fort*, 115–70.

Arapahoes, who displayed their hostile feelings by not shaking hands but did not molest them.

Garrard and his companion later encountered about thirty Arapahoes, whom they mistook for Mexicans because they were wearing sombreros. The white men advanced and offered to shake hands, but the Indians turned away coldly. One spoke out bitterly against the white man, who had run the buffalo out of the country and starved his people. When Smith tried to explain that he was a "squaw man," married to a Cheyenne woman, and that he loved the Indians and intended to live and die among them, the chief replied by signs that the white man "has a forked tongue." He raised his hand to his mouth and sent it out in direct line, with two fingers opened and stretched apart.

As the Arapahoes were riding away, they attempted to drive the white men's horses before them, but Smith prevented this. The Indians, who had just returned from a successful raid into New Mexico, had several fresh scalps dangling from the points of their lances. They also had two prisoners and thirty mules and horses they had captured. Pedro, the ox driver for the Garrard party, was some distance behind. When he caught up, he was terrified from his meeting with these same Indians, who wanted meat, guns, and, last but not least, his scalp. They threatened him and pulled his hair, but when he flourished his knife, they freed him.

Garrard later had an opportunity to play host to Warratoria, whom he first met in a Cheyenne village. He was not with the first Arapahoes to arrive, those who asked for *veheo-mah-pe* (whiskey) and were refused, but he soon followed. Garrard was favorably impressed by his benign expression and the slight furrows of age, which gave his countenance a cast of deep thought. His expressive brow, which was slightly receding, was "worthy of a statesman." Garrard was filled with reverence for the old man, who spoke in short sentences only, so different from "the volubility of most savages."

Young Garrard was delighted with the hilarity he found in the Indian encampment. Within an hour the bare spot of turf was transformed into a village with eighty lodges, about three hundred Indians, and eleven hundred horses. The girls from twelve to womanhood, who crossed and recrossed the river as they carried water or sticks for fuel, were laughing, talking, and splashing. Boys were either playing their favorite game of arrows or running races over the prairie. Garrard characterized the scene as one commingled with comfort, youth, and hilarity, exemplifying a carefree life which would appeal to any young man.

Garrard later noted an Indian boy about thirteen years old, a boy whose features were "mild and manly" and whose eyes studied him so intelligently that he was prompted to show his appreciation of him. Taking from his luggage a bright blue shirt, Garrard dressed him in it and then tied a colored kerchief around his neck. The boy was a rare sight, from his neatly groomed hair to his well-made moccasins. When Garrard sent him away with an added prize of some brown sugar, he appeared to be the happiest lad in the world.[32]

George F. Ruxton, who wintered in the mountains in 1846–47, feared the Arapahoes, "the deadly enemies of the Utes."[33] One day while he was hunting, he discovered that he was being stalked by an Indian. He hesitated to fire because he thought that the Indian might be a friendly Ute or one of the two Arapahoes he had met on the Arkansas among a party of traders—which happened to be the case. The Indian tapped his breast and exclaimed loudly, "Arapaho. Arapaho." Soon Coho and his war party came loping down the trail. They were bedecked with war paint and feathers after an unsuccessful foray against the Utes, whom they had not been able to find. They were badly in need of food, which the white men gladly supplied. Ruxton says there were twenty-one of them, the oldest, with the exception of the chief, being under thirty. They made a fine appearance. "Not one but could have sat as a model for Apollo," Ruxton declared. He saw quite a difference between them and the bandy-legged Comanches, who

[32] Lewis H. Garrard, *Wah-To-Yah and the Taos Trail*, 136–37, 165, 347, 350.
[33] Abert, "Report," *loc. cit.*, 7–14; Ruxton, *Ruxton of the Rockies*, 239–40; Grinnell, "Bent's Old Fort and Its Builders," *Kansas Historical Collections*, XV (1919–22), 32.

were such great riders that their leg muscles lacked development.

Ruxton made many contacts with the Arapahoes, whom he mentions frequently in his writings. His legendary account of Manito (Manitou, Colorado) indicates that the shrine might at one time have belonged to the Shoshonis. According to legend, a Comanche became infuriated when he saw a Shoshoni drink above the spring and drowned him. Wan-kan-aga (the Shoshonean counterpart of Manito) came out of the vapor that arose from the disturbed water and killed the Comanche. When he fell into the water, the taste became bitter. As a memorial to the young Shoshoni warrior, Wan-kan-aga smote the rock about the spring and pure water poured forth.

Parties of Arapahoes on their way to make war on the Utes would stop at the mysterious springs to bestow their offerings upon Manito, as they called it. At the time of Ruxton's visit, the spring was filled with pieces of red cloth and knives, and in the surrounding trees were moccasins, bits of cloth, and strips of deerskin. The area was so hallowed that the Arapahoes and Utes could meet there without bloodshed. Elsewhere, either tribe was at the mercy of the one that had the momentary advantage.

The year 1846 was especially important to the Arapahoes, for it was the year that Broken Hand (Thomas Fitzpatrick) was appointed their agent. His district included the Platte, the Arkansas, and all lands lying between. His special duties lay just east of the Rockies, along the great thoroughfare of Indians and whites for trade, war, hunting, and intercourse with Mexico. When he arrived at his post, he found only a few Arapahoes; the majority were with the Comanches, raiding along the Santa Fé Trail. Coho was the probable leader in their depredations of 1847–48, though he denied taking part in the Comanche raids. The success with which these were carried out led Fitzpatrick to consider the Arapahoes more dangerous than the Cheyennes.[34]

[34] Fitzpatrick's earliest experiences as an Indian agent are found in a series of letters to T. A. Harvey, Superintendent of Indian Affairs, dated February 4, April 30, September 18, and December 18, 1847, and February 13 and 15, 1848, IOR, NA. For his biography, see LeRoy R. Hafen and W. J. Ghent, *Broken Hand: The Life Story of Thomas Fitzpatrick.*

Bent's Fort was Fitzpatrick's principal station because it was nearer Mexico than the other strategic trading posts in his territory (St. Vrain on the South Platte and Fort Laramie, at the mouth of the Laramie River on the North Platte). Recognizing the necessity of having help in such a vast area, Fitzpatrick recommended that a military post be established at or near the vicinity of Laramie, as it was approximately in the center of the buffalo range. There, he predicted, the Platte River Indians, and the large influx of Sioux leaving the Missouri would become involved in a great struggle for survival. He began his official duties by attempting to find the guilty tribes who had been raiding on the Santa Fé Trail.

Frémont was overenthusiastic when he predicted, two years after Fitzpatrick had become agent, that within a few years Broken Hand would have the Indians farming, since he knew them so well.[35] Fitzpatrick was not as optimistic. He feared that the real character of the Indian could never be understood, that Christians could not comprehend how so much "depravity, wickedness, and folly could possibly belong to human beings." He was a realist who thought the Christians should, if possible, divest themselves of all partiality and prejudice and view the Indian as they found him. The Indians' innate qualities, he believed, were hastening their destruction. His pessimism reached its height when he said: "All the aid from the wealthiest countries in Europe, united with the United States, could not redeem the people in as much as I consider them a doomed race that must fulfil their destiny. And yet it is a generous and praiseworthy thing for the government to do all it can."[36]

Fitzpatrick was apprehensive of the union of the tribes under his jurisdiction. He estimated that among his charges there were thirty-three hundred warriors, the Sioux having two thousand, the Arapahoes eight hundred, and the Cheyennes five hundred. Should trouble arise, the Cheyennes had offered to fight in the white man's behalf, but Fitzpatrick was doubtful. "I have made a

[35] John Bigelow, *Memory of the Life and Public Service of John Charles Frémont*, 359.
[36] Fitzpatrick to Commissioner of Indian Affairs, Report, 1848, IOR, NA.

rule in all my intercourse with the Indians, whenever I find them very officious and professing great friendship, to double the guard."

Besides being skeptical of the Indians, the new agent was critical of the missionaries, for he knew the Indians far better than the inexperienced churchmen. He believed they were missing a great opportunity to improve physical and moral conditions, which should have been their first objective. Instead, they began "at the very place they aught to give the last touch." They gloried in regeneration rather than education. The truth of his theory was later proved when an epidemic claimed many lives among the Arapahoes De Smet had converted at Fort Laramie. The Indians immediately believed that the white man's religion had been bad medicine.

Fitzpatrick, who had lived among the Indians about a quarter of a century, had a deeper understanding of those in his charge than any of the transient writers. For this reason, his summary of their manners and customs is especially important. To him, the Medicine Lodge, or Offerings-Lodge, could be compared with the tabernacle of the ancient Jews in sacrificial offerings, purification rites, and ablutions. Mourning was a variant of "sack cloth and ashes," with women cutting their hair and otherwise disfiguring themselves by slashing their faces, arms, and legs and allowing the blood to flow but not washing it off until the end of the mourning period.

Broken Hand thought the Indians should be held accountable for their acts, for he was convinced that the "law of retaliation" was the only one they recognized. He gave as an example an incident of petty quarreling between the Arapahoes and Cheyennes. The latter were in the midst of a dance when an old woman interrupted and pleaded piteously that atonement be made for the killing of her son in the spring by the Arapahoes. Just then a courier brought news of an approaching party of the tribe. The warriors abandoned their dance, jumped on their fastest horses, and met the accused. When they returned, they had two Arapaho scalps and a woman prisoner. Thus the mother was reconciled over the loss of her only son and the Arapahoes received what they considered just treatment. Both tribes were satisfied.

The agent was convinced that nothing had been more detrimental to the welfare and improvement of the Indians than the great forbearance and constant humoring of all of their whims, together with the erroneous opinions then existing that nothing but the introduction of Christianity was wanting to make them happy and prosperous. He stated: "I am well aware that they will have to pass through a long and protracted ordeal before they can ever attain any part of civilization, and I have yet to learn and decide whether the full-blooded Indian is capable of such a change."

Also a skeptic regarding the value of treaties, Fitzpatrick said of them: "There is not a single day in the whole year that I could not make a treaty with any of these Indian tribes if I happen to have sufficient merchandise on hand to make presents worthy of the inconvenience and trouble of assembling the nation; and let the stipulation to that treaty be whatever I might choose to propose, it would be solemnly and apparently in good faith ratified and agreed to, but not for one single moment longer than a favorable opportunity offers for its violation."

In spite of his convictions, he went about the business of trying to reconcile the Indians under his jurisdiction. When the Arapahoes told him the Sioux were encamped along the South Platte in such great numbers that they extended below the confluence of the two streams (the North and South forks), he set out to visit them. He discovered that their encampment extended not only eighty miles along the river, but also along Pole Creek, a tributary. He was without an interpreter, but through signs he was able to communicate with them satisfactorily. They assured him of their good will and gratitude for having stopped the liquor traffic.

Reshaw had previously boasted that all the agents the government could send against him could not stop his liquor peddling. Apparently, Fitzpatrick had been successful, for as he said in an earlier report, he intended to teach "these gentlemen" (Reshaw and the illegal liquor peddlers at the present site of Pueblo) that a compliance with the law was a profitable course.

Fitzpatrick held frequent interviews with Coho, but it was Watogen (Two Mountains) who, in 1849, accompanied him to St. Louis, where he was called at the insistence of Robert Campbell to explain the true situation in his country. The agent thought he had passed all the bands and was out of reach of the chieftains when he was visited by Two Mountains, his wife, and their fourteen-year-old son.

Watogen insisted upon accompanying him to St. Louis, saying he wanted to see for himself the great powers and resources of the whites so that he could inform his people. He was a man of influence, not only with his own people, but also with the neighboring tribes, and he had always shown friendship for the whites. Such determination could not be denied, so Fitzpatrick allowed him to go. Watogen, who was the first Arapaho to be taken to the States, was well received and given presents. Superintendent D. D. Mitchell gave him fifty dollars' worth of goods, which pleased him greatly, and he returned to his people with an exalted opinion of the white man. His visit proved so uplifting that Fitzpatrick recommended that other leaders be given similar opportunity to witness the wonders of the white man.

On the way to St. Louis, Fitzpatrick met Solomon Sublette and apparently apprised him of the object of his trip.[37] Sublette said in a letter to his wife he had learned that Fitzpatrick had agreed to meet the Sioux, Cheyennes, and Arapahoes in council in about six weeks. Broken Hand was on his way to St. Louis to be invested with the power to meet in council and make treaties with the Indians. Sublette, who likewise knew the tribes in his charge, felt that such a venture was not worth the least consideration. "As soon as they get their presents," he predicted, "they will commence war."

When Fitzpatrick returned to Bent's Fort, he found a large assembly of Arapahoes, Cheyennes, Kiowas, and Apaches, as well as a few Sioux, who had been waiting some time for the "big talk,"

[37] Solomon Sublette to wife, Santa Fé, May 29, 1849. Sublette Papers, MHS.

an event he would gladly have avoided because of lack of presents. But hesitancy would have jeopardized his position, so he had to act at once. Alone and without resources, he was in a bad situation. He had not even been adequately provided with interpreters, but his council with the Indians proved satisfactory.

In his report, Fitzpatrick protested against maintaining an agency without some degree of respectability, whether with armed military force or means to recompense the Indians for trespass. He felt that the Indians had just cause for complaint concerning the destruction of their game and the cutting down of their timber. As a result of his recommendations, Mitchell suggested a council at Bent's Fort in October, 1849, but it did not materialize until two years later—at Fort Laramie.

While Fitzpatrick was attempting to determine what was best for his Indians, migrations to the West Coast were accelerated by the discovery of gold in California. The goldseekers who streamed along the trail brought further hardship and privation, as well as cholera, to the natives through whose country they traveled. The Arapaho soothsayers, with their mystic powers, could see that the bees now flying westward would eventually swarm into their honey tree.

CHAPTER SEVEN

Big Talk

THE ARAPAHOES were among those "wild and barbarous" tribes that excited attention around 1850 "because they inhabited the frontier and were capable of being brought in hostility against it." This Henry R. Schoolcraft found in his gigantic study of the Indian tribes of America.[1] The Arapaho proper totaled about three thousand souls, but until Schoolcraft was commissioned by Congress to make his study, there had been no "distinctive" account of their manners, customs, traditions, or language, nor had they entered into any official treaty with the government, other than the unofficial Gantt treaty. It was certainly not the fault of Thomas Fitzpatrick, who had worked toward that end the past three years.

In the spring of 1850 the Arapahoes and Cheyennes met in council with their agent near the Santa Fé Trail crossing of the Arkansas at a common meeting ground of the Plains tribes.[2] Since the government had failed to act on his request for funds, Fitzpatrick was not prepared for such a gathering. He had hoped—and had unfortunately led the Indians to believe—there would be a grand council long before this. He protested in his official report that putting off matters of this kind with the Indians could hardly be tolerated, since they invariably attributed such delay to "a course of tampering and temporizing in order to gain time for the purpose of maturing some plan or occasion for their disadvantage or injury." Said Broken Hand: "The Indians are exceedingly jealous and selfish, as well as full of deception, yet, strange to say,

[1] Henry R. Schoolcraft, *Information Respecting the History, Conditions, and Prospects of the Indian Tribes of the United States*, III, 533.
[2] Fitzpatrick to D. D. Mitchell, Superintendent, Central Agency, Report, IOR, NA. See also *Sen. Exec. Doc.* No. 1, 31 Cong., 2 sess., 52.

there is nothing they abhor more than to find such characteristics in a white man."

In the same report, he expressed his regret that some of the impressionable chiefs had not been given a chance to witness the power and strength of the United States. Until the Indians could realize the great power of the government, they might be expected to construe all favors and overtures as signs of weakness and inability to protect white emigrants. He conceded that a great injustice had been done to them by the Oregon Trail, which had impoverished their country within the last two years, and he deemed it a matter of justice that they be compensated for their loss. Finally, $100,000 was appropriated for the proposed council, and D. D. Mitchell, Superintendent of Indian Affairs at St. Louis, and Fitzpatrick were commissioned to treat with the Plains tribes, the place and time of meeting designated as Fort Laramie, September 1, 1851.[3]

The Arapahoes and Cheyennes were well pleased with the prospects of such a council, but the Kiowas, Comanches, and Apaches refused to go among the Crow and Sioux "horse thieves." Six weeks before the scheduled event, Indians began assembling at the mouth of the Laramie, with the Platte River Indians the first on the scene. With them were John Poisal and John Smith, interpreters. Poisal, whose descendants in Oklahoma bear the name *Pizzel*, had married an Arapaho, Snake Woman, sister of Left Hand, sometime around 1830, and she had borne him several children. One was Margaret (Maggie), who was sent to school in St. Louis by her father and became a recognized interpreter for her mother's people. Though many years his junior, she had become the wife of Fitzpatrick, and they had an infant son whom they named Andrew Jackson, or Jack, as he was known until the time of his death in Oklahoma.

The vast number of horses belonging to the ten thousand Indians who assembled at Fort Laramie necessitated that the council be moved to a grassy valley on Horse Creek before it convened, and it was consequently known as the Horse Creek Council,

[3] *Report of the Commissioner of Indian Affairs*, 1850, 51–52.

distinguishing it from other councils held at the fort. After the colorful cavalcade had been completed and the various tribes had been assigned to their allotted places, feasting and dancing began. Although the few Shoshonis present abhorred the thought of eating dog flesh, such feasts were held by the various Plains tribes. As a prelude to the proceedings, official calls were made on the commissioners. These were a part of the pageantry.

The usual pattern of the Camp Circle was observed, and there was a brush-walled arbor in the center where the dignitaries received the chieftains of the various tribes. On September 8, a cannon boomed and the council was officially opened. After the Superintendent of Indian Affairs had given his word of greeting, the Calumet was brought out, and Mitchell said it should be smoked only by those whose hearts were free of deceit. An interpreter, after lighting it, handed it first to Mitchell, then to Fitzpatrick, after which it made the rounds. Many added to their ceremonial smoke a symbolic gesture—that of drawing the right hand slowly from the bowl toward their throat—to signify their truthfulness.

When Mitchell addressed the council, he told the chieftains that he and Fitzpatrick had been sent by the Great Father in Washington to make peace and that they (the Indians) would be duly compensated by the government for the grass eaten by the emigrants' cattle, as well as for the destruction of the buffalo. On the other hand, the Great Father wanted the right to travel unmolested on the roads to the West and to build military posts for the protection of the emigrants. He also told them that certain areas would be designated as tribal lands. Fitzpatrick spoke a few words, urging peace and a thorough understanding of the treaty stipulations. Then a number of chiefs expressed their pleasure over the prospects of lasting peace.

They were given an opportunity to talk over the proposals with their people in tribal council the following day. On the third day, the Crows arrived in all their splendor, and for genuine elegance, they must have outclassed the "grandly savage" Shoshonis. They possessed fine horses which they rode with more grace than any of the other Indians. These were the horse thieves to whom the Kiowas and Comanches objected, but no issue was made of the fact that many of their mounts had previously belonged to the Platte River tribes or had come from the States through the medium of the white man. All hard feelings had been laid aside by the chieftains, who welcomed the Crow enemies with a smoke.

When the chiefs were granted the privilege of expressing their views, they alluded to the loss of the buffalo and their subsequent poverty. They also expressed their ignorance of this thing the white men called farming. Some of the speeches, including one by Cut Nose of the Arapahoes, were eloquent, though some writers attribute such oratory to the embellishment of interpreters and historians. And yet the dignity and general purpose were there, and the speech of Cut Nose was that of a statesman. He said:

> Grand Father, I thank the Great Spirit, the Sun, and the Moon for putting me on this earth. It is a good earth, and I hope there will be no more fighting on it—that the grass will grow and the water fall, and plenty of buffalo. You, Grand Father, are doing well for your children in coming so far and taking so much trouble about them. I think you will do us much good; I will go home satisfied. I will sleep sound and not have to watch my horses in the night, or be afraid for my squaws and children. We have to live on these streams and in the hills, and I would be glad if the whites would pick out a place for themselves and not come through our country; they should give us game for what they drive off.[4]

The wistful remarks of Cut Nose may have aroused the sympathy of the commissioners, but they could not stem the tide of progress. Fitzpatrick, Robert Campbell (by now a St. Louis businessman), and Jim Bridger—all former owners of Fort Laramie—had the important job of designating boundaries, which had always been a matter of tribal contention. But the three men, with their knowledge of the country and its river and mountains, were

[4] *Missouri Republican*, September, October, and November, 1851, MHS.

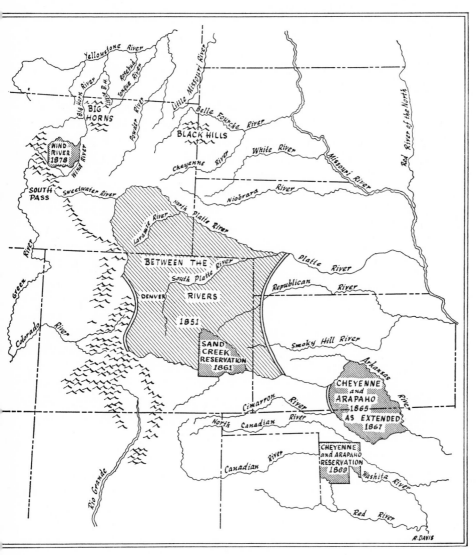

Arapaho Reservations

finally able to map out areas to which the participating tribes agreed. The territory assigned to the Arapahoes and Cheyennes was roughly between the Platte and the Arkansas rivers, the country the Arapahoes had claimed ever since crossing the Missouri. More specifically, it was designated: "Beginning at Red Butte, or the place where the road leaves the North Fork of the Platte River; thence up the North Fork of the Platte River to its source; thence along the range of Rocky Mountains to the headwaters of the Arkansas River; thence down the Arkansas River to the crossing of the Santa Fé Road; thence in a northeasterly direction to the forks of the Platte River; and thence up the Platte River to the place of beginning."[5]

The treaty, which was ready for signature on the seventeenth, provided for lasting peace, the right of the government to build posts, punishment (and restoration of property) for depredations, specified boundaries for each of the tribes but open fishing and hunting rights, and the payment of annuities in the amount of fifty thousand dollars in goods for fifty years. Indian violators of the treaty were to have their annuities withheld, but no reference was made to white violators. (Without either the knowledge or consent of the Indians, the Senate, in May, 1852, reduced the years of payment from fifty to fifteen, and it became Fitzpatrick's task to seek the Indians' agreement to the treaty change.)

The Horse Creek Council was thus concluded and "ratified" when twenty-seven heavily loaded wagons belatedly arrived with presents. When the distribution of gifts was completed, the tribes began to move away in various directions. In bidding each other adieu, the members of the various tribes showed their mutual confidence. Mitchell noted: "Invitations were freely given, and as freely accepted by each of the tribes to interchange visits, talk and smoke together like brothers, upon ground where they had never before met but for the purpose of scalping each other. This, to my mind, was conclusive evidence of the sincerity of the In-

---

[5] 11 *U.S. Stat.* 749; D. D. Mitchell to Commissioner of Indian Affairs, November 11, 1851, IOR, NA; Charles J. Kappler, *Indian Affairs; Laws and Treaties,* II, 55–60.

dians, and nothing but bad management, or some untoward misfortune can ever break it."[6]

Fitzpatrick also had reason to feel pleased over the outcome of the council, and he had the added satisfaction of taking eleven influential members of the Platte River tribes to Washington to call on the Great Father. Among them were Friday, Tempest, and Eagle's Head of the Arapahoes.[7] On their way, they stopped briefly with the Loup Pawnees, with whom Fitzpatrick hoped to make peace. De Smet, who accompanied the expedition, had baptized 305 Arapaho infants at Fort Laramie and he, too, was anxious to see the tribes at peace. Big Fatty, the Pawnee chief, welcomed his guests by saying: "My heart leaps with joy because I find myself in the presence of those that from my infancy I have been taught to consider my mortal foes."

Alights-on-the-Cloud, a young Cheyenne standing beneath the banner of his father, refused to accept the pipe with the enemy, but the other Cheyennes accepted for their people and a spirit of jubilation lasted late into the night.

When the Platte River delegation reached St. Mary's Mission among the Potawatomis, the Indians were introduced to the products of farming: potatoes, carrots, turnips, squash, parsnips, melons, apples, and peaches. Never had they tasted such food! They were so impressed that Eagle's Head said his ears were now open—now that he had eaten the products of the soil—and he understood what the white man meant when he said they must reap their subsistence from the earth, for he now saw a happy people, well fed and well clothed.

The Secretary of the Interior conceded in his annual report for 1851 that most of the depredations committed by the Indians on the frontier were the offspring of dire necessity.[8] With the advance of the white man, the Indians were compelled to relinquish their fertile lands and seek refuge in sterile regions which

[6] Mitchell to Commissioner, November 11, 1851, IOR, NA; *Sen. Exec. Doc.*, No. 1, 31 Cong., 1 sess., 288–90.

[7] De Smet, *Life, Letters, and Travels*, II, 683, 687–88, 689–90.

[8] *Annual Report of the Commissioner of Indian Affairs*, 1851, 65.

furnished little in the way of food. Driven by hunger, they committed numerous offenses, seizing horses, mules, and cattle to satisfy their natural cravings. When they were overtaken and punished, they got their revenge by committing outrages on the persons and property of peaceable inhabitants.

His idea of a solution to the problem of civilizing a wandering race was to tame the savage. "You must tie him down to the soil. You must make him understand the value of property and the benefits of its separate ownership. You must appeal to those selfish principles implanted by Divine Providence in the nature of man for the wisest purposes and make them minister to civilization and refinement," he declared. He went on to say that the Indian should be taught the uses of agriculture and the arts of peace. Best of all, he should be encouraged to look forward to the day when he could be elevated to American citizenship.

During the winter of 1852–53, the Pawnees stole some Arapaho horses, then attacked a band on Smoky Hill Fork. As they were returning victoriously, they were surprised by a war party of Cheyennes, who killed them all. Thus the war cycle was to begin all over again in spite of the good feeling engendered at the Horse Creek Council.[9]

Since the Kiowas, Comanches, and Apaches would not attend the Fort Laramie council, Congress appropriated twenty thousand dollars for a treaty council (1853) with these "Frontier Indians" at Fort Atkinson. The Arapahoes were not directly involved, but one of their number made a valuable contribution by serving as an interpreter.[10] Maggie Fitzpatrick is not mentioned, but it is probable that the words spoken were further interpreted by the English-speaking wife of the agent. He was master of the sign language, which was common to all tribes of the West, but he admitted that he was handicapped by its limitations. While signs answered the purpose of barter, they could not be relied upon in matters of so much importance and delicacy as a treaty.

[9] Hyde, *The Pawnee Indians*, 174–76; Grinnell, "Bent's Old Fort," *loc. cit.*, 84.

[10] Fitzpatrick to Commissioner, November 19, 1853, and Fitzpatrick, Annual Report for 1853, IOR, NA.

Fitzpatrick strongly urged military posts, for he believed there were only two policies—"an army or an annuity"—and that there could be no compromise between the two systems without producing the miseries of failure.[11] He concluded that the only course promising any permanent relief to the Indians was to modify the intercourse laws, to invite resident traders among them, and to open the whole territory to settlement. He had decided trade was the only civilizer. In his last report before his untimely death, Fitzpatrick said of the reservation system that Indians penned up in such small secluded colonies would become hospital wards of cholera and smallpox and would have to be supported at a tremendous cost to the government. He termed it "legalized murder of a whole nation."[12]

The Plains tribes were beset at this time by another problem, the influx of eastern immigrant Indians who engaged in buffalo hunting in the area they claimed. In the summer of 1853 a fight which began with an attack on a small band of Pawnees turned out to be against the Potawatomis, who came to their defense, well armed. Both the Arapahoes and Cheyennes lost heavily.

The following year, a grand council was held among the allied tribes—the Arapahoes, Cheyennes, and Sioux, as well as the Kiowas, Comanches, Apaches, and Osages with whom they were then at peace.[13] The council, which convened on Pawnee Fork at the crossing of the Santa Fé Trail, was the largest that had ever been held on the Arkansas. There were between twelve and fifteen hundred lodges and about forty-five thousand horses. The war pipe was passed, and plans were laid to wipe out all of the immigrant Indians who could be found on the plains. The losses sustained at the hands of the Potawatomis the preceding year may explain why there were only two bands of Cheyennes and one of Arapahoes and why no casualties were suffered by either tribe. They were token representatives sent to show the good faith of their people. Confident of victory, the great war party set out,

[11] *Sen. Exec. Doc.* No. 34, 33 Cong., 2 sess., 368.

[12] *American State Papers*, VI, 460. Fitzpatrick died January 4, 1854. See Hafen and Ghent, *Broken Hand*, 260.

[13] *Annual Report of the Commissioner of Indian Affairs*, 1854, 89–90.

but it was routed by a well-armed but comparatively small band of Sac and Foxes, whose arms were unlike anything the Plains tribes had ever seen.

Aside from the influx of eastern Indians, the Southern Plains tribes had cause to be disgruntled by the constant flow of traffic on the trails through their hunting grounds. Added to this was the irresponsible if not hostile action of soldiers at the forts along the trails. It seemed that certain military men were actually looking for excuses to attack. Lieutenant Henry Heath, the commander at Fort Atkinson on the Upper Arkansas, said casually in one of his reports he had intended to attack an Indian village that morning but that at five o'clock the afternoon before, word was received from William Bent that a trader with a Spanish train stated that a murder of which the Indians were accused was committed by his companion instead of the Cheyennes. The Lieutenant still thought the Indians were guilty, but in view of the message and "in the cause of humanity," he reluctantly called off the raid.[14]

Another feverish desire for action resulted in the unfortunate Grattan Massacre, nine miles below Fort Laramie. One of the Sioux killed a stray cow belonging to an emigrant, and all of his people feasted on the meat. Although the matter was reported to the fort by the contrite, half-starved Indians, who saw no reason why the meat should go to waste, young Grattan and his twenty-nine men marched to the village to demand the surrender of the guilty Indian. Perhaps the matter might have been settled satisfactorily had not the drunken interpreter told the Indians that the soldiers had come "to eat their hearts raw."[15] In the subsequent battle, all of the soldiers were killed but one, who died of his injuries. The Sioux then went on a rampage and looted the trading post at Bordeaux Bend and a near-by post belonging to the American Fur Company. Here they helped themselves to the 1854 annuities intended for the three Platte River tribes.

[14] Henry Heath to Captain I. McDowell, Jefferson Barracks, Mo., April 4, 1853, War Department Records (cited hereafter as WDR, NA).
[15] L. B. Dougherty to Major John Dougherty, August 29, 1854, Major John Dougherty Papers, MHS; *Annual Report of the Commissioner of Indian Affairs*, 1854, 92–98.

The military attitude is reflected in the opinion of Major O. F. Winship of Fort Laramie, who considered the remarks of the interpreter but an "irritating circumstance."[16] He termed the incident a "deeply matured scheme" resulting from hatred for the government and consequent hostility toward all its officers, agents, and instruments. Following the Grattan incident, the Sioux withdrew from the Fort Laramie area, but the Arapahoes and Cheyennes, who had come to receive their annuities, remained until Agent J. W. Whitfield (Fitzpatrick's successor) arrived with fifteen thousand pounds of goods. In council he found the Indians sullen. A Cheyenne spokesman for the two tribes demanded that travel on the Platte Road be stopped and that next year the agent bring four thousand dollars in cash and the balance of their annuities in guns, ammunition, and one thousand white women. The Indians, who were in a disagreeable mood because of the Grattan incident, had a more personal grievance because Whitfield had forced them to give up a prisoner. They complained that next year he would force them to give up their horses.

Whitfield was convinced that the Northern and Southern Arapahoes could never be induced to live together as one nation. At that time they were as hostile toward each other as almost any other nation on the plains. The hostility may have been caused indirectly by the white man and his liquor. Cut Nose, whose oration at the Horse Creek Council was unsurpassed in eloquence, became intoxicated and offensive. When he aroused the ire of one of the band leaders, the warriors took sides and a free-for-all resulted. When one of the Arapahoes was killed, the Nam-e-sum (Cut Nose) band fled north and the main body continued southward as originally planned.[17] With the dissension of the Northern and Southern Arapahoes in mind, Whitfield recommended that the Platte and Arkansas Agency be divided into three units: the Arkansas Agency for the five Prairie tribes—the Southern Arapahoes and Cheyennes and the Comanches, Kiowas, and Apaches;

[16] O. F. Winship statement witnessed by J. W. Whitfield, August 29, 1854, IOR, NA; *Annual Report of the Commissioner of Indian Affairs*, 1854, 89–90.
[17] De. B. Randolph Keim, *Sheridan's Troopers on the Border*, 187–88.

the South Platte Agency to include the balance of the Arapahoes, or the Northern bands; and the North Platte Agency the Sioux.

When Agent Thomas S. Twiss took charge of the Platte River tribes, they numbered sixty-five hundred Sioux, sixteen hundred Arapahoes, and fourteen hundred Cheyennes who contended with each other over their hunting grounds while opposing white encroachment. Judging by the number of Arapahoes, other bands had come north. Twiss hoped to establish peace with his Indians, but he found that while the civil authorities favored peace through a great council, the military believed in force or chastisement. Fearing that trouble would result, he assembled several hundred lodges of friendly Sioux at Deer Creek, a safe distance from Fort Laramie. Here he established what he called the Upper Platte River Agency.

Twiss urged that the Sioux be placed on a reservation on the North Platte and that the Arapaho and Cheyenne allies be settled on the South Fork of the Platte, where farms might be provided for them.[18] This was his idea of dissolving their combined strength and breaking their predatory habits. The following year, he stressed the urgency of the matter, for, as he explained, the Platte River Indians were deteriorating and becoming worse every year. He found that they had been exposed to the influences and examples of whites sufficiently to learn and practice to perfection all of their vices and none of their virtues. Also, he maintained that the whites who lived among the Indians were not pioneers of civilization but fugitives from justice.

The agent also urged that some of the most influential chieftains be sent to see the Great Father in Washington so that they could see for themselves the wonders of white civilization. No one had been sent since 1851, but those still living who had made the trip were listened to and their words were believed by the young and the old. Twiss noted that the bands whose respected men had not seen the President branded those who had as "liars" and "humbug."

Like Fitzpatrick, Twiss, who was thoroughly familiar with

[18] *Sen. Exec. Doc.*, No. 91, 34 Cong., 1 sess., 398; *ibid.*, 3 sess., 386.

Indian ways, favored punishment for their misdemeanors because it was expected, but at the same time he believed the friendlies should have a chance to live in peace. Colonel William S. Harney made a merciless attack upon an encampment of Sioux at Blue Water. Then he marched deep into the Sioux country, where he found the Indians farther removed from the white men's trails more peaceful. But the treaty comsummated with the Sioux at Fort Pierre on March 1, 1856, further complicated matters by including three unenforceable articles: the Indians were not to "lurk" in the vicinity of the trails; the chiefs must compel their bands to obey; and the Sioux should make peace with the Pawnees. This obligated the Arapahoes and Cheyennes to fall in line, for the dominant tribe determined the conduct of its allies.[19]

The Arapahoes seem to have taken little part in the Cheyenne depredations of 1856, although their rations were denied them because in the previous year they had killed twenty-two hundred head of sheep in one drive along the trail.[20] They gave as their reason that they were starving and so ill from smallpox that they were unable to provide for their women and children. They were, however, guilty—along with the Cheyennes, Kiowas, and Apaches —of killing or driving away more than eighty head of cattle belonging to William Bent.[21] The Cheyennes boasted of this accomplishment on the Platte Road, where they whipped one white man, took powder from another, and forced a third to give them coffee. The Indians were so restless that Bent refused to permit the storing of their annuities at his fort. When he left the area in 1857 with his family, Robert C. Miller, the new agent for the Upper Arkansas, was left without defense. The Indians were so hostile that he had to store their annuity goods.

That spring, Twiss protested against the proposed establish-

19 Fort Pierre Treaty, March 1, 1856, *House Exec. Doc.* No. 130, 34 Cong., 1 sess., 1–39.
20 Whitfield to Superintendent of Indian Affairs, from Bent's Fort, August 6, 1855, IOR, NA; *Annual Report of the Commissioner of Indian Affairs*, 1856, 90–100.
21 Robert E. Miller to Superintendent, Upper Arkansas Agency, May, 1856, and July, 1857, Reports, IOR, NA.

ment of Mormon mail stations at intervals of one hundred miles between Fort Laramie and Salt Lake.[22] He said the Mormons proposed to build houses, plow the ground, plant crops, and keep large herds of cattle and horses and a large store to outfit emigrants along the trail. Each proposed station was to be occupied by about fifty or sixty men, who he claimed would usurp the rights of the Indians. He felt there were already too many traders holding talks with the Indians and stirring up trouble. He predicted that there would be no peace if the chain were allowed. Nevertheless, the mail stations were established, though they were later either abandoned or burned.

Twiss reported in November that the Mormons were "tampering" with the Arapahoes. One of the band chiefs had informed him that the Mormons who had begun to settle on Deer Creek had held talks with the Indians and had said they should be more closely united. The Indians were told that the Great Father was sending troops to Utah to take away their country and that when this was accomplished, it would be a simple matter to take the Indians' land. The Mormons had already held talks with the Snakes, Crows, Flatheads, and Nez Percés, and although they had no presents to give, they were planting corn and would soon have plenty to give to all. Twiss was so disturbed by this news that he sent runners to the Snakes and Crows and urged them to meet him in council. The Arapahoes, who he says were true to the government, would gladly accompany the troops. Nevertheless, when Colonel Albert Sidney Johnston's Utah Expedition arrived, the Indians were not permitted to join.

One of the soldiers with Johnston's army wrote of a meeting with about forty Arapahoes.[23] After they had unsaddled their horses and turned them out, they sat down for a talk, which was interpreted by Friday. The Indian said he had come five hundred miles from the Platte River in the Black Hills and had been on the trail of "thieving Utes." The soldiers, impressed by the "tall, noble

[22] Twiss to Commissioner, May 14 and November 1, 1857, IOR, NA.
[23] John Pulsipher, "Diary of John Pulsipher," in *Far West and the Rockies,* VIII, 34.

looking man, well dressed in skins and with good buffalo robes for blankets," mentioned the band chief as Wattoma (Black Bear), who later played a prominent role in the Indian wars in Wyoming.

The Cheyennes were proving so troublesome that the Arapahoes, who were usually found hunting on the tributaries of the South Platte, were directed by their agent to move to the parks in the western part of their territory to avoid becoming involved. By heeding his advice, they managed to stay out of the trouble that resulted in Colonel E. V. Sumner's campaign against the Cheyennes.

Robert C. Miller, who became agent for the Arkansas River Indians in the summer of 1857, found three hundred lodges of Southern Arapahoes in a starving condition about ten miles above Fort Atkinson.[24] Instead of requiring them to proceed to the usual point of distribution for their annuities, he issued these at once to the grateful Indians. Little Raven, who was among them, expressed a wish for his people to cultivate the soil and become farmers, for he knew that the buffalo would be entirely gone from the prairie in a few years. He hoped the Great Father would send thereafter farming implements and instructors to teach the Indians how to use them.

In the council with the chiefs, Miller spoke of the behavior of the young men at Bent's Fort the previous year when they were demanding and troublesome. Little Raven explained that they had waited many days for the arrival of the Cheyennes and could not wait longer because their women and children were faint with hunger. The Arapahoes were so pleased with the many presents the Great Father had sent through Agent Miller that they vowed they would never be seen making war on the whites, like the Cheyennes, or murdering and stealing, like the Kiowas.

The next year, Miller found fifteen hundred lodges of Arapahoes and Cheyennes on the green banks of the Arkansas, extending up and down the river as far as eye could see.[25] He was so impressed by the pastoral scene that he felt the Indian should be

[24] *Annual Report of the Commissioner of Indian Affairs*, 1857, 141–48.
[25] *Ibid.*, 1858, 96–100.

"pardoned for his egotism" in believing his people better than the whites. "It is seldom," he said, "that you can find one who is not fully satisfied of his superiority." He did not dwell long upon the beauty of the scene in his report, turning instead to a sordid picture of the Indian and his health problems. The agent said the Arapahoes had suffered heavily from cholera and smallpox and told how venereal disease was thinning them out. He predicted that the once great tribe would eventually disappear.

From Deer Creek came word that the Platte River Indians were strictly observing the stipulations of the 1851 treaty but that the Crows and Blackfeet were persistently sending war parties against them. While veteran trader Bill Hamilton was among the Crows, he listened to their boasting of recent engagements with the Sioux, Arapahoes, and Cheyennes in which they claimed they took many scalps, mules, and horses.[26] They showed him two fresh scalps, apparently all they had. Hamilton offered them a blanket if they could show more, but they refused. He commented that the boasters were no match for the Platte River Indians, observing that the Arapahoes and Cheyennes could whip them three to five, while the Sioux could hold them in even numbers.

The invasion of Cheyenne and Arapaho country by goldseekers began in the spring of 1858, and townsites were established on Indian lands without regard for the owners. By 1859, immigrants were pouring into the Pikes Peak area by the thousands. William Bent protested to the Superintendent of Indian Affairs that the Cheyennes and Arapahoes were uneasy about the whites' building towns all over the best part of their hunting grounds. Auraria, Denver, Montana City, and other settlements were going up, and the Indians were bewildered because they had not signed a treaty including such provisions. Bent reported they had been "talking very strong" against the whites.[27]

The first postmaster at the settlement of Auraria and his party encountered a large deputation of Arapahoes, on whose

[26] William T. Hamilton, "A Trading Expedition Among the Indians in 1858," Montana Historical Society *Contributions*, III (1900), 65–66.
[27] Bent to Superintendent, Bent's Fort, December 17, 1858, IOR, NA.

lands they were camping. The Indians appeared friendly and pleased to have the whites come among them, but their pleasure would not have been so great had they known that another resident predicted on November 20, 1858, that Colorado would soon be second to California in population and wealth and that by next fall there would be fifty thousand immigrants.[28]

In the winter of 1858, prospector George A. Jackson discovered gold near Idaho Springs. He mentions in his diary that Left Hand (Niwot) had moved up the South Fork of the St. Vrain. Neva, his brother, was with him. Jackson was apparently impressed by the latter, for after he gave him his dinner, he named a peak in his honor.[29]

Left Hand became alarmed upon seeing the white men in the neighborhood of his encampment on St. Vrain Creek. "Go away," he ordered. "You come to get our gold, eat our grass, burn our timber, and kill and drive off our game."[30] A white man, knowing of Left Hand's love of sugar and coffee, told him that he was now paying a dollar a pound, but when the whites should arrive, these articles would be cheap. They could all live together in peace because there was ample room, the white man told him.

After Left Hand had been fed and flattered, he excited the white men's imagination by tales of gold "away back in the mountains"—tales that were as false as they were romantic. Several of the more imaginative of the group listened and believed. Lured by the prospect, they followed Neva, who led them toward the head of the Little Thompson. There the trek ended, for Neva said that he must return to his starving wife and children. He took with him the deer they had killed and left the prospectors to find their own wealth.

Many Whips, another outstanding Arapaho, demanded of the white men an occasional "fat ox."[31] Finding them in no mood to comply, he ordered them to leave within three days or fight.

[28] LeRoy R. Hafen, *Colorado and Its People*, 62.
[29] Louisa W. Arps and Elinor E. Kingery, *High Country Names*, 136.
[30] LeRoy R. Hafen and Ann W. Hafen (eds.), *Relations with the Indians of the Plains*, 173–76.
[31] *Rocky Mountain News*, October 29, 1863.

During the allotted time, he harangued his people and concluded each remark with a plea that "something must be done." Then, in chorus, the women would give vent to their grief with a long, mournful wail.

After having a vision, Bear Head was of a different opinion. On the final day, when the whites were scheduled to leave or fight, he came out of his camp and sauntered toward the fortified cabin. There he bowed down and, feigning much distress, proclaimed that he had a fearful dream in which he stood on a near-by knoll and saw a great flood come down Boulder Canyon. It drowned all of the Indians, but left the whites on dry ground. He interpreted this as the Great Spirit's way of telling him that if they were to fight, the Indians would be the losers. "Let us have peace," he urged.

In an off-the-record agreement—ratified by a feast—the whites pledged that they would not waste game by killing more than they needed, nor would they chase it away. They also agreed not to kindle fires in the timber, lest they get out of control. The reporter for the occasion admitted that the treaty was not well kept, that the way white hunters chased game over the range and the prospectors set fire in the mountains was enough "to start up the Arapaho ghosts."

Our People may have reached the point of starvation, but they were still rich in horses and mules.[32] Their agent observed that individuals would frequently possess as many as one hundred head. These they loved next to their children, and they parted with them only in case of absolute starvation or when they desired to pay a high compliment to a friend or reward someone for a great favor. Whitfield estimated that the twenty-four hundred Arapahoes had a total of fifteen thousand horses.

The last battle between the Arapahoes and Pawnees in Larimer County, Colorado, took place in August, 1858.[33] The Arapahoes and Cheyennes, who claimed all lands east of the Rockies in

[32] *Annual Report of the Commissioner of Indian Affairs*, 1858, 98.
[33] *Dawson Scrapbooks*, Colorado State Historical Society Library, III, 9.

Colorado for their hunting grounds, would allow the Comanches
and Kiowas to hunt there after peace was made in 1840, but never
the Pawnees. Upon this occasion, about twenty Pawnees were
hunting in the vicinity of La Porte, where they killed several deer.
The Arapahoes, hearing the shots, started after them. The Pawnees, rushing up a hogback, threw up breastworks at the edge
of the ridge. As night approached, the Arapahoes, confident of
victory the next day, bedded themselves down at the base of the
ridge. In the darkness, the Pawnees escaped on the opposite side, a
trick every tribe on the plains is credited with executing at least
once. This is the second time on record that the Pawnees succeeded in this maneuver.

Friday and his independent band of Arapahoes, numbering
about 250 braves, roamed on the upper waters of the Cache la
Poudre and the Big Thompson in Colorado. In the fall of 1858, his
band, too, met the Pawnees in battle, with both sides suffering
losses.[34] Friday was sometimes seen among the Arapahoes still in
the vicinity of Clear Creek, about two miles east of present-day
Golden, where Arapaho City was founded in 1858.

Marshall Cook and George A. Jackson, whose camp was
twelve miles west of Auraria at the base of the Table Mountains,
had frequent contacts with the Arapahoes in the area.[35] Cook was
accompanied to the site by Left Hand, who, with his wife and
family, had been on an extended tour into Nebraska and Iowa to
see how the white man lived. Since he spoke good English, he was
at ease among the whites.

Cook, a reputable pioneer, gives an account which cannot
otherwise be substantiated because no records have come to light
to prove it. And yet until it is disproved, it should be accepted on
Cook's word since it might indicate why Friday's once large band
had dwindled. According to Cook, before the abandonment of Fort
St. Vrain, the owners returned to St. Louis to dispose of their

[34] Ansel Watrous, *History of Larimer County* (Colorado), 83–84.
[35] Agnes Wright Spring (re Marshall Cook) in "Rush to the Rockies, 1859,"
Colorado Magazine, XXXVI, 2 (April, 1959), 99; George A. Jackson, "Diary,"
Colorado Magazine, XII, 6 (November, 1935), 201–14.

robes and pelts.[36] They left the Indian wife and child belonging to one of them (probably Marcellin St. Vrain) with others to look after the fort in their absence. A large band of Arapahoes, assembled at the post to await their return, discovered that the Indian woman belonged to an enemy tribe, so they proceeded to avenge the wrongs her people had done them by killing and scalping both woman and child. Unaware that they had committed a crime, they remained until the St. Vrains returned.

When the traders learned what had happened, they sent an employee to invite the Indians to a feast. Meanwhile, the cannon in the watchtower was loaded and the employees, about seventy-five able-bodied men, stationed themselves in positions to fire into the Indians at a given signal. St. Vrain then barbecued an elk in the center of the courtyard. As the smell of the cooking meat permeated the air, the unsuspecting Arapahoes drew near the gate. They were not permitted to enter until all was ready. Then St. Vrain opened the gates, but he warned them that it was a social occasion and they were not to bring weapons of war. Makeshift tables had been set up in cannon range. After all had entered, the gates were closed and a signal was given to fire. When the smoke cleared, about half had fallen to the ground. Then the men at their stations opened fire, killing all but a few—Friday among them—who made their escape.

The bereaved chief would return annually to the site of the old fort, where he would paint his face black and sit on the old walls and mourn piteously. Sometimes he would rave and rend his clothing; at others he would sway and howl in agonizing lamentation. Cook was puzzled until he learned from him the cause of his sorrow.

The site of Denver was a favorite Arapaho campground, and in the city's early days the Indians would "persistently haunt" the place, according to its historian.[37] Sometimes there would be as many as fifteen hundred encamped there. There was no criti-

---

[36] Cook manuscript in Colorado State Historical Society (hereafter referred to as CSHS) Library. See also Hafen, "Fort St. Vrain," *loc. cit.*, 251–55.

[37] Jerome C. Smiley, *History of Denver*, 69, 71.

cism of their behavior unless they were under the influence of liquor. Left Hand, who was accused of being too much under the white man's influence, as well as the influence of his liquor, was said to have lost much of his prestige.

In January, 1859, there were so many miners in the Auraria area that they gave a great feast for five hundred Arapaho warriors and their people whose lands they occupied. By spring, the gold rush was on, and as people came swarming into Colorado, they displayed no concern for the Indians and their rights. The frenzied goldseekers, ever anxious for a shorter route, sometimes followed the Smoky Hill Trail, which in itself offered more hazards than the Indians through whose country it ran.[38] One party had to resort to cannibalism, and the lone survivor would have perished had it not been for the sympathy of the Arapahoes, who nursed him back to health. The gold rush not only brought such men as Daniel Blue, the cannibal, but it also enticed a multitude of men from all walks of life to follow the trail to the diggings.

Among the motley crew were three important newspaper men of the day: Horace Greeley of the *New York Tribune*; Albert D. Richardson, roving reporter for the *Boston Journal*; and Henry Villard, newspaperman and later president of the Northern Pacific Railroad.

Greeley visited his first Arapaho camp when he came through Kansas.[39] The men were away, but he had an opportunity to study the women and children, the latter of whom he observed to be "thorough savages" with a small allowance of clothing, amounting to an average of no more than six inches of buffalo skin for each. At Denver he had an opportunity to interview Left Hand, whom he quotes as saying that he could not remember that the Utes and Arapahoes had ever been at peace.

The editor found about two or three hundred lodges of Arapahoes encamped in and about the log city of Denver. They

[38] Margaret Long, *The Smoky Hill Trail*, 13–14.
[39] Martha B. Caldwell (ed.), "When Horace Greeley Visited Kansas in 1859," *Kansas Historical Quarterly* (cited hereafter as *KHQ*), IX, 2 (May, 1940), 115–40. See also Horace Greeley, *An Overland Journey from New York to San Francisco in the Summer of 1859*, 149–56.

were planning to leave their wives and children in the protection of the whites while they made an onslaught upon the Utes. The Arapahoes, Greeley observed, unlike other Indians on the war-path, who ride mainly by night, would resort to the cover of darkness only after they were within the shadows of the mountains. This caused Greeley to comment that the Utes, whom he says were confessedly stronger, could ambush and destroy any Arapaho force "by the help of a good spyglass and a little white forecast."

After seeing the lands of the Delawares and Potawatomis, "the very best corn lands on earth," Greeley formulated his plan for civilizing the Indian. He thought the idle owners were not entitled to the land, which is God's gift to those who will subdue and cultivate it. He considered it a righteous decree and the Indians would have to abide by it. In other words, they should cultivate the soil or relinquish it to those who would.

Since Left Hand was the only English-speaking Indian he could find, Greeley tried to sound him out on the idea of an Arapaho tribal farm of about two hundred acres for a beginning. But Left Hand, "though shrewd in his way, was an Indian and every whit as conservative as Boston's Beacon Street or our Fifth Avenue." Greeley was subsequently convinced that nothing could be done about the lot of the male Indians, that the only chance for survival of the race lay in the women, who were neither too proud nor too indolent to work.

Richardson, in covering the gold rush, gives a most colorful account of the Indians with whom he came in contact. He was especially interested in Little Raven, whom he believed to be the nearest approximation to an ideal Indian he had ever met. He describes him as having a fine manly form and a "human, trust-worthy face." Each afternoon the Chief would call for a chat in sign language with the newspaperman, whose knowledge of Arapaho was as deficient as the Chief's of English. When they felt the need of a linguist, they sent for Left Hand, who had acquired his knowledge of the language from white traders as a boy.

Richardson tells of one of his interviews with Little Raven, during the course of which the Chief questioned him about the Great Father in Washington and asked that he be shown his whereabouts on the map they had been perusing. Then the Chief questioned him on personal matters: his lodge, the number of his wives and children, and the number of his horses and revolvers.

Unable to impress the Chief except for the revolvers, Richardson asked how many locomotives he had. He shook his head sadly and said that he had heard of them but he had not seen one. Richardson, playing upon his incredulity, told him about the fiery monster which could take him farther in one sleep than the Chief's fastest horses could in ten, leaving the Chief with the impression that he was the owner of several such monsters. Thereafter Little Raven treated the newspaperman with the respect due a chief.[40]

In a news item dated May 25, 1859, the *Missouri Democrat* states that Little Raven had made peace.[41] The following month, the *Leavenworth Times*, in an account probably written by correspondent Villard, tells of a dinner party given in his honor after the negotiations. He had with him four distinguished warriors, one of whom was his interpreter, Left Hand. The article states: "Little Raven is a very sensible and friendly disposed man. He handles knife and fork and smokes his cigars like a white man."

That same year, Left Hand was encamped west of Boulder City, protesting the building of "strong tipis" on Indian lands.[42] But after he had been given his dinner (and perhaps a drink or two), he was in such good spirits that he refused to accept gold dust and small nuggets the white men offered him for the use of the land. When he returned about a week later, the whites again offered to pay, but still he refused. He even told them that they could build their tipis on his land, and a deep friendship resulted.

In the fall of 1859 the Arapahoes met defeat in a battle with

40 Albert D. Richardson, *Beyond the Mississippi*, 190–93, and "Leavenworth and Pike's Peak Route," *SWHC*, XI, 255–56.

41 *Missouri Democrat*, May 25, 1859; *Leavenworth Times*, June 4, 1859.

42 Mary L. Geffs, *Under Ten Flags* (a history of Weld County, Colorado), 238–39.

the Utes near Tarryall Creek.[43] The score was even, for the Arapahoes had captured Ute Susan (Chief Ouray's sister) and Cotoan (his son) some time before. This was the year William Bent became agent on the Upper Arkansas.[44] The confederate band of Arapahoes and Cheyennes, who had intermarried, now occupied and claimed exclusively the area between the North and South Platte. When he talked to the tribal leaders in the fall, Bent found them ready and willing to settle down to farming, but they insisted upon being paid for the large district known to contain gold, the area already occupied by the whites who had established Arapaho County, Colorado. They also wanted annuities for the lands they would relinquish. Bent had to use his influence to keep the Indians quiet.

He thought that if the Northern and Southern bands wished to remain separated as two distinct tribes, a favorable place for the Northern division would be between Cache la Poudre and Chugwater, an area later requested by the Northern Arapahoes for a reservation. He summarized the difficulties that had beset the tribes by stating that a desperate war of survival was imminent and inevitable, a prediction Fitzpatrick had made earlier. Only prompt action could prevent it.

The Platte River Indians unsuccessfully tried to stop the white men, even the U.S. Topographical Engineers, from penetrating their hunting grounds. Agent Twiss explained the situation, saying the Indians gave as their reason that the buffalo would not return to the same place after scenting a white man. In a conscientious effort to bring about a peaceful solution to the Indian problem, Twiss held a council at Deer Creek, Nebraska Territory, on September 18.[45]

Apparently he had been authorized to negotiate such a treaty, though nothing came of it. Even so, it did add an item of interest to Arapaho history, for the chiefs present were Medicine Man,

43 F. W. Cragen, "Early Far West" (28 notebooks in the Pioneer Museum, Colorado Springs, Colorado), XVIII, 34.

44 William Bent to Superintendent of Indian Affairs, October 5, 1859, IOR, NA.

45 Twiss, Deer Creek council; see *Far West and the Rockies*, IX, 176–79.

Black Bear, Cut Nose, Little Owl, and Friday, plus about thirty of their leading men. Medicine Man came to the fore upon this occasion, and while it may have been just another "talk" to the white man, it was a "big talk" to him as he spoke in behalf of the three Platte River tribes. That an Arapaho should be permitted to speak for the Sioux was in itself unprecedented. In response to the opening remarks made by Twiss, Medicine Man said:

> Father (Twiss), the words which you have given us from our Great Father are good. We listen to his voice. Our country for hunting game has become very small. We see the white men everywhere; their rifles kill some of the game, and the smoke of their Camp fires scares the rest away. . . . It is but a few years ago, when we camped here, in this valley of Deer Creek, and remained many moons, for the Buffalo were plenty and made the prairie look black all around us. Now, none are seen and we are obliged to go to the Yellow Stone, ten days travel, and then find only a few, for the Crow Tribe of Indians show hostile feelings towards us when we hunt there; oftentimes scaring away the game and stealing our horses. . . . Our sufferings are increasing every winter. Our horses, too, are dying because we ride them so far to get a little game for our Lodges. We wish to live. . . .
>
> We are willing that our people should plant and raise corn for food, and settle on small farms and live in Cabins. We ask our Great Father to help us until we can labor like the white people. The Arapaho Tribe wish to settle on the Laramie River, above Fort Laramie. The Oglalas will settle on Horse Creek, in part; and another part on Deer Creek, the present Agency. . . . We request that our Great Father will supply us for a few years with a Blacksmith, Carpenter, farmers, physicians, Missionaries of the gospel, and teachers; seeds, agricultural implements and stock; and such annuity goods as our necessities may require.
>
> With this assistance and a good disposition on our part, we shall in a few years be able to raise corn and live like the White man, without any further aid from our Great Father. Father, we give all the rest of our Country to our Great Father, except the reservations above named. It is no longer any use to us, as nearly all the game has disappeared. We would ask our Father to permit us to hunt where the White man has not settled.

CHAPTER EIGHT

"They Must Go"

The Indians saw their former homes and hunting grounds overrun by a greedy population, thirsting for gold. They saw their game driven east to the plains, and soon found themselves the object of jealousy and hatred. *They must go.*[1]

Aᶠᵀᴱᴿ ɢᴏʟᴅ was discovered in the Colorado mountains, the whites began to question the rights of the Indian. Even the agents echoed the question of whether the red men should remain on their ceded lands because of their conduct. "They kill cattle, steal horses, threaten the people, yet they claim the right to remain in Colorado."[2] By the same token, would white men and their families have been excluded from lands to which they were legally entitled? Horse stealing was a pattern followed by all Plains tribes, but it is evident that the killing of cattle and the threatening of lives was brought on by starvation.

Albert D. Richardson found Denver's Blake Street in 1860 "a busy scene, a mingled maze of various life."[3] After passing stores and saloons and marveling at the tremendous size of the vegetables and melons, all locally grown, he found, a few yards beyond the busy street, an Arapaho village where "barbarism" thus far had maintained its ground against the advancement of (nominal) civilization, but he predicted that before long it would be crowded out. Although Richardson characterized the Arapahoes as poorer and more wretched than most other Plains tribes, he conceded a

[1] *Annual Report of the Commissioner of Indian Affairs*, 1868, 32.
[2] *Ibid.*, 1860, 100.
[3] Richardson, *Beyond the Mississippi*, 300.

certain amount of picturesque splendor to a warrior prepared for the warpath, and he felt that the women were rich at least in the number of children playing about their lodges.

One of the old-timers, Oliver P. Wiggins, on his way up the Platte, stopped among the Arapahoes at the camp of Chief Roaring Winds, where he witnessed a scene more piteous than amusing.[4] The half-starved children grabbed and ate the corn the horses slobbered from their mouths. A white woman whose heart was stirred by their destitution went to a wagon to get them some dried apples. A sack of red peppers rolled out, and one of the boys grabbed several and shared them with his companions, who started screaming and running about, their hands clapped over their mouths. Roaring Winds came at once to find the cause of the commotion. Wiggins took one of the peppers, tasted it, and handed it to the chief, who did likewise. Then he exclaimed, "Whoop! Poo! Heap hot!" as he passed it around so that others could place their tongues to the object to obtain the effect.

Some of the women in the emigrant train wanted to give everything they owned to the Arapahoes, since they were sure they would be killed anyway. When the Indians unhitched the horses and drove them away, the pessimists in the train were convinced they would never see them again. Wiggins, who had spent a winter in charge of a camp near Arapahoes under Slim Face and Big Thunder, assured them they had nothing to fear. At sunup next morning, here came the Indians with the horses. When the whites left, they scattered corn like chicken feed to see the children scamper for it. But when they offered the peppers to them, the children ran away screaming. The whites then gave the peppers to Roaring Winds, who, with a laugh, commented that they would make "heap good firewater."

The white men who flooded the Indian country showed a general disregard for the Indians. Besides destroying their only means of subsistence, they cheated them in trade and debauched them with liquor. With starvation their only alternative, the Arapahoes showed a surprising amount of restraint when one

[4] Cragen, "Early Far West," XXI, 23–30.

considers that there was little actual trouble before 1860. Historians would have us believe that the hostiles were saving up for a major engagement, which may have been the case, but there occurred provocative incidents that could have set off a chain of battles much earlier. We find casual mention of "shameful outrages" to which the Arapahoes in the Denver area were subjected. Upon more than one occasion in the winter of 1859–60, one authority tells us, their camps were invaded by brutal, half-drunk white ruffians who overpowered the braves and subjected the women to nameless indignities.[5] Had the tables been turned, as they later were, the whole country would have been ablaze with news of Indian atrocities.

In June the Arapahoes, leaving their families in Denver in the care of the white men, whom they still seemed to trust, set out in a large war party against the Utes. Accompanied by an undetermined number of Apache warriors, they made a surprise attack on an enemy village and killed several women and children. Rallying their forces, the Utes drove them back and later made a successful night attack on their encampment. After six of the Arapaho and Apache warriors had been killed, the others withdrew. On their way back to Denver, they are said to have insulted several emigrants by compelling them to give them provisions, and they drew revolvers on a defenseless woman they found alone in a log house.[6] The comment of the journalist reporting the incident was: "Unless the Arapahoes very soon abandon such proceedings, they will find a more formidable enemy in the field than the Utes."

A similar statement appears in another newspaper, which claims the settlers were suffering daily from the Indians' operations.[7] The occasion for the remark was a "bloody fight" between the Arapahoes and Cheyennes on the one side and the Delawares and Potawatomis on the other, which took place about one

[5] Smiley, *History of Denver*, 402; *Rocky Mountain News*, April 18, 1860.

[6] Albert D. Richardson, "Letters on the Pike's Peak Gold Region" (to the editor), *Lawrence* (Kansas) *Republican*, May 22 to August 15, 1860; Louise Barry (ed.), "Letters on the Pikes Peak Gold Region," *KHQ*, XII, 1 (February, 1943), 29–31.

[7] *Neosho Valley Register* (Burlington, Kansas), August 11, 1860.

hundred miles above Fort Riley. Some three hundred of the latter were killed, including prominent Indians well known to the whites in eastern Kansas.

During the summer, Buffalo Belly, one of the lesser Arapaho chiefs, was killed when he came into the possession of a quantity of bad whiskey while he was camped with his band on Cherry Creek.[8] There were no whites involved in the incident except the unknown trader who brought the liquor into camp.

William Bent, who was aware of the scarcity of game and the restlessness of the Southern tribes, hoped to protect their rights and interests, but he believed that the only solution to their problem was to settle them away from the trails and transform them into an agricultural people. He felt that the Indians would be satisfied with lands bordering on the Arkansas, from Fountain Creek to the Raton Mountains. Since the whites had already appropriated and settled their principal hunting grounds on the South Platte, Cherry Creek, and the Arkansas, he urged that measures be taken at once to avert a desperate war.[9]

At Bent's insistence that a treaty be made and at the Arapahoes' and Cheyennes' expression of willingness to attend such a council, Commissioner A. B. Greenwood, armed with a $35,000 congressional appropriation, was dispatched to Bent's Fort to conduct negotiations. Upon his arrival he found Little Raven, Storm, Big Mouth, and Left Hand with their Arapahoes on hand to greet him, but most of the Cheyennes were two hundred miles away on a buffalo hunt. Greenwood distributed medals featuring James Buchanan, then occupying the presidential chair, and some of the wags in the party gave campaign buttons of the two contenders for the office. Just how highly these relics were prized was revealed when Little Raven offered ten horses for the recovery of his "lost Buchanan." The Indians enlivened the occasion by bringing a Pawnee scalp and holding a night-long dance.[10]

Black Kettle, White Antelope, and three minor chiefs of the

[8] Smiley, *History of Denver*, 71.
[9] *Annual Report of the Commissioner of Indian Affairs*, 1859, 137–39.
[10] *Ibid.*, 1860, 228–30; Greenwood to Commissioner, October 25, 1860, IOR, NA; Richardson, *Beyond the Mississippi*, 303.

Cheyennes arrived later, and in council Greenwood distributed about a third of the treaty goods and promised the rest after the document was signed. The Cheyenne chiefs were willing to accept the proposals made to them, but they would not make commitments for all of their people until they had been given an opportunity to discuss the question.

The Arapaho and Cheyenne representatives present agreed verbally to a greatly reduced reservation and to accept $450,000 over a fifteen-year period for the vast cession. Greenwood proposed to settle them on both sides of the Arkansas above Purgatory, up to the vicinity of Huerfano, and so to the north line of New Mexico and on that line east to the Purgatory, and to include the creek north of the Arkansas called Sand Creek. The Sand Creek Reservation, as it was to be known, was considered more than adequate for the Arapahoes and Cheyennes of the Upper Arkansas, though it had little to offer from the Indian point of view. And yet when the chiefs were shown a diagram of the 1851 reserve "between the rivers" and the diminished one, they offered no protest. Greenwood showed his undisguised enthusiasm when he said the Arapahoes had exhibited a "degree of intelligence seldom to be found among uncivilized tribes." When he told them that they should settle down, engage in agriculture, and eventually abandon the chase as a means of support, they agreed and stated that such was their wish. They had also "noticed" the approach of the whites, and felt that they must soon conform to white habits.[11]

Greenwood represented the Indians as being fully aware of the rich mines discovered in their country, and yet they were disposed to yield up their claims without reluctance. He felt they certainly deserved "the fostering hand of the government and should be liberally encouraged in their new sphere of life." This enthusiasm was not shared by William Bent, who tendered his resignation. The legality of the land transfer was posed by Article VI of the so-called Fort Wise Treaty, which states that continued effort be made to obtain cession agreements from all Cheyennes

11 *Annual Report of the Commissioner of Indian Affairs*, 1860, 452–54.

and Arapahoes of the Upper Arkansas, implying that until such signatures were gained, the treaty had accomplished no change in the status of the land in question.[12]

For years the Arapahoes, as well as the Cheyennes, had enjoyed occupancy rights as separate tribal units, the Northern bands on the Platte and the Southern on the Arkansas. The division had been recognized by the creation of the Upper Platte and Upper Arkansas agencies serving the two geographic divisions. An attempt to clarify boundary lines created a further dilemma until Commissioner William P. Dole finally gave Superintendent of Indian Affairs John Evans, governor of Colorado, blanket authority to settle the problem. At the same time, Dole informed the Governor that the Fort Wise Treaty ceded by its terms all lands previously owned, claimed, or possessed by the Cheyennes and Arapahoes, wherever situated. He considered the congressional appropriation too great for the few Indians embraced by the treaty, and he therefore ruled that it was meant for all—both the Northern and Southern bands of the allied tribes. Still, he said, "you must now go ahead and get the rest of the signatures."

Bent was succeeded by Albert G. Boone, Daniel's grandson, who played a leading role in negotiating the ultimate Fort Wise (or Boone) Treaty on February 18, 1861.[13] To this were affixed the rude X's of four Arapahoes (Little Raven, Storm, Shave-Head, and Big Mouth). Among the six Cheyennes who signed was a chief named Left Hand (Namos), sometimes confused with Left Hand (Niwot), the popular Arapaho band chief.

Big Mouth had become exceedingly fond of liquor and was soon in disrepute. He was the first to climb on a whiskey wagon and seize two and one-half barrels when his warriors pillaged a Mexican train about thirteen miles west of Fort Larned in August. Besides his own followers, he was aided by Wolf's band, but the leader was exonerated because he was at Fort Larned at the time.

---

[12] Evans to W. P. Dole, April 10, 1863, and Dole to Evans, May 18, 1863, IOR, NA. For a detailed discussion of the land problem posed by the Fort Wise Treaty, see William E. Unrau, "A Prelude to War," *Colorado Magazine*, XLI, 4 (October, 1964), 299–313.

[13] Kappler, *Indian Affairs*, II, 807–11; *12 U.S. Stat. 1168–69.*

Little Raven had passed the same train earlier but had resisted the temptation to attack. The infantryman who reported the incident suggested that Big Mouth and fifteen or twenty of his men be seized and held as hostages until a stop could be put to such acts. If the Arapahoes were not checked, the Kiowas were bound to follow the lead.[14]

The Indian situation in Colorado was complicated when Major S. G. Colley was sent from Washington to head the same agency to which Boone had already been appointed by William Gilpin, who had served as the first territorial governor of Colorado. One operated from Fort Wise (Fort Lyon), the other from Denver, and both were so concerned over their personal aspirations that they seemed to lose sight of the Indians, whose welfare they were supposed to safeguard.

The Census of 1862 shows the Northern Arapahoes as a minority group. Of the 10,395 Platte River Indians, 7,875 were Sioux, 1,800 Cheyennes, and only 720 Arapahoes.[15] Though few in number at the time, John Loree, then agent, found them "the most honorable tribe at the Upper Platte Agency." In proving his point, he said they had found six mules bearing the Overland Stage Company's brand. These they brought to the agency and asked that they be turned over to the company. The same census showed the Southern tribes to include 1,500 Arapahoes, 1,600 Cheyennes, 1,800 Comanches, 1,800 Kiowas, and 500 Apaches. With an average of four ponies each, the combined herds of the Arkansas River Indians amounted to 28,800 head.

With such a formidable array of mounted warriors as the above would suggest, it is not surprising that Agent Boone was concerned when the Kiowas and Comanches were in his vicinity, near the Cheyennes and Arapahoes.[16] Together they were spending their time cutting lodge poles while their warriors fought the Snakes and Pawnees. Reports of depredations were coming to him hourly, but he was unable to name the guilty Indians. As timber

14 J. Hayden to A. J. Boone, Fort Larned, August 3, 1861, IOR, NA.
15 John Loree to H. B. Branch, September 1, 1862, *ibid.*; *Annual Report of the Commissioner of Indian Affairs*, 1862, 225–30.
16 Boone to Commissioner, April 26, 1861, IOR, NA.

and grass became scarce and buffalo less plentiful, the Indians of the Arkansas began accusing each other of violating their rights. For this reason, as well as the advisability of keeping the Indians away from the white settlements in eastern Colorado and farther from their enemies, the Utes, it was necessary to distribute their annuities at Fort Larned, Kansas.

The Northern bands, who watched the Oregon settlers, the Mormon zealots, and the California goldseekers stream westward along the great Emigrant Trail, were mystified by the Pony Express rider, who dashed from one station to another, with only two minutes allowed for change of mail and horses. "Pony Express —9 Days from San Francisco to New York" was one of the marvels of the age. Then, eighteen months after its inception, there followed the Overland Telegraph, or "singing wires," which never ceased to perplex and annoy the Indians.

In 1862 the road along the Platte had to be abandoned because of the hostile Sioux. The Overland Stage Line then dipped southward into Colorado to follow the Cherokee Trail up to the Laramie Plains, then went due west along the course later followed by the Union Pacific Railroad. The new route avoided the Sioux, but it bisected Arapaho country as it followed the South Platte to the Cache la Poudre and entered the Laramie Plains. In the summer, a post (named Fort Halleck, for a Union general) was built at the base of Elk Mountain, where the Cherokee Trail rounded the Medicine Bow Range. This infringed on the rights of the Arapahoes, who, with their allies, frequented the Medicine Bow area, where they camped while they replenished their weapons. Several Arapaho trails can be followed to this day through the Laramie Mountains. These the Indians used in going back and forth from the Black Hills to the Medicine Bow campgrounds, as well as to the Laramie Plains, where they hunted buffalo.

The *Rocky Mountain News* assumed a conciliatory tone in the spring of 1862 when it told of twelve lodges of Arapahoes under Spotted Wolf who, destitute of provisions, were stranded in the Denver area.[17] A hasty council was called and the chief

[17] *Rocky Mountain News*, April 5, 1862.

agreed to leave on Monday, assuming the Indians could obtain the ammunition they needed to defend themselves from enemy tribes and to procure food. They were fearful of an attack by the Utes. The editor suggested that the citizens "relieve them somewhat" should they appear at the door, as "conciliation was the best policy." The once proud Indians who inhabited the land had now been reduced to the status of beggars.

Adding to the miseries of the Indians on the Arkansas in the early spring of 1862 was another outbreak of smallpox, which Little Raven reported at Fort Wise to be raging in a camp of Kiowas and Comanches twelve miles downriver.[18] He feared that if the Indians reached Denver, the epidemic might spread among the whites. A month later, Little Raven again visited the fort. He had come to find out if facilities were forthcoming to help his Indians settle down to a life of farming. He said, quite logically, that if the Great Father expected them to farm, they must have the necessary equipment and training. He expressed his willingness to lead out, and Boone was so impressed by his manner that he suggested in his report that he not be "overlooked."

According to Agent Colley, all of the Colorado bands of Arapahoes seemed anxious to settle on a reservation with the exception of Little Owl's and Friday's.[19] Little Owl, with about fifty lodges, had not been present at the signing of the Fort Wise Treaty and refused to recognize it as binding. Friday, who had for many years lived on the Cache la Poudre, hoped to round out his life there. Medicine Man later agreed to a reservation on the same stream, but at no time would he hear to moving to the Sand Creek Reservation.

Apparently there must have been other "disaffected" bands of Arapahoes, for John Evans estimated that they constituted nearly half the tribe. He held councils with several, explained the treaty to them, and sought their approval, but they denied having

[18] Boone to Commissioner, February 2, 1862, IOR, NA.
[19] Samuel G. Colley, Report, June 30, 1862, IOR, NA; Evans to William P. Dole, November 9, and Evans to John Loree, November 24, 1863, John Evans Collection, CSHS Library.

any part in it and were still dissatisfied.[20] Evans listed two principal reasons for the disaffection. In the first place, he feared he might have caused it by insisting upon their cessation of war with the Utes. Since hostilities had been the rule from the time they first met, his efforts were regarded as unwarranted intervention, even though they agreed to respect his wishes. Second, some of the bands were not present when the treaty was made and refused to have any part in it.

In July, Evans had sent a detachment of twenty-five men down the South Platte to disperse the Indians and stop all outrages.[21] The unofficial report of this assignment indicates that it turned into an enjoyable outing. The men took a "6-pounder" to impress the Indians, but it was the whites who were more impressed. Through John Smith (Blackfoot John, the interpreter), Colley was introduced to Cut Nose, whose camp comprised about seventy lodges of docile Arapahoes. Smith interpreted the Chief as saying that he was sorry not to have left the Platte as he had promised the Governor, but the Great Spirit had intervened and had demanded that he call a Medicine Lodge and have a Buffalo Dance. If Colley would permit, he would be through and ready to leave early Thursday morning.

The soldiers were fascinated by the Buffalo Dance, in which a woman and two girls, about ten years of age, represented a white cow and her two calves. The forty women taking part were dressed to represent buffalo. At the conclusion of the dance, a foot race was run, the last woman out being pelted with sticks, stones, dirt, or anything loose by the crowd of men, women, and children.

Immediately after receiving their annuity goods, the Southern Arapahoes and Cheyennes left for their hunting grounds on the Pawnee and Republican rivers near Fort Larned. Again Friday is mentioned, this time as the "lone dissenter" among the Arapahoes, though Evans had given the impression that half of the tribe was opposed to the treaty stipulations. Refusing a reservation on

---

[20] Colley to Commissioner, September 30, 1863, IOR, NA.
[21] *Rocky Mountain News*, July 19, 1862.

the Arkansas, Friday stubbornly returned to the Cache la Poudre.

January, 1863, found Boone still waiting for the Platte River Indians to come to the Sand Creek Reservation. The chiefs of the Southern Arapahoes informed him that they were unwilling to await the Northerners, "a small band who lived and hung around Fort Laramie, scarcely ever going on the hunt and begging for a living or refusing to live on their own land."[22] Although the Northern and Southern bands appear to have fluctuated in numbers, there was still a feeling of bitterness between the two factions. Two months later, Evans reported that Little Owl and Friday had not been reconciled to going on the Sand Creek Reservation. The general lack of interest on the part of both the Arapahoes and Cheyennes in the newly created reservation is reflected in the statement that only one Indian family had settled there by midsummer.

A few weeks later, John J. Saville, surgeon of the Second Cavalry Volunteers, wrote a significant letter to the Bureau of Indian Affairs, copies of which were sent to Governor Evans and Agent Colley.[23] Saville recounted many grievances of the Arapahoes and Cheyennes, whose confidence he had gained, his chief means of communication being Left Hand and his brother Neva.

Saville stated that in the spring of 1862, Neva had come to him with the complaint that his people had been treated badly in creating the Fort Wise Treaty; he asked to consult the new governor. Saville took Neva to see Evans so that he would have a chance to voice his protest that the Indians had been deceived. Left Hand had previously claimed that both Agent Colley and Smith had lied to the Arapahoes and had made promises they had not kept.

Neva wanted the Governor to know that the Arapahoes disliked "Lying John" Smith (otherwise known as Blackfoot John or Uncle John) and would not believe a word he said. They flatly refused to have him as their interpreter. Instead, they wanted

---

[22] Colley to Evans, December 31, 1862, Boone to Evans, January 16, 1863, and Evans to Dole, March 9, 1863, IOR, NA; *Annual Report of the Commissioner of Indian Affairs*, 1863, 122–26, 240.

[23] John J. Saville, Report, April 15, 1863, IOR, NA.

Colonel William Bent. Although the same complaints were later registered by Left Hand, the Governor appointed John Smith as their official interpreter. Smith's son Jack and Bent's son Robert were made richer by being given 640 acres each of valuable land bordering the Arkansas following the Boone Treaty. To add to the intrigue, Colley's son was in partnership with John Smith in a lucrative hide and cattle business near Fort Lyon.

Left Hand argued that the treaty was negotiated while he was away and that he did not know the terms, which his people accepted without his consent. He pointed out that the Left Hand (Namos) whose signature appeared on the treaty was a Cheyenne. According to Saville, John Smith had told the Great Father in Washington that Left Hand (Niwot) was of no consequence, though he was a "principal man," that is, a band chief and influential leader. Politically, Little Raven was the civil chief, and although Left Hand may have considered himself at the top, he was but a band leader and his name does not appear on any of the various treaties signed by the Arapaho chiefs. The fact that he was an intelligent, English-speaking member of the tribe added greatly to his importance, and it is possible that he might have served his people better as an interpreter than John Smith, whose motives were questionable.

Saville says that a few days after Colley left the post to collect the Indians for their trip to Washington, Left Hand arrived, expecting to accompany him. He maintained that Colley had promised to wait twenty-four days for him. At that he had arrived two days before the time agreed upon, yet Colley had been gone seven or eight days. Left Hand was "chagrined and disappointed," for he had hoped to talk to the Great Father in English and tell him how the agent and John Smith had been misrepresenting matters to the Indians. He was convinced that Colley did not want him to go because he knew he would disclose what had taken place. (He might also have named the swindlers who had acquired annuity goods which they later sold to the Indians.)

Evans had exacted a promise that the Arapahoes discontinue their attacks upon the Utes. The summer before, the Governor had promised the Arapahoes and Cheyennes that Colonel Jesse H. Leavenworth would protect them if they would discontinue their expeditions into Ute country. Leavenworth even stopped an expedition then on its way to attack the enemy. In calling off the raid, the Arapahoes were guaranteed protection, but near Fort Lyon a party of Utes stole seventy of their horses, leaving them without means of procuring food. The raid took place in sight of the fort, but nothing was done to prevent it, the commanding officer disclaiming any knowledge of such a promise. The Indians could not understand why the white men had broken this agreement. They considered it bad faith on the part of the government.

A few days before Saville wrote his letter, the Arapahoes came to him excited and angry. They claimed that Colonel John M. Chivington had burned nine of their lodges on the Platte River. The surgeon said he did not want to bring charges against any of the officers in the territory but felt that there was a "strange and most unaccountable disregard of the feelings and wishes of the Indians." He admitted that the Arapahoes were jealous because of the reception accorded the Ute chiefs at Denver and the military escort and train of wagons used to take them to the States. The last straw consisted of leaving Left Hand. This convinced the Arapahoes and Cheyennes that Governor Evans wanted to favor the Utes at their expense. At the time of Saville's writing, the Arapahoes, in righteous indignation, had organized a war party, under Left Hand, against the Utes.

The year 1863, known to the Indians as "the year of hunger," was one in which the most peaceful of the Arkansas Indians had reached a point of desperation. The much lauded Sand Creek Reservation was destitute of game; there was not a buffalo within one hundred miles of it. Colley admitted that the depredations committed by the Arapahoes were caused for the most part by starvation. He claimed they were so destitute there was a possibility of their joining the Sioux in a war against the whites.[24] Major

<hr/>

[24] Colley to Dole, September 30, 1863, IOR, NA; *Annual Report of the Commissioner of Indian Affairs*, 1863, 134–35; *The War of the Rebellion* (cited hereafter as *WR*), Series One, Vol. XXII, Pt. 2, 511–72.

Scott J. Anthony at Fort Lyon also reported the Indians as impoverished. He believed the government would be forced to subsist them or let them starve to death, "which would probably be the easier way of disposing of them."

The usually passive Black Kettle and White Antelope seemed on the verge of joining the Sioux, who were bringing pressure against Medicine Man, Many Whips, Little Owl, and Friday. The disturbance was so general that Evans was instructed by the Bureau of Indian Affairs to treat with the Indians in order to restore peace. Even the Arapahoes and the Cheyennes, in their general state of frustration, were reported to be temporarily at war with each other.[25]

During the summer, two squaw men, Elbridge Gerry (Little Gerry) and Antoine Janice, were sent to round up the Indians and induce them to come to a council on the Arkansas the middle of September. Both were reputable Indian traders. Gerry went south to the Arkansas, and Robert North, substituting for Janice, tried to contact scattered bands as far away as the headwaters of the Yellowstone.[26]

North had married into the Northern Arapaho tribe. While the two men scoured the country and talked with indifferent people, unverified word began to sift into Denver of negotiations between the dissatisfied Arapahoes and Cheyennes and the hostile Sioux. According to Agent Simeon Whitely, after North had failed to find the Arapahoes under Roman Nose, Friday sent four of his young men to induce him to come in with his people.[27] Friday, ever anxious for a treaty to provide permanent settlement on the Cache la Poudre, had already been joined by two bands, those under Many Whips and White Wolf. After talking with the latter, Whitely and Evans, who accompanied him, were convinced that the Arapahoes wanted to keep the peace, but more from motives of prudence than friendship.

[25] Zebulon M. Pike, *The Expedition of Zebulon Montgomery Pike*, II, 435.

[26] For the report of Robert North, see Evans Collection, CSHS; *Annual Report of the Commissioner of Indian Affairs*, 1864, 224–25.

[27] Simeon Whitely, Report, August 20, 1864, IOR, NA; *Annual Report of the Commissioner of Indian Affairs*, 1864, 136, 219, 236.

The agent had learned that Little Raven, Left Hand, and Storm were at Fort Larned, there receiving full army rations though they had been warned by the Cheyennes to leave. With the Kiowas, Comanches, and Apaches helping, the Cheyennes intended to take all the forts on the Arkansas. Even though they were threatened by this powerful alliance, the Arapahoes would not join in a war against the whites, the three chiefs affirmed.

A council of the allied tribes was held on Horse Creek about one hundred miles north of Denver.[28] Medicine Man (or Roman Nose, as Evans consistently called him) talked with the Governor upon several occasions, each time stating that he and his people opposed war. In the late summer, Evans sent for the Northern Arapaho chiefs, then in a large village about seventy-five miles north of Denver, and impressed upon them the folly of war. Colley wrote from Fort Lyon that most of the Northern Arapahoes were there in August and that he was at a loss to know what to do with them. He held a council with the headmen, who appeared to have no definite plan of aggression, and he was convinced that the Northern and Southern Arapahoes were one people. The visitors were poor and hungry, but not hostile. He claimed it was "beg, beg, all the time."

Before Colley permitted them to receive rations, he required that they sign the following statement:

> We, the undersigned chiefs and principal men of the Cheyenne and Arapaho Indians of the Upper Platte Agency, agree that we will abide by any treaty that has been or may be made by our people with the United States, as we have due notice of a pending treaty by our agent, John Loree; and in consideration of the above agreement, we have our annuities distributed to us. All above has been duly explained, and in witness thereof we append our signatures or marks.[29]

The agreement was signed by Medicine Man, Black Bear, and Friday of the Arapahoes and by two lesser chiefs of the Chey-

---

[28] *WR*, Vol. XXII, Pt. 2, 294; *Annual Report of the Commissioner of Indian Affairs*, 1863, 239–46.
[29] Colley to Evans, August 22, 1864, IOR, NA.

ennes. It was witnessed by Samuel Smith and James Bordean (probably James Bordeau[x]). After placing their X marks on the agreement and receiving their much needed food, the Northerners, whom Janice had succeeded in sending to Fort Lyon, departed.

Gerry was not as fortunate. When the appointed day arrived and the delegation came for a big talk, it found only Little Gerry and his wagonload of annuities. He held out small hope that his charges, the Southerners, would appear. After the Governor had sent him to locate the Indians, he had found them otherwise engaged—that is, they were in the midst of their fall hunt.[30] Gerry conferred with Bull Bear, the recognized leader of the Dog Soldiers, a roving society made up chiefly of members of his tribe, the Cheyennes, and some of the more hostile Arapahoes and Sioux. When Gerry tried to explain that the White Father wanted the Indians to settle down on their reservation, build wooden tipis, and live at peace, the war chief was incredulous. Twice he asked if the Great Father wanted the Indians to live like white men, and twice Gerry assured him that he did. "You tell white chief, Indian maybe not so low yet!" was Bull Bear's scornful reply.

The Indians had further reason for not going to the council: they had recently lost thirty-five of their children from diarrhea and whooping cough. Black Kettle, who was too ill to go, and White Antelope both denied signing the Fort Wise Treaty. They emphatically stated that they had not sold their country at the headwaters of the Republican and Smoky Hill. Then they alluded to the recent killing of a Cheyenne brave to prove that the white man's hand "dripped with blood." The incident took place July 19 at Fort Larned.

After this, depredations by the Cheyennes and Arapahoes became more frequent. Robert North finally brought to Governor Evans news of a great Medicine Dance held jointly by the Platte River Indians and the Kiowas.[31] The combination of these forces

---

[30] Edger C. McMechen, *Life of Governor Evans*, 115.
[31] *WR*, Vol. XXII, Pt. 2, 400–401; *ibid.*, Vol. XXIV, Pt. 4, 100; *Annual Report of the Commissioner of Indian Affairs*, 1864, 224–25.

was so ominous that Evans instructed Colley not to issue any more arms and ammunition until further notice. North, who could neither read nor write, dictated a statement that the chiefs had agreed to be friendly until they had obtained the necessary guns and ammunition and that they had invited him to join in their attack. He claimed that he was a witness to their agreement, but no attempt was made to verify his statements.

Little Raven and Yellow Buffalo, a Kiowa chief, probably reported the matter with a greater degree of accuracy to Major Anthony.[32] They stated that the Sioux proposed an all-out attack in the spring of 1864 on the two major routes along the Platte and Arkansas, but the pipe had been refused by all but the Cheyennes. Later Anthony met about two thousand Arapahoes (a combination of Northern and Southern bands) on their way to Fort Lyon for annunities. In all probability, the Northerners were attempting to escape the hostile Sioux influence so that they could stay out of trouble.

Evans and Colley had both reported only a short time before that the Indians were generally friendly. After mulling over the Robert North report a month, Evans wrote to the Secretary of War for military aid and the authority to call out the militia of Colorado. He also urged that troops be stationed along the various routes in order to safeguard travel and keep freight moving. As a result, one company of cavalry was placed on the Cache la Poudre. In addition, eight companies of Iowa Cavalry were distributed at strategic points along the Emigrant Road.

Oddly enough, Evans had held a council with Medicine Man only the day before North made his sworn statement and had found him professing friendship for the Governor but he had said that the disposition of his allies, the Sioux, Cheyennes, and Kiowas, was for war. Although Roman Nose proposed to remain friendly and true to the whites, he declined to enter into a treaty before having an opportunity to find out the wishes of all of his people.

[32] Anthony to Lieutenant G. H. Stilwell, September 2, 14, 24, 1863, *WR*, Vol. XXII, Pt. 2, 532–33, 571–72.

Frankly, he admitted, he was "not much disposed to the Arkansas."[33]

Two days later, the Governor held still another conference with the chiefs of the Northern Arapaho bands, who demanded a reservation on the Cache la Poudre as the only condition under which they would talk of a treaty. Late in November, Evans again stated that Roman Nose positively refused to make any treaty until he was given his reservation on the Cache la Poudre.[34] This might have been construed as stubbornness, but it was in no way a sign of hostility. Meanwhile, the stage was being set for trouble with the Oglala Sioux, who were spurred on by their kinsmen, the Yankton Sioux, who had been driven from Minnesota two years earlier. The withholding of ammunition for the hunt, the shortage of annuities, and various fraudulent practices attributed to their agent, John Loree, had disillusioned the Sioux and the Northern bands of Cheyennes and Arapahoes. War appeared to be the only course, but they held off while they counseled with their Arapaho and Cheyenne allies in the south.

One of the first depredations involving the Arapahoes was committed at the Van Wormer ranch thirty-five miles east of Denver.[35] Here the Indians stole several head of cattle, horses, and some of the rancher's worldly goods. Van Wormer, with North as his interpreter, visited the Arapaho village, where the Indians readily admitted butchering the cattle. They turned over one horse they had stolen. Since it did not belong to Van Wormer, he took it to Denver and advertised for the owner. This was the beginning of a number of incidents which, for the most part, involved the Cheyennes and the Dog Soldiers.

January, 1864, three years after the Fort Wise Treaty, found the allied tribes still wandering and the buffalo fast disappearing.[36] The Southern bands expressed a willingness to farm, but they said this would be impossible as long as troops were stationed at Fort

[33] *Annual Report of the Commissioner of Indian Affairs*, 1863, 412, 540–41; Evans *Collection*, November 9 and 11, 1863, CSHS.
[34] Evans to Loree, November 29, 1863, IOR, NA.
[35] *Annual Report of the Commissioner of Indian Affairs*, 1863, 543–44.
[36] H. P. Bennet to Dole, January 28, 1864, IOR, NA.

Lyon. They requested their removal to some point where they would be of more service in preserving the peace and in preventing an outbreak between the Indians and the whites. The chiefs expressed themselves as favoring peace, but they were concerned about their young people. If permitted to visit the military post without restraint, the men would obtain whiskey and the women would become immoral.

Little Raven reportedly had been drunk on several occasions, and it was claimed that he and Left Hand could obtain whiskey by the bottle from the sutler's store at Fort Lyon.[37] A special agent (H. Y. Ketcham) visiting that post and Fort Larned in the spring described the drunken behavior of the soldiers and citizens who were debasing the Indians and spreading venereal diseases among them. He believed that little peace could be expected when the commanding officer at Fort Larned got drunk every day and insulted and abused the leading men of the tribes. The special agent, who noted that the Arapahoes in particular "suffered terribly" from smallpox, vaccinated all Indians at the Upper Arkansas Agency. Although he found them poor, sick, and starving, they still were friendly and treated him with the greatest kindness. And yet he noted that traders were swindling them by buying their few robes with whiskey.

The Indians' suggestion that the troops be posted on government lands just above the Cheyenne and Arapaho Reservation, between the whites and the Indians, met no response, though supplies could have been obtained more reasonably and a major cause of Indian complaint might have been removed. As if all were serene, Colley reported (April 17) that the irrigation ditch on the Sand Creek Reservation was ready to hold water. He asserted that not even the Arapahoes, who showed more inclination to accept the white man's ways than the Cheyennes, were ready to farm. But by leasing their farm lands, they could learn by example. Meanwhile, petty jealousies and disagreements between Colonel Chivington, in command of the District of Colorado, and his

[37] *Annual Report of the Commissioner of Indian Affairs,* 1864, 216–18, 240, 256, 257.

officers over a matter of authority resulted in a turmoil among the army personnel which overshadowed, for a time, the Indian difficulties.

Except for the usual warfare of the Arapahoes and Cheyennes against the Utes and temporary hostility between the Arapahoes and the Kiowas, who had killed some of their warriors, there was little indication of impending hostilities in the Colorado area in the spring of 1864. Just how important a role the Civil War played in the subsequent troubles cannot be estimated, but it is significant that instead of troops being sent to defend the frontier as Evans had asked, much available manpower was being drawn from Colorado to implement Civil War efforts. Still, the Governor, the settlers, and the military personnel were convinced of a planned war by the consolidated tribes.

The Indians did not strike as North had predicted; rather, the War of 1864 began with a series of cattle thefts. White Antelope, later speaking at Camp Weld, insisted that it began April 12 at Fremont's Orchard on the Platte.[38] He asked Governor Evans "what it was for—a soldier fired first." When Evans told him that the soldiers had gone to recover about forty head of stolen horses and that the Indians had fired a volley into their ranks, White Antelope protested. "That is all a mistake," he stoutly maintained. The Indians were coming down the Bijou and found one horse and one mule. He went on to explain that before they reached Gerry's, they met a white man, to whom they gave the horse. Then they went on to the ranch, where they expected to surrender the mule. When they heard that the soldiers and the Indians were fighting somewhere down the Platte, they "took a fright" and all fled.

Whatever the circumstances, the Cheyennes were the Indians principally involved in this and a similar incident in which they reportedly stole 175 head of stock belonging to a government contractor on the Smoky Hill River.[39] They were incensed by the

38 "The Sand Creek Massacre," *Sen. Exec. Doc.* No. 26, 39 Cong., 2 sess., 215–17; *Annual Report of the Commissioner of Indian Affairs*, 1864, 218.

39 *Rocky Mountain News*, April 27, 1864; Curtis to Chivington, April 8, 1864, *WR*, Vol. XXXIV, Pt. 3, 98. For the Cheyenne side of the story, see Lieu-

soldiers' burning four of their villages. When Black Kettle still refused to fight, the Dog Soldiers took matters into their own hands. One of Bull Bear's principal lieutenants was the fearless Bird (also known as Bird Chief), an Arapaho.

Unable to pinpoint the difficulty, the Commissioner of Indian Affairs attributed it to the "active efforts upon the savage nations by the emissaries from the hostile Northern tribes (principally the Sioux)."[40] Bull Bear blamed the Yankton Sioux, driven from Minnesota by the whites, and the Missouri River Sioux, who had crossed the Platte to stir up hostilities among the Southern tribes. North's story further emphasized the certainty of a Sioux uprising involving both the Arapahoes and Cheyennes. But neither General S. R. Curtis, commanding the Department of Kansas at Fort Leavenworth, nor Chivington seemed to anticipate any large-scale offensive.

Evans, on the other hand, continued to dwell upon the possibility of a united effort on the part of the two Upper Arkansas River tribes in league with the Kiowas and Comanches. He wrote to General Curtis, urging that troops not be withdrawn. "In the name of humanity," he pleaded, "I ask that our troops now on the border of Kansas may not be taken away from us just as they have been specially prepared to defend us . . . and at a time of our greatest need of their service since the settlement of the country." Evans not only urged that troops not be removed from the Kansas border, but called for a force to chastise the combined alliance of Indians at once to prevent a long "bloody" war and the loss of many lives and untold amounts of property. He predicted that the lines of communciation, the main "dependence for subsistence" in the territory, would be plundered and the trains driven off the route. To a people so remote, the situation appeared desperate.

Although most of the war talk centered in Colorado, shocking depredations were committed in Kansas, where various mili-

tenant J. A. Cramer in "The Sand Creek Massacre," *loc. cit.*, 32, and John Smith's testimony, *ibid.*, 116. For the military angle, see Lieutenant Clark Dunn, Report, April 18, 1864, *WR*, Vol. XXXIV, Pt. 11, 884–88.

[40] *Annual Report of the Commissioner of Indian Affairs*, 1864, 167; *WR*, Vol. XXXIV, Pt. 4, 97–99.

tary expeditions were sent against the Cheyennes.[41] At a council
of Arapahoes, Comanches, and Kiowas held at Fort Larned in
May, the Comanches were the only ones who censured the Cheyennes for their conduct. While professing their friendship, these
bands were thought to have been the Indians who robbed a train
of wagons within a few miles of the fort and later a corn train on
its way to Fort Lyon.

Major T. I. McKenney, who was sent to investigate affairs
at Fort Larned, reported that the commanding officer was a confirmed drunkard.[42] As to Indian difficulties, he believed that unless
great caution were exercised, there would be war. He suggested
conciliation and the establishment of guards for the mails and the
immigrant trains to prevent theft. He emphasized the necessity of
putting an end to army scouting parties, which had been roaming
over the country, because they did not know one tribe from
another and would kill anything resembling an Indian. He was
sure that a few more murders on the part of the troops would
unite all warlike tribes on the plains.

The truth of McKenney's statement was illustrated when one
of the most peaceful and respected chiefs of the Cheyennes, Lean
Bear, was shot and killed when he came forward in sign of peace.
He was wearing a medal given to him by the Great Father in
Washington. Because of resulting hostility, several attacks were
made upon Indian villages. In one near Fort Larned, twenty-five
to thirty Indians were killed; in another, twenty-six were killed
and thirty wounded. Retaliatory raids, which were to be expected,
soon followed, with considerable loss of life and property. Young
Arapaho warriors who could not be controlled by their elders
were fighting with the Cheyennes in ever increasing numbers.

Brigadier General Robert B. Mitchell, commander of the
Department of Nebraska, made three separate attempts to treat
with the Cheyennes in the spring and summer, but all he could
get from them was a demand to close the Smoky Hill Road

[41] Marvin H. Garfield, "Defense of Kansas," *KHQ*, I, 4 (1931), 34; *Annual
Report of the Commissioner of Indian Affairs*, 1864, 239; *WR*, Pt. 4, 402–404.
[42] Whitely's report of proceedings at Camp Weld, is in "The Sand Creek
Massacre," *loc. cit.*, 215.

through their hunting grounds.[43] So far, there had been no major outbreak along the North Platte, but troops at Fort Laramie were kept busy scouting and guarding the Emigrant Road. Only one attack, if it might be called that, ever took place at the fort. One day after some of the scouting soldiers had returned from their assignment, they unsaddled their horses and allowed them to roll and nibble the grass while they themselves rested. Suddenly, without warning, a war whoop sounded and a daring party of Indians (believed to be Sioux) rushed over the parade ground and succeeded in driving away the horses.

The most serious Arapaho involvement in the War of 1864 came in June, again at the Van Wormer ranch, where Ward Hungate, the ranch manager, and his wife were brutally murdered. The Hungates, including their two small children, were apparently killed by four Arapahoes going north from a Southern camp. Just who they were is uncertain. Neva blamed Medicine Man and three others, but Robert North accused John Notee, also a Northern Arapaho.[44] Inasmuch as Agent Whitely could establish the whereabouts of Medicine Man at the time—and he stated emphatically that Medicine Man could not have been there—the chances are that it was the work of Notee. The implication is strong, for he was known to have been in a sullen mood because he had been compelled to return some stolen stock. Had the whites been able to locate the thirty head of horses and mules driven away during the attack on the defenseless family, the identity of the guilty Indians might have been established. As it was, the consolidated tribes were blamed for the fiendish work of four outlaw Indians.

Another theory, that the Hungate family was killed "by a party of Arapahoes under Friday, who was permitted to remain on the Cache la Poudre," is inconsistent with his behavior pattern.[45] The band chief was so dedicated to peace that he drove his own son and his wives from his camp to avoid trouble when they

[43] Eugene F. Ware, *The Indian War of 1864*, 144–61, 286–90.
[44] *Annual Report of the Commissioner of Indian Affairs*, 1864, 228; *WR*, Vol. XXXIV, Pt. 4, 354–55; "The Sand Creek Massacre," *loc. cit.*, 216.
[45] Berthrong, *The Southern Cheyennes*, 210–11.

demonstrated their hostile attitude toward the whites. He worked tirelessly to induce Medicine Man, Little Owl, and Many Whips to join his peaceful band, but Many Whips was the only one who chose to tarry with the friendlies on the Cache la Poudre. Medicine Man and Little Owl preferred the Platte, where they were under the dominant influence of the Sioux.

The scalped and badly mutilated bodies of the Hungates were taken to Denver and put on public display. No better recruiting device could have been found, for everyone who saw the exhibit cried out for vengeance. People from isolated areas flocked to Denver. Chivington, in a verbose order to the captain of the company sent in pursuit of the guilty Indians, told him: "Do not keep your command out longer than there is prospect of success nor encumber your command with prisoner Indians."[46]

Two days after the Hungate incident, a man galloped through the streets of Denver and sounded an alarm that Indians were coming to murder and burn.[47] The news swept the town like a prairie fire, and people were frantic with apprehension. The Governor issued an order closing all business houses at 6:30 P.M. and all able-bodied men were ordered to assemble daily for drill. Women and children in east Denver were rushed to the mint, those in west Denver to the upper story of the Commissary Building on Ferry Street. Here men patrolled the buildings.

When the search outside the city limits proved fruitless, some families returned to their homes; others remained until morning. In their desperation, many of the citizens left doors and windows open and lamps burning, but the reports were so ominous and the people so shocked that no one thought of looting. The excitement was traced to a frightened rancher who had mistaken a camp of freighters for Indians.

Evans should be given credit for at least attempting to separate the friendlies from the hostiles. He specifically directed Colley to care for the former and keep them at peace at Fort Lyon

---

[46] *WR*, Vol. XXXIV, Pt. 4, 318; *ibid.*, Vol. XLI, Pt. 1, 963–64; Evans to Dole, June 14 and 15, 1864, Evans Collection, CSHS.
[47] Smiley, *History of Denver*, 405.

so that war against the hostiles could be advanced with vigor. Then he issued a proclamation (June 27) to the friendlies.[48] The Arapahoes and Cheyennes of the Upper Arkansas were directed to report to Major Colley at Fort Lyon, the Kiowas and Comanches at Fort Larned, the Sioux at Fort Laramie, and the Arapahoes and Cheyennes of the Upper Platte at Camp Collins on the Cache la Poudre, there to be assigned to places of safety and provided for while the hostiles were being subdued. The object of his directive, he explained, was to prevent peaceful Indians from being killed by mistake. He emphasized that the war against the hostiles would continue until their resistance was broken.

Not even the Jim Reynolds gang of desperadoes and their pillaging in Colorado in July could divert Evans from his contention that the combined Plains tribes were preparing all-out war.[49] "Please," he begged the War Department, "bring all the force of your department to bear in favor of speeding re-enforcements of our troops, and get me authority to raise a regiment of 100-day mounted men." Evans' request was granted.

George Bent's description of the activity he found in the intertribal camp on Solomon Fork in central Kansas, where he arrived in early summer, indicates that the Governor had cause for alarm.[50] The camp, which was made up of Cheyennes, Sioux, Dog Soldiers, and Arapahoes, was one of the largest the halfblood Bent had ever seen. Spoils taken from the great trail along the Platte were unbelievable, for war parties were setting out and returning daily. Their depredations had become a major problem, since the small raiding parties were elusive. Not even General Mitchell could locate their main camp.

In late summer, while the raiders were still active, the Cheyennes and Arapahoes held a council at which the older men, contrary to the wishes of the warriors, decided on peace. At Black

[48] *WR*, Vol. XLI, Pt. 1, 964; *Annual Report of the Commissioner of Indian Affairs*, 1864, 218; Evans to Colley, June 29, 1864, "The Sand Creek Massacre," *loc. cit.*, 55.
[49] *WR*, Vol. XLI, Pt. 2, 644, 753–54, Pt. 3, 47, and Pt. 4, 149–50.
[50] Hyde, *Life of George Bent*, 140–42; *Annual Report of the Commissioner of Indian Affairs*, 1864, 230–32, 254–55.

Kettle's dictation, two identical letters were written, one by Edmund Guerrier, to be delivered to the commanding officer at Fort Lyon, the other by George Bent, to be delivered to Colley.

Major General Curtis, moving against the Indians of western Kansas, met with little success. They scattered before his force of four hundred men, and the soldiers were unable to give them the chastisement he promised. The General implicated Big Mouth's Arapahoes, together with Kiowas and Comanches, in raids along the Santa Fé Trail. Settlers in both Kansas and Nebraska were in a state of near panic after a series of serious outbreaks.

Evans, unmindful of the platitude "Indian time, no time," felt that he had waited long enough—45 days—for the friendlies to agree to his terms. When there was little response, he interpreted this to mean that the Indians, except for the few at Fort Lyon and Camp Collins, were hostile, and he proceeded without further delay to issue a second proclamation nullifying the first.[51] In it he gave the citizens of Colorado authority to pursue all hostile Indians on the plains, "scrupulously avoiding" those who responded to his call to go to one or the other of the indicated points. His order was "to kill and destroy" all hostiles, the reward being, besides soldier's pay, all property which might be captured. He concluded his proclamation with this statement: "The conflict is upon us, and all good citizens are called upon to do their duty for the defense of their homes and families." A Denver newspaper added its stamp of approval by saying that a few months of active extermination of the "red devils" would bring quiet and that nothing else would. Since the Hungate murders all Indians were red devils to the press.

Evans said in a wire (dated August 18) to the War Department: "It is impossible to exaggerate our danger."[52] And yet he seemed to be doing a fair job by reporting "extensive Indian depredations" and the "murder of families" occurring thirty miles south of Denver the day before. The "families" amounted to one

51 *WR*, Vol. XLI, Pt. 3, 47; *Rocky Mountain News*, August 10, 1864.
52 *Annual Report of the Commissioner of Indian Affairs*, 1864, 230–31; *WR*, Vol. XLI, Pt. 2, 694.

man and one boy killed on Running Creek, but again the Governor was convincing.

Meanwhile, William Bent, learning of a planned major engagement against the Cheyennes, conferred with Black Kettle, who professed that he did not know what the fight was about. Bent then discussed the matter with Chivington, who was almost as vague, though he indicated that he was in no mood to discuss peace. When Bent conferred with Colley, he was asked to bring his friendlies to Fort Lyon, where protection was promised. Bent found the consolidated tribes in the vicinity of Fort Larned and, for the moment, at peace, which was spoiled in late July when the Kiowas made a raid on the Fort Larned horse herd and a sentinel was killed.

Left Hand showed his friendly intent by going to the post with twenty-five men to offer his services in recovering the stolen stock.[53] Advancing with a white flag to a spot within a few hundred yards of the fort, he met a soldier, whom he dispatched to the commanding officer with his offer. The reply was a blast from a howitzer which caused the Arapahoes to flee for their lives. Although Left Hand still persisted in his friendship, some of his followers used this as an excuse to join the Dog Soldiers. A retaliatory raid was made by the Arapahoes at Point of Rocks, below Fort Lyon. There they took a herd of horses and frightened the ranchmen from their homes, but no one was killed.

On August 11, soldiers from Fort Lyon had their first encounter with the Arapahoes near the mouth of Sand Creek.[54] An ordnance sergeant in search of stray horses spotted the Indians riding toward him. He rushed back to the fort, with the small group following. He was unaware that they were friendlies, for he was too frightened to interpret their gestures. They were led by Neva, who had come with the letter from Black Kettle to Colley. In it the Cheyenne chief wanted to explain that he did not want to fight and would not, unless attacked.

Neva called and waved the letter, but he had no chance to

[53] "The Sand Creek Massacre," *loc. cit.*, 30.
[54] *WR*, Vol. XLI, Pt. 2, 238–39.

explain. As soon as the soldier reached the fort, the commanding officer, Major Edward W. Wynkoop, dispatched thirty troops to rout the Indians. A running fight covering four miles ensued, but no serious damage was inflicted on either side beyond the wounding of four Indians, none seriously, the capture of one of their ponies, and the creation of another reason for bitterness. Although more Arapahoes were stirred to vengeance, Neva later reported: "I know the value of presents which we receive from Washington; we cannot live without them. That is why I try so hard to keep peace with the whites."[55] He reported that his men wanted to return and fight the soldiers for firing on them without cause, but he was opposed. Four days later, the Indians forced the closing of all mail lines from the East, and these were not reopened until September 29.

On August 19, two friendly Cheyennes came to warn Elbridge Gerry that he should move his stock from the mouth of Crow Creek, on the South Platte, because an attack would take place "two sleeps" later. Gerry made a rush trip to Denver (sixty-five miles away) to spread the news and alert all threatened localities. When the Indians arrived and found their secret plans had been discovered, they settled matters by driving away all of the horses belonging to Gerry. Three days later, Evans wired the Secretary of War that he had "unlimited" information of a large-scale Indian uprising.[56]

The general superintendent of the Overland Mail Line outlined the difficulties already suffered by his company in a frantic letter to the Commissioner of Indian Affairs.[57] In addition to expressing his alarm over depredations on the trail, he feared the Indians might burn the grass along the route as they became increasingly troublesome. For about six weeks, a four-hundred-mile stretch of the Emigrant Road was controlled by the Platte River Indians, thus causing the Overland Stage Company to remove all

[55] "The Sand Creek Massacre," *loc. cit.*, 33, 215–17; Evans to Curtis, August 18, 1864, *WR*, Vol. XLI, Pt. 2, 765–66.

[56] *Annual Report of the Commissioner of Indian Affairs*, 1864, 232.

[57] George L. Curtis, Report, August 31, 1864, IOR, NA; *Rocky Mountain News*, August 24 and September 24, 1864.

stock that had not been captured. Mail going east from Denver had to be sent by stage to San Francisco, then by way of Panama to New York.

Six days after Neva was fired upon, a small ambulance was attacked near Fort Lyon by one of Little Raven's sons.[58] Two men were killed and scalped, and one woman, a Mrs. Snyder, who later hanged herself, was captured. One of the wheel mules was shot and the other three were missing. The day before, these same Indians took twenty-eight head of stock from the agency and several horses from a near-by ranch. A week later, two men were scalped eighteen miles west of the fort. Depredations committed by Arapahoes were becoming so frequent that it looked to Colley as if the soldiers might have to fight them all.

In September, three Indians (two men and one woman) approached Fort Lyon.[59] A soldier was about to fire when one of the Indians held up a paper and pointed to it. The soldiers who took the Indians to Major Wynkoop were reprimanded for not killing them, since that was the standing order. John Smith, serving as interpreter, found the prisoners to be One-Eye, his wife, and Minimic (all Cheyennes). They bore the second letter dictated by Black Kettle, dated Cheyenne Village, August 29, in which he told of the recent council where the Cheyennes had concluded to make peace, "providing you make peace with the Kiowas, Comanches, Arapahoes, Apaches, and Sioux." Furthermore, the Indians would give up the prisoners they held, "providing you give up yours." The message was not phrased in the most diplomatic style, but little did the Chief know of such matters. At least it showed his peaceful intent.

According to One-Eye, there were about two thousand Cheyennes and Arapahoes at the headwaters of the Smoky Hill River and they wanted a big talk, a lead that Wynkoop was quick

---

[58] Julia S. Lambert, "Plain Tales of the Plains," *The Trail*, VII, 12 (January-September, 1916), 216; *Annual Report of the Commissioner of Indian Affairs*, 1864, 375.

[59] *Annual Report of the Commissioner of Indian Affairs*, 1864, 22–23; *WR*, Vol. XL., Pt. 3, 242–43; *Rocky Mountain News*, September 21 and 28, 1864.

to follow.[60] But when he arrived, he was greeted with signs of hostility. Nevertheless, a council was held. Bull Bear of the Dog Soldiers was sulky and maintained that the whites were to blame for the trouble—that all the Indians could do now was to fight. To this, One-Eye responded gallantly that he had risked his life trying to bring about a peaceful understanding and that he would now stake his life as a pledge of good faith on the part of the Indians. If the Cheyennes did not stand by their word previously made to him, he did not care to live. He even went so far as to offer to go with the soldiers to fight against his own people. When Bull Bear continued to grumble, One-Eye offered him the choice of his best horses if he would keep quiet, an offer which Bull Bear accepted.

Left Hand was still unhappy about his recent experience at Fort Larned, for he had done what he could to prevent trouble and yet was fired upon. His followers, now hostile, had subsequently carried out raids on the Arkansas. Surprisingly, Little Raven sanctioned the words of Bull Bear. Even though he might like to shake the hand of the whites, he was doubtful of peace. His usual loyalty was obviously shaken by the treatment Left Hand had received. Black Kettle attributed the trouble to bad men on both sides. Although he was opposed to fighting, he said that the Indians were forced to it.

At noon the second day after the council, Left Hand came bringing a captive, Laura Roper, and stated that Black Kettle would arrive the following day with others—three children ranging in age from four to eight. When the Cheyenne chief arrived with the children, he said a Mrs. Morton and a Mrs. Eubanks and her baby had been taken to the Platte and he was unable to reach them. Accounts of Mrs. Eubanks are legion in the early horror stories of the time. One credits her with flying into a rage when one of the Indians grabbed her baby and attempted to dash its brains out against a tree. She is said to have fought so savagely that she caused him to lose his balance and fall. When he tried to knife

---

[60] Edward W. Wynkoop, "Colorado History," unfinished manuscript in CSHS, 27–28; "The Sand Creek Massacre," *loc. cit.*, 30–32, 169.

her, his chief (Two-Face) intervened. What kind of a warrior was he, the Chief asked, "to be thrown by a squaw"? Two-Face, according to the fictitious account, then took the woman as his wife. More reliable accounts state that the two Sioux (Two-Face and Blackfoot) purchased the woman and her child, presumably from Bull Bear's band, and brought them to Fort Laramie (August 11, 1864) to prove their friendliness. The "drunken officer in charge" had the two hanged in chains.[61]

Wynkoop had said earlier in a report to Chivington: "My intention is to kill all Indians I may come across until I receive orders to the contrary from headquarters."[62] Such orders were unlikely to be forthcoming. Wynkoop by now had reversed his judgment, and although skirmishes were taking place between the soldiers and roving bands of Cheyennes and Arapahoes, he decided to do all in his power to bring about peace. Accompanied by such tribal leaders as Black Kettle, Bull Bear, and White Antelope of the Cheyennes and Neva, Bosse, Heap of Buffalo, and No-ta-nee (Knock Knee, the soldiers called him) of the Arapahoes, Wynkoop made his way to Denver. Little Raven and Left Hand remained on the Smoky Hill River. Just why they did not go is not clear, unless they were still smarting over the unjust treatment Left Hand had received. Neva may have been more forgiving.

When Wynkoop finally had an opportunity to confer with Evans, his hopes were thwarted. The Governor argued that the Indians had declared war against the United States and that it was not a good policy to make peace until they were sufficiently punished. When Wynkoop told him he had brought them four hundred miles to confer with him, he still refused to see them. The crux of the matter, he admitted, according to Wynkoop, was that if peace were restored, it would appear in Washington that he had misrepresented matters.[63] Evans wired Curtis that he felt the Indians should be required to make full restitution, then be forced

---

[61] Frank A. Root and William E. Connelley, *The Overland Stage to California*, 150, 155–56; Grinnell, *The Fighting Cheyennes*, 181 n.
[62] *WR*, Vol. XLI, Pt. 1, 237–38.
[63] *Ibid.*, Pt. 3, 462; "The Sand Creek Massacre," *loc. cit.*, 77.

on the reservation, to which the General replied: "I want no peace until the Indians suffer more. . . . Left Hand is said to be a good chief, but Big Mouth is a rascal. . . . No peace must be made without my directions." Big Mouth had recently eluded military pursuit.

In spite of his wishes, there was nothing Evans could do but meet with the Indians, hence the Camp Weld Council (September 28, 1864), at which Agent Whitely served as clerk and John Smith as interpreter. Black Kettle arose and made a plea for peace. Then he said: "We must live near the buffalo or starve. When we came here we came free, without any apprehension, to see you, and when I go home and tell my people that I have taken your hand and the hands of all the chiefs here in Denver, they will feel well, and so will all the different tribes of Indians on the plains, after we have eaten and drunk with them."

Evans accused the Indians of smoking the war pipe with the Sioux, to which Black Kettle and others protested. When they asked who had told him so, the Governor did not give his source, but he did back down sufficiently to admit that he thought their conduct had been such as to show they had an understanding with the other tribes.

Neva asked of John Smith, who had known him since childhood, if he had ever known of his committing depredations on the whites. He added: "I went to Washington last year, receiving good counsel; I hold on to it. I am determined always to keep peace with the whites. Now, when I shake hands with them they seem to pull away. I came here to seek peace, and nothing else."[64]

Chivington made little comment, saying merely: "I am not a big war chief, but all of the soldiers in this country are at my command. My rule of fighting white men or Indians is to fight them until they lay down their arms and submit to military authority. You are nearer Major Wynkoop than any one else, and you can go to him when you get ready to do that."

In a follow-up wire, Curtis stated: "I shall require the bad

---

[64] "The Sand Creek Massacre," *loc. cit.*, 213–17; "Massacre of Cheyenne Indians," *Senate Report* No. 142, 38 Cong., 2 sess., 87–90.

189

Indians delivered up; restoration of equal numbers of stock, also hostages to secure. I want no peace till the Indians suffer more."[65]

By the time Wynkoop returned to Fort Lyon, he had won the chief's complete confidence and his attitude had changed from the day One-Eye had so nobly staked his life on the word of his people. His display of patriotism had caused the Major to say that he felt as if he were in the presence of a "superior being." One-Eye was a representative of a race Wynkoop admitted he had once looked upon as being "cruel, treacherous, and blood-thirsty."[66]

While Wynkoop and his delegation were in Denver, the Arapahoes and Cheyennes, who were camped together, sent out raiding parties against the Pawnees. One such party had an encounter with cavalrymen under Major J. Scott Anthony. One Arapaho (White Horse) was killed in the ensuing skirmish. But when General James G. Blunt's column appeared, the outnumbered warriors withdrew.

Soon after Wynkoop's return to Fort Lyon, Little Raven, Spotted Wolf, and Storm arrived with 113 lodges, all in destitute condition. They brought some buffalo skins which they traded for supplies. Otherwise, they subsisted on prisoners' rations, but they came and went freely at the fort. In fact, Left Hand, who was with Little Raven's band, was so popular that Chivington was prompted to quip that he, instead of Wynkoop, was really in charge at the fort, until Wynkoop was transferred and succeeded by Anthony.[67]

Red Eye, as the Arapahoes called the new commanding officer, did not measure up to his predecessor in their estimation. The Cheyennes, concerned by their appraisal, came to see for themselves. They established their camp on Sand Creek, about forty miles northeast of Fort Lyon. At first, Anthony seemed friendly toward the Arapahoes, whom he permitted to camp near the fort with the status of unarmed prisoners. Pressure may have

[65] *Annual Report of the Commissioner of Indian Affairs*, 1864, 221; Chivington to Curtis, September 26, 1864, *WR*, Vol. XLI, Pt. 3, 399.
[66] Wynkoop, "Colorado History," 28.
[67] "The Sand Creek Massacre," *loc. cit.*, 115–18.

been brought to bear because he changed his attitude and ordered the surprised Arapahoes to move away from the post. Puzzled by his change of mind, most of them left at once for a hunt, after which they settled in a winter camp south of the Arkansas. Left Hand, who is said to have been ill at the time, remained on Sand Creek with the Cheyennes. He had with him eight or ten lodges of his people.

Although Anthony created the impression that he was interested in the Indians, he gave himself away in the following report to Curtis:

> I have told them [the Indians] that I was not authorized as yet to say that any permanent peace could be established, but that no war would be waged against them until your pleasure had been heard. . . . I have been trying to let the Indians that I have talked with think that I have no desire for trouble with them, but that I could not agree upon a permanent peace until I was authorized by you, thus keeping matters quiet for the present until troops enough are sent out to enforce any demand we may choose to make. It would be easy for us to fight the few Indian warriors that have come into the post, but as soon as we assume a hostile attitude the travel upon the road will be cut off, and the settlements about and upon the different streams will be completely broken up, as we are not strong enough to follow them and fight them upon their own ground. Some of the Cheyenne and Arapaho Indians can be made useful to me. . . . My intention, however, is to let matters remain dormant until troops can be sent out to take the field against all the tribes.[68]

Although suspicious of Anthony's motives, the Indians remained loyal to their friend Tall Chief (Wynkoop), whom they befriended a final time along the road from Fort Lyon. No-ta-nee and two companions were sent by Black Kettle to warn him that two hundred hostile Sioux were on their way to make war along the Arkansas and that he should proceed with caution. When the Major reached Fort Larned, he learned the Sioux had been seen along the river, but they did not molest him.[69]

[68] *WR*, Vol. XLI, Pt. 1, 914.
[69] "The Sand Creek Massacre," *loc. cit.*, 87.

Silas Soule, second in command at Fort Lyon, stayed on with Anthony, but like Wynkoop, he had been won over by the Indians. On November 27, Soule was out on reconnaissance and met Colonel Chivington approaching with his cavalry.[70] Chivington inquired of Soule whether there were any Indians at the fort, and Soule replied that there were some Cheyennes and Arapahoes who were considered prisoners. According to Soule, one of the officers boasted: "They won't be prisoners long after we get there."

Lieutenant Joseph A. Cramer and several others agreed with Soule that Chivington should be talked out of an unwarranted attack upon the peaceful Indians, who, unarmed, would be completely at their mercy. To his surprise, he found Anthony in full agreement with the Colonel. The commanding officer reported the arrival of the expedition to headquarters at Fort Riley by stating that one thousand men had arrived with two howitzers. "This number of men," he affirmed, "has been required for some time, and is appreciated by me now, as I believe the Indians will be properly punished—what they have for some time deserved."[71] George Bent's defense of Anthony seems unwarranted. It took no persuasion on the part of Chivington to enlist Anthony's aid, as his reports show.

Several of the officers at the fort, besides feeling obligated to keep Wynkoop's promises, actually credited the Indians with saving their lives. Soule, Major Colley, and others openly opposed Chivington's plan, but they were rewarded by his explosive oath: "Damn anyone in sympathy with Indians!"[72] When Cramer continued to protest, Chivington replied that it was "right and honorable" to use any means "under God's heaven" to kill Indians who killed women and children.

The air was crisp and cold on the morning of November 29, and women were building their campfires when they noticed in the distance what they thought to be a herd of buffalo coming steadily toward them. Before an alarm could be sounded, a large

---

[70] *Ibid.*, 10–11.
[71] *WR*, Vol. XLI, Pt. 4, 708; Hyde, *Life of George Bent*, 151.
[72] "The Sand Creek Massacre," *loc. cit.*, 47.

body of troops rushed in from the south, fanned out, and began to encircle them. All was confusion as the Indians, some not yet clothed, tried to arm and defend themselves. Women and children moaned and screamed at the sight of the soldiers. Some of the braves rushed to save the horse herd, grazing to the southwest, and others sought to defend themselves and their families. Black Kettle, who was still unable to realize the true situation, tried to calm the frenzied people as he ran up a flag before his lodge. White Antelope, with whom he had visited the Great Father in Washington the year before, made no effort to defend himself. He sang his death song as the soldiers shot him down.

The Indians scattered in all directions, many taking to the dry creek bed, where some could hide along the edge, while others, digging rifle pits in the loose sand, attempted to defend themselves. Chivington gives them credit for stubbornly contesting every step of the way.[73] The troops gave up trying to pursue those fleeing to the hills and concentrated on those in the creek bed, although Black Kettle, George Bent, and some of the others managed to escape.

Soule, refusing to order his men to fire, followed the south bank of the creek while the holocaust was in progress.[74] Chivington's loss amounted to nine men killed and thirty-eight wounded. "All did nobly," he reported.

The Colonel was either lacking in knowledge of Indian life or he was trying to impress General Curtis with the fact that he had subdued a camp with an overwhelming number of warriors. He claimed that the Cheyenne village of 130 lodges had from 900 to 1,000 warriors, a disproportionate number in view of the number of lodges. In reality, there were perhaps half that number

[73] *WR*, Vol. XLI, Pt. 1, 949; Grinnell, *The Fighting Cheyennes*, 170–73; Hyde, *Life of George Bent*, 155–68.

[74] Edward E. Wynkoop, "Edward Wanshier Wynkoop," *Kansas Historical Collections*, XIII (1913–14), 76–77; "Report of the Secretary of War," *Sen. Exec. Doc.* No. 26, 39 Cong., 2 sess., 47. Edmund Guerrier, Testimony, "Conditions of the Indian Tribes," March 3, 1865, *Senate Report* No. 156, 39 Cong., 2 sess. Guerrier estimates that 148 Indians were killed, 60 of them braves. Tappan's estimate (Manuscript diary, CSHS) is 144 Indians, of whom 35 were braves. See also *WR*, Vol. XLI, Pt. 1, 948.

of Indians all told, with only one-third of them warriors. Against his force of about 750 to 1,000 men, the figure is inglorious.

To the *Rocky Mountain News*, Chivington sent a dispatch claiming victory in one of the "most bloody Indian battles ever fought on the plains."[75] The number of Indians killed finally simmered down to around 150 instead of the more than 400 he claimed, with probably two-thirds women and children. One-Eye, who had converted Wynkoop to the Indian cause, was among the dead, but Black Kettle, Little Robe, No-ta-nee, and Left Hand escaped. The last two were said to have been killed, a report that was as erroneous as Richardson's assertion that Little Raven was killed by the Utes a year after his visit to Denver.

It is not known how Left Hand, No-ta-nee, and a few other Arapahoes made their escape, but George Bent's map of the Sand Creek encampment shows Left Hand's lodges to be back from the creek, in the northeast sector of the camp. Since most warriors kept horses picketed near their doors, the men in question could have made their getaway without trouble before the soldiers encircled the camp. Few in Chief Sand Hill's band, camped immediately to the east, were killed. Perhaps at Sand Creek, Left Hand remained true to his word, once given to Colley: "I will not fight the whites, and you cannot make me do it. You may imprison me or kill me, but I will not fight the whites."[76] Among the Arapahoes who reached safety was a woman holding a baby at her breast, carrying another on her back, and leading a third child by the hand. She managed to save the first, but the other two were killed. Her body, bearing the scars of battle until she died in Oklahoma at the reported age of 104, was a constant reminder of the cruelty at Sand Creek. Kohiss was her name, and she is said to have outlived all other Arapaho survivors of the massacre.

The Indian village on Sand Creek was burned, but the bodies of the men, women, and children, mutilated this time by the white men, were not taken to Denver for display, as the Hungates' had been. Instead, they were left for the hungry dogs and wolves to

---

[75] *Rocky Mountain News*, December 17, 1864.
[76] "Massacre of Cheyenne Indians," *loc. cit.*, 31.

devour. Three round-eyed children (no prisoners were taken) were later found and exhibited before curiosity seekers in Denver and elsewhere. The Cheyennes demanded the return of two; the third was an Arapaho boy.

Chivington had hoped to add to his glory by overtaking a large encampment of Arapahoes under Little Raven. He marched as far as the Kansas border, but was unable to locate them. On December 7 he decided to give up the chase because his horses and men were in poor condition. Back in Denver, he was quick to censure Soule, whom he quoted as saying that he "thanked God he had killed no Indians," thereby proving himself more in sympathy with the Indians than with the whites. Lieutenant Colonel Samuel F. Tappan, who had been removed from command at Fort Lyon the year before, could have reiterated Soule's statement. He happened to be at the fort at the time, but he was grounded because of an injured foot. Long a foe of Chivington, he was made chairman of the military commission investigating the Sand Creek affair, which was to the Colonel's disadvantage.[77]

The seven hundred pages of testimony produced by the two congressional committees investigating the debacle would probably have resulted in Chivington's court-martial had it not been time for his retirement and his subsequent resignation.[78] When the *Rocky Mountain News* eulogized the Colonel, it said in part: "A thousand incidents of individual daring and the passing events of the day [at Sand Creek] might be told, but space forbids. We leave the task for eye-witnesses to chronicle." The editor must have been amazed by the incredible accounts that came to light in the military and congressional investigations. Although records clearly show that others besides Chivington were to blame, he was to carry the stigma the rest of his days, which he spent trying to vindicate himself.

[77] Wynkoop, "Colorado History," 20, 36.
[78] Synopsis of Military Commission Report, prepared by Chivington and printed in the *Rocky Mountain News*, June 24, 1865; Report of Congressional Committee Investigating the Sand Creek Massacre, Senator Ben Wade, Chairman. This resulted in the resignation of Governor Evans and Wynkoop's reassignment to Fort Lyon. For answers by Evans and the editor, see *Rocky Mountain News*, August 6 and 19, 1865.

Soule's outspoken criticism may have cost him his life, for he was shot and killed April 23, 1865, on a Denver street. He had been threatened as far back as the time he expressed himself so openly at Fort Lyon. His assassin was apprehended, but he escaped and was never brought to trial.

In August (before Sand Creek), Left Hand, who claimed land in the Boulder area, had visited his friend Robert Hauck, and, as usual, the two had discussed Indian problems.[79] He told Hauck he was going to the Arkansas to get the Indians to make peace with the white man, which he was confident he could do. When Left Hand bade farewell to his friend the next morning, it was the last time he was ever seen around Boulder. Hauck and many others took the word of the soldiers who reported his death at Sand Creek. The fact that he did not return to visit his white friends has been used as conclusive proof that he was killed. After Sand Creek, the Indians no longer considered that they had white friends in Colorado. They had learned a bitter lesson—*they must go!*

[79] Augusta Hauck Block, "Lower Boulder and St. Vrain Home Guards and Fort Junction," *Colorado Magazine*, XVI, 5 (September, 1939), 189. Left Hand's name remains in Colorado in the form of Niwot Mountain, but Left Hand Creek was named for Andrew Sublette in the 1830's. Arps and Kingery, *High Country Names*, 137–38.

CHAPTER NINE

Retaliation

AFTER SAND CREEK, Black Kettle and Little Raven were temporarily set aside by members of their vengeful tribes, and the warriors among the Southern bands, together with the Dog Soldiers, followed their own hostile chiefs. The Dog Soldiers, comprised principally of Cheyennes, were an organized band made up of the "turbulent and uncontrollable spirits of all of the tribes," men who were never satisfied unless they were at war. Colonel George A. Custer considered them "fine looking braves of magnificent physique, and in appearance and demeanor [they] more nearly conformed to the ideal warrior than those of any other tribe."[1]

A great war council was held near Cherry Creek, a tributary of the South Fork of the Arkansas, near the Colorado-Kansas border just below the Nebraska line. There were perhaps as many as one thousand warriors among the combined tribes. Included among the hostiles were eighty lodges of Northern Arapahoes who had come south to winter with their kinsmen. Finding the main body in the Kiowa country, they remained with the Sioux, who were represented at the council by their well-known chiefs Spotted Tail and Pawnee Killer. Since the Sioux were the first to smoke the war pipe, they were, according to Indian protocol, the ones to lead in subsequent events.

The first major attack was made January 7, 1865, at Julesburg, Colorado. The small settlement on the South Platte consisted of a stage station, an express and telegraph office, a large store, a well-stocked warehouse, and adequate stables and corrals.[2] One

[1] George A. Custer, *My Life on the Plains*, 125.
[2] Ware, *The Indian War of 1864*; Grinnell, *The Fighting Cheyennes*, 174–83.

mile to the west was a military camp (Fort Rankin, later Fort Sedgwick), where the action began. At daybreak the Indians fired on several soldiers just outside the camp. Soon about sixty cavalrymen rode out of the stockade to charge the hostiles, who hoped to lead them into a trap and ambush them, but they turned back toward the stockade and the Indians were unable to intercept them. After killing fifteen or sixteen soldiers, the Indians kept the remainder pinned down at the post while they pillaged the store. George Bent, who was one of the warriors, reports they were so loaded down with plunder that it took them three days to return to their camp on Cherry Creek.[3]

Attempting to locate them, General Mitchell believed they had gone to the Republican River in southwestern Nebraska Territory. His troops suffered so much from the cold, however, that they were finally forced to turn back to the Platte. The General, who had a frozen toe, complained that the thermometer stood two successive days at twenty to twenty-four degrees below zero. If he could not catch the hostiles, he decided that the next best thing would be to roast them.

In desperation, he masterminded "the great prairie fire," but opinions differ concerning its extent and damage. Mitchell waited for a day when the wind was blowing from the northwest. Then (on January 27) he wired instructions up and down the river that fire details be sent in order to connect and that at sundown the prairies be simultaneously fired from Fort Kearny to Denver. His lieutenant, Eugene F. Ware, reported that the country for three hundred miles was soon ablaze. He claimed the fire ravaged the country to the banks of the Arkansas, far to the south, then ran out in the Texas Panhandle. "The Indians managed to save themselves," he reported, "though their game was gone—swept ahead of the terrific blaze."

That the fire was less extensive than Ware would lead us to think is shown in Mitchell's modest report that he destroyed grass for animals for more than a hundred miles, "making it exceedingly difficult for Indians to remain in that locality for want of sub-

[3] Hyde, *Life of George Bent*, 173.

sistence for their animals."[4] But Bent, who was in the area in question, maintains that he did not see a sign of the fire nor did he find an Indian who knew anything about it. From this it would seem that General Mitchell had once again met with frustration.

When the General received word the Indians had been seen east of Denver, he sent Captain C. J. O'Brian and Lieutenant Ware from his Cottonwood headquarters to Julesburg. Nearing the settlement on February 2, they unwittingly rode headlong into a second major attack. Simultaneous raids were being made on a fifty-mile stretch of the Platte, with the Cheyennes to the west, the Sioux to the east, and the Arapahoes in between. The soldiers went to the crest of a hill to determine the cause of smoke in the distance, and to their amazement, they saw Indians everywhere in front of them.[5] Some were crossing the river, others running around the stage station, blacksmith shop, and telegraph office, which, together with some haystacks, were ablaze. Proceeding cautiously to within a couple of miles of the post, the soldiers made a run for it. As they passed the stage station, they saw Indians carrying away corn. Even the trail across the ice on the river had been sanded so that the unshod ponies could cross with their burdens.

The Indians gave way when the detail at the post started firing, enabling O'Brian and his men to reach safety. Perhaps the dense smoke from the burning stacks kept the hostiles from being fully aware of what was taking place. On the other hand, they may have been too preoccupied to pay attention to the soldiers who rushed past them. At any rate, their firing was described as "halfhearted." Arriving at the post, the soldiers learned that the Indian encampment was located across the river at the mouth of Lodgepole Creek. Fifty citizens who had been driven from their homes and were temporarily at the post identified the attackers as a mixture of Cheyennes and Arapahoes who, coming up from

[4] Mitchell to Curtis, January 29, 1865, letter printed in the *Lawrence* (Kansas) *Weekly Tribune*, February 2, 1865; Hyde, *Life of George Bent*, 177.
[5] Ware, *The Indian War of 1864*, 450; Grinnell, *The Fighting Cheyennes*, 174–94. George Bent gives a first-hand account of the Julesburg raids in Hyde, *Life of George Bent*, 168–75.

the south, had struck the river some distance above Julesburg and wrought destruction all along their way.

Liquor, destined for Denver but confiscated by the hostiles, enlivened the Scalp Dance before the campfire that night. Ware describes the scene as "thrilling," yet he believed that if they had the courage to make a dash on the post, there would not be any soldiers left by daylight. The pioneers, whose knowledge of Indians was better than his, assured him the Indians would not attack by night but that an onslaught could be expected at sunup. This would indicate that the warriors were not without courage, but merely opposed to fighting in the dark. No outside help could be expected at the post, since the Indians had destroyed the telegraph line.

The settlers were as surprised as the soldiers, for just before dawn, the hostiles disappeared. When the troops inspected the scene, they found among the plunder that was left behind the heads of fifty-six cattle the Indians had butchered. Tracks indicated they had gone up Lodgepole (or Pole) Creek. The explanation for their sudden departure was that they had learned, through their runners, something that the soldiers did not know: a large detachment of troops was within thirty miles of Julesburg.

On their northern sweep, the hostiles killed when they could and otherwise destroyed property. While the warriors and the Dog Soldiers were pillaging the countryside, their families, ahead of them, were being driven to safety. The destruction was so great that General Grenville M. Dodge, commanding the Department of the Missouri, was convinced that a war was imminent. Troops in the field seemed unable to cope with the Indians, who finally found their first effective resistance at Mud Springs Station. Although they captured the horses, they could not dislodge the telegrapher and the few soldiers stationed in the stronghold.

When reinforcements arrived, the hostiles again attacked, but they could not rout the soldiers from their hastily constructed rifle pits or steal their horses, encircled by the relief wagon train. The allied tribes proceeded northward until they reached the vicinity of Bear Lodge, where they separated, with the Arapahoes going toward Powder River, north of the Cheyenne camp, where a runner had located an encampment of their people. Here they spent the winter in relative calm.

By March, General Dodge had formulated his plan of striking a staggering blow to the Indians concentrated in the Powder River area.[6] Three columns under General P. E. Connor were to move against the Northerners, while a fourth under General John B. Sanborn was to advance against the Southerners. Dodge began by placing Connor in charge of the District of the Plains, but his war plans were momentarily thwarted by an equally opinionated agent, Jesse H. Leavenworth, who urged peace negotiations. Further depredations, however, caused the Secretary of the Interior and the Secretary of War to decide in Dodge's favor.[7]

When the grass was green and the horses were in traveling condition, many of the Arapahoes returned to their old haunt, the Medicine Bow area.[8] They were reported to be "thick," with more coming. And yet they were not too troublesome, for the soldiers reached Fort Halleck without incident. Writing from Fort Laramie in May, Lieutenant Colonel W. O. Collins reported that all of the Arapahoes seemed friendly and that he believed the Northern bands would continue to be peaceful unless provoked. He listed as their principal chiefs Medicine Man, Black Bear, White Bull, and Little Shield. Collins feared the hostile Cheyennes and Arapahoes from the south might exercise a bad influence by telling of their wrongs, "pretended or otherwise," and might persuade or force the Northern bands into a war against the whites. He realized that the Indians' patience was worn thin, for he said they were all liable to become hostile because of the rush of the emigrants through their lands and the rapid destruction of their game.

[6] Grenville M. Dodge to Miles, July 19, 1895, in Nelson A. Miles, *The Personal Recollections and Observations of General Nelson A. Miles*, 7.
[7] *WR*, 48, II, 243–44; *Annual Report of the Commissioner of Indian Affairs*, 1865, 398–400.
[8] Collins to Commissioner, Report, May 12, 1865, IOR, NA; Agnes Wright Spring, *Caspar Collins*, 167; Lewis B. Hull, "Soldiering on the High Plains," *KHQ*, VII, 1 (1938), 53.

The Upper Arkansas Indians were so scattered that Leavenworth still held nearly half the 1864 annuity goods at Fort Larned, where he considered them unsafe. He advised holding the 1865 annuities on the Missouri River. To this and to General Sanborn's proposal to transfer the Cheyenne and Arapaho Indians to the Kansas superintendency, Evans cried, "Absurd!"[9] He later called the placing of these Indians, "whose reservation and improvements thereon are in the heart of Colorado," under a superintendency six hundred miles distant an insult and "an injustice to the public service."

In May, about two hundred Indians attacked Deer Creek and were repulsed, but not before they had driven away twenty-six head of horses.[10] Thirty soldiers gave chase; one soldier and one Indian were killed. On June 1, troops operating from Fort Laramie west stated that Rock Ridge Station (near Fort Halleck) had been burned by Indians, the stock run off, and the telegraph wires cut. Connecting Fort Halleck with Fort Laramie was a military road that served as a shortcut between the two. Leaving Fort Laramie, it went west across a wide expanse of land (now known as the Wheatland Flats), through Halleck Canyon, and on to the Laramie Plains. This important supply road, which followed one of the still visible Arapaho trails through the Laramie Mountains, was in constant danger.

St. Mary's Station (in the Sweetwater country) was attacked and burned May 27 by 150 "savages," but the garrison managed to escape to South Pass. After destroying four hundred yards of telegraph wire the Indians set fire to the posts. In June a peaceful village of Brulé Sioux, who had surrendered at Fort Laramie lest they be mistaken for hostiles, were being transferred to Fort Kearny, where they could be subsisted more economically. Suddenly, at a signal, the Indians revolted at the thought of going into the country of their old enemies, the Pawnees. Since they had not been disarmed, they immediately killed the captain in charge and

[9] Evans to Secretary of the Interior, November 18, 1865, Evans Collection, CSHS.
[10] Spring, *Caspar Collins*, 75–77; Connor to Dodge, June 15 and July 13, 1865, WDR, NA.

four of the soldiers. Before the uprising was over, they had lost 19 of their number, four of them their own chiefs, whom they had killed because the headmen were not in sympathy with their plan. Then they fled westward to join the Arapahoes. Colonel Thomas Moonlight, who gave chase, was robbed of his horses while they were grazing and had to return to Fort Laramie ingloriously on foot.

A month later, Connor said in a wire to Dodge that a number of Sioux and Arapahoes whom the government had been feeding at Camp Collins and Fort Halleck were guilty of most of the depredations committed on the mail routes. In view of these and other circumstances, he sought permission to launch his long-planned offensive, at the same time taking a slap at the Indian agents whose swindling, he believed, had been partly responsible for the trouble. Vital Jarrot, who was then agent for the Upper Platte, received a wire from Connor stating that all the Indians congregated at Fort Halleck and Camp Collins, with the exception of Friday's band, had taken to the warpath.[11]

Shortly after this, 120 lodges under Medicine Man were reported on the Little Chug (now known as North Chug, in southeastern Wyoming), where Agent Simeon Whitely of the Upper Arkansas had learned the Chief wanted a reservation. Evans suggested sending Whitely to investigate the possibility of a reservation for the Arapahoes on the headwaters of Chugwater Creek. Jarrot, who knew the terrain, was outspoken in his disapproval of the location, which possessed none of the requirements to justify it as an Indian reservation. In the first place, he opposed the idea because the land was between the two great roads, along which the Indians would constantly be brought into contact with travelers. Second, he pointed out, the quantity of tillable soil—the government was obsessed with the idea of making farmers of the Indians—was so small that there was not enough on the whole creek to support half the Arapahoes. In view of the gold discovery in the general Rocky Mountain area, Jarrot believed no suitable reservation could be found except on the Missouri.

[11] Vital Jarrot to Connor, July 15, 1865, WDR, NA.

In his long letter the agent reviewed some of the Indian complaints. The buffalo were fast disappearing or leaving their hunting grounds, and the annuities were either insufficient or not forthcoming. The year before, the Cheyennes and Arapahoes had said the small pittance paid them did not justify the injury done their horses in coming for it. Those who did come left in a bad mood. Not until a great deal of persuasion was used could they be induced to sign receipts. They gave as their reason that a previous agent had given them only a small portion of their annuities, but he had made them sign a receipt for all on the assurance that the balance would be available later. Then he had sold the rest of the goods to them at double their value, thus cheating them. Jarrot found that a number of irregularities of this sort had caused more Indians to take to the warpath.

Five days after he made his report, Circular No. 11 was ready for distribution at Fort Laramie.[12] It stated that parleys would no longer be held with the Indians because they must first be severely chastised. Punishment, not presents, was to be the order for the future. This was justified by the following charges: "They [the Platte River Indians] have massacred our men, women, and children; burned, stolen, and otherwise destroyed our property; and committed outrages upon innocent women, which sicken the soul and crush the pleadings of mercy." The order was not as severe as Chivington's had been, for there was a promise that no outrages would be perpetrated upon Indian women and children; neither would they be killed. Instead, they would be imprisoned, subject to orders from higher headquarters.

The Powder River campaign to subdue the Platte River Indians was carried out in the summer of 1865 by Connor, Colonel Nelson Cole, and Lieutenant Colonel Samuel Walker. The three commanders planned to converge upon the Indians at the same time, but the General, pausing to build a stockade at Camp Connor (later Fort Reno), failed to establish connections with the other two columns. As a result, they nearly perished.

The major attack of the summer, involving the principal

12 Connor, Fort Laramie, July 15, 1865, WDR, NA.

fighting forces of the three allied tribes, occurred at Platte Bridge on July 25.[13] The Indians began by using a decoy and trying unsuccessfully to lead the soldiers into ambush. Now, the Sioux had been the first to smoke the war pipe and were consequently honored by being in charge. George Bent credits Roman Nose (a Cheyenne) with being a leader, along with two seasoned Sioux warriors, Red Cloud and Old Man Afraid (or Old Man Afraid of his Horses, as he was more generally known). The warriors, approximately three thousand in number, were perfectly organized, with the Dog Soldiers acting as police and guards and "severely soldiering" anyone who disobeyed commands.

At dawn the next day, the warriors divided into three units, one moving farther west to hide behind the hills about due north of the bridge and another going down the creek. The third, or main body, moved up behind the bluffs, there to await developments. About nine o'clock, a small body of soldiers under young Lieutenant Caspar Collins, sent to the relief of a wood train, marched across the bridge and turned left on a road that paralleled the river. As they approached the hill beyond which the main body of warriors was stationed, Indians came swarming toward them. Though the Indians were perhaps a mile away, the soldiers whirled and galloped back toward the bridge. By this time, all three divisions of the hostiles were converging upon the troops from the north, northwest, and northeast. At the fort a cannon was brought into action, but it could do little in the way of helping the men escape. Collins' horse bolted and carried him straight into the Indian ranks. Through the dust and smoke, Bent saw Collins, an arrow protruding from his forehead. Then he fell into the hands of the warriors. Only a few escaped the savage onslaught. Bodies of dead soldiers and horses were strewn a mile along the road.

Accounts differ, but Bent, who recalls the incident in detail, says the cannon prevented the Indians from crossing the bridge. They did not like the big guns, so they withdrew. Soon scouts told

[13] For detailed accounts of the Battle of Platte Bridge, see J. W. Vaughn, *The Battle of Platte Bridge*; Grinnell, *The Fighting Cheyennes*, 228–29; Hyde, *Life of George Bent*, 214–22; Spring, *Caspar Collins*, 214–22.

them that more soldiers were coming from the west. They were dismounted cavalrymen to whose relief Collins had been assigned. The Indians surrounded them, and although they fought fiercely from their rifle pits, only two managed to escape. The battle was over in a half-hour.

Two Cheyennes distinguished themselves in battle: Roman Nose, a daring young warrior, and High Backed Wolf.[14] The latter fought bravely, but in the heat of the battle he failed to heed the advice of the medicine man, who had warned the warriors not to hold anything metallic in their mouths. Apparently forgetting this, High Backed Wolf put a bullet in his mouth while loading his revolver; he was killed. His body was recovered by his people and later buried in a well-drained crevice in the Big Horn Mountains of north-central Wyoming, where it was found many years later in a mummified state. The body of the Chief and all of the trappings found with it were eventually taken to a museum in Hastings, Nebraska.

Two years before the Battle of Platte Bridge, John Bozeman, returning to the gold fields at Virginia City (Montana), had followed a route east of the mountains, branching from the old Oregon Trail. It traversed the Powder River hunting grounds of the Sioux, and the danger of traveling it became obvious when Bozeman and his companions were attacked and driven back to Sweetwater. A year later, Jim Bridger, who considered such a road an affront to the Indians, proposed another route—west of the mountains. In a test trip to see which was the more practical, Bridger started earlier than Bozeman but arrived at the same time.[15] To the impatient white man, this was sufficient reason to justify the Bozeman Trail as the shorter and better route to the Montana gold fields, though it threatened the existence of the Indians.

It was along this trail that Connor led his troops north to the

14 The Roman Nose for whom Roman Nose Park in Oklahoma is named was Henry Roman Nose, who was among the Cheyenne and Arapaho prisoners sent to Fort Marion, Florida, in 1875. He served as a delegate to Washington in 1899. See Cohoe, *A Cheyenne Sketchbook*, 36, 93.
15 Grace Raymond Hebard and E. A. Brininstool, *The Bozeman Trail*, I, 219, 219n. Bozeman was killed by Indians on April 19, 1867.

ARAPAHOES (except for two Shoshonis in hats) on arrival at Carlisle in 1881. Dickens, son of Chief Sharp Nose, is second from left, top row. On his left (No. 4) is Grant, grandson of Friday, and next to him is Lincoln (No. 5), son of Little Wolf. Front row, third from left, is Garfield (No. 9), son of Wolf Moccasin. On his left (No. 10), is Shakespeare, son of Scar Face. No. 11 is Summer Black Coal (*sitting*) and No. 13 is Horse, son of Washington.

Courtesy Colorado State Historical Society Library

Lone Woman, an Arapaho. This unusual picture, without further identification, is in the files of the Oklahoma Historical Society, Oklahoma City.

Courtesy
Oklahoma State Historical
Society

JOHN BROKENHORN AND HIS WIFE LIZZIE FLETCHER, a captive.

Courtesy Riverton (*Wyoming*) Ranger

UTE, the last of the Water-Sprinkling Old Men.

Courtesy Gus and Mary Yellowhair

Kooɪsʜ, said to have been the last Arapaho survivor of the Sand Creek Massacre.

Courtesy University of Oklahoma Library Manuscript Division

THE INTERIOR OF THE OFFERINGS-LODGE. The Flat-Pipe bundle is to the right of the Center-Pole.

Courtesy Wyoming State Archives and Historical Department

PREPARING THE ALTAR in the Offerings-Lodge.

Courtesy Chicago Natural History Museum

BLACK COYOTE (Watonga), Southern Arapaho band chief, police officer, and Ghost Dance leader. Note tattoos on his chest, the Arapaho symbol. Scars on his arms indicate flesh offerings to the sun, and the crow is emblematic of the Ghost Dance.

Courtesy Bureau of American Ethnology

Tongue River country, where, on August 29, 1865, the major attack of his campaign took place. His Pawnee scouts discovered an Indian trail over which a large camp had recently moved. On investigation, it was found that about twenty-five miles ahead was a village comprising approximately 250 lodges of Arapahoes. Connor proceeded toward it with his four hundred men and two pieces of artillery. The soldiers were within three-quarters of a mile of the camp before they were observed by the Indians.

Earlier, a Cheyenne and his wife and son, who were on their way to the Arapaho village, had spotted the column and had ridden fast to alert the camp. Black Bear and Old David, who felt secure in the remote area to which they had taken their families, believed their informant was mistaken, that he might have seen other Indians coming over the trail or perhaps some buffalo at a distance. But when an Arapaho riding a fast horse arrived with the same disquieting news, the camp was thrown into a state of panic. Many of the women and children, caught without means of escape, hid in the underbrush along the river and waited. Others were soon mounted and ready to leave.

At the sight of the soldiers, the ponies covering the tableland near the camp set up a tremendous whinnying and galloped down toward the village, with the Pawnee scouts attempting to capture them. Dogs began barking and the hills echoed the fearful yells of the Indians. Captain H. E. Palmer, describing the scene, says most of the warriors and perhaps half the women were mounted and, he believed, had taken up a march up the stream toward a new camp.[16] They could not have been moving camp, since their lodges were still standing. They were obviously attempting a hasty escape. While the women fled, the warriors fought fiercely, but they were finally forced from the village. As they retreated up Wolf Creek, a tributary of Tongue River, they were closely pressed by the troops.

In reviewing the battle, Palmer states that it began about 9:00

[16] The most complete account of the battle is by Captain H. E. Palmer, "History of the Powder River Indian Expedition of 1865," *Nebraska State Historical Society Transactions and Reports*, II, (1887), 103–52. See also Robert B. David, *Finn Burnett, Frontiersman*, 81–93.

A.M. and the soldiers were on the offensive until the General was driven back into camp. While the soldiers had the advantage, they captured eleven hundred ponies, and the Pawnees plundered the village. In the immense amount of Indian property destroyed were 250 lodges and their contents. Blankets, buffalo robes, and furs were heaped up on lodge poles, dried meat was piled on top, and the whole thing was burned. To keep the hostiles from multilating the bodies of the dead, they, too, were placed on a burning pyre and cremated. The battle seemed to be over, but the Arapahoes had not given up hope. They managed to recover some of their horses and dislodge the soldiers from the burning village. Palmer admits that the soldiers were on the defensive from the time the General was driven back into his camp until midnight, when the Indians withdrew.

The Arapahoes made a brave attempt to recover their families and their ponies. They succeeded in regaining their women and children when they made a peaceful visit to Connor's camp a few days later, but the Pawnees claimed the horses as their spoils of war.

After the Battle of Tongue River, "medicine wolves" plagued the soldiers. Palmer reported that from the time they left Fort Laramie to attack the Arapaho camp, they had been surrounded by thousands of wolves, which had made the night "hideous with their infernal howling." But when the medicine wolves appeared with their unusual sounds, it was too much for superstitious Bridger and Janice, who were serving as guides. They took their blankets and struck out, reasoning that it was the only way of escaping the danger that was sure to follow when the supernatural animal howled. With a like-minded companion, they went down the river about a half-mile and camped alone, without fear of the Arapahoes.[17]

Connor, who had declared that the guilty Indians must be hunted down like wolves, had little to show for his expedition other than the destruction of the Arapaho village. A Kansas news-

[17] Palmer, "History of the Powder River Indian Expedition of 1865," *loc. cit.*, 152.

paper, advocating "force not negotiation," defended Connor's merciless attack upon the Arapahoes. Its editor supposed a "sniffling" Congress would send an investigating committee after the General.[18] It advocated a short residence upon the plains and the loss of a scalp or two to remove romantic ideas from the heads of the senators in regard to the "dirty red devils."

Connor's success at Tongue River was more than offset by the bitter losses sustained by the men under Cole and Walker, who became bogged down and were actually starving when overtaken by Major Frank North and his Pawnee scouts. Thoroughly unfamiliar with the country, they had wandered aimlessly, fighting only when necessary. All that saved them from annihilation was their artillery, which boomed threateningly from time to time. Unable to turn their horses loose to graze because they might be driven away, they watched them die by the hundreds in the picket lines. The six hundred cavalry horses left were considered unfit for military service.[19]

While the Powder River Expedition was under way, Colonel James A. Sawyers and his military escort attempted to blaze a new trail from the Missouri up the Niobrara River and on to the Montana mines.[20] As it was approaching Powder River, the party was attacked by a force of several hundred Indians. The expedition was harassed almost daily by the Cheyennes, who were bought off, as George Bent expresses it, so that the whites could reach Connor's Fort. The Indians were incensed when they learned that a fort had been built in the heart of their hunting grounds.

Reinforced, the expedition moved northward without further difficulty until it met a contingent of angry Arapahoes who forced them to corral. After repeatedly attacking and withdrawing, the Indians signified their willingness to talk. Three warriors, still hoping to recover ponies lost in the recent attack on their camp, agreed to go as hostages to Connor's Fort, where they received

[18] *Kansas Daily Tribune*, August 25, 1865.
[19] Connor to Dodge, July 3 and 5, 1865, WDR, NA; Cole to Grant, February 10, 1867, *WR*, Vol. XLVIII, Pt. 1, 366–80.
[20] Grinnell, *The Fighting Cheyennes*, 199, 202.

nothing for their efforts but a stronger protective force for the expedition.[21]

Earlier in August, the vanguard of the Arapahoes had caused trouble in the Fort Halleck area. In one attack, four whites were killed near Rock Creek. The hospital steward at the fort reported that one of the captured men was scalped and tied to a wheel of a wagon. Bacon was piled around him and set on fire, consuming him in its flames.[22]

Meanwhile, the southern campaign under General Sanborn was meeting with difficulties. Knowing that Dodge proposed to send him against the Upper Arkansas Indians, Agent Leavenworth requested that troops not be dispatched until he had been given a chance to visit the tribes to determine their intentions, whether for peace or war. Dodge, nevertheless, ordered Sanborn to proceed. He said in a letter to the Secretary of the Interior: "The place to make a treaty is down in the heart of their country where we can dictate the terms; not they in our country."[23] Dodge was again restrained by news that the President of the United States had authorized the creation of a peace commission and that the policy was to shift from force to negotiation. When the commissioners met with Kit Carson and William Bent, the latter said he would guarantee peace "with his head."

The first overture was made by representatives of the Kiowas —four men and four women—who contacted Leavenworth at the mouth of the Little Arkansas, but Dodge had little faith in a treaty, such as Leavenworth proposed, before the Indians had been whipped and made to give up stolen stock. "It appears to me," he said, "a treaty is a bid for them to commence again as soon as we take our troops off." In spite of this, Sanborn was ordered (August 4) by Major General John Pope of the Department of the Missouri to suspend all movement and arrange for a peace treaty with the Indians.[24]

---

21 Dodge to Pope, September 15, 1865, *WR*, Vol. XLVIII, Pt. 2, 1229.
22 *Rocky Mountains News*, August 6 and 10, 1865.
23 *WR*, Vol. XLVIII, Pt. 1, 360–61; Pt. 2, 1075–76, 1094.
24 Pope to Sanborn, *ibid.*, Pt. 1, 361.

The council which followed on August 15, 1865, at the mouth of the Little Arkansas concerned the Kiowas, Comanches, and Kiowa-Apaches for the most part, with Big Mouth alone representing the Cheyennes and Arapahoes in signing the truce.[25] He made no promises for the Northern bands, for he was not sure they would come south even after a treaty was made. According to this agreement, the Indians promised to cease all acts of violence toward travelers on the Santa Fé Trail and the frontier settlements and to be present at a council on October 11 at Bluff Creek, about forty miles south of the Arkansas River. Furthermore, they promised to use their influence to induce all of their bands north of the Platte to join them in perpetual peace.

When a second truce was negotiated with the Arapahoes and Cheyennes three days later at the same site, the former were represented by Little Raven, Spotted Wolf, and Storm, the latter by Black Kettle and Little Robe. The document they were asked to sign differed from the one offered previously, for it recognized the Sand Creek Massacre as the cause of present hostilities. In signing it, the chiefs stated that they hoped to restore peace between their people and the government and that they would be present for the big talk at Bluff Creek.

The commissioners included such dignitaries as Sanborn, General W. S. Harney, Colonels Kit Carson and William Bent, Agent Leavenworth, and Judge James Steele. John Smith served as interpreter for the Cheyennes and Maggie Poisal (Fitzpatrick) Wilmarth for the Arapahoes. Samuel A. Kingman, a lawyer from Atchison, Kansas, who was with the commissioners, considered the Cheyennes and Arapahoes the best Indians on the plains.[26] He declared they were the white man's friends until driven into hostilities by the Sand Creek Massacre. Writing before the council convened, he predicted that the commissioners would "treat with them gently and use them liberally."

After Sanborn had given his opening address, in which he

[25] *Annual Report of the Commissioner of Indian Affairs*, 1865, 394–95, 517–25.

[26] Samuel A. Kingman, "Diary of Samuel A. Kingman in 1865," *KHQ*, I, 5 (November, 1932), 442–50.

outlined the purpose of the council, he expressed the desire of the Great Father to have the Indians reside on a designated reservation. Big Mouth replied: "As for sitting down upon any one piece of ground, I cannot now say or understand how it will be."

Little Raven, showing his concern for the bands in the north, asked what could be done for them. Sanborn replied that he would give them five months to come in and join the tribe. "If you live in peace and do well, all the Indians will come and join you. We desire to have your reservations so large that you can subsist by hunting for many years. You will not have so small a tract as heretofore."

The southern boundary of the proposed reservation was not clarified, but in general the reservation line was to begin at the mouth of the Cimarron River on the Arkansas, then go up that stream to a point opposite Buffalo Creek, then north to the Arkansas and down that river to the confluence of the Cimarron and the Arkansas. Again the Sand Creek Massacre was mentioned, and 160 acres of land were given to survivors who had lost either a husband or a parent.[27]

Little Raven said sadly: "It will be a very hard thing to leave the country that God gave us on the Arkansas; our friends are buried there, and we have to leave these grounds." (He was obviously referring to the area in Colorado which was claimed by the Arapahoes, but he later claimed that he still considered the Colorado lands as part of his reservation.)

Sanborn answered: "We have all got to submit to the tide of emigration and civilization. . . . We fully appreciate the trial that it is to you to separate from the graves of your ancestors, but events over which you have no control make it necessary for you to do so."

Little Raven expressed himself as glad that men had been sent from Washington—that they "took so much pains" to come and see the Arapahoes, for they did not like to fight with the

[27] *Annual Report of the Commissioner of Indian Affairs*, 1865, 517–27; Kappler, *Indian Affairs*, II, 887–89. The Arapahoes signing the treaty were Little Raven, Storm, Big Mouth, Spotted Wolf, Black Man, Chief in Everything, and Haversack.

whites. He was "much grieved" by the treatment his people had received from Chivington. He thought the Cheyennes and Arapahoes (that is, those who were present) were "good Indians" and he wanted it understood that they should not be held accountable for acts committed by their kinsmen to the north. And yet he believed it was only fair to wait until spring, when both Northern and Southern bands could assemble to decide upon a reservation.

The Arapaho chief was convinced that when it came to peacemaking, his people would stand by their bargain better than the whites. Furthermore, he complained about their being swindled by agents who had sold their goods to them. When asked to name the guilty agents, Little Raven did not answer directly. "The Arapahoes and Cheyennes," he countered, "had only one fair agent—Major Fitzpatrick." He wanted Mrs. Wilmarth to remain with the Arapahoes as interpreter and live with them and be paid by the government.

The Chief, with the shrewd business sense of an Arapaho, reminded Sanborn that if the President intended to treat for their lands, he must give a good price because the settlers were digging for gold. While admitting he knew it was wrong, he claimed he did not trouble the whites because he thought the government would make up for his loss. As for the Boone Treaty, Little Raven said Boone came out and got the Indians to sign "the paper," although they did not know what it was about. "That is one reason why I want an interpreter," he maintained, "so that I can know what I sign." According to both chiefs, the Arapahoes on the Arkansas represented in council comprised 190 lodges, the Cheyennes 80, with the usual figure of five to a lodge. In the north there were 480 lodges of Southern Arapahoes and Cheyennes combined. This shows that the chiefs present represented a minor portion of the allied tribes.

Regarding Sand Creek, Little Raven said: "There is something strong for us [hard on us]—that fool band of soldiers that cleared out our lodges and killed our women and children. This is strong [hard] on us. There, at Sand Creek, is [was?] one [Arapaho] chief Left Hand, [by changing the comma after "Left

Hand" to a period, it would seem that Little Raven meant that the Arapahoes were represented by an important chief, Left Hand, for he goes on to say] White Antelope and many others lie there; our women and children lie there, and I do not feel disposed to go right off in a new country and leave them." In his concluding speech, he said the Arapahoes wanted Colonel Thomas Murphy as superintendent to see that they got their proper goods.

Still smarting with a spirit of retaliation, the Cheyennes and Arapahoes began to sift southward in the fall of 1865. About fifteen hundred Indians crossed the Smoky Hill Road, attacked and burned a coach, and killed six men.[28] They then drove off all the stock from five stations on the line. Just how many hostiles were involved in the difficulties of farmer-contractor J. H. Haynes at the site of the old Sand Creek Reservation we do not know, but the Indians, identified as Arapahoes, harassed him so constantly that he had to abandon his investment in materials and crops and flee for his life. Two of his workmen were killed on their way to the field, and he lost eleven head of mules, some of which he had bought from Colley for $125 each. Three of the mules were reported by Colley's son, Dexter, to have been seen in the hands of the Arapahoes. One of the Indians later told him the stock was driven to Kansas.

Haynes returned in September to estimate his property damage, which he claimed amounted to $18,864.66, and to harvest whatever crops might have matured in his absence. With not more than five hundred bushels to show for his effort, he again fled, this time because he was informed that he would not have military protection. The Cheyennes and Arapahoes, he claimed, were murdering all whites they found unprotected.

On the supposition that the level-headed chiefs who had recently signed the treaty might have a good influence over the dissidents, plans were made to unite the Southern bands of Cheyennes and Arapahoes. Major Wynkoop was assigned as special agent and later resident agent for the Kiowas and Apaches, as well

[28] Colley, Testimony Taken in Kansas, Letters from J. H. Haynes and His Lawyer, Beginning March, 1865, Asking Reimbursement for Loss, IOR, NA.

as the Upper Arkansas tribes. He maintained that the absentee Indians had been misinformed; they had been told that the treaty of 1865 was null and void.[29]

A treaty council was held with the Sioux at Fort Laramie in 1866, but the spirit of the occasion was marred when Colonel Henry B. Carrington arrived with a wagon train (226 mule teams) loaded with supplies and equipment for the construction of Forts Phil Kearny, Reno, and C. F. Smith on the Bozeman Road. Red Cloud angrily stalked from the council and thus became the supreme leader, not only of the Sioux, but also of the other two Platte River tribes. The Arapahoes who came into Fort Laramie later in the month to declare themselves for peace did not want to be drawn into a major conflict by the Sioux.

By December, all hopes that the strife on the plains might be ended were dispelled when Red Cloud's forces wiped out a detachment of eighty-one officers and men, including Captain W. J. Fetterman, near Fort Phil Kearny.[30] Although the Sioux could control their allies, they were unable to draw the Crows into the conflict, since the latter had not forgiven the Sioux for driving them from the disputed area, the land above the Platte east of the Big Horns.

Involved in the Fetterman Massacre were about two thousand warriors, with the Sioux outnumbering their allies three to one. Little Chief and Sorrel Horse of the Arapahoes were known to have taken part, though their contributions seem to have been made largely through raids in which they drove horses and cattle from the garrison. Their war leader was the spectacular Robert North, Evans' erstwhile informant, who had earned a name for himself: "murderous white chief."[31] As the leader of an outlawed band, he had been implicated in 1853 in the killing of ten miners near the mouth of Powder River. He and his Arapaho wife were

[29] Wynkoop to General John Pope, Fort Larned, March 12, 1866, IOR, NA.

[30] *Sen. Exec. Doc.* No. 97, 49 Cong., 2 sess., 1–6; Carrington to Litchfield, Report, December 6 and 16, 1866, WDR, NA.

[31] Joseph H. Taylor, "The Renegade Chief," in *Sketches of Frontier and Indian Life on the Upper Missouri and Great Plains*, 1863–1889, 224–30.

finally hanged by desperadoes in Kansas (1869) as they were making their way to a Southern Arapaho camp.

In a prepared statement, Bridger claimed the Platte River Indians had been planning their attack for weeks.[32] The Indians began, as usual, by leading the soldiers into a trap and ambushing them. Then they made their escape with twenty-three head of horses. Two fights, minor as far as the white man was concerned, were even more significant from the Indian viewpoint than the Fetterman Massacre. They took place in midsummer, 1867, following a Sun Dance at which plans were made to wipe out two of the despised military posts on the Bozeman Trail, Fort Phil Kearny on the Little Piney and Fort C. F. Smith on the Little Big Horn.

The first attack was made by four hundred to five hundred Cheyenne and Arapaho warriors upon a hay crew near Fort C. F. Smith. The captain commanding the detachment and two privates were killed before a relief party arrived from the fort. Armed with new breech-loading rifles, they succeeded in driving the Indians away without further loss to themselves. The second attack was made the following day by the Sioux upon a wagon-box fortress protecting wood cutters five miles from Fort Phil Kearny. Little did the Indians realize at either place that several hundred repeating rifles, covered by grain, had been smuggled into the fort. The Platte River Indians were unable to cope with the new firearms. The numbers of Indians killed in the two engagements has not been firmly established—estimates vary widely—but the loss was greater than they had expected, so they withdrew after capturing a number of horses and mules. The new weapons discouraged further attacks on detachments in the immediate area. The Indians then turned their efforts to the south, where they harassed the Union Pacific Railroad, then building west. In order to halt depredations, the commissioners again sought a peaceful solution.

[32] Captain T. B. Burrows to Post Adjutant, Fort C. F. Smith, August 3, 1867, and Captain James Powell to Post Adjutant, Fort Phil Kearny, August 4, 1867, IOR, NA.

Conditions were somewhat different in the south. Major General W. S. Hancock of the Department of the Missouri was impatient to launch a new military campaign. After his inspection of the Smoky Hill route, he revealed that every station 170 miles each side of Fort Wallace had been attacked at least four times.[33] Hancock was short tempered, and when his council with the hostiles proved unsuccessful, he made a surprise attack on a Cheyenne-Sioux encampment. Using it as an object lesson, he destroyed it. The loss to the Indians paralleled that of the Arapahoes at Tongue River, for 140 Sioux and 111 Cheyenne lodges and their contents were destroyed. Tempers flared anew, and there were charges and countercharges among the whites and retaliations from the Indians. Ten days after the attack, Hancock held a talk with Little Raven, Yellow Bear, Beardy, Cut Nose, and some of their warriors at Fort Dodge. Although they signified their desire for peace, there is little doubt their sympathy was with the Dog Soldiers and Sioux, who had been trying to prevent the construction of a railroad through Smoky Hill Valley. The Arapahoes claimed they had taken no part in recent troubles and that they planned to stay south of the Arkansas, well out of the troubled area.

Wynkoop was critical of Hancock's action, since the General had assured him the village would not be destroyed. The trouble stirred up by this incident was bound to cause a chain reaction from the Indians and prove costly in lives and property. By remaining, for the most part, south of the Arkansas, the Arapahoes were only indirectly involved in the Cheyenne war that followed. General Sherman's offensive, designed to push the Indians from the Platte and the Arkansas, was finally brought to a halt when once again the attitude of the government turned from war to

[33] Hancock to Sherman, April 19, 1867, Sherman Papers, Library of Congress (cited hereafter as LC). Theodore R. Davis, artist for *Harper's Weekly*, was so impressed at the Arapaho council (April 28, 1867) that he sketched the four leading chiefs smoking with Hancock. He said the pipe was "loaded with a fragrant preparation of sumach leaves, willow bark, sage leaf, and tobacco, the whole saturated with some preparation made from the morrow taken from buffalo bones." See *Harper's Weekly*, June 29, 1867. Talk Held with Little Raven, Fort Dodge, Office of Adjutant General, WDR, NA.

negotiation. No wonder the Indians were confused by the irresolute white man when the Indian Peace Commission of 1867 was created by Congress. In line with the new policy, messengers contacted Little Raven, Black Kettle, and Poor Bear (chief of the Kiowa-Apaches), assuring them the Peace Commissioners would settle their problems and "mark out a straight road for the future" if they would but come to another treaty council, this time at Fort Larned, after the full moon in October.[34]

Little Raven and Yellow Bear, who reached Fort Larned the first week in September, were in a deplorable condition. They blamed the Cheyennes for all of the depredations during the summer, which meant they had no peace to make, not having been at war.[35] According to George Bent, who was living with the Arapahoes after forsaking his role as warrior, the various chiefs had tried to use their influence to stop the fighting until "they were worn out."

A preliminary council was held at Fort Larned on September 8, 1867, between the Peace Commissioners and the head chiefs of the Arapahoes, Cheyennes, and Kiowas.[36] The chiefs insisted that the main council be held on Medicine Lodge Creek because the Indians were reluctant to move their people near the army posts, where troops did not always distinguish between friendlies and hostiles. Complying with their wishes, the officials moved to the council grounds on Medicine Lodge Creek, sixty miles south of Fort Larned. Here Thomas Murphy found fourteen hundred Indians, mostly Arapahoes, who immediately assumed the responsibility of protecting the officials, as well as the treaty provisions.

The Cheyennes brought to the Arapaho village by Guerrier were not amicable. One chief stated sarcastically: "A dog will rush to eat provisions. The provisions you bring us make us sick;

[34] Murphy to Little Raven, Black Kettle, and Poor Bear, Indian Peace Commission Records (cited hereafter as PCR), NA.

[35] *Annual Report of the Commissioner of Indian Affairs*, 1867, 314–15; George Bent to Wynkoop, PCR, NA; Murphy to Taylor, September 21, 1867, *ibid.*

[36] *House Exec. Doc.* No. 97, 40 Cong., 2 sess., 6; Alfred A. Taylor, "Medicine Lodge Peace Council," *Chronicles of Oklahoma*, II, 2 (March, 1924), 99.

we can live on buffalo but the main articles that we need we do not see, powder, lead and caps. When you bring us these we will believe you are sincere."[37] Gray Bear, a Cheyenne who had defected from Roman Nose's camp, urged Murphy to "keep a strong heart," as the decision was up to Chief Medicine Arrow, who was a forceful leader of the Soldier Society. He was sure the Cheyennes would abide by Medicine Arrow's word.

When the Medicine Lodge council finally convened on October 16, it was an impressive affair, with Brigadier General C. C. Augur taking charge in Sherman's absence.[38] Also present were the governor of Kansas with two other officials, besides eleven newspapermen and one photographer. The opening session was marred when the Kaws stole some of the Arapahoes' horses, which aroused Little Raven into sending some of his men in pursuit. He rejoiced three days later when he learned they had overtaken the Kaws and had returned with the horses and some fresh scalps. He warned the whites not to become alarmed by their victory dance.

At the end of the first day's hearings, which concerned Hancock's campaign against the Cheyennes, Little Raven entertained several reporters with a dance at his camp. At its conclusion, the artist for *Harper's Weekly*, who was one of the guests, noticed that someone had taken his revolver. The Chief, who was embarrassed by the incident, offered him one of his own.

During the time Little Raven was sitting as a delegate through the Kiowa-Comanche grand council, he entertained the hope that the Arapahoes would be treated separately from the Cheyennes. He had made such a request but had received no answer. Events of the following days showed that the commissioners intended to create only two reservations—one for the Kiowas, Comanches, and Plains Apaches, the other for the Cheyennes and Arapahoes.

The grand council for the two tribes of the Upper Arkansas

---

[37] Proceedings of Council Held at Arapaho Village, September 27, 1867, PCR, NA.

[38] For an account of the Medicine Lodge treaty council as it was reported in the newspapers of the day, see Douglas C. Jones, *The Treaty of Medicine Lodge*.

was delayed by the Cheyennes' failure to appear. They finally arrived on October 28, and the leaders of the two tribes signed the treaty.[39] It assured the safety of railroad construction crews and travelers on the emigrant roads by removing the Indians from Kansas. Their new reservation was bounded by the thirty-seventh parallel and by the Cimarron and Arkansas rivers and included part of the Cherokee Outlet. In return for the Indians' guarantee of peace, the government agreed to provide buildings, schools, instructors, doctors, farmers, blacksmiths, carpenters, engineers, and millers. Besides furnishing clothing, the government agreed to expend twenty thousand dollars annually for the benefit of the Indians over a period of twenty-five years.

The Arapahoes gave a lively farewell dance in honor of the commissioners.[40] Dressed in their war regalia, they were unmindful of an approaching electrical storm. Lightning set fire to the prairie grass, but the Indians kept up their dancing. The rain fell and the winds blew, but still they kept dancing. The white men, who were driven to their tents by the storm, could hear the Indians singing until nearly dawn, when the storm subsided and the Indians left.

After the Medicine Lodge council, intertribal warfare was resumed, with a foray against the offending Kaws first on the agenda. The commissioners proceeded to Fort Laramie, where they hoped to treat with the Sioux and their allies, as well as with the Crows. But Red Cloud sent word that he would not appear unless troops were withdrawn from the Bozeman Road. Louis L. Simonin, a French mining engineer visiting in the Rockies at the time, gives a rare account of the Fort Laramie meeting with the Arapahoes and the Crows, held at the fort on November 14.[41] General Harney did not consider the three hundred Indians present representative of the people with whom he had come to deal. Nevertheless, the formality of a council was observed, and to the Indians, at least, it was an important occasion. The Arapahoes

[39] Kappler, *Indian Affairs*, II, 189–90, 984–89.
[40] Jones, *The Treaty of Medicine Lodge*, 189–90.
[41] Louis L. Simonin, *The Rocky Mountain West in 1867*, 100–90.

were represented by Sorrel Horse (spokesman) and Black Coal, with Friday serving as their interpreter.

There is little evidence to substantiate Simonin's belief that Little Shield was "the great chief" at the time. He was a war chief, but as far as can be determined, he was never head chief, an honor belonging to Medicine Man, who was not present. Simonin was surprised by the calm with which Sorrel Horse spoke. Remaining seated, he discussed the problems of his people in the manner of an after-dinner talk. He expressed his love for the white man and his desire to live south of the Platte, and he vowed that at the next moon he would go with some of his men to "plant" his tent near Fort Sanders (in the present-day Laramie, Wyoming, area). Apparently he considered this "south of the Platte," for he showed no inclination to join the Southern bands in Indian Territory. Saying that he must hunt to live, he asked for provisions and ammunition, both of which were given to him.

A more important council was held at Fort Laramie on April 29, 1868, wherein the Northern Cheyennes and Arapahoes agreed to accept as a "permanent home" some portion of the country set aside for the Cheyennes and Arapahoes at Medicine Lodge or that designated as a reservation for the Brulés and other bands of Sioux.[42] The Arapaho chiefs signing the treaty were Medicine Man, Black Bear, Sorrel Horse, and Little Shield.

On June 16 the greater portion of the Northern Arapahoes, comprising 119 lodges, arrived at the fort from the Powder River country. They were on their way to join the Southern bands, but they were ill prepared for such a journey because they lacked horses and were without sufficient clothing and ammunition. Nevertheless, they expressed their great friendship for the government and their satisfaction at the prospects of peace. Although the treaty had already been concluded (May 10), the chiefs insisted that the following add their marks: Tall Bear, Neva, Wounded Bear, Whirlwind, The Fox, The Dog, Big Mouth, Spotted Wolf, Big Wolf, Knock Knee (No-ta-nee), Little Old Man, Paul, Black Bull, Big Track, The Foot, Black White, Yellow Hair, Wolf

[42] *Annual Report of the Commissioner of Indian Affairs,* 1868, 252–54.

Moccasin, Big Robe, and Wolf Chief. A number of Southern
Arapahoes, including Neva, Big Mouth, Spotted Wolf, and
No-ta-nee, are on the list. Left Hand was not with his brother
(Neva); he was with White Eyed Antelope, Row of Lodges, and
White Snake in Lincoln County, Kansas. Depredations committed
elsewhere but attributed to him were found to have been com-
mitted by the Sioux.[43]

In January, 1868, Wynkoop had been unable to induce any
of the allied chiefs to go to Washington.[44] They gave as their
reason that they were at war with the Kaws and Osages. Under
such circumstances, it was the duty of the tribal leaders to remain
with their people. Murphy suggested that a council be called to
work out a peace, but it would not be possible before May, for
belligerent tribes had fired the grass. The Indians were agreeable
to such a plan if their war was over by then. A month later, John
Smith suggested to Murphy that annuities be given to the Cheyennes and Arapahoes sixty miles south of Fort Dodge to keep them
away from the fort, where they had been obtaining whiskey.

A short time later, Murphy, writing to the Commissioner of
Indian Affairs, said he had promised a small spring wagon ($150)
and a set of harness ($40) to the Kiowa chief and to Little Raven,
and he was anxious to carry through in order to keep the confidence of the two worthy Indians. The $190 for each chief was
to be paid out of the tribes' funds. Murphy also complained that
whiskey was being furnished in vast quantities at Fort Dodge
and unless a stop were put to it, there would be trouble the coming
season. I. L. Butterfield, whose express company had suffered
heavily at the hands of the Cheyennes, complained that Big Mouth,
who had obtained eighteen bottles and one keg of whiskey at Fort
Dodge, had brought it into the Cheyenne camp and that it was
endangering everyone.

[43] Keim, *Sheridan's Troopers on the Border*, 32–33; G. D. Williams to Commissioner, March 2, 1887, Cheyenne and Arapaho Agency Letterbooks, No. 20,
OHS.
[44] Murphy to Acting Commissioner, Atchison, Kansas, January 7 and 14,
1868, Smith to Murphy, February 5, 1868, and Murphy to Commissioner, February 20, 1868, IOR, NA.

Wynkoop found the Cheyennes and Arapahoes determined to take to the warpath as soon as grass was green.[45] He told the Indians that the government wanted them to make peace with their enemies (then the Kaws and Osages, with whom they were at war), to which they replied that they did not want peace. They had grievances against their enemies, and they intended to chastise them.

Efforts were also made in the spring of 1868 to bring about peace between the Cheyennes and Arapahoes and bands of Utes and Apaches attached to the agency at Cimarron Springs, New Mexico. George Bent, representing Black Kettle and Little Raven, held council with the enemy Indians and told them the two chiefs stood in readiness to effect such a peace.[46] Although the Utes remained hostile, some of the Apaches later showed their friendliness by joining the Arapahoes in Indian Territory.

The Indians had remained relatively quiet during the winter and the spring of 1868 as far as the whites were concerned, but trouble started on the Solomon in midsummer.[47] A war party of two hundred Cheyennes and four Arapahoes (including one of Little Raven's sons) left their camp on Walnut Creek, apparently to attack the Pawnees. They crossed the Smoky Hill River near Fort Hays, then proceeded to the Saline. A brother of White Antelope, who was killed at Sand Creek, kidnaped a woman, whom he raped before returning her to her home. The party then left the Saline and went north to the settlements on the South Fork of the Solomon.

The Indians, who were kindly received and fed, caused no trouble until they were fired upon. Their victims in this case were a man and a woman. At a second house, they killed two men and captured two little girls, whom they took with them when they turned south. On the way they encountered mounted soldiers. In the subsequent attack, they abandoned the children. Then they

[45] Murphy to Commissioner, February 26, 1868, and Butterfield to Murphy from Cheyenne Camp, February 5, 1868, IOR, NA.
[46] Wynkoop to Murphy, April 10, May 15, 1868, and J. B. Dennison, Cimarron Springs, to Superintendent, April 3, 1868, IOR, NA.
[47] Wynkoop, Report, August 19, 1868, IOR, NA.

split their ranks, the majority going north to continue their depre-
dations and a few returning contritely to Black Kettle's camp.
The rampaging Indians were so successful that the Kiowas and
Comanches were reported to be joining in the "Cheyenne and
Arapaho War," although there were only a few outlaw Arapahoes
among the hostiles.[48]

The Indian outbreak in Kansas was so violent, officials concluded that the only remedy was to root out the guilty Indians
and destroy them.[49] Even Murphy despaired of inducing the
allied tribes to abandon their "savage habits." He was so angered
by their conduct that he believed the Arapahoes and Cheyennes
should be held accountable for each other's acts, a policy the army
had long advocated. He even went so far as to favor leaving them
to the "tender mercies" of the army.

On September 19, an official declaration of war was issued.[50]
It stated that a "vital part" of the Cheyenne and Arapaho tribes
was committing murders and robberies from Kansas to Colorado.
It was deemed "in excess of generosity to be feeding and supplying
the old, young, and feeble while their young men were at war."
Even so, the Department of the Interior insisted upon separating
the innocent from the guilty, and the friendlies were to be taken
to Fort Cobb, out of the line of action. But Sheridan was determined to make war on both the Arapahoes and Cheyennes, though
as a tribe the former had not committed hostile acts.

When the General opened his campaign, Murphy extolled
the virtues of Black Kettle, "one of the best and truest friends the
white man ever had."[51] The Chief had purchased with his own
ponies the white women and children captured on the Blue and
Platte rivers by the Dog Soldiers and the Sioux. He had been
threatened by his tribesmen and had been forced to steal away
with his family to the lodges of the friendly Arapahoes. After

[48] A. C. Farnham (telegram) to Charles E. Mix, Acting Commissioner, October 6, 1868, IOR, NA.
[49] Keim, *Sheridan's Troopers on the Border*, 33.
[50] W. T. Sherman, Headquarters, Military Division of the Missouri, Declaration of War, September 19, 1868.
[51] Murphy to Commissioner, Atchison, Kansas, December 4, 1868, IOR,
NA.

Saline and Solomon, he tore his hair and clothing in grief and apprehension.

Reports had apparently been circulated that Little Raven had taken part in the Saline atrocities and that he was then a prisoner of Sheridan. Murphy was highly indignant, for he believed that no Arapahoes would have been involved if the Chief could have prevented it. He recalled how Little Raven had protected the white delegation at the Medicine Lodge council, where he had watched over them day and night. He was continually sending messengers to hostile Indians to urge them to come to the council and meet with the commissioners.

While General Sheridan was encamped on a hill north of Fort Dodge in September, he looked through his binoculars at what appeared to be an apparition.[52] When he could make out what it was, he saw that it was an ambulance with a long pole lashed to it. Attached to the pole was a wagon sheet, a flag of truce. The driver was Little Raven, who was arriving for an official visit. He had come to tell the General that he wanted two days to bring in the guilty tribesmen who had joined in the Cheyenne war but that he himself wanted no part in it. The General told him he could have a week if necessary, but the Chief insisted that all he needed was two sleeps in order to call in the culprits. Well laden with supplies, he departed the following day. The officers believed his visit was merely a ruse to allow the Arapaho women and children time to scatter into broken country, where there was little chance they would be overtaken by soldiers.

In spite of the Peace Commissioners, the years 1868 and 1869 were, statistically, the worst two years, from the white man's point of view, experienced on the plains.[53] Principally involved were the Sioux, Cheyennes, and Dog Soldiers, with whom some of the Arapahoes were still affiliated. One, at least (Little Man), was killed as he took part in the Battle of Beecher's Island on September

[52] Robert M. Wright, "Reminiscences of Dodge," *Kansas Historical Collections*, X (1905–1906), 441–42.

[53] For a list of depredations, see "Report of Secretary of War," 41 Cong., 2 sess., Vol. II, Pt. 1, 52–55; Walter S. Campbell (Stanley Vestal), "The Cheyenne Dog Soldiers," *Chronicles of Oklahoma*, I, 1 (January, 1923), 95.

17, 1868. In this fight, also known as the Battle of the Arikaree, Major George A. Forsyth and fifty hardy frontiersmen were able to fight creditably against an overwhelming number of Sioux, Cheyennes, and Dog Soldiers. In their unsuccessful effort to dislodge Forsyth's hard-pressed men, the Indians lost one of their celebrated warriors, Roman Nose of the Dog Soldiers.[54]

Little Raven's band was the first to signify its intention to go onto the reservation.[55] The Indians hoped to leave as soon as their horses were able to carry them, going by way of Camp Supply to receive their rations. Sheridan, who provided a "safe guard" to accompany them, was anxious to see them settled before the not-so-peaceful Platte River Indians aroused them. The Southern Arapahoes in general were tired of war.

Besides Little Raven, others who came to Fort Dodge in September were Standing Bear, Spotted Wolf, and Bull, all Arapahoes. This seemed to have little effect upon General Sherman's war effort, for he still considered the Arapahoes, as well as the Cheyennes, to be at war.[56] He admitted they were not all equally guilty of criminal offenses, but all were guilty, except the very old, young, and feeble, in that they had done nothing to restrain the offenders, nor had they given them up as agreed. And yet he gave assurance that all who congregated at Fort Cobb, situated on the Washita River, would be safe from harm.

In November, Big Mouth and Spotted Wolf, accompanied by Black Kettle and Little Robe of the Cheyennes, arrived at the fort. Big Mouth, the spokesman, told General W. B. Hazen that he had returned to the land of his childhood because the agent had sent for him, but no sooner had he arrived than trouble broke out. "I do not want war," he protested, "and my people do not, but

54 George A. Forsyth, "A Frontier Fight," *Harper's New Monthly Magazine*, XCI, 541 (June, 1895); John Hurst and Sigmund Schlesinger, "Battle of the Arikaree," *Kansas Historical Collections*, XV (1923), 532.

55 Sheridan to Major General B. H. Grierson, in the Field, Medicine Lodge Bluff, February 23, 1869, and Sheridan to General E. D. Townsend, Headquarters, Division of the Missouri, Chicago, Ill., April 17, 1869, Sheridan Papers, LC.

56 Sherman to John M. Schofield, September 19, 1868, and Hazen to Sheridan, November 22, 1868, Sheridan Papers, LC.

although we have came back south of the Arkansas the soldiers follow us and keep fighting, and we want you to send out and stop those soldiers from coming against us. I want you to send a letter to the Great Father at Washington at once, to tell him to have this fighting stopped—that we want no more of it."

Yellow Robe, an Arapaho statesman, said: "I want peace and am pushing for peace. . . . The old men at home whom we left in the villages are all looking this way and will be glad when these Indians return to them with good news." Then Little Shield added: "We want to throw fighting to one side and cut it off."

Since a full-scale offensive was in the making, Hazen had no authority to treat with the Indians. Sheridan, who had assumed command of the Department of the Missouri in March, had chosen as field commander of the Seventh Cavalry Colonel George A. Custer, whose name and that of his regiment will never be forgotten by the Cheyennes and Arapahoes. With band playing, the flamboyant Colonel and his troops set out for their objective, a Cheyenne village located on the south bank of the Washita River.[57] Here, on November 27, 1868, the Battle of the Washita— or, as the Indians call it, the Washita Massacre—took place. Black Kettle was among the undetermined number of Indians killed. Fifty-one lodges, fully equipped, and nine hundred head of horses were destroyed. The attack on the village concerned the Cheyennes alone, but the Arapahoes took part in the sequel. While the battle was in progress at Black Kettle's camp, Major Joel H. Elliott and about fifteen of his troops dashed in pursuit of several Cheyennes who were attempting to lead some of their women and children to safety. The sound of battle had already alerted the nearest Arapaho camp, and the Indians were coming to the defense of their allies.

It was Elliott's misfortune to run into them.[58] Soon sur-

[57] Official Report of the Battle of Washita, Colonel G. A. Custer, Sheridan Papers, LC; Custer, *My Life on the Plains,* 226–98.

[58] Little Raven, who was not present at the time, claimed the older Indians sought a truce, but the young warriors, who could not be restrained, rushed in and killed Elliott's soldiers "to the last man." Wright, "Reminiscences of Dodge," *loc. cit.,* 72; W. S. Nye, *Carbine and Lance,* 71.

rounded, he ordered his men to dismount and lie in a circle and fire from a tall-grass screen. The grass which protected them from sight also obstructed their view in aiming, so their shots went wild, and the Indians were able to creep up on them—in fact, to point-blank range. Within a matter of minutes, the troops were slain and the Indian women rushed to the scene to mutilate the bodies. The Arapahoes then fled to escape the power of the white man's army.

On December 7, Sheridan's forces, refitted and ready for battle, set out to follow the Indians. First they inspected the site of Black Kettle's village where Custer reported he killed 103 Cheyennes and took 53 captives. Then they rode on in search of a trace of Elliott's detachment. They found the bodies naked, frozen, and badly mutilated. In an abandoned Indian camp, they also found the body of a young white woman and a small boy. She was identified as Mrs. Clara Blinn, about twenty-two, whom the Arapahoes had captured near Fort Lyon. She had been shot in the forehead and the boy's head had been crushed against a tree.

Custer left Camp Wichita on January 21 with a small group of men, reasoning that a large number of soldiers would frighten away the Indians.[59] He was accompanied by Little Robe of the Cheyennes and Yellow Robe of the Arapahoes. The former, on the pretext of going in search of the Cheyenne camp, disappeared after Custer had traveled about 180 miles. Lack of food forced the troops to return to camp. On the way, Custer encountered Little Raven and his band, who were going to Fort Sill to surrender. Their horses were in such poor condition that they had to be hurried along by two companies of the Seventh Cavalry.

By December, there was little fight left, in the "Fighting Cheyennes," for they had been kept on the move by troops and had been unable to make their usual hunt. When Sheridan sent messengers to induce the hostiles to come to Fort Cobb, Little Robe, representing the Cheyennes; Yellow Bear, speaking for the Arapahoes; and a small delegation of tribal leaders came on foot. Sheridan was so insistent upon total war or total peace—he did not

[59] Sheridan to Sherman, Report, January 25, 1869, Sherman Papers, LC.

want the Indians to resume hostilities in the spring—that his harshness may have deterred other members of the tribe from following their lead.

In April, 1869, Medicine Man, Little Big Mouth, Yellow Bear, Storm, and six hundred of their people expressed themselves as ready to go on the reservation.[60] When General B. H. Grierson had a talk with Medicine Man, "their principal chief," the Arapaho said his people wished "to follow the face of the white man and learn his ways; that they would welcome teachers on their reservation and treat them as brothers." Medicine Man apparently remained in the south long enough to have his picture taken at Fort Sill, but when he was next heard of officially, he had returned to the north.

Questioned by Grierson about his knowledge of the location of the reservation allotted to the Arapahoes and Cheyennes in the Medicine Lodge Treaty, Little Raven affirmed that at the time he signed, he assumed that the land on the Upper Arkansas between Bent's Fort and the Rocky Mountains was included in the reservation. He believed the Cheyennes were of the same opinion. Until he met and talked with General Sheridan at the latter's Medicine Bluff headquarters on February 15, 1869, Little Raven did not know precisely where the new reservation was located. He was sure a false idea might have resulted from the hasty way in which the treaty was made, or perhaps it had been mistakenly interpreted. This may explain why he persistently spoke of his Colorado reservation during the Medicine Lodge council.[61]

By April, 1869, most of the Southern Arapahoes, as well as some of the Northern bands, were at Fort Sill, seemingly ready to take up life on the reservation. Four months later, on August 10, President Grant issued a proclamation assigning a new reservation to the Southern Arapahoes and Cheyennes along the North Canadian and the Upper Washita rivers, lying west of the 98th meridian.[62] Its boundary on the north was the Cherokee Outlet, on

[60] *Annual Report of the Commissioner of Indian Affairs*, 1869, 82.
[61] Jones, *The Treaty of Medicine Lodge*, 175.
[62] Office Records, Cheyenne and Arapaho Agency, Concho, Oklahoma.

the east the Cimarron, on the south the Kiowa-Comanche Reservation, and on the west the Texas state line.

In December, some of the Osages, Comanches, and Kiowas, while out on a hunting trip, discussed the matter of peace with the now docile Arapaho Powder Face, who had forsaken all hostile ways. He advised them to be friendly because "the father" wanted them to be. They shook hands and agreed to peace.[63] The following month, the Arapahoes were put on foot by the Pawnees, who stole 150 head of their ponies; as a result, the Arapahoes could not come in for rations. They appealed to their agent, who arranged for the return of the horses through the Pawnees' agent.

It was difficult for Little Raven to understand why peace terms with the whites should have any bearing upon his attitude toward his traditional enemies. At Camp Supply he had made it clear in a council (August 10) with Felix R. Brunot of the Board of Indian Commissioners that he wanted peace with the whites but that this in no way included the Pawnees and Utes. He had asked permission for his young men to go against the latter. He wanted a piece of paper so that when his warriors were on the warpath, they could show it in order to keep out of trouble with the whites. The commanding officer tried to explain that the Great Father would not tolerate fighting of any sort.

To this, Medicine Arrow of the Dog Soldiers replied: "It is a poor rule that will not work both ways. Why do your soldiers fight our Cheyennes in the north?"

"Because they fight our soldiers," was the answer.

[63] Darlington to Hoag, Camp Supply, December 12, 1869, IOR, NA.

CHAPTER TEN

"*A Little Piece of Land*"

A PEACE TREATY was concluded between the Shoshonis and Arapahoes on February 17, 1870, largely through the efforts of Medicine Man, Black Bear, and Little Wolf. The Shoshonis favored amicable relations but refused to permit the Arapahoes to settle on their reservation. After reaching an agreement whereby each could travel unmolested in the other's country, both tribes expressed a desire to see the Wyoming Superintendent of Indian Affairs, Governor J. A. Campbell, with the Arapahoes agreeing to remain until his arrival.

Lieutenant G. W. Fleming, the agent, urged such a meeting as a measure of peace.[1] When Campbell arrived, he was impressed by the Arapahoes' seemingly sincere desire to settle down. They hoped for a treaty like the one at Fort Bridger (1868), which created the Wind River Reservation (known for a number of years as the Shoshoni-Bannock Reservation, though the Bannocks preferred to reside at Fort Hall).

In March the restless young Arapaho warriors began raiding and ranging at will. They struck first at a mining camp near Atlantic City, then at St. Mary's Station on the Sweetwater.[2] Eight citizens were killed and considerable property was taken. At first the Arapahoes denied the accusation, but later they admitted to Washakie that they had killed the whites.

Medicine Man and Friday, who had been encamped about

[1] Fleming to J. A. Campbell, February 17, 1870, Campbell Letterbooks, National Archives and Wyoming State Archives and Historical Department, Cheyenne; "Arapahoes Join Shoshones on Reservation," *House Executive Documents*, Vol. I (1870–71), Pt. 2, 31–35, and Pt. 4, 638–45.
[2] H. G. Nickerson, "Early History of Fremont County, Wyoming," *Wyoming State Historical Society Bulletins*, II, 1 (1924), 1–5.

thirty miles below the present site of Lander, Wyoming, had promised friendly relations with the settlers as well as the Shoshonis. They had also agreed to notify both in case of the approach of hostiles. When depredations continued, they named the marauders as Sioux and Cheyennes, but stolen stock found in their camp indicated that they alone were guilty. When accused, they claimed they bought the plunder from their allies.

On the last day of March, Captain H. G. Nickerson, set out to investigate the atrocities, stopping first at the camp of Friday, who, with about twenty lodges, was located a short distance from Medicine Man's camp. Nickerson had saved Friday's life the autumn before. When Friday's horse came into Miner's Delight without a rider, the Captain went to look for him and found him helplessly drunk by the wayside. After lifting him onto his horse, Nickerson took him to his home and provided for him until he had recovered sufficiently to return to his camp. Consequently, Friday was happy to have his benefactor visit him, for he believed him to be on a friendly mission. Not so with Medicine Man, who wanted him killed, but Friday managed to protect him and spirit him away before the Indians could do him harm.

While in the Arapaho camp, Nickerson learned that Little Shield and his warriors had gone over to the Sweetwater, ostensibly on a buffalo hunt. Since the killings at Atlantic City and St. Mary's coincided with his excursion, the miners were convinced that he was implicated. So a raid against the Arapahoes was decided upon.

A force of about 275 men was raised, with Bill Smith, a daredevil miner, in charge of 75 mounted men. Nickerson was supposed to follow on foot with 200 men. Smith struck out in full daylight to find the guilty Indians, who, in the level country, could have seen him twenty miles away. Had the Arapahoes he encountered been guilty, they could have run, or at least tried to defend themselves. Since they comprised a small, unarmed party going to Camp Brown (at the present site of Lander) to trade, fighting seems to have been far from their minds. Smith's men killed Chief Black Bear, who had survived the attack on his camp on Tongue River, two women, and all of the grown males, 14 in number. They captured Black Bear's wife and child besides seven other children.[3]

One of the small captives was Swiftest Runner (E-tus-che-wa-ah), whose name the army surgeon changed to William Tecumseh Sherman. Soon afterwards he was adopted by Captain and Mrs. Charles A. Coolidge and renamed Sherman Coolidge.[4] Black Bear, who had signified his desire for peace by signing the Fort Laramie Treaty of 1868, was the most important man in the Northern Arapaho tribe next to Medicine Man. His "murder," as it was termed in Bureau of Indian Affairs records, made the Arapahoes more bitter than ever. In one of their attacks in April, No-ta-nee (Knock Knee) was fatally injured.

Following this, 160 lodges under Medicine Man, who a short time before had asked for a reservation near Fort Caspar, started toward the Gros Ventre Agency at Milk River (Montana).[5] The Arapahoes had previously tried, without success, to enlist the aid of the Gros Ventres in their hostilities. Whether or not they were planning to make yet another attempt cannot be determined. There is a chance that they might have gone with the intention of casting their lot with their Northern kinsmen, for they did not want to stay with the Sioux or go to Indian Territory. Only ten lodges completed the journey to the Gros Ventre country. When most of the Indians in this small delegation died of smallpox, those in the main camp, then at the Musselshell, became alarmed and fled back into the country from which they came.

Friday, who preferred to take his chances once again in Colorado, moved south with twenty lodges. A short time later, a

[3] Chief Black Bear was killed April 8, 1870, "Arapahoes Join Shoshones," *loc. cit.*, Pt. 4, 640; *Annual Report of the Commissioner of Indian Affairs*, 1870, 176; *Rocky Mountain News*, April 20, 1870.

[4] W. H. Ziegler, *Wyoming Indians*, 28–30. For a novel based on the life of Sherman Coolidge, see Helen Butler, *A Stone on His Shoulder*. Mrs. Sherman Coolidge (*Tepee Neighbors*, by Grace Coolidge) recounts her experiences at Wind River during the time her husband was serving as missionary among the Arapahoes.

[5] *Annual Report of the Commissioner of Indian Affairs*, 1870, 201; Bradley, "Lieutenant Bradley's Journal," *loc. cit.*, 313.

fight with some of the settlers occurred at Middle Park.⁶ According to the press, the Indians questioned the rights of the settlers, and a fight ensued. After two Arapahoes had been killed and carried away by their tribesmen, Friday again returned to the Fort Fetterman area.

While visiting the Utes about this time, Felix R. Brunot found Chief Ouray deeply grieved because he had been unable to find his only child (Cotoan), a son who had been captured by the Arapahoes and Cheyennes as an infant fifteen years before.⁷ His only clue was that he had been reported as living with Friday, whose name he had been given. When the Chief was located in the Owl Mountains of Wyoming, he said the boy had been taken to the Staked Plains by the Southern Arapahoes. Arrangements were finally made by Brunot to bring father and son to Washington, where they met at the Bureau of Indian Affairs. The likeness was unmistakable, but the youth was at first unable to believe that he was a Ute, whom he had been taught to despise. Finally accepting his father, he agreed to return with him, but according to one report, he died on the way.

The Arapahoes were especially antagonistic toward the small, dark-skinned Utes because the latter would take their women and girls, the Arapahoes maintain to this day, to improve the stature and color of their race. Ute Susan, Ouray's sister, would have been burned at the stake had not a white officer intervened. One of Little Raven's sons was numbered among those captured by the enemy tribe, but details are lacking.

By August 1, 1870, the Northern Arapahoes had joined the other Platte River Indians on Powder River and were preparing

⁶ *Central City* (Colorado) *Register*, August 27, October 1 and 22, 1870.
⁷ Charles L. Slattery, *Felix Reville Brunot*, 192–93; "Friday, the Ute Boy," Miles to Hoag, March 3, 1873, IOR, NA. Accounts of Cotoan differ, the one above being that given by Slattery. Marshall Sprague (*Massacre: The Tragedy of White River*, 334) says Brunot was unsuccessful in his attempt to find the boy. LeRoy R. Hafen and Ann W. Hafen (*The Colorado Story*, 258) say Cotoan had been trained to hate the Utes and because of this, Ouray did not claim him. Sprague (p. 89) states that the Arapahoes were in the process of burning Ute Susan, Ouray's sister, when troops arrived in time to save her. He gives as their reason that they had been rebuffed by a settler who would not buy her for an old hat and a looking glass.

a campaign against the Crows.[8] A month later, F. V. Hayden, on a geologic survey assignment, was granted permission by the Indians to travel the old California Trail, but they were infuriated when Nelson Story made his celebrated cattle drive through their country with a thousand head of cattle. The Sioux announced that no more intrusions of any sort would be permitted. Medicine Man, lest he become involved in another Sioux war, agreed to meet Governor Campbell in Cheyenne but he refused to go to Fort Laramie. Red Cloud, after a visit to Washington in the summer of 1870, became reconciled to existing conditions and willingly went onto his reservation a year later. But this had little to do with the difficulties of the Sioux and their allies, who turned to more hostile leaders.

Fort Fetterman had served as a supply depot for the three forts on the Bozeman Trail, and although they were abandoned to conform with Red Cloud's demand before he signed the Fort Laramie Treaty of 1868, Fetterman continued as a garrison. It was an ideal place for the roving bands to congregate.[9] According to Colonel George A. Woodward, who was stationed there, Red Cloud claimed the Arapahoes and Cheyennes were under his jurisdiction, but they repudiated this and as a result were permitted to receive their supplies at Fetterman. The post had practically become their agency, with the commanding officer their ex officio agent. The only hostile acts that took place while Woodward was there were an attack made on a small party at La Bonte Creek in May, 1872, and the killing of a soldier who was in charge of the mail en route to Horseshoe Creek. When he rode ahead alone, he was killed by Indians believed to be Cheyennes. This was later confirmed when they returned the mule he had been riding.

Woodward tried to persuade the Arapahoes and Cheyennes to ask permission to send a delegation to Washington, which they finally did, but it proved to be an inopportune time, for Red Cloud was there on one of his periodic visits. He insisted that a delegation

[8] Campbell to Commissioner, August 1 and September 5, 1870, Campbell Letterbooks, NA.

[9] George A. Woodward, "The Northern Cheyennes at Fort Fetterman," *Montana Magazine*, (Spring 1959), 18–21.

from his allies was unnecessary—that they belonged to him and he would represent them. Both the Northern Cheyennes and Arapahoes refrained from joining the Sioux in their village life because they were weaker in number and, consequently, subject to their whims. They did not want to be "robbed and lorded over" by their more powerful ally. Even after they were assigned to Red Cloud Agency, the Arapahoes continued to visit Fetterman while hunting or making forays against the Shoshonis.

Woodward reported the Arapahoes and Cheyennes peaceful toward each other, with the former only about half as numerous as the latter. He believed that the Arapahoes, once among the "fierce and warlike Indians of the Plains," were assuming a milder type of manner and character. Their declining numbers partly accounted for this. Also he attributed some of it to the influence of Friday. Unfortunately, their mild-mannered attitude did not extend far beyond the reaches of Fetterman.

They continued to make raids against the freighters, miners, and settlers in the Sweetwater area, as well as against the Shoshonis.[10] On May 10, they attacked freighters on Twin Creek Hill, near Sweetwater, and took all of their horses, which were grazing near by. Major David Gordon, then stationed near Atlantic City, pursued them and a heated engagement followed. Several Indians who had been killed or wounded were spirited away, and for a time the body of Lieutenant Stambaugh (for whom Fort Stambaugh was later named) was in the hands of the hostiles. They robbed it of all its possessions and shot it several times before it could be recovered by the soldiers. A sergeant was severely wounded, part of his jaw shot away, before the Indians made good their escape with all of the stock. A month later, they ambushed two men on the Point of Rocks Road thirty miles south of Atlantic City. They killed one with a volley of fire, but the other escaped by keeping the attackers at a distance with his well-aimed rifle.

In August, two hundred Arapaho wariors went on a marauding expedition, first attacking three men near Willow Creek between the Big and Little Popo Agie. Unable to reach shelter, the

10 Nickerson, "Early History of Fremont County," *loc. cit.*, 4.

whites were killed and their horses and provisions taken. Although one of the victims was known to the Indians, whom he had be-friended, they cut the sinews from his back, legs, and arms for bowstrings and drove a bolt so far into his forehead that it could not be pulled out by those who found the body.

Next they stopped at a ranch near Red Canyon, where they succeeded only in shooting through a ranchman's beard. They found him too strongly fortified, so they left. Going on to South Pass, they captured two hundred head of horses and mules belonging to the miners and prospectors. Lieutenant Robinson and a company of cavalrymen from Fort Washakie pursued them, but again they made their escape with the stock.

While this was taking place, the various Indian agencies were experiencing a period of reform under what was known as the Grant Policy. After the inauguration of President U. S. Grant, the agencies were placed in the hands of the denominations already having established missions or those that would undertake the work on a missionary basis. Wind River was assigned to the Episcopal church, and the Cheyenne and Arapaho Agency to the Society of Friends under Enoch Hoag of the central superintendency, with Brinton Darlington as agent for the Upper Arkansas. Darlington's original task was gigantic, but the mild-mannered Quaker, through conscientious effort, was later to win the respect of his charges. His first worry concerned the 1,800 Cheyennes and 1,344 Arapahoes at Camp Supply, where all appeared satisfied to remain and draw rations. The commanding officer stated that all the cavalry in the department could not drive them to Round Pond Creek, where Darlington hoped to establish headquarters. The agent believed that should such an attempt be made, the Indians would scatter.

A Quaker delegation soon arrived to look after the interests of the agent, who, according to a report, had yet to find his Indians. In August, 1869, Brunot and two other special Indian commissioners held a talk with the Cheyennes and Arapahoes at Camp Supply.[11] Little Raven, serving as spokesman for both tribes, urged

[11] Cheyenne and Arapaho Files, "The Society of Friends," OHS; "Darling-

them to settle down and live in peace. In his talk he expressed his dissatisfaction with the reservation designated in the Medicine Lodge Treaty, as the two tribes preferred lands along the North Canadian River. According to Little Raven, they were ready for reservation life, though they still intended to continue warring against the Utes and Pawnees. When he was approached on the subject of getting Arapaho Indians as laborers to herd cattle, haul timber, and build a storehouse at the proposed agency, he replied: "They don't know how to work. . . . They get tired too easy."

Since Darlington knew nothing of issuing rations, a task he had not anticipated, his only recourse was to permit the Indians to leave on a hunting expedition. Taking with him several of the chiefs, he located a spot for his agency about one hundred miles from Camp Supply on the North Fork of the Canadian.[12] The area was sufficient to provide a farm of eighty acres for every male over eighteen years of age.

Still the Indians were unable to restrain their wild inclinations. On September 1, 1869, they stampeded 128 head of government cattle to the bluffs, although six herders were present. At the time of the transfer to their new agency (near present El Reno, Oklahoma), the Arapaho enrollment (June 20, 1870) amounted to 1,877. The increase in numbers from the year before may be explained by the arrival of Northern bands.

The year 1870 was even more difficult for the Southern Cheyennes than it was for the Arapahoes, for their young men were more unmanageable. Both tribes were disappointed in the new reservation, though the Arapahoes did little more than complain. They were not pleased to share the same reservation—their "little piece of land"—with Indians not as deserving as they, and they were jealous of certain favors they believed were accorded the Cheyennes. To make matters worse, Little Raven persistently

ton" (leaflet printed in Low Ausgate, New York, 1873); *Annual Report of the Commissioner of Indian Affairs*, 1869, 11–15; Darlington to Parker, Upper Arkansas Agency, August 13, 1869, IOR, NA. For a detailed study of the Grant Policy, see Loring B. Priest, *Uncle Sam's Stepchildren.*

12 Fort Supply Letterbook, OHS.

assured his people that it was not the intention of the government to make the Arapahoes work, but that the white men (that is, the employees at the agency) were sent there for the purpose of raising corn for them.[13]

This same logic is found in a treaty said to have been written by an Indian and presented to the commissioners at Fort Laramie in June, 1866. It specified the terms under which the Sioux would permit the white man to make a road through the Powder River country. The Indians demanded one thousand "Marcon" horses, one hundred wagons loaded with Indian goods, one thousand "Rivels," five hundred head of cattle, two thousand head of "Seaps," one thousand head of hogs, five hundred "rusters," one thousand chickens, and two hundred "Culed men to rais corn."[14]

By February, 1870, Darlington was gratified by the uniform profession of willingness on the part of the agency Indians to follow government regulations, but he was not as well pleased with some of the Arapaho warriors who were determined to take to the warpath.[15] Left Hand asked his permission to lead a spring attack against the Utes, as some of the young men were anxious to distinguish themselves after having been at peace so long. Yellow Bear and Cut Finger, who had been noted for their friendliness, agreed to accompany the expedition to see that no harm was done to white settlers along the way. Following the Battle of the Washita, Custer had been so favorably impressed by Yellow Bear that he had asserted: "Little Raven continues to exercise the powers of head chief of the Arapahoes, although he is too old and infirm to exercise active command. My former friend and companion, Yellow Bear, is second in rank to Little Raven and probably will succeed him."[16] Custer was wrong in his prediction.

Not wishing to offend Left Hand and Yellow Bear with a flat refusal, Darlington agreed to refer the request to the Interior

13 *Annual Report of the Commissioner of Indian Affairs*, 1871, 470.
14 Photographic copy of "Indian Treaty," Wyoming State Archives and Historical Department, Cheyenne.
15 Left Hand's Autobiography, OHS.
16 *Chronicles of Oklahoma*, I, 3 (June, 1923), 271–73. Custer, *My Life on the Plains*, 379.

Department in Washington, hoping that if matters were delayed, Left Hand would reconsider. The Chief waited for what he considered a reasonable length of time, then left for the Ute country with Cut Finger.

Three days after their departure, Darlington received a letter from the Commissioner of Indian Affairs telling him to stop the raid at all costs, so he sent John Murphy, an employee at the agency, and Yellow Bear to overtake the war party. After a hard ride, they caught up with Left Hand and explained that he must turn back. The warriors held a council and decided to obey the agent's directions. In his memoirs, Murphy describes Left Hand as "handsome, lithe, and athletic, a man of strong magnetism when it came to enlisting the support and following of his fellow tribes-men." A precocious warrior, he is said to have begun his career at fifteen.[17]

In early spring Darlington reported that the Arapahoes were coming to the agency in great numbers with the avowed intention of remaining. He seemed well pleased with their behavior, but he was convinced that a band of Cheyennes had taken part in recent depredations.[18] Little Raven and 78 lodges (making 240 lodges of his tribe then at the agency) arrived from a hunt the first week in April. Darlington stated in a letter to Superintendent Hoag: "This is the darkest hour I have experienced in Indian Affairs." He was nearly out of almost everything, worst of all beef, which was badly needed because the Indians' hunt had not been a success. They behaved remarkably well for "hungry savages," and he added that "few whites would have conducted themselves as well."

By May, the old grudge against the Utes had seemingly been dropped. The Arapahoes were afraid they might be drawn into contemplated disturbances by the Cheyennes. In order to avoid this, they decided to remain at the agency in a body. Reports arrived that some of the Cheyennes had joined the Kiowas and Apaches and were again raiding in Texas, but for the most part,

[17] Left Hand's Autobiography, OHS.
[18] Darlington to Hoag, April 1, 16, 25, and May 10, 21, 1871, IOR, NA.

the Arapahoes were complacent and law abiding. The agent recommended the following for medals: Little Raven, Big Mouth, Left Hand, Bird Chief, Cut Finger, Spotted Wolf, Powder Face, Yellow Bear, Curly, and Yellow Horse. He considered that they were worthy of such an honor for having co-operated with him in his peace efforts.

When the head chiefs of the Arapahoes, Cheyennes, and Wichitas were taken east in June, Little Raven, a natural diplomat, had several opportunities to show his eloquence in Boston, New York, and Washington.[19] Speaking to the governor of Massachusetts, he said in part that he had been received with great kindness by the people of the East and that he was much pleased with all that he had seen. He would carry it back to his people and tell them to live in peace with the whites.

He was definitely impressed, but not in the way Darlington had hoped. In fact, on his return he became an "evil influence." He stated persistently that "Washington" did not expect the Indian to raise corn because the Great Father had a "heap" of money to hire help for the Indians. Furthermore, he decided that he would no longer care to live in a little tipi. He wanted a big strong one like the President's mansion. When the agent tried to explain that there was not enough money in the treasury, Little Raven scoffed at the idea. Had he not seen the Great Father making money at the mint?

It is impossible to determine Little Raven's exact age, but Custer considered him too old to be an active leader. He may have been in his dotage, for he was considered a "fat, tiresome old man" by the reporters at the Medicine Lodge council, where he continually harped on the Cheyennes, who committed all the depredations while the Arapahoes were guiltless.[20] Nevertheless, he seems to have had reason for complaint. Yellow Bear joined him in August to protest that the Cheyennes, who had constantly

[19] Little Raven's long speeches are recorded in *Annual Report of the Commissioner of Indian Affairs*, 1871, 31–37.
[20] Jones, *The Treaty of Medicine Lodge*, 205; Little Raven and Yellow Bear to Commanding Officer, Camp Supply, August 23, 1870, Fort Supply Letterbook, OHS.

proved troublesome, were supplied equally. This did not seem fair when the Arapahoes had remained peacefully at the agency, far from the buffalo herds.

In spite of Big Mouth's part in the Elliott attack—he was still riding the Major's horse—he was more amenable than Little Raven. Politically, Yellow Bear may have been in line to succeed Little Raven, but it was Big Mouth who was top man when it came to leadership on the "corn road," for he had fenced eighty acres and plowed and planted it, doing much of the work himself with his own team in spite of tribal ridicule. Taking pride in his accomplishment, he said later: "I have just been gathering my corn, and it does me good to look at it and think what we might do. I have been tired several times, but I am well paid."[21] He persisted even after disaster beset him. When his fence burned, cattle destroyed his crop. The next year, his land was laid bare by grasshoppers and drought, but he refused to be discouraged. For his efforts, Darlington maintained that he owed Big Mouth much. It was beneath the usual dignity of a chief even to herd his own horses. Not so with Big Mouth, the "rascal" General Curtis had failed to capture.

The total number of Indians on the Cheyenne and Arapaho Reservation in July, 1871, was 3,540, including 540 Northern Arapahoes who had recently arrived.[22] Darlington said their physical and moral condition compared favorably with that of the whites and that they were on the increase. After reviewing their prevailing habits and beliefs, he found "little openness" to Christianity.

When William D. Nicholson visited the various agencies on his tour of inspection for the Society of Friends, he was particularly impressed by three Arapahoes—Big Mouth, White Crow, and Yellow Horse—who, in spite of tribal opposition, were determined to follow the corn road.[23] They wanted chickens, plows,

---

21 Hoag to Commissioner, November 11, 1871, IOR, NA; *Annual Report of the Commissioner of Indian Affairs,* 1871, 472–74.

22 *Annual Report of the Commissioner of Indian Affairs,* 1873, 220–23; Darlington to William Nicholson, July 17, 1871, IOR, NA; *Annual Report of the Commissioner of Indian Affairs,* 1871, 470.

and wagons. Nicholson listed the band leaders of the Arapahoes as Little Raven, Left Hand, Spotted Wolf, Storm, Ice, Powder Face, White Crow, Yellow Horse, Bird Chief, Tall Bear, and Yellow Bear, making eleven bands in all. Some of these were later consolidated.

In September, three hundred Pawnees, well armed, mounted, and driving five hundred horses they were bringing from the south, arrived at the agency and announced their intention of wintering in the vicinity.[24] Darlington was gravely concerned, for he knew that the Cheyennes were not to be trifled with. Once aroused, as they could be by the Pawnees, he might have war "at his own back door." When the Pawnees left, some of the Cheyennes followed. They found two separated from the main body and returned with their scalps.

Later that fall, two hundred wandering Apaches reached the agency. They were so poor that Big Mouth took pity on them. He had met them at Camp Supply in 1869, and he now declared that he loved them as brothers and wanted them to stay. Darlington issued rations and wrote to the department for an opinion, which finally permitted the friendlies to remain.

About the middle of November, a band of sixty Arapahoes headed by Many Birds, a younger brother of Powder Face, started out on another expedition against the Utes, but when they were ordered not to proceed, they disbanded.[25] To discourage other such ventures, Darlington refused to issue rations to any warriors taking part in raids against enemy tribes.

The Cheyennes and Arapahoes had to go some distance from the agency to find buffalo during their winter hunt the following year. By February, Big Mouth, Tall Bear, Cut Finger, and their bands had returned to the agency. Little Raven's was twelve miles from Fort Supply, Left Hand's on the Cimarron, and Bird Chief's

23 Darlington, July Report, 1871, IOR, NA; William Nicholson, "A Tour of Indian Agencies in Kansas and Indian Territory," *KHQ*, III, 3 (August, 1934), 34–48.
24 Darlington to Hoag, September 21, October 21, and November 13, 1871, IOR, NA.
25 Lieutenant M. M. Moxan to Darlington, December 25, 1871, IOR, NA.

and Powder Face's combined bands were on a tributary of the Red Fork of the Arkansas. While these Indians were away from the agency, seventeen whites filed claims against the Arapahoes for depredations said to have been committed by them. When accused, the Arapahoes blamed the Kiowas, who were furious with them because they would not join in Kiowa war efforts. Darlington believed them. Ten days later, the claims against both the Arapahoes and Cheyennes amounted to fifty.[26]

The Quaker agent, who died from a severe attack of brain fever on May 1, 1872, was beloved by all. One thing he did—removing his teeth from his mouth and replacing them—so intrigued his charges that the gesture became their sign for "agent." All of the Indians in both tribes grieved over his death, and it was fitting that he should be buried in Darlington Cemetery, not far from the present agency at Concho, Oklahoma. His successor was John D. Miles, also a Quaker, who took office May 31, 1872. He worked tirelessly for many years in an effort to help the Indians adjust from the buffalo to the corn and cattle road.

Miles's first problem involved a reservation issue. He had hoped to extend the boundary eastward, since much of the western portion was useless for farming. In May the Secretary of the Interior was authorized to make an agreement with the two allied tribes confirming them in the reservation given them in 1869 in exchange for the one in 1867. Then Miles found himself embroiled in a problem that he had not foreseen. He postponed the council after learning that Henry E. Alvord, special commissioner, was planning to take a delegation of Arapahoes to Washington. Just why Alvord chose "unauthorized" Arapaho agents to speak for the Arapahoes, much less for both tribes, is not clear, unless it might have been that the less tractable Cheyennes were hard to find. Alvord was apparently unaware of any existing jealousy between the two tribes.

After his return, Big Mouth, leader of the unauthorized delegates (the others are not named in the records), reported that the Arapahoes had made a treaty with Washington whereby they

[26] Darlington to Hoag, February 23 and March 12, 1872, IOR, NA.

were to have a reservation separate from the Cheyennes and that theirs would include the major portion of the arable lands.[27] But the part that "capped the climax," according to Miles, was that the Arapahoes had told Washington they wanted the separate reservation because the Cheyennes were constantly getting their young men into trouble. Miles commented: "There could not have been a greater insult thrown at the Cheyennes, for they believe that they are equally as deserving as the Arapahoes."[28]

Now that the delegates had expressed themselves publicly and their remarks had appeared in the press, which the Cheyennes seemed to resent most of all, they were equally anxious for a separate reservation. The matter reached treaty stage and agreements were formulated in October, 1872, and November, 1873, but since they were not ratified, they did little besides stir up antagonism between the allies. The hard feelings so easily aroused were not as easily dismissed.

Another serious problem was the illegal liquor traffic, which seemed impossible to control. Miles declared that if it were not stopped, the Indians would become completely demoralized. He visited the camps of Big Mouth, Cut Finger, and Tall Bear and tried to impress upon them the importance of trading with licensed traders who would not cheat them by giving them whiskey for their robes. Some of the Indian men would watch and wait while their women prepared the hides; then, as soon as the women had finished, they would take the hides and trade them for liquor. This so infuriated the women that they not only cut down on their production, but were also willing to reveal the names of the ranches and individuals guilty of the illegal trade. As a result, eight men were arrested.

Three murders had lately been attributed to liquor traffic, but

27 *House Exec. Doc.* No. 1, 42 Cong., 3 sess., III. 489. Proposed Arapaho Reservation, December 16, 1872, IOR, NA. See also Miles's seven-page protest, Miles to Hoag, March 12, 1873, IOR, NA; *House Exec. Doc.* No. 12, 43 Cong., 1 sess., 1–5.

28 Miles to Hoag, November 4 and 14, 1872, January 28, 1873, and January-February Report, 1873, IOR, NA. Carl Sweezy (*The Arapaho Way*, 19) names the four leading chiefs at the Medicine Lodge council as Little Raven, Spotted Wolf, Yellow Bear, and Powder Face.

Big Mouth, the conformist, was the Arapaho who suffered most. His brother-in-law, Walk-a-Bet, was killed in a brawl during the winter. Tragedy again visited him when his daughter, Emma Morrison, died of consumption. Emma, like her father, had made quite a record for herself. She wore "American clothes" made on a sewing machine and was considered a good housekeeper, a devoted mother, and an excellent cook. Miles tried to arrange a Christian funeral, but it had to be conducted amid loudly keening kinsmen, who gashed their arms and legs and killed their favorite ponies.

The six bands listed by Miles in January, 1873, were Little Raven's, with 64 lodges; Big Mouth's, 65; Powder Face's, 25; Left Hand's, 30; Bird Chief's, 70; and Keith Poisal's, 9—a total of 263 lodges. Yellow Bear and Spotted Wolf, two of the four principal chiefs at the Medicine Lodge council, the others being Little Raven and Powder Face, were not named; they were in the north.

In the spring of 1873, another cloud of gloom was cast over the agency in the murder of Big Mouth's adopted son, Leon Williams, a Mexican, by an Arapaho who bore him a personal grudge.[29] Williams, an employee at the agency, was well respected. Had he been a white man, the agent would have demanded that the murderer be apprehended and punished. Since Indians alone were involved, a council was called and the difficulty was settled between Big Mouth and the accused through the payment of the required number of horses.

Speaking for the agent at the council, William Evans explained to the Indians how the white man would handle such a crime and said he wanted positive assurance that the employees would be safe thereafter. The chiefs expressed their regret that the unfortunate incident had occurred. Powder Face, for one, asked that the whites not lose confidence in the Indians, but since they claimed Leon in their tribe, it was their privilege to settle the difficulty according to their own custom. Commenting upon the matter, Miles said: "We entertain no fears in the future other than

[29] Miles to Hoag, June 1 and 13, July 18, 21, and 28, and September 22, 1873, IOR, NA. See also John H. Seger, *Early Days Among the Cheyennes and Arapaho Indians*, 30.

is common in any community where unrestrained passions come in contact."

A few weeks later, a band of restless Arapaho warriors took to the warpath. Miles sent several members of the Soldier Society after them, and although they returned with thirty-seven, others managed to slip through. They surprised a small number of Ponca Indians, whom they attacked. The Indian they killed and scalped proved to be second to the chief of the tribe and he was carrying a pass permitting him to go to the Osages to effect a truce. Powder Face sent word to the agent that "his heart was on the ground" over such an occurrence, and at the same time, Spotted Wolf proceeded to bring in the marauders. After the young Arapahoes had been punished by the Soldier Society for their conduct, Left Hand and Powder Face, indicating that they did not want trouble, said they would not permit their young men to leave camp again. Big Mouth and Yellow Horse promised to take measures to see that nothing like it happened in the future.

Friction between the Arapahoes and Osages took on ominous proportions in July. There had been several minor difficulties between the two tribes, the most recent being the theft of thirty horses belonging to Left Hand and Big Crow. The soldier element was described as "spunky" and "cross-grained." Yellow Bear, in particular, was out of sorts. The soldiers under Left Hand would not even promise to refrain from retaliation against the Osages. Feelings ran so high that Miles was convinced that if the Wichitas called on the Arapahoes to fight their common enemy, they could enlist the help of the whole tribe.

Relations had been strained between the the Arapahoes and Cheyennes since the reservation issue had come between them. A number of incidents added fuel to the fire. An Arapaho in a drunken brawl was killed by a Cheyenne, and the Cheyenne wife of the interpreter, Ben Clark, was shot and made a permanent invalid by an Arapaho. In addition, both tribes were in a disagreeable mood because their annuities had not arrived. Instead there came four surveyors, whom the Cheyennes proceeded to kill. They gave as their excuse that the whites had not first consulted them and they thought the surveyors had come to take their land.

Two separate groups of Arapahoes from the north rejoined the Southern bands in September, one led by Spotted Wolf and one by Yellow Horse. Yellow Bear had already returned to his people. These Southern Arapaho dignitaries had evidently gone north to visit their kinsmen. They found that because of numerical weakness, the Northerners feared the Sioux, who permitted them to share their rations on sufferance. Yellow Horse told of trouble along the way when the whites claimed some stray ponies in their possession. When the Arapahoes refused to give them up, the whites opened fire, killing four Indians. One was related to Powder Face, who, according to the custom of his people, should avenge his death. It was a crucial time for the Arapaho war chief, who had been trying hard to conform to the white man's rules. But his pledge had been given, and he stayed at peace.

Before the new arrivals left the Northern bands, the latter were estimated to number 1,515 Arapahoes and 1,342 Cheyennes, compared to 6,320 Sioux among the Platte River Indians. Provisions had been withheld from the Northern Cheyennes and Arapahoes until they could be moved to Indian Territory. The bands mentioned above came through safely, but before the main trek could get under way, war broke out in the south. The Cheyennes, Comanches, and Kiowas left their reservations for a final stand in the spring of 1874, but the Arapahoes refused to take part in the disturbance.[30]

When Plenty Bear arrived in April with twenty-five lodges of Northern Arapahoes, he carried a letter from General John E. Smith stating that the transfer of such a large number of Indians was approved. They endured great suffering along the way, for no buffalo were to be found and their ponies were so jaded that they had to walk. But they arrived in time to join the Southerners in the concluding ritual of their Medicine Lodge Ceremony. Although supplies were alarmingly low, the Arapahoes

[30] Hubert E. Collins, "Ben Williams, Frontier Peace Officer," *Chronicles of Oklahoma*, X, (1932), 542–71.

stoutly maintained that they would stay even if they starved.[31] They had incurred the further displeasure of the Cheyennes by their fidelity to the government and their refusal to join the hostiles.

When a small party of sympathetic young warriors tried to slip out to join the Cheyennes, the chiefs issued an order to bring them back. Little Wolf carried out the order, and when they returned, they were duly punished. By using the rigid methods of discipline of his war society, Powder Face was able to keep matters fairly well under control. He calmed the fears of the agency employees by telling them that they belonged to him and that he would protect them.[32]

In defiance of Powder Face, Yellow Horse left Darlington in a hostile mood with twenty-two young warriors and joined the Cheyennes, who (in June, 1873) were holding their Sun Dance on the headwaters of the Washita River.[33] These were the only Arapahoes known to have taken part in an attack upon the hide hunters, horse thieves, and liquor dealers at Adobe Walls (old, abandoned Fort Adobe) on June 9. Following the initial attack, the Indians conducted a series of raids on the Kansas frontier, only to return confidently to Adobe Walls on June 27. Under the leadership of a Comanche soothsayer who promised easy victory, they attacked but failed to rout the occupants. The Comanches and Cheyennes both lost six warriors in the battle, which disillusioned those who had listened to the medicine man. The Arapahoes, who had been given a chance to work off their hostility, returned to the tribe to take their punishment for disobedience. From then on, no Arapahoes, other than a few Dog Soldiers, took any part in the war of 1874–75.

While the Southerners were conscientiously attempting to keep out of trouble, war clouds were gathering for the remaining bands in the north. Numerous depredations were attributed to them in the Wind River area, the most alarming of which occurred

31 Miles to Hoag, April 1 and June 16, 1874, IOR, NA. See also Sabin, *Kit Carson Days*, II, 736.
32 Miles to Smith, June 16, 18, and 30, 1874, IOR, NA.
33 Hyde, *Life of George Bent*, 358.

in a small settlement where Lander, Wyoming, now stands. Here two women were cruelly murdered, their house plundered, and a horse and mule driven away.[34] When raids continued, Captain A. E. Bates and his company of cavalry, guided by Shoshoni scouts, set out to locate the hostiles. General E. O. C. Ord, who, with General Philip H. Sheridan, was at Camp Brown at the time, gives a terse account of the engagement. He says that when the Shoshonis trailed the raiders to their encampment, a company of cavalry under Captain Bates was sent "to attack the camp and break it up." Their loss was two soldiers killed and one officer and three privates wounded. The enemy's loss was reported to be twenty-six killed and a proportionate number wounded, with twenty-one of the wounded later reported to have died.

General Philip H. Sheridan, in a telegraphic dispatch; Bates, in his official report; and Ord do not identify the hostiles by tribe, but James I. Patten, who was at Wind River then and a number of years afterwards as teacher, lay missionary, and later agent, calls them Arapahoes. Patten, who got his information from the Indians themselves when they were finally placed on the reservation, said the three Platte River tribes started from the Black Hills on a raid against the Shoshonis but argued along the way and separated before the Arapahoes made camp at Nowood, a tributary of Wind River. The bands attacked in this encampment constituted the major portion of the Northern Arapahoes under Black Coal, who had become head chief following the death of Medicine Man in the winter of 1871–72. Unfortunately, no account of the affair from the Indian point of view is available, but we do know that Black Coal's horse was shot from under him. He sustained a chest wound which finally contributed to his death. Previous to the Bates Battle, three of his fingers had been shot off, causing him to be called Tag-ge-tha-the (Shot-off-Fingers). He got the name Black Coal when, as a young warrior, he rolled in ashes after a victorious battle with the Utes until he was "black as coal."

[34] Nickerson, "Early History of Fremont County," *loc. cit.*, 5.

The reports of both Ord and Bates leave much to be desired.[35]
Ord praised the military and Bates excused himself for not having
achieved a complete victory by blaming the Shoshonis. To this,
and to Sheridan's statement that the Shoshonis failed to carry out
orders, Agent James Irwin objected strenuously. He claimed Bates
talked so fast that not even the interpreter could understand his
orders.

Lone Star, the reporter with Bates, wrote to please the reader
and colored his story accordingly. For example, he said that when
the camp was located, "we knew that this village was the rendezvous—the infernal nest of the hellish murdering scoundrels that
have infested this country since the white people have attempted
to make an honest living here." Such terms as "fiends," "mur-
derers," "fiendish red devils" were trite expressions in the newspapers of the day.

When the attack began at dawn on July 4, 1874, the Shoshonis sounded their war cry and alerted the Arapahoes, who
poured forth from their tipis. To the north of the village were
two rock-capped buttes, the key to the defense of the camp, and
as such they should have been manned by trained soldiers instead
of Indian scouts. The soldiers lost the advantage of a surprise
attack when the Arapahoes managed to gain the heights, where
they rained lead down upon them. The Shoshonis, who were
blamed for not scaling the buttes as ordered, were busily driving
away the horses. Meanwhile, some of the soldiers, in a flanking
movement, attempted to dislodge the Arapahoes, who had reached
the top of one of the buttes. Captain Bates captured and held the
village for half an hour, during which time the post surgeon cared

35 Ord's report (*House Exec. Doc.* No. 12, 43 Cong., 2 sess., Serial 1635, I,
Pt. 2, 32–33) and Irwin's account (*House Exec. Doc.* No. 12, 43 Cong., I, Pt.
5, 578) were both published. Bates's official report, Sheridan's telegram, and the
report of Captain R. A. Torrey, commanding officer at Camp Brown, are in
WDR, NA. For further accounts of the Bates Battle, the *Cheyenne Daily Leader*,
July 14 and 16, 1874, and James I. Patten, "Bates' Famous Battle," *The (Big Horn)
Rustler* (October 1899). Irwin's reply to General Sheridan's telegram (July 9) is
given in his letter to Commissioner E. P. Smith. Irwin to Smith, September 18,
1874. IOR, NA.

for the wounded in a tipi, but he was soon forced to evacuate.

Irwin points out that aside from failing to understand orders, the Shoshonis wore no distinguishing garb and thus may have been reluctant to expose themselves to the fire of the reckless soldiers, who could not distinguish one Indian from another. The Shoshoni loss was as heavy as the military, the agent pointed out. He made no excuse for the Arapahoes, who brought it all on themselves by their depredations.

Lone Star says 100 Indians were killed and 175 wounded, a figure as exaggerated as his statement that Bates "whipped the Indians soundly." It is true that the Shoshonis ran off perhaps 250 head of horses and that about 50 Arapahoes were killed. But when Bates withdrew—because of a lack of ammunition and the loss of two men killed and an officer seriously wounded—the Arapahoes believed themselves the victors. All that prevented their following up their advantage was that they had been put on foot by the Shoshonis. Following this episode, the Arapahoes returned to Red Cloud Agency, where they were forced to endure the taunts of their allies for not having kept with them in their original plan to attack the Shoshonis.

When the magic word *gold* was sounded, this time in the Black Hills, the excitement was matched only by Indian resentment. The discovery was attributed to Custer's command, which had been sent on a reconnaissance mission the same month as the Bates Battle. Another commission was formed to provide Congress with just such a report as it needed. It determined that the unceded territory north of the North Platte (the vast hunting grounds claimed by the Sioux) was of "little advantage to the Indians." If this were abrogated, it would pave the way for settlement. The Indians would benefit from reservation life and depredations would cease. This was the attitude that resulted in the Indian wars of 1876.

The great buffalo herds of the plains were being depleted so rapidly that by now there were more hunters than buffalo. Colonel Richard I. Dodge claimed that in a three-year period (1872–74), at least five million buffalo were slaughtered for their hides. Although this was in violation of the law, no one had the special duty of putting a stop to it. The Bureau of Indian Affairs gave up after a feeble effort.[36] General Nelson A. Miles claimed the vast numbers of buffalo and wild horses which once wandered the plains were practically exterminated in the Southwest between 1872 and 1877 and in the Northwest between 1878 and 1885. Carl Sweezy, Arapaho, gives the date of the last satisfactory buffalo hunt on the Cheyenne and Arapaho Reservation as 1874.

Although the Arapahoes had little part in the Cheyenne-Comanche-Kiowa war which ended in the spring of 1875, two of their number were found guilty of violating the white man's laws and taken to Fort Marion, Florida, by Lieutenant P. H. Pratt of the Tenth Cavalry. During the three years Pratt worked with the Indians, he was a teacher rather than a jailer. His experience resulted in the founding of Carlisle Indian School in Pennsylvania, in 1879, the first boarding school to be established by the government.

With the imprisonment of two of their number, the Arapahoes learned for the first time that murder charges could not be dismissed by the relinquishment of a few horses. Packer (initials not given), who had killed Leon Williams without provocation, and White Bear, who had made an assault with intent to commit murder upon F. H. Williams, an agency employee, were the two Arapahoes with Pratt's prisoners. Left Hand, who was imprisoned for killing a hunter, was a Cheyenne, not an Arapaho. Agent Miles considered the moral effect of the arrests good.[37]

Following the Cheyenne war, the matter of separate reservations was again discussed. Miles agreed with those who thought the Arapahoes could progress more rapidly when not disturbed by the restless Cheyennes, but the issue remained undecided. Drawing rations with the 1,658 Arapahoes in May were 120 Apaches. Eighty of the original number had returned to their own people, but those who stayed continued to be friendly.[38]

In May, Miles was gratified when Left Hand, Big Mouth,

36 Dodge, *Our Wild Indians*, 295; Miles, *Personal Recollections*, 134; Oliver Nelson, *The Cowman's Southwest*, 296–300.
37 Miles to Hoag, May 1, 1875, IOR, NA.
38 *Annual Report of the Commissioner of Indian Affairs*, 1875, 43–44.

Tall Bear, Heap of Bears, Yellow Bear, and Spotted Wolf attended a general council at what is now Okmulgee, Oklahoma.[39] He felt that the contact with more civilized tribes would benefit them because they would see that they, too, could progress by traveling the same road to civilization. Left Hand gave a speech in which he expressed his desire to follow the example of the Cherokees, Creeks, and Choctaws. He was for peace with the red man and the white, and he hoped that the Indians and the agents might better understand each other. Furthermore, he wanted a good white man to teach him how to farm, for he was strongly in favor of the white man's way of life.

Estimated statistics for 1875 showed a total of 3,229 Arapahoes—1,664 in Indian Territory, the remaining 1,565 in the Dakotas.[40] The Northern bands, demanding that rations be issued through their chiefs, persistently refused to be counted, which resulted in generalizations rather than actual numbers. It also encouraged corruption, for unscrupulous agents were known to up the number of Indians in order to receive additional annuity goods which they could dispose of at profit. A special investigation conducted at the Red Cloud Agency did not prove that the agent was guilty of this, but it found deplorable conditions and established with certainty the fact that he was inefficient and that the Indians suffered accordingly. Black Coal and Little Wolf, with Friday as their interpreter, testified that they were given spoiled food and blankets too short for issue.

Coal of Fire (Fire) and nineteen companions, who left the Cheyenne and Arapaho Agency in August without permission, returned about six weeks later to tell of their harrowing experiences.[41] It took them seventeen days to reach the Northern Arapaho village in the vicinity of Red Cloud Agency. As they neared it, they had a brush with the soldiers and lost several ponies, which were later returned to them. Thirty men and five women joined

---

[39] Miles to Smith, June 1, 1875, IOR, NA; Okmulgee Intertribal Council, Indian Archives, OHS.

[40] *Annual Report of the Commissioner of Indian Affairs*, 1875, 752; *Report of the Special Commission to Investigate the Affairs of the Red Cloud Agency*, 375.

[41] Miles to Hoag, November 5 and December 8, 1875, IOR, NA.

Fire's expedition when it returned to the south. One of the leaders was given a pass by the agent, for every means of encouragement was being used to induce the Northerners to join the bands in Indian Territory.

Soon after the Indians entered Kansas, they saw troops and went into camp on a tributary of the Republican. While the man carrying the pass was seeking to recover some of the tired ponies they had left on the trail the day before, the soldiers struck the main camp. A woman who could speak English went out to talk to the commanding officer, to whom she explained that the agent had given them a pass, which was being carried by one of the men who had gone in search of their ponies.

The officer, setting out to locate him, demanded that the Indian guiding him surrender his gun. This he refused to do, and the officer opened fire. Hearing the sound, the soldiers also began firing; one Indian was killed. Fire believed the troops were worsted because one of their horses was killed and two others, captured by the Indians, had empty saddles. The officer obviously did not know that a warrior would choose death to the surrender of his weapons. Ten of the Arapahoes were arrested and held until Miles made a second request for a hearing. Yellow Horse, their band chief, wanted to meet the officers with whom they had the conflict. He vowed that if his story did not agree with the officers', he was willing to suffer the consequences.

In his message to Congress on December 7, 1875, President Grant stated:

> The discovery of gold in the Black Hills, a portion of the Sioux Reservation, has had the effect to induce a large emigration of miners to that point. Thus far, the effort to protect the treaty rights of the Indians to that section has been successful, but the next year will certainly witness a large increase of such emigration. The negotiations for the relinquishment of the gold fields having failed, it will be necessary for Congress to adopt some measures to relieve the embarrassment growing out of the causes named.[42]

[42] James D. Richardson, *Messages and Papers of the Presidents*, VII, 352.

The Interior Department sent word to the Platte River Indians in December to come to the reservation or be considered hostile. The Sioux, who were hunting at the time, sent back word that they could be expected "when the snow melts." In the meantime, plans were being formulated by the military authorities to force the allied tribes onto the reservation. After the Bates Battle, the commanding officer at Camp Brown had urged, "in the interest of humanity and civilization," that the Arapahoes be compelled to go to their reservation.[43]

In the spring of 1876, three expeditions were launched: one from the east under the command of General Alfred H. Terry, a second from the north under Colonel John Gibbon, and a third from the south under General George Crook. Thus plans were formulated for another major drive against the Plains Indians. When Crook reached Fort Fetterman, he was visited by Black Coal, who told him of a hostile camp some 150 miles north of the post and just below the site of Fort Reno. Telegraphic reports had advised him that three hundred lodges of Sioux had just come in to the Red Cloud Agency, that supplies were low, and that no more would be forthcoming until Congress could make another appropriation. Black Coal's information was interpreted by Crook to mean that there would be only a small number of Sioux and Cheyennes to drive back to the reservation.[44]

He began by placing Major General J. J. Reynolds in charge of the Big Horn Expedition. While plans were being formulated, Plenty Bear and about a dozen lodges of his Arapahoes came to the post to express their desire for peace.[45] He was on his way to the Red Cloud Agency to show his sincerity, and he reported the Sioux as having so many lodges that it made him tired to count them. Black Crow, another Arapaho chief, came with thirty-six lodges of his people to tell of his peaceful intentions. He was afraid something

[43] Irwin to Commissioner, July 6, 1874, IOR, NA; Torrey to U.S. Assistant Adjutant General, Headquarters, Department of the Platte, July 7, 1874, WDR, NA.

[44] Robert C. Strahorn, *Rocky Mountain News* dispatch, February 29, 1876.

[45] *Annals of Wyoming*, IV (January, 1927), 359; John G. Bourke, *On the Border with Crook*, 250, 391–93, 404–408.

was about to happen, and he did not want to be drawn into a Sioux war. From among this number, ten scouts were conscripted. Their most painful assignment was to appear each morning in full military dress, which soon lost its glamor. Little Dog was described by Captain A. B. Cain, who imposed the order, as a "good soldier but a poor scout," though he was the only one who conformed.

On March 17, apparently hoping for a Tongue River-type victory over what he thought to be Crazy Horse's village, Reynolds launched an attack on an encampment of Indians on the banks of the Powder River. They proved to be Cheyennes, who, after being routed, swarmed like angry hornets to the Oglala camp farther north of them. Although Reynolds destroyed their village and all the supplies therein, his success was hollow, for he not only burned blankets and food needed by his troops, but also aroused the antagonism of the Cheyennes. They rallied their forces, and with the help of the Sioux, forced the soldiers to retire. The timely arrival of General Crook was all that saved the day.

The Sioux, infuriated by the attack on the Cheyenne village, began preparing for a major offensive. In spite of the efforts of their chiefs to restrain them, warriors began leaving the reservation with the avowed purpose of forming a war camp at the Big Bend of the Rosebud. By May, Red Cloud Agency had been drained of its young men, and by June, all Sioux bands had smoked the war pipe and were united for a battle of survival.

On May 29, General Crook, in personal command of 1,000 troops, launched his Big Horn and Yellowstone Expedition from Fetterman. Along the way, he was joined by more than 250 Shoshoni and Crow scouts, the latter bringing news of the concentration of hostiles at the Big Bend. In the Battle of the Rosebud, which took place June 17, Crook again met with frustration, if not humiliating defeat, for he was forced by the Sioux and Cheyennes to retire to his supply base to await reinforcements. He had not even reached Crazy Horse's camp, for the Indians had rushed toward him in surprising numbers.

Eight days later, Custer, who was not as cautious as Crook, disregarded orders not to follow an Indian trail if it led in the direction of the Little Big Horn, but to wait reinforcements. Consequently, he and his entire command were killed. The loss of 268 soldiers at the Battle of the Little Big Horn on June 25 surpassed that of the Fetterman disaster. The Arapahoes had no part in the Battle of the Rosebud, but a few may have died while serving Custer at the Little Big Horn. An Arapaho woman, telling of her brother, who was said to have been among those slain, says the only time the Arapahoes ever feared the Cheyennes was when they were fighting with Custer. On the other hand, a short time before the battle seven Arapaho braves offered their services to the Sioux, who accepted them with caution. According to the Southern Arapahoes, these were some of their number who had stalked Custer since the Battle of the Washita.

On his second Powder River campaign, Crook sent General R. S. Mackenzie on a reconnaissance mission, from the General's base on Crazy Woman Creek to locate the hostiles. Mackenzie found Dull Knife's camp on the Red Fork of Powder River. At dawn on November 26, more than one thousand troops surprised the Cheyennes and drove them from their village, where many articles belonging to Custer's forces were found. Although the warriors rallied and fought desperately until midafternoon, the camp and all of its contents were destroyed. Almost naked and with their means of defense exhausted, the Cheyennes retreated through the deep snow to Crazy Horse's camp, about seventy miles away.

In addition to the Shoshoni and Crow scouts who had previously served with Crook, he now had a number of Arapahoes and a few Sioux and Cheyenne friendlies. Captain John G. Bourke says of the scouting force: "It was an improvement over that of the preceding summer, not in bravery or energy, but in complete familiarity with the plans and designs of the hostile Sioux and Cheyennes whom we were to hunt down."

The Arapaho scouts with Crook's expedition were Medicine Man (Sorrel Horse) Coal (Black Coal), Sharp Nose, Old Eagle, Six Feathers, Little Fox, Shell-on-the-Neck, White Horse, Wolf Moccasin, Sleeping Wolf, Friday, Red Beaver, Driving Down

Hill, Yellow Bull, Wild Sage (Sage), Eagle Chief, Sitting Bull, Short Head, Arrow Quiver (Quiver), Yellow Owl, Strong Bear, Spotted Crow, White Bear, Old Man, Painted Man, Left Hand (a Northern Arapaho), Long Hair, Ground Bear, Walking Water, Young Chief, Bull Robe, Crying Dog, Flat Foot, Flint Breaker, Singing Beaver, Fat Belly (Gros Ventre), Crazy, Blind Man, Foot, Hungry Man, Wrinkled Forehead, Fast Wolf, Big Man, White Plume, Sleeping Bear, Little Owl, Butcher, Broken Horn, Bear's Backbone, Head Warrior, Big Ridge, Black Man, Strong Man, Whole Robe, and Bear Wolf.

The hostiles resented the scouts. Captain Bourke tells of Chief Dull Knife's shouting to them, "Go home—you have no business here; we can whip the white soldiers alone, but can't fight you, too." One of his warriors also cried out: "You have killed and hurt a heap of our people, and you may as well stay now and kill the rest of us." After the Sioux suffered losses at the hands of General Nelson A. Miles, more and more of their number returned to the agency. In order to have a complete victory over the Indians, the army called for the surrender of Crazy Horse.

While the soldiers and scouts waited at Fort Robinson (Nebraska) for Red Cloud and Spotted Tail to effect the surrender of Crazy Horse, Captain Bourke had an opportunity to observe the Arapaho scouts, whom he found to be "of fine mental calibre." He states: "In all that galaxy of gallant soldiers, white and copper-colored, whom I met . . . none stands out more clearly in my recollection than Sharp Nose. He was the inspiration of the battlefield. He reminded me of a blacksmith; he struck with a sledge-hammer, but intelligently, at the right spot and right moment. He handled men with rare judgment and coolness, and was as modest as he was brave."

Bourke also provides insight into the nature of some of the other Arapaho leaders. He speaks of Black Coal as an able and respected chief; the handsome Washington as one with a desire to walk "in the new road"; Friday as Friday Fitzpatrick; Sorrel Horse as a medicine man, ventriloquist, magician, and card shark; and White Horse as a "grim sort of wag but something of a linguist." White Horse proved to Bourke that his difficult language was a "well constructed dialect, inferior to none of the aboriginal tongues in North America." Six Feathers, who became Crook's "brother," profited more from the experience than did the General.

After the war of 1876, the Arapahoes for a time accepted rations with the Sioux at Red Cloud Agency. Then, in 1878, they reluctantly agreed to go to Indian Territory. Anything seemed preferable to being dominated by the Sioux. But when they reached the Platte, they divided, part going south, the rest refusing to move farther until they had a chance to talk to Washington. They wanted a reservation near the site of old Fort Caspar. Reduced to poverty and depleted in numbers, they made camp near Fort Fetterman. The governor of Wyoming urged that they be placed temporarily upon the Wind River Reservation, a plan that was satisfactory to the Indians, who had already attempted to deal with Chief Washakie on two occasions.

The first delegation to be sent to Wind River for that purpose had included Medicine Man, Sorrel Horse, Friday, Little Wolf, and Cut Foot, who returned to their people after spending twelve unsuccessful days trying to locate the Shoshoni chief. The second, three months later, had included Medicine Man, Knock Knees, Little Wolf, Black Bear, Little Robe, and Sorrel Horse. All they accomplished was a temporary peace, in 1870, which was soon broken. Bitter enmity had existed between the two tribes since that time.

Agent James Patten of the Shoshoni Agency had no knowledge of a government plan to move the Arapahoes from Fetterman to Fort Washakie until he received a telegram instructing him to proceed to their encampment with the necessary supplies.[46] Upon arrival, he found they were adequately supplied with meat—they had just completed a successful hunt—but were without ammunition and the staples, flour, sugar, and coffee, which had become a

[46] Commissioner of Indian Affairs (telegram) to Agent Patten, December 4, 1877.

necessary part of their diet. Their lodge skins were so old and worn that two or three families were crowded into each tipi. Through Friday, the Indians claimed they no longer wanted to suffer the abuse of the Sioux but would like to have a reservation of their own where they could learn to farm. Plenty Bear, who had visited Washington the year before with Black Coal, said the whites had captured three boys and one girl at the time Black Bear was killed and their mothers wanted them returned if they were still alive.[47]

Black Coal referred to the President's promising him an agent, which he had now wanted four years, and said he was glad finally to see him. He maintained that the Arapahoes wanted peace but the Sioux would not let them have it. At the time of Patten's visit, the tribe was mourning the death of Black Coal's "brother."

The agent, with Friday as his guide, visited every tipi and made an official count. Well received, he was impressed by the character of Black Coal, Sharp Nose, and Six Feathers, who, he predicted, would lead in the civilization of their people.

When the agent was advised to return to his reservation, he sent ahead a four-month supply of rations and asked whether the move was to be temporary or permanent.[48] He suggested that peace be effected between the Shoshonis and Arapahoes before the latter were permitted to enter the reservation. Later he said the Shoshonis strongly objected to the Arapahoes' being brought to Wind River. They were willing to make peace a second time, but they wanted the Arapahoes on a separate reservation.

The autumn before, the agent (then Dr. James Irwin) had alleviated the fears of the Shoshonis by telling them that the government had not the remotest intention of placing the Arapahoes on their reservation. He thought they would be placed on a piece of land at Sweetwater. When he heard that plans were being formulated to take them to Wind River, he protested (from

[47] *New York Times* (account of Arapaho visit in Washington), September 26 and 28, 1877.
[48] Commissioner of Indian Affairs to Patten (telegram), January 4, 1878; Patten to Commissioner (telegram), February 21, 1878.

Philadelphia, where he was at the time) that even if the Shoshonis agreed, it would not be fair.[49]

Eventually, Washakie, who had "too great a heart to say no," reluctantly consented to the Arapahoes' being placed on his land until other arrangements could be made.[50] But he was not on hand to greet them when they arrived. His absence may account for the fact that they were placed on the more fertile lands in the Wind River Valley, with the two bands, one under Black Coal, the other under Sharp Nose, camping apart.

Ed Farlow, who lived and worked among the Indians many years, met scout Frank Grouard, on Beaver Creek in March, 1878, and Grouard told him that what he feared to be a bunch of hostiles in the distance was a band of Northern Arapahoes being moved from the present site of Casper, Wyoming, to Wind River until a reservation could be found for them.[51]

Grouard also told Farlow that there were two white captives among the Indians, a boy and a girl. The boy proved to be Charlie Whiteman, then twelve or fourteen years of age, who spoke only Arapaho. Charlie, whose parentage was never known, lived with the Indians until his death, and his descendants may still be found among the Northern Arapahoes. The girl, fifteen-year-old Lizzie Fletcher was blue-eyed and sandy haired but tanned almost as dark as an Indian. She may even then have been the wife of John Broken Horn, who had served as a scout under Crook. Later (at Casper, Wyoming) she was positively identified by her sister (Mary), who was captured with her in 1865 but ransomed sometime later. Through an interpreter, Lizzie denied being white. She was an Arapaho, she maintained, and as such she lived and died.

[49] Irwin to Patten, in *Annual Report of the Commissioner of Indian Affairs*, 1877, 19. The Arapahoes arrived at Wind River March 18 and April 6 and 11, 1878.
[50] Hoyt (July 17, 1878) conferred with Washakie, Black Coal, Sharp Nose, and Friday. Hoyt Letterbooks, NA; Hoyt, Autobiography, Wyoming Archives and Historical Department, Cheyenne. For his twelve-page report of his visit to the Wind River Reservation, see Wyoming Superintendency, IOR, NA.
[51] E. J. Farlow, "Memoirs," Wyoming State Archives and Historical Department, Cheyenne, 244; Mary J. Allen, *Twentieth Century Pioneering* (experiences at Riverton, Wyoming), 23, 24.

CHAPTER ELEVEN

The New Road

Religious acculturation was fostered by the Grant Policy, which resulted in the opening of schools by church groups to which the various agencies were assigned. These were managed under contract with the financial aid of the government, but the mild-mannered Quakers at Darlington proved no match for the capricious young Indians. John H. Seger, who came to the agency in 1872 to do masonry work, became superintendent of the school three years later through sheer ability to cope with the Indians.[1] He could perform feats that made him nothing less than a medicine man in the eyes of the incredulous natives. They called him Johnny Smoker because of a ditty he sang to gain the attention of the rowdy boys, over whom the smiling Quaker superintendent had no control. It was a round, demonstrating in pantomime how Johnny blew his horn, beat his drum, played his violin, and smoked his pipe. In his fearless handling of the Indians, Seger at length won the respect of even the most fractious.

In the fall of 1877, S. S. Haury, a Mennonite missionary, conducted a study of the Arapahoes and Cheyennes and spent three days visiting Powder Face. As a result, he decided that mission work should be undertaken among the Arapahoes. He had also been well received by Cut Finger, who promised him land for his mission.[2] Haury gave as his good reasons for wanting to work among the Arapahoes that they seemed more receptive than

---

[1] Seger, *Early Days*, 23–24; Seger material, Manuscript Division, University of Oklahoma, and OHS; Interview with Miss Genevieve Seger, Geary, Oklahoma, 1966.

[2] H. P. Krehbiel, *The History of the General Conference of the Mennonites of North America* (cited hereafter as *General Conference*), 249, 250–52, 282–322.

the Cheyennes, that the Indian agent advised his starting there, and that he felt himself drawn to the tribe. He went east for the necessary permission from the church board; while there, he had serious eye trouble, delaying his return three months. Once back in Indian Territory, he discovered that a month after his departure the Quakers had entered the field and had located a mission at Darlington. Discouraged, he turned his attention elsewhere.

The year 1880, the "time of short rations," was especially trying for Agent Miles, for the Indians increased their demands and he was without instructions from the commissioner to meet them.[3] As a result, some of his disgruntled charges quirted him and fled to the sandhills southeast of Fort Reno. Major George Randall and about three hundred soldiers prepared for action, but first the Major decided to talk with the Indians. Accompanied by Ben Clark, the interpreter, he set out toward a large Cheyenne encampment, where he believed the trouble had originated.

Clark reported that when they arrived, the Major ordered him to stand on a box and tell the Indians that he had on the march from the end of the railroad at Caldwell, Kansas, "more soldiers than there were blades of grass" and that if they chose to fight, the troops would "wipe them off the face of the earth." The bluff worked, and the Indians dispersed.

Miles sent word to Haury that his denomination (the Quaker) proposed to confine its activities to the Cheyennes and urged that the Mennonites, through Haury, take up their work among the Arapahoes. On his return to Darlington, Haury was greeted as an old friend by the agent and his Indians, and Big Mouth embraced him with a tenderness that surprised the spectators. Miles observed that Big Mouth was always one of the very first to give his support to anything that was suggested for the betterment of his people, even to accepting the white man's religion. As a consequence, a house was built for him before the housing was completed for the agency employees. Big Mouth's dwelling was a story and a half, with two rooms on both the first and second floors. It was the

[3] H. C. Keeling, "My Experience with the Cheyenne Indians," *KHQ*, IX (1909-10), 313; *Annual Report of the Secretary of War*, 1880, 89-90.

most comfortable house at the agency, as well as one of the most pretentious, for it had a fireplace and plastered walls.

When it was ready for occupancy and the keys were turned over to him, Big Mouth looked it over carefully. Then he said it was too small for his family—he had seven wives and each wife had seven children. He claimed that he should have at least one room for each wife so that there would be no discord. When the agent looked crestfallen, the Arapaho hastened to console him by saying: "I'll tell you what I'll do, I'll move my camp close to the house and use it for my dogs to sleep in, and I will store my raw buffalo hides there while my seven wives are engaged in tanning them."[4] This is what he did.

Powder Face, the noted war chief, was perhaps the most progressive chieftain among the Southern Arapahoes. He had been so impressed by his visit to Washington that he resolved to follow the white man's ways. This proved profitable, for by 1880 he had 107 head of cattle on his own farm on the Canadian. He believed that the young men of the tribe would follow the example of their chiefs if they would wear white men's clothing.[5]

The Mennonite mission, which was built large enough to accommodate the Haury family and twenty-five Arapaho children, was completed at Darlington in August, 1881.[6] Six months later, it was destroyed by fire, and four small children, including the Haurys' infant son, were overcome by fumes. While plans were being made to rebuild, Miles informed the Mennonites that Fort Cantonment, located about sixty miles northwest of Darlington, was to be abandoned by the government. Since the most prominent Arapaho chiefs had camps in that vicinity, he thought it would be wise to establish a mission there; he added that the vacated buildings could be used without charge for mission purposes.

Fort Cantonment (Canton, Oklahoma) was abandoned by the government October 2, 1882, and missionary H. R. Voth was

[4] Seger, *Early Days*, 16–19.
[5] *Cheyenne Transporter*, December 24, 1880.
[6] Krehbiel, *General Conference*, 287–90.

sent to look after the property until the transfer could be completed.[7] There were twenty-five buildings of different sizes, including two constructed of brick, the hospital and the bakery. The former, built at a cost of twelve thousand dollars to the government, was given to Little Raven for his faithfulness to the cause of peace. His new home was not in the style of the President's mansion, but it was commodious and he was greatly pleased. It proved an excellent place to keep his horses while he camped in the yard. Among his descendants in Oklahoma, the story is told that the Cheyennes highly resented his being thus favored and sent word that they were coming to destroy both the building and its owner. The old chief and his family dressed in their best clothing. They were prepared to die, for there was no purpose in trying to fight their allies. Little Raven's calm acceptance of the inevitable disconcerted the Cheyennes, who withdrew, leaving him to enjoy his mansion in any way he saw fit for the remainder of his days.[8]

Missionary work among the Arapahoes and Cheyennes was difficult. The Indians who had so recently roamed at will were now confined to their reservation and kept under strict military surveillance, which to them was a form of captivity. Speaking of the two tribes in general, Haury comments: "Can we wonder that they hated the whites—their oppressors? Or that they were rebellious and repelled everything originating with the palefaces? Filled with the bitterest animosity . . . they also repelled the Gospel, for was not that the religion of their hated oppressors?"[9] This evalua-

[7] Cantonment was established by Colonel Dodge on March 6, 1879, and it was here that he completed his book *Our Wild Indians*. See "Seventy-five Years of General Mission Work among the Cheyennes and Arapahoes," Bethel College Library, North Newton, Kansas (copy furnished through the kindness of Gus Yellow Hair, Geary, Oklahoma).

[8] Interviews with Gus Yellow Hair (Little Raven's great-grandson), Geary, Oklahoma, 1965 and 1966. "Little Raven," BAE *Bulletin 30*, 770–71. A notation on the back of the picture of Big Mouth (Manuscript Division, University of Oklahoma) states that he was succeeded by Left Hand. If so, Big Mouth must have been a "talking chief" only, for no other source speaks of him as having succeeded Little Raven. Sweezy (*The Arapaho Way*) does not mention Big Mouth as head chief, although he speaks at length of Little Raven and Left Hand as the principal men of the tribe.

[9] Haury in Krehbiel, *General Conference*, 302–303.

tion, so aptly expressed, may explain in part why the Arapahoes later turned with fervor to peyotism and to the Ghost Dance religion, which swept the plains in 1890.

The nomadic habits of the Indians also made life difficult for the missionaries. A family might have its tipi at a certain place for a month or two, long enough to become acquainted with a missionary, then move miles away. This practice complicated matters for Yellow Horse, who had entered into the poultry business with enthusiasm after being given a "squaw hen" and a hatching of eggs. He kept the hen at the head of his bed, where he watched over her carefully. When his band decided to move camp, he protested that it would spoil his poultry business. As a result, the Indians agreed that he could stay only by putting on a feast for the entire band. Yellow Horse was so delighted with their decision that he sold his best buffalo horse and used the money to buy the food.

The hog business suffered in a similar manner. When the Indians decided to go on a buffalo hunt and had no place to leave their hogs, they asked the agent if he would tend them until their return. The request was granted, but after an unsuccessful hunt, they butchered the hogs and had a big feast.[10]

Miles, who found that much of the country was better for ranching than farming, had helped some of his charges to start on the cattle road, and several were beginning to make a "respectable showing." Besides Powder Face, Left Hand, Yellow Bear, Curly, and others had small herds and were improving them by introducing bulls of superior breed.[11] They were not without problems, since rustling and encroaching were universal. Drovers would carry food for the day, but they would stop in overnight camps and turn their stock loose to graze. In addition to range cattle, the agency also boasted of a dairy herd. At the industrial school, three Indian boys, to whom three calves were given in

[10] Seger, *Early Days*, 13–14.
[11] *Annual Report of the Commissioner of Indian Affairs*, 1880, 67–69; Nelson, *The Cowman's Southwest*, 35–38, 42.

1875 for milking an equal number of cows, had started the venture. Five years later, the school had acquired 1,526 head of cattle.

The first count of the Northern Arapahoes after they were placed on the Wind River Reservation showed 913 drawing rations at the Shoshoni Agency at Fort Washakie.[12] Here, too, was friction, for the Arapahoes were subjected to the animosity of the Shoshonis, who considered them interlopers. They railed at them when they came to the agency and spitefully called them Beggers and Dog Eaters. So bitter was the feeling between the two tribes that it was finally necessary to establish a subagency at Arapaho, Wyoming, commonly called Lower Arapaho.

Lieutenant H. R. Lemley of Fort Washakie, writing for *Harper's New Monthly Magazine*, had a high regard for Black Coal, Sharp Nose, Six Feathers, and Washington.[13] It is impossible to establish with certainty what caused the death of Medicine Man, whom Black Coal succeeded. One story has it that he died at Fort Fetterman from eating the white man's food. Another (the one told by his descendants) is that he was accidentally shot and killed by an Indian who fired into a tipi with the intention of hitting someone else.

Lemley found Black Coal remarkably intelligent. Ordinarily he wore his native costume, but on special occasions he would discard this for a broadcloth suit presented to him by the Secretary of the Interior when he was in Washington. His outfit was completed with a watch and chain and a white felt hat, to the crown of which was attached an eagle feather. His tipi, the largest in the village, was decorated with beaded circles from the centers of which dangled scalplocks taken in battle against the Utes. At one time it was proposed that a poster of Black Coal be made to show that an Indian could be civilized.

Six Feathers, who was hospitable and friendly, invited young Lemley to dinner, which was served on plain white china. The meat consisted of stewed dog, slightly sweetened boiled rice, bread

[12] *Annual Report of the Commissioner of Indian Affairs*, 1880, 176. The subagency was founded at Lower Arapaho (Arapaho, Wyoming) about 1890.

[13] H. R. Lemley, "Among the Arapahoes," *Harper's New Monthly Magazine*, XL (March, 1880), 494–501.

"baked by reflection," and tea. When Lemley stated that Washington resembled the "Father of his Country," the artist for *Harper's* attempted to prove his point by adding a three-cornered hat above his noble brow. Lemley said Washington was a medicine man who, whatever the diagnosis, would invariably administer the same treatment, consisting of beating his own accompaniment while he sang and danced wildly about the patient, who was either frightened to death or recovered by natural process. If the former, the evil spirit triumphed; if the latter, the good.

In speaking of Sharp Nose, Black Coal's head soldier, Lemley says: "His eyes are as bright and as piercing as an eagle's. Nothing escapes his vision. Sharp Nose rendered invaluable service to Colonel Mackenzie in his winter campaign against the Cheyennes, in 1876–77. His 8-year-old son, an intelligent and active lad, frequently accompanies him on less hostile expeditions." This son was among the Arapahoes sent to Carlisle Indian School in Pennsylvania by his progressive father.

Lemley, whom Friday served as an interpreter, was one of the last to write of him, and what he had to say was not flattering. He claimed Friday had relapsed into barbarism and that he had forgotten how to read and write. Yet his knowledge of the English language provided him with a vocation, for he was official interpreter at the agency. When he died of a heart ailment May 13, 1881, at the probable age of fifty-nine, he was greatly missed. As an interpreter of his difficult language, he was the most useful Indian on the reservation. He was never head chief, but in his constant effort to maintain harmonious relations with the whites, he was recognized as a peace chief. It was because of his long acquaintance with Washakie that the Shoshoni chief allowed the Arapahoes to come to his reservation on a temporary basis. Perhaps the Arapahoes have purposely misled the whites into thinking his grave has been lost. Robert Friday, grandson of Friday Fitzpatrick, as Bourke called him, said it had been.[14] The grave shows evidence of having been disturbed, perhaps by souvenir hunters.

[14] Statement of Robert Friday in "Arapaho," No. 4445, BAE, Smithsonian Institution. Robert Friday, grandson of Chief Friday, was also an outstanding tribal leader.

Seeking trade with the Wind River Indians, William A. Baillie-Grohman found Black Coal as jealous as he was intelligent.[15] The trader was invited into his big tipi, where the Chief received him in the usual stoic manner. With Black Coal were two wives, "very superior personages." When Baillie-Grohman showed his wares, the Chief gathered up several papers of vermilion and put them in the pocket of his old soldier's cape. The trader commented: "Now to allow this would have been madness, for if ever a white man lets a wild Indian possess himself of the proverbial finger, he is apt to want not only the hand, but also the body of the finger's owner." So he flourished his revolver and told him that he wanted the paint returned. It was. At the conclusion of the business deal, Baillie-Grohman thoughtlessly dropped the two remaining paints into the laps of the women opposite him. With a bound, Black Coal was on his feet, and had the revolver not been in evidence, the gesture might have cost the white man his life. The Chief raised himself to his full height and, stretching out his arm, pointed to the door. "Go!" he ordered, and his visitor left with alacrity.

Black Coal was considered the "hidden hero of the Rockies" by the Reverend John Roberts of the Episcopal mission at Fort Washakie.[16] He maintained that he would never have been able to establish a government school had it not been for Black Coal's aid. He considered him a peer of the great Shoshoni Chief Washakie, for he was "brave and calm and magnanimous, a fine fellow."

In the south, when one of the Cheyennes made an attempt upon the life of Agent Miles in 1882, a cry went up to disarm the Arapahoes and Cheyennes.[17] According to Miles, this could have been accomplished by nothing short of war. He estimated that the Arapahoes alone, exclusive of the Indian police, had 181 breech-loading and magazine guns, 1,108 other arms of various kinds, and about 1,800 rounds of ammunition. He was convinced that the

15 William A. Baillie-Grohman, *Camp in the Rockies*, 278–80.

16 Ziegler, *Wyoming Indians*, 41–42.

17 Miles Report, January 25, 1882; Miles to Commissioner, May 17, 1882; IOR, NA; Seger, *Early Days*, 58–88.

Indians would resist to the death. Before any action was taken, Miles thought it would be well to consider that the Indians of both tribes were armed and mounted. If they were required to give up their arms, all because one Indian had demonstrated hostile action, it would show complete lack of faith and those who worked with them so arduously would be the first to suffer.

Miles advocated establishing a "Court of Justice" within easy reach of the agency. He felt that the guilty Indians should be held accountable by law instead of launching a military offensive against the whole tribe. If the Indians were punished individually, their tribesmen would have more wholesome regard for those trying to help them. Hippy, the obstreperous Cheyenne who had tried to kill Miles, was arrested and sent to Fort Smith, where he spent two years working on the rock pile. The agent reflected: "Time was when the disgruntled Indians would proceed to some remote place on the frontier to retaliate for wrongs, imaginary or real, but as subsistence beyond the agency is cut off, they will seek revenge for all their grievances upon those who have charge of their management." Apparently the Cheyennes were not in sympathy with Hippy, who had repeatedly caused trouble, for there were no retaliations.

Following the fire that destroyed the Mennonite mission, fourteen Arapaho boys were taken to Halstead, Kansas, and placed in the home of Christian Krehbiel in what was doubtless the forerunner of the "outing system." This was perfected by Richard H. Pratt, founder of Carlisle Indian School.[18] The thrifty Mennonites called theirs an industrial school, where they taught the boys the self-satisfaction of personal labor.

The Arapahoes favored the rich bottom lands on the North and South Canadian rivers about ten miles from the agency. Powder Face, Left Hand, and some of the other tribal leaders were continuing to improve their herds, which were surpassed by few.[19] They were less easily discouraged than the Cheyennes, and some of the younger members of the tribe were beginning

18 Cheyenne and Arapaho Files, OHS.
19 *Annual Report of the Commissioner of Indian Affairs*, 1883, 60–61, 66.

to follow the example of their leaders by taking an interest in agriculture.

In his concluding report in 1883, Miles mentioned some of the events during his twelve years of conscientious service. In summary, he said he felt that some of his efforts in the Arapahoes' and Cheyennes' behalf had been a success while others had not, but in all things he had tried to do his duty in accordance with his best judgment. To this the Arapahoes would have agreed, for they thought well of their agent.

Hubert E. Collins, who came to Darlington in 1883 to be with relatives, gives an excellent account of the agency as he saw it. He was chiefly impressed by beef issue day, which he re-creates in all of its exciting detail.[20] He spoke most favorably of the war chief Powder Face, who was second only to Left Hand when the latter became head chief following Little Raven's death.

The first definite step toward forced acculturation was taken on the Wind River Reservation in 1884 when the government built a boarding school for the children of both tribes. The Catholics of Omaha, who gave five thousand dollars toward its furnishings, had been granted permission to operate the school. But when Father John Jutz, arrived, he learned it had been turned over to the Episcopalians.[21] With the agent's permission, he then decided to start a mission (St. Stephen's Catholic Mission) among the Arapahoes. When he chose the site for his camp and set up an altar for Mass, Black Coal, his two wives, and their two children witnessed the celebration of the Divine Mysteries. A mission house, consisting of four rooms on the ground floor and one in the attic, was built, but the priest was soon transferred. He sold the furnishings and left the house in Black Coal's care. The next priest had to pay the chief thirty dollars for the property, as Black Coal claimed it "by right of prescription."

In 1886 a convent was built, but in 1887 it was discovered that the structure had been built on sand and one wall was unsafe. A new location on solid rock was selected and construction begun.

[20] Collins, *Warpath and Cattle Trail*, 180–224.
[21] Patrick A. McGovern, *History of the Diocese of Cheyenne*, 196–217.

Eleven months later, in 1888, the building was completed and ninety children were enrolled in the Catholic school. Mentioning this in his report, Agent Thomas M. Jones said: "The building is among the Arapahoes, and I trust after the varied trials and hardships they have had it will prove a blessing."[22] Black Coal was as active in his support of the Catholic school as he had been of the Protestant. Though blind and around ninety years of age, Mike Goggles, Sr., of Arapaho, Wyoming, reminiscing about his childhood, recalled in 1966 the way in which Black Coal used to come into the classroom and encourage the children to work hard and learn all they could. His influence still lingers at Wind River.

D. B. Dyer, who succeeded Miles on August 9, 1884, found the Southern Arapahoes "quite tractable, good-natured, and inclined to be progressive, but like all Indians lacking in adhesion and zeal and aggressive habits."[23] The agent had neither sympathy nor understanding of the Indian and his problems. As a consequence, there was constant conflict during the two years he was there. He was as jittery as Governor Evans had been in Colorado. When the Indians donned their paint and feathers and galloped through the streets, he was sure an outbreak was to be expected momentarily. His plea for military protection was so frantic that troops were sent to quell a nonexistent disturbance. The Indians enjoyed this as a big joke.

During Dyer's time, a delegation of Cheyennes and Arapahoes was sent to Washington, with Left Hand and Row-of-Lodges representing the latter.[24] Cleaver Warden was their interpreter. Left Hand had obviously gone to discuss money and allotments, for he was not happy over either. The Indians, he claimed, were in a "bad fix" financially and families were being scattered through allotments. Furthermore, he wanted his land looked after better

[22] *Annual Report of the Commissioner of Indian Affairs*, 1886, 88; Interview with Mike Goggles, Sr., Lower Arapaho (Arapaho, Wyoming), 1966.
[23] *Annual Report of the Commissioner of Indian Affairs*, 1884, 73. The Indians seem to have made the most of Dyer's state of nerves. See Sweezy, *The Arapaho Way*, 58–59.
[24] Talks with Cheyennes and Arapahoes, Bureau of Indian Affairs, March 16, 20, and 21, 1895, IOR, NA.

in the future. "It seems to me," he complained, "that the white man got the allotments instead of the Indian." While he was away from home on a trip to the agency, a number of whites cut his timber and stole furniture and cooking utensils from his house. "It is a shame," he declared, "to a white man to do so because he should have the same respect to an Indian as to a white man. . . . Heretofore a good many of our Indians have had trouble with the white people; in fact they have been beaten in every case that has been in the courts no matter how strong the evidence has been. It might be because the white man speaks his own language and understands the ways of giving testimony in the case, and the Indian has not got so much intelligence to tell his own case, and so he gets beaten."

Left Hand was glad that milch cows were being bought for the Arapaho schools, but he displayed resentment at corporal punishment and he wanted the superintendent removed. Punishment of any sort was unknown except in the age societies, which were gradually dying out. All children were uninhibited. Left Hand was also displeased with the agency doctor, as he felt the physician was not accomplishing anything. Then, in a final plea, he asked for wagons, harness, and farming inplements, which the Indians had no money to buy but without which they could not become self-sufficient.

Dyer was thought to be in sympathy with the cattlemen, who had been leasing Indian lands. The leases had been paid half in cash and half in cattle, but the Cheyennes, through their delegates in Washington, demanded that all be in cash. Dyer said in opposition: "Easy money breeds indolence." After gaining their point, some of the Indians felt they did not need to work. Dyer, following two highly competent agents (Darlington and Miles), was at a disadvantage. Even the Indians recognized his inadequacy.[25]

In 1885, President Grover Cleveland issued a proclamation ordering the removal of all cattle from the Cheyenne and Arapaho Reservation. General Sheridan was on hand to enforce the order,

25 Sweezy, *The Arapaho Way*, 58.

which meant the displacement of 210,000 head of cattle, subsequently thrown into a depressed market or sent to overstocked ranges in the Cherokee Outlet or to the Panhandle of Texas.[26]

Captain J. M. Lee, who succeeded Dyer, arrived at a time when the "grass money" had been cut off and the Indians were without funds. The government hired one hundred scouts at twenty-five dollars a month to help clear the cattle from the country when the stockmen were forced to leave. This helped those concerned, but Lee was worried about the "Darlington Loafers," who seemed content to stay around the agency and draw rations. He felt their only salvation lay in removal from the vicinity. Perhaps the most important accomplishment during his stay was the relocation of the "nonprogressive" Indians fifty miles from the agency. John Seger took 120 of them to what was later to be known as Seger Colony (Colony, Oklahoma).[27]

Lee found the Arapahoes and Cheyennes as unlike as "the phlegmatic German and the mercurial Frenchman."[28] He predicted that the Cheyennes as a race would outlast the "fast disappearing" Arapahoes, for he said that if their disease and death rate of the last ten or fifteen years continued, there would be only a handful of them left. He attributed the causes to contacts with the vicious elements of the whites and to lack of sanitation. No adequate facilities had been provided for their care.

Little Raven, the chief without whom the Medicine Dance could not ordinarily be held, pleased his agent by leaving while it was in progress and coming to the agency to transact business. He stayed overnight and slept as unconcernedly as if there were no Medicine Dance. The next day, he told Haury that his young men were gambling with the Cheyennes and that he considered it went "hand in hand" with drinking whiskey. He asked the missionary to do all he could to put a stop to it.

Many of the schoolchildren, H. R. Voth reported, died in school of consumption "principally caused by syphilitic disease."[29]

26 Nelson, *The Cowman's Southwest*, 240.
27 Seger, *Early Days*, 101–107.
28 *Annual Report of the Commissioner of Indian Affairs*, 1886, 88, 114.
29 H. R. Voth's Report, *ibid.*, 1886, 94, 127.

The missionary said Little Raven claimed that when he was a young man, syphilis was unknown. The white man had brought it to the Indians, he said, and unless it could be checked, extermination would follow. The native doctors had no cure.

Ethelbert Talbot, the first missionary bishop in Wyoming and Idaho for the Episcopal church, was impressed by the methods used by the native doctors. He said that the Arapaho medicine man would hypnotize his patient and sometimes resort to a faith cure. Or he would blow chewed roots from his mouth on the bare body of the patient. Then he might suck the blood through the skin. His most beneficial treatment, Talbot believed, was his herb teas. The missionary was told the way in which the famous Medicine Man once received his "diploma from the powers of the air."[30] He heard a voice calling him from above. Stepping outside his tipi, he saw a paper floating down toward him. This paper, which the Northern Arapahoes still mention with awe, was reportedly shown to the soldiers when they attempted to make Medicine Man move his people to Indian Territory. It was so powerful that they had to grasp it firmly while it was being read. Through the magic of its words, the officers said no more to Medicine Man about moving south. The message on the document remains a mystery. When asked what became of the paper, the Arapahoes say it was torn to bits and distributed among the headmen of the tribe.

This legend is similar to one told about Little Raven, who, according to the Southern Arapahoes, had a scroll that he alone could read. It forecast the arrival of the white man and was said to have been buried with him, but when his body was disinterred and moved from its original grave along the river to higher ground, no trace of the document could be found. It is presumed that it disintegrated in the moist soil.

Bishop Talbot spoke highly of Sherman Coolidge, the ordained full-blooded Arapaho priest then associated with the Reverend Mr. Roberts in missionary work. He considered the worthy clergyman "a cultivated, Christian gentleman" and an honor to

[30] Ethelbert Talbot, *My People of the Plains*, 262–63.

his race. In physical form and feature, Coolidge was a fine specimen of the Arapaho tribe: tall, erect, broad shouldered, and full chested. His presence was commanding and dignified.

In 1887 the General Allotment Act (also called the Dawes Act) was passed, its object being to lead the Indian to self-support and worth-while citizenship, responsibility, and pride—all necessary for his emergence into the general population.[31] According to the agent's report, as early as 1888 both the Arapahoes and Shoshonis at Wind River had asked "of their own free will" for lands in severalty. T. M. Jones, the agent, believed that unless the Sioux, "or some other foreign element," should interfere, there was no reason why this should not be accomplished at an early date. This seems to have been wishful thinking on his part, for elsewhere is found evidence that Washakie actively opposed such a plan. Well he might, for he considered the entire reservation the communal property of the Shoshonis. From his point of view. the Arapahoes had the status of unwelcome guests. On the other hand, it is not surprising that Black Coal and Sharp Nose favored the plan. Land in severalty would assure them a place to call their own.

In his report, Jones says that the Northern Arapahoes, having no taste for intoxicating liquors, had given no trouble on that score. As a tribe they had kept farther removed from the white man's influence than the Southern bands. Friday seems to have been an exception, having become demoralized through white contact. Had it not been for Captain Nickerson, he would have frozen to death while intoxicated. His dissipation no doubt caused Lemley to say that at fifty he not only had relapsed into barbarism, but also possessed as many wives as fingers.[32]

In the spring of 1890, Father Scollen of St. Stephen's Mission attempted to record an Arapaho vocabulary. Optimistically, he predicted that he could accomplish his undertaking in four months and that when it was completed, "any white man with ordinary

[31] The Dawes Act, *24 U.S. Stat.,* February 8, 1887; *Annual Report of the Commissioner of Indian Affairs,* 1888, 243-45; *Wyoming Historical Collections,* I (1907), 108.
[32] Lemley, "Among the Arapahoes," *loc. cit.,* 494-501.

intelligence and some application" could master the language without trouble.[33] Whether the priest overestimated his ability or the white man's capability is not known, since his undertaking was not published.

Sherman Coolidge, who was a religious leader at Wind River in 1890, gives a summary of the history and civilization of his people in an important miscellaneous document.[34] The Sun Dance, he claims, had no religious character but was merely an occasion for national jubilance. He speaks of the dancers as heroes gaining a certain notoriety which was so dear to their natures. He dismisses the ceremony in the same paragraph with the statement that the Arapahoes have many such ceremonies: the Buffalo, Wolf, Hungry, and War dances. His years among the whites and his dedication to the Christian religion had obviously influenced him. He was not like Carl Sweezy, who, until his death, believed that Man-Above and God were the same and that the Indian's religion differed from the white's no more than denominations differ.[35] When Left Hand tried to explain his attitude to Major George W. Stouch, then agent, the Major was so impressed that he did little to stamp out the native religion. Said Left Hand:

> Our way has come down to us through many generations, and is the only way we know. Among white people there are many ways of worshipping, and many kinds of belief about God. They are all tolerated, but our way is not tolerated. Our children go to school and learn your way and will worship as they are taught. But many of us are old, and can not change our ways. When we die, our way of worship will end. We are so sure that our God and your God are the same that we do not try to take our children away from you; we know your way is good, but we do not understand it. We want you to teach our children your way and let us follow our own. We invite you to come and visit our ceremonies, and to see that they are ancient and reverent and contain nothing harmful.

[33] *Laramie Weekly Boomerang*, May 1, 1890.
[34] "Report of Indians Taxed and Indians Not Taxed in the United States," *Misc. Doc.* No. 340, 52 Cong., 1 sess., 542–43, 627–32.
[35] Sweezy, *The Arapaho Way*, 56–76.

When Sherman Coolidge later proposed to the Northern Arapahoes the possibility of establishing an Episcopal mission among them, they replied "Ethete [good]." Thus the mission, named St. Michael's for Michael Whitehawk, a fullblood Arapaho, came into being at Ethete, Wyoming.

The Cheyenne and Arapaho Reservation encompassed an area amounting to more than 4,000,000 acres, which seemed unnecessarily large to the land-hungry settlers who were clamoring for a homestead. They wanted the allotment question settled so that the "surplus" lands might be thrown open for their use. Under the Act of February 8, 1887, as amended by the Act of March 3, 1891, the Southern Cheyennes and Arapahoes were allotted 528,652.94 acres out of the original reservation.[36] Approximately 3,500,000 acres, for which the government paid $1,500,000 (to be placed to the credit of the two tribes), were opened for settlement. The balance was set aside in reserve for such miscellaneous purposes as schools, agencies, military needs, and missions. Each allottee was to receive 160 acres. At this time, there was but one agency, but in 1903 it was divided into three: one at Cantonment, another at Colony, and the original agency at Darlington. In 1912, Darlington Agency was moved to its present location at Concho, Oklahoma, where the agencies were eventually consolidated.

John Seger was appointed special agent to allot lands to the Cheyennes and Arapahoes. Left Hand, Row-of-Lodges, White Eyed Antelope, Scabby Bull, and Bull Thunder petitioned that W. T. Darlington, son of Brinton Darlington, also be chosen as an allotting agent.[37] Although the Allotment Act was later termed a swindle, Charles F. Meserve, former superintendent of Haskell Institute at Lawrence, Kansas, had praise for it. When he spoke in October, 1902, at a meeting of the Lake Mohonk Indian Conference, he used Seger Colony as an example of how it worked.[38]

[36] Records at the Cheyenne and Arapaho Agency, Concho, Oklahoma.
[37] Allotment Files (1889–92), May 14, 1890, and March 21, 1891, NA.
[38] Charles F. Meserve, "The First Allotment of Land in Severalty among the Oklahoma Cheyenne and Arapaho Indians," *Chronicles of Oklahoma*, XI, 4 (1933), 1040–43.

Meserve said more than 70 per cent of the two hundred Indians at Seger Colony were living on their allotted lands, nearly all of them in houses which had been built since 1888. He said further: "I do not wish to convey to you the impression that these Seger Colony Indians are hungering and thirsting for an opportunity to labor—far from it. But I do wish you to understand that they have made progress in the last ten or fifteen years and it is my opinion, formed from observation that if the Government rations and other aid now granted were withdrawn, they would become independent and self-supporting. . . . The enactment of the 'Land in Severalty Act' as wisely administered as in the Seger Colony is anything but a failure."

The keynote to the active program of forced acculturation was sounded in 1889, the year Little Raven died. The government edict stated: "The tribal relations should be broken up, socialism destroyed, and the family and the autonomy of the individual substituted."[39] Many proposals were made concerning how this might be accomplished. As a first measure, a course of study was proposed and "Rules for Indian Schools" were formulated. The abolishment of all Indian books was included. This did not affect the Arapahoes, for they had no written language, but the prohibition against the use of their native tongue distressed them. They were proud of their difficult language, which few outside their tribe could master. No Indian child was permitted to speak a word in his own tongue under penalty of severe punishment. One Southern Arapaho woman, in telling of her experiences in the government school, says she was so afraid of losing her language that she used to go to the furnace room and talk to herself.

The general plan was to scatter the Indians and discourage their passion for gathering together and holding grand dog feasts and powwows. Such disposition had not been found conducive to the good and quiet of the people, or so the authorities claimed. They also believed that it "facilities the efforts of chiefs and

[39] *Annual Report of the Commissioner of Indian Affairs*, 1889, 3–19. Circulars issued by the U.S. Indian Service, December 1, 1899, and January 25, 1900, were considered too harsh and were revoked January 26, 1900 (Cheyenne and Arapaho Files, OHS), but others of similar nature followed.

demagogues to inflame them [their followers] and set them against Christianity and enlightenment."[40]

On March 19, 1890, the Commissioner of Indian Affairs proposed yet another plan: changing Indian names. The Arapahoes, who were accustomed to ceremonial name-changing, were to have little to say in the matter. As far as possible, the scheme was to provide an English Christian name and retain the surname, unless it might be obscene or of such a nature that it might bring ridicule upon the person. If the Indian's name were long and difficult, it might be shortened—for example, Row-of-Lodges to Rowlodge. Nicknames were to be discarded and a permanent designation made. All names thus decided upon were to be fully explained to the Indians. One wonders what reasons the agent could give for changing such colorful names as Lone Bear to Lon Brown, Night Horse to Henry Lee Tyler, or Yellow Calf to George Caldwell. Captain Nickerson, who was largely responsible for the name-changing task at Wind River, must have had free rein, for we find both Cornelius Vanderbilt and William Shakespeare on the early tribal rolls.

Not only was the Indian supposed to accept and use the English language and adopt his new name, he was also directed to cut his hair and dress like a white man.[41] He was puzzled by these rulings because the white man's clothing was drab and uncomfortable. Shoes were difficult to wear after the pliable softness of the moccasin. Though the Indian found little satisfaction in the white man's attire, he tried to make the best of it, but cutting his hair was a different matter. If it were unsanitary, as the agent told him, to have long hair on his head, was it not also "unhealthy and

---

40 Indian Rights Association, *Annual Report*, X (1893), 29.
41 "Indian Customs" (Cheyenne and Arapaho Files, OHS), U.S. Indian Service Circular, 1902. Charles F. Ashley to C. F. Meserve, Superintendent of Indian School, Lawrence, Kansas, December 10, 1891. Cheyenne and Arapaho Agency Letterbooks, No. 31, 489-90, OHS. In 1890, nine Arapahoes (Left Hand, Row-of-Lodges, Bull Thunder, Black Coyote, White Eyed Antelope, Scabby Bull, Little Chief, White Snake, and White Buffalo) were measured for suits to be made at the Indian school. Left Hand's measurements follow: coat, breast 42 inches, waist 40 inches, length 43 inches; arms, 37 inches; vest, breast 41 inches, length 31 inches; pants, waist 39 inches, hips 41 inches, inseam 33 inches.

unclean" to have a bushy growth of hair on the face? Nothing short of force could induce the older Indians to cut their hair, for it had been instilled in them that it was cowardly to deprive the enemy of a possible scalplock. As one old Indian said bitterly, "I would rather die than part with my hair!" Finally, when it became mandatory that all boys have their hair cut before entering school, the parents would take them to the Sun Dance to have it done ceremonially.

A serious effort was also made to stop the practice of painting. The rule against it was not rigidly enforced, though the commissioner, through the agents, told the Indians that paint was a direct cause of eye trouble.

The most drastic edict of all concerned the banning of ceremonial practices, such as feasts and dances—in fact, gatherings of any sort that might be detrimental to the civilizing influence. This was difficult to enforce, for a religious revival such as the Indians had never known was soon to engulf the plains like a tidal wave.

CHAPTER TWELVE

"Many Ways to God"

T HE NORTHERN Arapahoes were receptive to the stirring tales brought to Wind River by the Bannocks of Idaho. They said the Messiah, still bearing the scars of His crucifixion, had returned to the Nevada desert in the person of a Paiute prophet, Wovoka. He had come to instruct the Indians so that they would love one another. If they would repeat the Ghost Dance, as Wovoka called it, at frequent intervals, use the sacred red paint he prescribed, and practice the principles of brotherly love, the millennium would come and the earth would be restored to the Indian and the buffalo. What better prophecy could be made to a down-trodden people?

Sage was the first representative of the Northern Arapahoes to be sent to visit Wovoka, the founder of the new faith, to learn the ritual.[1] Leaving Wyoming in the spring of 1889, he went to Nevada, where he obtained the original songs of the dance, which he taught to his people on his return. He and the several Shoshonis who accompanied him were so convincing in their reports that the new religion was adopted immediately at Wind River.

Since smoke had always been a medium through which the Indians' prayers were delivered to Man-Above, the great prophecy was given impetus by a dense "supernatural" smoke caused by a forest fire then raging. As the skies cleared, the Shoshonis, like the Comanches, who were never in complete accord with the move, became disillusioned and gradually abandoned the new cult. The Cheyennes, who were also more skeptical by nature, received it, but not with the same exuberance as the Arapahoes, who accepted it unreservedly.

1 Mooney, *The Ghost Dance Religion*, 807–808.

Then a second delegation, including Arapahoes, Sioux, and Cheyennes, was sent to be instructed by Wovoka. This time the Northern Arapahoes were Friday and Sitting Bull (not to be confused with the well-known Sioux chief also of Ghost Dance fame). Leaving Wind River in December, 1889, the delegates finally returned three months later with further convincing evidence.

Meanwhile, the Southern Arapahoes sent Black Coyote (Watanga) and Washee to investigate. Washee, a scout at Fort Reno, went home after being disillusioned at Fort Hall (Idaho) by the report that Wovoka was a halfblood; but Black Coyote, unwilling to take the word of anyone else, went on to Nevada, where he joined other delegates whose enthusiasm he shared. When he returned in April, 1890, he brought the new songs and teachings. He is said to have inaugurated the first Ghost Dance among the Southern Arapahoes. Excitement was at its peak when Sitting Bull came from Wind River to teach the doctrine. He arrived at a propitious time when the Indians were prepared to believe anything. Consequently, they accepted him as a great prophet, second in importance only to Wovoka.[2]

C. C. Painter, general agent of the Indian Rights Association, says in his eyewitness account of the "craze" among the Southern tribes that Sitting Bull had an eagle feather given to him by the new Christ.[3] A skeptic among the Cheyennes laughed at him and his "Messiah." Sitting Bull shook the feather at him, and the Cheyenne tumbled down in a swoon. While in a trance, he, too, saw the Messiah and was converted. A Carlisle student said that although Sitting Bull did not point the feather at him, when the Northern Arapaho looked at him, he trembled.

The commanding officer at Fort Sill instructed Captain Hugh L. Scott to appraise the situation among the prairie tribes and see that the dance did not assume warlike proportions as it did among the Sioux. When news came of the Battle of Wounded Knee, which effectively suppressed the Ghost Dance among the Sioux,

2 Hugh L. Scott, *Some Memories of a Soldier*, 150.
3 C. C. Painter, *Kansas City Times*, November 20, 1890.

the press urged that the Southern Indians be disarmed. Scott recommended patience and caution, for he was convinced that the fire would harmlessly burn itself out. He was anxious to meet the Arapaho Sitting Bull, who had taught the Messiah Dance up and down the plains. Putting four mules on a light buckboard, he drove fifty miles in one day to overtake him.

Scott found Sitting Bull remarkable in that he had light eyes. He was affable, obliging, and an excellent sign talker. The captain established his camp near Sitting Bull's lodge and spent a great deal of time with him so that he might watch him and his proceedings. There he saw the Bible scenes depicting the life of Jesus. The Wichita and Caddo women (in whose camp he found Sitting Bull) would surround him, weeping, and touch him "to get some of the virtue out of him." Presents of every kind were heaped on him. It was even said that he had deposited six thousand dollars with a trader at Fort Reno. After studying the leader and his cult, Scott said:

> Many preposterous and impossible statements were made by Sitting Bull, which he evidently expected to have believed, but which no white man would consider for a moment. The Indian, however, could and did believe them and was willing to stake his life on their truth without a particle of proof. I am convinced that, impossible as they were from the standpoint of our superior knowledge, Sitting Bull himself believed the whole thing implicitly.

James Mooney said in Sitting Bull's favor that he had given the people of the Southern Plains a better religion than they ever had before. He taught them precepts which, if faithfully carried out, would bring them into better accord with their white neighbors and prepared them for final Christianization.[4]

When Sitting Bull came south in the fall of 1890, excitement was so great that an estimated three thousand Indians assembled to take part in the largest Ghost Dance ever held on the Southern

---

[4] Mooney, *The Ghost Dance Religion*, 897, 899; Scott, *Some Memories of a Soldier*, 148–51, 155.

Plains. It took place on the South Canadian River about two miles below the agency at Darlington. Practically all of the Arapahoes and Cheyennes were in attendance, as were many representatives of neighboring tribes. Sitting Bull's hypnotic powers were a marvel to all present.

While the Ghost Dance leader was at the height of his career, Chief Left Hand sought his advice, which was freely given. A commission had arrived from the government to negotiate with the Southern Cheyennes and Arapahoes for the sale of their reservation.[5] Sitting Bull, who was thoroughly convinced of the truth of his doctrine, advised the Chief to sign the agreement, for the Indians were badly in need of the money. Besides, in a short time the whole Indian race, both the living and the dead, would be reunited on a regenerated earth free from death, misery, and the white man. Left Hand signed, but the Cheyennes refused to have anything to do with the transaction, nor did they recognize its validity even after the whites moved onto the land. Through false hopes and unwise guidance, the Arapahoes thus brought further difficulties upon themselves.

The fact that not all of the Southern Indians were in accord with Sitting Bull is seen in a dramatic debate which took place at Anadarko (Oklahoma), in the heart of the Kiowa country, on February 19, 1891. The Kiowas had also sent a representative, Wooden Lance (Apiatan), to investigate the truth of the messiah claims. He wrote from Fort Hall on his way home that he had found Wovoka to be a fraud, but the Kiowas awaited his return to learn the details of his story. Meanwhile, they sent for Sitting Bull, who arrived with a delegation of Arapahoes to present his side of the case. Indians swarmed over the prairie by the thousands as they came to listen to the great Sitting Bull and find out what he had to say in response to the claims of Wooden Lance, who had returned to his people completely disillusioned.

Mooney, who was present at the assembly, gives insight into what transpired. Wooden Lance testified that he found the

[5] For Left Hand's remarks on the relinquishment of the reservation, see Cheyenne and Arapaho Agency Letterbooks, No. 33, May 3, 1892, OHS.

Nevada prophet lying down, singing one of his songs.[6] His face
was covered with a blanket, which he removed at the end of the
song. Then he questioned the Kiowa through an interpreter.
When he asked his name and the purpose of his visit, Wooden
Lance was abashed, for he had thought of a messiah as omniscient
and able to read his innermost thoughts. He told him who he was
and why he had come: to see his little child who had recently died.
Wovoka shattered his confidence by saying that he could not
see spirits.

When the Kiowa observed that there were no scars on the
prophet's hands, he expressed doubt, but Wovoka assured him that
there was no other Messiah. He had preached and had given the
Ghost Dance songs to Sitting Bull and many others, he said, but
the Sioux had "twisted things and made trouble." Then he
admonished Wooden Lance to return to his people and tell them
"to quit the whole business."

It took some time to interpret the report into the languages of
the various tribes. At last Sitting Bull was called upon for his
statement, in which he told of visiting Wovoka the year before
and recounted what he had said to him. He insisted that he spoke
the truth, but he was challenged by Wooden Lance, who accused
him of deceiving the people so that they would give him their
property. To this Sitting Bull replied that he had asked nothing.
All of the presents he had received were freely given; those who
disbelieved could reclaim their gifts. Wooden Lance retorted that
it was not the "Kiowa road" to give and take back.

Mooney, as well as Scott, was impressed by the Ghost Dance
leader, of whom he said: "Sitting Bull spoke in a low musical voice,
and the soft Arapaho syllables contrasted pleasantly with the
choking sounds of the Kiowa and the boisterous loudness of the
Wichita. I could not help a feeling of pity for him when at the
close of the council he drew his blanket around him and went

<hr>

[6] Mooney, *The Ghost Dance Religion*, 775–898, 1901. Mooney (see "Songs
of the Arapaho" in *The Ghost Dance Religion*, 955–1013) says that "for number,
richness of reference, beauty of sentiment, and rhythm of language," the Arapaho
songs rank first. For Ghost Dance and other songs of the Arapahoes, see Frances
Densmore, "Cheyenne and Arapaho Music," *Southwest Museum Papers*, No. 10.

out from the gathering to cross the river to the Caddo camp, attended only by his faithful Arapahoes."

When Wovoka's predictions failed to materialize, Sitting Bull lost his following and was succeeded by Black Coyote, who had dreams of being a great priest and medicine man. Mooney, who knew him well, said: "Black Coyote in full uniform with official badge, a Harrison medal, and an immense police overcoat, which he procured in Washington, and riding with his three wives in his own double-seated coach, is a spectacle magnificent and impressive. Black Coyote, in breechcloth, paint, and feathers, leading the Ghost Dance, or sitting flat on the ground and beating the earth with his hand in excess of religious fervor, is equally impressive." Along with his rise to fame, Black Coyote had acquired two more wives than he had in 1883, when he was merely an Indian policeman.

Black Coyote's arms were covered with multiple scars, self-inflicted during times of prayer for the health of his children, some of whom had died. The scars, seventy in number, were made to form lines, circles, and crosses and on one arm he bore the mark of the sacred Pipe. Two sun symbols, tattooed on his chest, were probably there before he experienced his self-torture.

By using Black Coyote and Tall Bull of the Cheyennes as examples, Mooney illustrates tribal characteristics and shows the difference in susceptibility of members of the two tribes to Wovoka's doctrine. Both were subjected to his hypnotic power at the same time, but they reacted quite differently. They had asked Wovoka to demonstrate some of his supernatural powers so that they could convince their people when they returned. The Paiute, sitting with his sombrero in front of him and his eagle feathers in his hand, quickly reached into the hat and took from it "something black." Tall Bull was unimpressed, but Black Coyote, true to the nature of his people, who were constantly having visions and experiencing dreams, said that when he looked inside the hat, he saw "the entire world." Recognizing the depth of religious belief of the Arapahoes and the skepticism of the Cheyennes, Mooney did not question the sincerity of either Indian.

Although the Battle of Wounded Knee (December 15, 1890) ended the Ghost Dance craze in that quarter, elsewhere there were those who continued to dance and believe. Various dates were given for the millennium, but moons waned and nothing happened. After repeatedly misleading his followers, the Nevada prophet set no further dates, but the stubborn believers would not give up their dance. There was still a faint hope that at some remote time their longings would be fulfilled if only they would dance and pray.

The Northern Arapahoes, unlike their Southern brothers, wore Ghost Dance shirts, which they discovered did not deflect bullets at Wounded Knee. The Ghost Dance was not warlike on the Southern Plains, but Ghost Dance dresses were worn by the women and Ghost Dance tipis were used for ceremonial purposes. These may have helped to create the mood for trances and dreams, in which the Indians envisioned an ideal life after death. They escaped, at least momentarily, the sordid reality of everyday life.

When Mooney returned from visiting Wovoka in 1892, news of his mission spread rapidly and the Indians came in great numbers to see the sacred articles he brought with him and to learn more about the prophet. They would grasp his hand and repeat a long earnest prayer, sometimes aloud, sometimes with lips silently moving. Frequently, tears would roll down their cheeks and their bodies would tremble violently from emotion. Before their prayer was ended, they were almost hysterical, little less than in the Ghost Dance itself. They prayed for a glimpse of "the coming glory," which they hoped might come to them by touching the hand of one who had been able to see and talk to the messiah.

The ethnologist was deeply stirred by a scene in Left Hand's tipi, where he told of his visit with the Nevada messiah. After prayers had been offered, he gave Left Hand some piñon nuts and told him they were the kind of food used by the Paiutes. The chief then handed a portion to his wife, and they both arose, stretched out their hands toward the northwest, the land of Wovoka, and prayed long and earnestly for a blessing of the sacred food and that his coming might be hastened. Mooney characterized the scene as "another of those impressive exhibitions of natural religion which it has been my fortune to witness of which the ordinary white observer never dreams."

When he visited the Northern Arapahoes, Mooney was greeted with the same reverence and awe. He does not name the chief, but he says that when he held out his hands toward him, the chief uttered the short exclamations "Hu! Hu! Hu!" as the Indians sometimes did toward a priest in the Ghost Dance in the hope of going into a trance. In all probability, the chief was Sharp Nose, an ardent believer in the Ghost Dance religion. Black Coal, who had responded to the Catholic influence, did not look favorably upon the cult. He did, however, propose sending Yellow Eagle, who had graduated from the government school, to learn the truth of the new doctrine. When Yellow Eagle reported against the movement (1891), Black Coal considered his suspicions well founded, though much of his tribe continued to believe.

During Mooney's visit to the Northern Arapahoes (June, 1892), he was told by the agent at Fort Washakie that the Ghost Dance had been strictly forbidden and that the Indians had abandoned it. The first Arapahoes whom he and his interpreter met professed their ignorance of the cult. Later in the evening, when Mooney was on his way to the lodge where, he was informed, he would find the elders of the tribe, he heard the unmistakable Ghost Dance songs from a neighboring hill. His interpreter then admitted that the Arapahoes were dancing the Ghost Dance, something he had never reported and never would. "It is their religion, and they have a right to it," he said.

This was also the opinion of Black Coal, head chief until his death on July 10, 1893, at the age of fifty. The following March, the Northern Arapaho tribe, represented by his successor, Sharp Nose, and headmen Lone Bear, Eagle Chief, Bull Gun, Plenty Bear, Eagle Head, and Tallow, erected at his grave on the bluffs west of St. Stephen's Mission a stone obelisk inscribed to the memory of Black Coal. On it, after his name, was an inscription: "Erected by the Northern Arapahoes in honor of a brave and honest man." The tribe set aside eighty acres around the monument as a burial place, "to be dedicated to that use forever and known as the Black Coal Cemetery."

When the Southern Cheyennes and Arapahoes lost their reservation and settlers began to plague them, there was desperation such as they had never known. They danced with increasing fervor, for their only solace lay in their religion. Making one last effort to establish the truth of the messiah, they sent a final delegation to Nevada. It was composed of Sitting Bull and his wife; Washee and two other Arapahoes; and Edward Guerrier, the halfblood Cheyenne. Wovoka, whose peaceful doctrine had resulted in tragedy among the Sioux, had become tired of it all and wanted to be left alone. When the Southern delegation arrived, he told them to go home and stop dancing, that he did not want to be bothered again with the incessant demands of the people.

Some of the Arapahoes were still reluctant to accept proof that the messiah was a hoax. In October, 1893, Black Coyote, through Mooney, dictated to Wovoka a letter in which he begged for some sacred paint, "or some good words to help us and our children." Most of all, he wanted assurance that the delegates sent to Nevada the previous year had brought back false reports. Mooney's comment was: "To one who knows these people, their simple religious faith is touching." Their depression, resulting in complete loss of hope, is expressed in one of their many Ghost Dance songs.

> *My Father, have pity on me!*
> *I have nothing to eat.*
> *I am dying of thirst—*
> *Everything is gone.*

When a Ghost Dance was to be held, a crier went about the camp announcing in a loud voice that everyone was to make ready.[7] Such preparations were elaborate, for each color and symbol had special significance. Second only to the Thunderbird

---

[7] Mooney, *The Ghost Dance Religion*, 920–22.

(the eagle), which was revered by the tribe, was the crow, the symbolic bird of the Ghost Dance. Other symbols commonly used were the turtle, the sun, stars, crescents, and crosses. The morning star was represented by a Maltese cross. When the leaders were ready, they joined hands and sang the opening song, first quietly, then again in full voice, always without instrumental accompaniment. Upon the second singing, they started shuffling their feet in a sideward dance, or "dragging" step, the Naroya Dance of the Shoshonean people. They stood still each time the song was sung for the first time; then they moved clockwise as they repeated it. People would join the circle until there would be fifty to five hundred taking part—so many that there would be large and small circles.

The Crow Dance, an afternoon prelude to the Ghost Dance, which usually began in the early evening, was a special innovation of the Southern Arapahoes and Cheyennes. It was a modified version of the Omaha Dance, which was organized by Grant Left Hand. Trances were also an essential part of the Omaha Dance, but, unlike the Ghost Dance, it was accompanied by an immense drum. The dance was highly colorful, for the participants stripped to their breechcloths, painted their entire bodies, and wore varicolored feathers from their waist in what the Indians termed "a crow."[8] The myth concerning the crow and the spirit world is told in one of the Ghost Dance songs, which credits the bird with bridging the water between this world and the hereafter so that people could return from the land of the dead. The crow was considered so sacred that upon one occasion the Indians in Left Hand's camp captured one that was thought to utter prophetic cries from the spirit world.

At least one blessing came from the "false religion," for Mooney, while studying the Ghost Dance cult and the Arapahoes embracing it, discovered a talented boy artist who painted for him during the summer of 1895. His name was Carl Sweezy.[9] He

[8] For a description of the "crow," see Kroeber, *The Arapaho*, 339. For an account of the Crow Dance, see Mooney, *The Ghost Dance Religion*, 982–83.
[9] Angie Debo, "Carl Sweezy" (an unpublished biographical sketch from her personal files). He gives his own account of his work with Mooney in *The Arap-*

was only fourteen years old, but he was encouraged by the ethnologist, who taught him to paint what he saw. His realism caused him to be criticized in the field of art for a lack of imagination. And yet to the prolific artist, the most outstanding in his tribe, we should be deeply grateful for a careful portrayal of Arapaho culture.

As Scott had predicted, the Ghost Dance gradually "burned itself out." He says: "The Indian was then most susceptible to conversion to Christianity; the name of Jesus was on every tongue, and had I been a missionary I could have led every Indian on the Plains into the church, but the missionaries were not awake to their opportunity." Perhaps he was right. At least he lived at a time when he could appraise the situation. Nevertheless, some of the missionaries were influential, and they made converts who worked conscientiously in the white man's church. Among those to accept the "Jesus road" was Left Hand, who said at the time he was converted at a Baptist revival meeting: "When the Ghost Dance religion came, and I was about ready to embrace it, then it stopped. This Christian religion," Left Hand predicted, "won't stop. . . . Just as I am blind in my eyes, so I have been blind in my heart. I am going to give myself to Jesus in old age."[10]

While the government was attempting to stamp out all ceremonial practices and the missionaries were trying to Christianize the Indians, a cult was growing virtually unnoticed in the Southwest.[11] In fact, it had already spread northward and was a fully developed native religion by the time it was reported among the Kiowas by Mooney in 1891. The Bureau of Indian Affairs and missionaries were unable to determine the nature of the new sacrament—that is, whether peyote and the mescal bean were one

---

aho Way, 62–64. His original sketches, made for Mooney, are to be found in the Bureau of American Ethnology, Smithsonian Institution.

[10] For an interview with J. B. Rounds, pioneer Baptist minister who converted Left Hand, see "Indian Pioneer History," XCVIII, 430, OHS. See also Left Hand's Autobiography, OHS.

[11] Weston La Barre, *The Peyote Cult*, 15, 105–23; Mooney, *Calendar History of the Kiowa Indians*.

and the same.[12] Whatever it was, they decided it was not good for the Indian. The law was on their side if they could but prove that peyote was a mescal intoxicant. Those who counted on the testimony of James Mooney were disappointed, for he insisted that peyote and mescal were not the same and that the former was not an intoxicant. As a result of the confusion and failure to brand the cactus either as a mescal bean or an intoxicant, the session law governing the matter was omitted from the General Statutes of Oklahoma in 1908, thereby removing all legal means suppressing the cult in that state.[13] It was through the initiative of James Mooney that the Native American Church was incorporated in Oklahoma on October 10, 1918.

In looking back over the history of the religious concept, one finds that it may have been new to the white man only when it was first brought to light in the 1890's.[14] Authorities seem to agree that the Comanches and Kiowas learned of peyote from the Mescalero Apaches in the early 1870's. The herb is carrot shaped, its uppermost portion (all that appears above the ground) a succulent green spineless cactus. It was no doubt confused with the mescal bean by early scholars because the Mescalero Apaches derived their name from the use of the bean in their pre-peyote Mescal Bean Cult. The peyote button, the head which has been sliced from the root and dried, has erroneously been referred to as the mescal button.

Mooney first became aware of peyotism among the Kiowas as early as 1886, probably two years after it had been introduced among the Southern Arapahoes. The latter, along with the Cheyennes, were second only to the Kiowas and Comanches in the diffusion of the standard rite of the cult. Quanah Parker, teaching his "Comanche Way," led meetings among the Southern Arapahoes and Cheyennes in 1884.

[12] Cheyenne and Arapaho Files, Vices, Indian Archives Division, OHS; Guthrie Conference, January 21, 1908, *ibid.*

[13] Carol Rachlin, "The Native American Church," *Chronicles of Oklahoma* (Autumn, 1964), 262–72.

[14] James Mooney, "Peyote," in Frederick Webb Hodge (ed.), *Handbook of American Indians North of Mexico*, BAE *Bulletin 30*, II, 237, 846; Kroeber, *The Arapaho*, 320–21, 398–410; La Barre, *The Peyote Cult*, 15, 111, 113 n., 202, 218.

According to a Northern Arapaho version, one of Our People discovered the herb in a vision after drifting into Mexico.[15] (The discoverer is generally believed to have been a Caddo Indian, a member of a war party against Indians in the interior of Mexico.) As one of the peyote priests at Wind River tells the story, two Arapahoes, who had with them nothing but extra moccasins, set out on a peaceful mission, "looking for something good." In their search, they parted. Whoever succeeded in his quest was to call to the other, but one of the men became lost. He was in desert country where there was neither water nor vegetation. The unfortunate Indian was so overcome by thirst and fatigue that he lay down to die. In his delirium, he could hear a voice from above saying, "My friend, what is the trouble?" The Indian replied that he had been looking for something good, but that he had become separated from his companion. Without food and water, he could not last. Suddenly he noticed several green spineless cactus plants protruding above the ground. When he tasted one, he found it refreshing, so he continued to eat until he had consumed four. Then he lay down to sleep. Again he heard the voice speaking to him. This time it said: "I am Peyote. I have come to help you." It told him that Peyote was sent by the Creator, who made every living thing, as well as the sun and the earth. He directed the Indian to carry the herb to his people and teach them its use. Then the eyes and the mind would be opened so that people would know that there is a Man-Above and that they should worship him.

Zoe Friday, who was the matriarch of her tribe (the Northern Arapaho), until her death, stressed the correlation between the sacred Pipe and peyotism. She said the Indian who saw the vision of peyote was told by the voice to return to his tribe and talk with the keeper of the Pipe and learn the full details of the story of the creation. This is legendary, but it shows that to the

---

[15] Mollie P. Stenberg, "The Peyote Culture among Wyoming Indians," University of Wyoming *Publications in Science*, XII, 4 (1946), 85–156. With the exception of the legend concerning the early discovery of peyote, the priests at Wind River tell substantially the same story John Goggles told Mollie Stenberg.

Arapahoes, peyote is subservient to Flat-Pipe, though both serve as intermediaries between the Indian and Man-Above.

The plant may have been worshiped directly by the Indians of Mexico before the coming of Christianity, but both Catholic and Protestant influences have become so much a part of the Peyote Cult ritual that it could not be labeled idolatrous. The Indian uses peyote, either dry or as a tea, just as the white man partakes of his sacrament. Both are offered as supplications to the one God. Though there is little conflict in principle, church opposition has been strong among the Catholics at Wind River and the Protestants in Oklahoma. The Episcopal church at Ethete has maintained an attitude of respectful tolerance, with some of its leading members being professed Peyote Men.

The Arapahoes attribute their knowledge of the ritual to Medicine Bird (Left Hand), who, because of illness, was determined to learn about "the medicine." He is said to have gone to the Caddoes, who took him in and conducted a "healing service" in his behalf. First he was given four plants, but as the evening wore on, he continued to partake until the medicine began to fight his disease. The internal struggle caused him to weaken, but he refused to give up because he was considered one of the bravest men in the tribe. As he said of himself, "My name kept getting bigger all the time."[16] Finally, when he had consumed a large number of plants, he fell asleep and in a vision saw a special tipi with a fireplace behind which was a half-moon, which were lacking at the Caddo meeting. The entire ritual was revealed to him as he saw the way in which meetings should be conducted. The chief (as the Arapahoes call the leader of the cult) told him that he should watch carefully so that he could show it to his people. When his dream was over, he found that he had been miraculously cured of tuberculosis. After remaining among the Caddoes long enough to learn all they could tell him about peyotism, he returned to his people.

The Northern Arapahoes give William Shakespeare credit

[16] Left Hand's Autobiography, 2, OHS.

for bringing the cult to Wind River about 1895. While in school, he became seriously ill and his father sent him south in the care of White Antelope to learn about peyotism. When he arrived, he found a cult meeting in progress, but he was not permitted to enter because the tipi was already crowded. After being refused entry three times, he appeared again and was admitted. When the chief asked why he was so persistent, he explained the nature of his illness. The glands in his neck were so badly swollen that he could not turn his head.

Shakespeare was given the herbs, four at a time. As he continued to consume them and the chief prayed for him, he could feel the power of the prayers and the strength of the medicine working within him. The glands in his neck broke open and drained, and the pain and swelling subsided. After the meeting, the chief directed him to take peyote to his people and teach them how to worship. Shakespeare taught the ritual to John Goggles, who later went to Indian Territory, where he studied under Cleaver Warden, who in turn had been taught by Left Hand. Thus evolved what is known as the Arapaho Way at Wind River.

Over the years there have been various "ways," depending primarily upon the tribes and secondarily on the leaders, who have introduced their own ideas.[17] Considering the nature of the Arapaho, it is not surprising that peyotism has had special appeal. Then, too, he is aware of the racial trend which it stresses. Peyotism through the years since its spread has served as a medium of uniting tribes, at the same time generally excluding the white man, a principle to which the Northern Arapahoes are particularly receptive. Coming into prominence at a time when the precepts of the Ghost Dance had proved false, it offered consolation and an opportunity for the Indian to escape from the monotony of reservation life into an imaginary world. According to one authority on the subject, we cannot be certain that "the religion spread as

[17] Stenberg ("The Peyote Culture among Wyoming Indians," *loc. cit.*, 119–27) explains the Kiowa and Comanche ways used at Wind River.

a substitute for the Ghost Dance, but it is plain that it diffused rapidly around the turn of the century."[18] He considers it in terms of accommodation.

The cult stresses a high moral code, and the priests insist that by "thinking good," one will see nothing but good, though it is not a panacea for everyone. Certain anthropologists believe that peyotism has kept down alcoholism. Unquestionably there are peyotists who drink, but probably not to the extent they would otherwise. The priests insist that if the Indian would "think right," he would not crave liquor.

Those who have unpleasant reactions or see fantastic or frightening objects during a meeting are said to have allowed their thoughts to wander. By controlling one's thinking, one finds inspiration in the quiet meditation of a meeting, where there is no dancing or hilarity of any sort. Music, a necessary part of the ritual, is subdued during the early hours, but it increases in tempo and volume after midnight, when it becomes spirited. The cult services among the Southern Arapahoes and Cheyennes became standardized through the Native American Church, with which the Northern Arapahoes are not affiliated. Each of their priests (there are about fifteen at Wind River) has his own idea of conducting the ritual, but since the Arapahoes are sticklers for form, the pattern for the Arapaho Way is more or less consistent, and it may not have changed greatly over the years.

As in the Covering the Pipe Ceremony and the Sun Dance, there must always be a vow for something of importance to the individual, to the tribe, or to the world as a whole. Vowing is a persistent pattern among the Algonquian-speaking peoples.[19] After the vow, the Indian "puts up" the service. This suggests the pitching of a tipi, though the ceremony may be held in a house, as it is during the winter months in Wyoming. Even so, the term *tipi* is still applicable, perhaps because the cult had its origin in the south, where meetings were generally held in one the year round.

---

[18] J. S. Slotkin, *The Peyote Religion*, 35.
[19] La Barre, *The Peyote Cult*, 58, 58n.

The prayer meeting, lasting from 8:00 P.M. to 8:00 A.M., requires certain paraphernalia, namely a three-foot staff, or symbol of the authority of the chief, a ceremonial fan, a decorated gourd rattle, and a special kettledrum. Fans are symbolic of birds, messengers from Man-Above. The Northern Arapahoes favor the feathers of the eagle, prairie chicken, hawk, pheasant, and magpie, the Southern the snake bird and the flycatcher. An impressive fan at Wind River consists of twenty-four shiny black magpie feathers, stripped halfway up the canes, which are painted white. In the center of the cluster is a Kennedy half-dollar, and added as a final touch is a scissortail feather, which, it is believed, will cause the music to resound.

The rattles are made of rounded gourds about five inches in diameter, usually with beaded handles about nine inches long. The drum, a three-legged iron kettle, is filled half full with water, into which a dozen live coals are thrown before the well-soaked buckskin head is stretched in place. Seven lug marbles or rocks suggest the points of a star outlined on the bottom of the drum by the thong or rope which holds the head in place. Other items necessary for a meeting are a small altar cloth, a smoke stick, tobacco, corn-husk cigarette papers, a bundle of sage, and powdered cedar for incense.

There is no fanfare before the meeting, no food taboo or fasting. The participants (about twenty-four in number in an ordinary meeting) assemble quietly and await instructions.[20] Meanwhile, they talk in subdued tones, for they have come to worship, not to visit. There may be a processional, or they may merely be instructed to "go in." Within a few moments, all of the space on the perimeter of the enclosure is filled.

When the meeting opens, the chief is seated west of the altar, which has previously been arranged in the center of the circle. On his right is the drummer, and on his left is the cedarman. The

[20] The above discussion concerns a ceremony attended by the author at Ethete, Wyoming, on November 29, 1966. For Southern Arapaho participation in the Native American Church, see Ruth Underhill, "Peyote," International Congress of Americanists *Proceedings*, XXX (1952), 143–48. An outline of a Peyote meeting, explained by Frank Sweezy, appears in *ibid.*, 147.

sponsor, or the one who is "putting up the meeting" is on the south. On the altar, there is a crescent-shaped moon with tips pointing east. A groove the full length of the top signifies the Peyote Road over which visions and thoughts pass to and from God.

The meeting opens with the cedarman offering a prayer and the chief placing "Chief Peyote" (a decorated or especially large peyote button) on the crisscrossed sprigs of sage, laid on the center of the crescent and pointing in the four directions. An impressive peyote button at Wind River is kept, when not in use, in a small, heart-shaped jewel box which has a crucifix inside the lid. Chief Peyote rests on a cushion of a sweet-sage leaves. The crown of the button is painted in such a way that sun rays ("God's light") extend from the downy center between pairs of tiny white tufts. On the back of the painted button is a miniature of Jesus, suggesting that peyote, like Jesus, serves as an intermediary between man and God. The Catholic influence is further noticed when some of the participants cross themselves.

A smoke establishes the mood of the meeting. A sack of tobacco is passed around and each participant "rolls his own" and takes four puffs, not for pleasure, but as part of the sacred rite. This is traditional and the only time there is a general smoke during the meeting. Sage is then passed, with each participant taking some, crushing it between his hands, and rubbing it on his body in a purification rite. After the sponsor of the meeting has explained his vow and asked that all pray for its fulfillment, he tells the chief, in detail, his need and the nature of the prayers he wishes him to offer in his behalf. Then, after the sponsor thanks all of those who have any part in the service, the chief offers a long prayer.

Cedar is put on the fire, and everyone "smokes" himself, that is, reaches out toward the fire in a symbolic gesture, then pats the smoke into his body. Next the chief starts the "peyote pan" around, and each participant helps himself to the ground substance with a spoon. The pan is followed closely by the peyote tea bucket. The participant—everyone must be one in order to attend a meeting—places the dry substance in the palm of his left hand, then in his mouth. Though the tea is as bitter and distasteful as the ground medicine, the liquid helps wash it down.

After the chief has served himself, he blows a whistle four times and lays out the ritual items on the altar cloth. Each is smoked as it is held toward the cedar fire. Then it is raised toward heaven four times. In order, the chief, the drummer, and the cedarman hold the staff and fan in their left hand and rattle the gourd with an up-and-down motion of their right, thus setting the pattern for the participants as they sing their four songs during each of the four periods in the meeting. The drummer accompanies the chief in the first group of Opening Songs; then the chief accompanies the drummer and the cedarman as they take their turns.

The ritual items (fan, rattle, and drum) are passed clockwise, with each man present singing his allotted number of songs in turn while the man next to him accompanies him on the kettle-drum. Women, if present, may hand the ritual objects from right to left, but they do not take part in the singing or oral prayers, except for the Morning Water Woman. The firechief collects the cigarette ends and piles them neatly at the points of the crescent. ("The Shoshonis have them all around," according to one Arapaho priest.)

During the singing, there is an occasional interruption by someone who wishes to offer a few words of prayer. Before praying, he smokes (four puffs) on a ceremonial cigarette. At the conclusion of his prayer, he takes four more puffs and hands the cigarette to the chief, who repeats the process, thus adding his prayers to those just offered.

Cedar is put on the coals directly east of the altar, and everyone smokes himself whenever he leaves and re-enters. Periodically through the evening, the firechief takes hot ashes to the altar as he shapes, with wood ashes, a majestic spread-eagle, with wings featheredged with black coal dust. As one of the priests says, it is "like shaping a body," when the firechief creates his work of art with a forked stick, a brush, and his bare hands.

After the Midnight Water Songs, the firechief brings in the water and sets it before the altar. Then he smokes ceremonially, using a corn-husk cigarette, and prays. After that, he passes the smoke to the drummer, then to the cedarman, with each taking four puffs. It is then passed to the chief, who, by taking part in the smoke, adds his prayers to those offered. After smoking, the chief hands the cigarette stub to the cedarman, who places it against the crescent on the west side. The whistle is blown by the chief four times, after which the bucket is passed around and everyone drinks.

Following this, the chief goes outside and blows his whistle toward each of the four cardinal points. At the same time, four songs are being sung inside the tipi. The meeting is resumed as before with the ritual items and the peyote pan and the tea bucket making their rounds. They make four complete circuits during the course of the meeting, with each participant helping himself each time to both the ground substance and the tea. It takes a great amount of controlled thinking to overcome the nausea that results.

As the music gains tempo and the singing becomes more lively, the firechief obliterates his spread-eagle, and in its place makes a conventional ash-eagle. Better than in words, he shows the temporal nature of beauty. He collects and burns the cigarette ends which are at the tips of the crescent. Unlike the Shoshonis, who lift the smokes used by the chief over Peyote Chief and leave one leaning against the inner crescent pointing toward the chief, the Araphoes do not go "over the top." This seems to be a fairly recent innovation, perhaps dating back to World War I.

The chief blows four loud blasts on his whistle before he sings the first of the four Morning Water Songs. Though the words elude interpretation, the first is "like an old man talking aloud to his Creator." He is calling attention to himself. "See me—that is, take pity on me. . . . Here she [Water Woman] comes. Pity her. Woman with water, welcome, *Ha Haa Yah*." This is the general idea conveyed in the Water Song, which calls upon Man-Above to bless the woman and the worshipers. When Water

COLONY MISSIONARIES ON THE TRAIL. At the mission chuck wagon (*seated, left to right*) are the Reverend Walter C. Roe ("Iron Eyes"), Mrs. Roe, and the Reverend F. H. Wright. Near Colony in 1900.

THE MISSIONARY INFLUENCE. Panting Horse, Sherman Coolidge (*standing*), and Black Coal (Shot-off-Fingers).

WATAN, Southern Arapaho band chief, as a deacon in the mission
church at Colony.

Courtesy University of Oklahoma Library Manuscript Division

ARAPAHO SUN DANCERS at Wind River. Note the Sun and Man-Above symbols and the "rabbit tracks."

Courtesy Wyoming Travel Commission

THE GHOST DANCE. Photograph of a painting by Mary I. Wright, made from photographs of the Ghost Dance taken by James Mooney in 1893.

Courtesy Bureau of American Ethnology

SITTING BULL, the Arapaho Ghost Dance leader.

Courtesy University of Oklahoma Library Manuscript Division

CLEAVER WARDEN (Hitunena, or Gros Ventre Man) with peyote fan and rattle.

Courtesy Bureau of American Ethnology

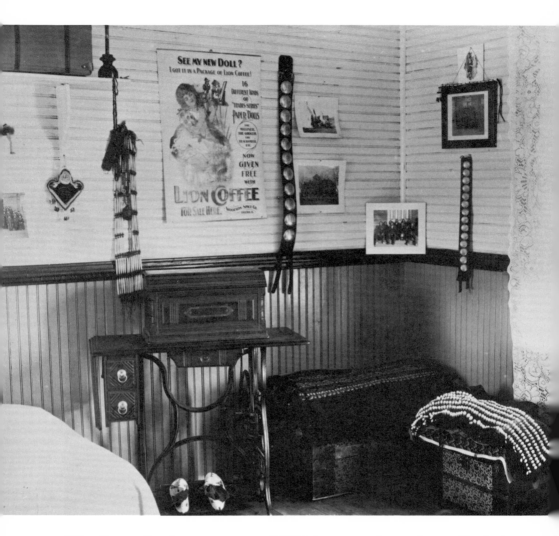

"Mrs. Little Bird's favorite room." With her moccasins on the treadle, she is prepared to travel the New Road. From the Seger Colony Album.

Courtesy National Archives

Woman enters, she carefully places the bucket at the cross (the four directions) made between the altar and the entrance.

As the sun comes up, the second Morning Song is sung and the door is opened wide to allow the sun's rays to enter. This is told in song and alludes to the light woman has brought into the world. The other two Morning Songs are in the nature of praise and thanksgiving for the gift of water. Following the songs, the woman prays, asking God's blessing through the medium of Chief Peyote, upon the sponsor, the chief, the other leaders, the participants, and anyone else whom she wishes to include. When she has finished, the chief takes her ceremonial smoke and adds his prayer.

Breakfast, consisting of three symbolic foods—corn, meat, and fruit (water is the fourth)—is passed around the circle and all partake. The first of the four Quitting Songs in the Arapaho Way suggests a group of Indians camping. They are talking in a loud voice so that all may hear. There are three other songs evoking God's mercy. As the meeting nears an end, there is a burst of music. Although the songs and prayers are nearly all in Arapaho, the spirit is unmistakable. Carl Sweezy says:

> When the service ends at sunrise, and the fast is broken with the water and the food that the woman (Water Woman) brings, those who have taken part face the day and the world before them with a new sense of beauty and hope and goodness in their hearts. Left Hand spoke the truth: There are many ways to God.[21]

Not all of the Arapahoes were as pliable as Left Hand, the Reverend Frank H. Wright discovered when he arrived by hack in 1894 to work among the Cheyennes and Arapahoes as a missionary-teacher.[22] There was nothing but a well at his mission, so he would harness his team and start out in pursuit of his Indians. Usually they knew in advance of his coming and would

[21] Sweezy, *The Arapaho Way*, 76.
[22] Interview with Elizabeth Page Harris (daughter of Elizabeth M. Page and niece of the Roes), Thermopolis, Wyoming, 1965. Mrs. Harris has rich memories of the summers she spent with the Cheyennes and Arapahoes near Colony when she was a girl.

pack up and slip away, often leaving warm campfires. When he would overtake them to visit with them in their tipis, he would be met with silence, although the moment before there might have been laughter. Still he persisted, and by performing kindly services, he gradually won their confidence. Ill health forced him to go to a different climate in the winter, but he would return in the spring. It was two years before he was accepted.

A church was built for him in 1896 by the Dutch Reformed Church of America. It was a mission church, adjoining the Seger Indian Boarding School, where he preached and sang. Those who remember him at Colony still speak of his fine voice. In 1897 he was joined by Mr. and Mrs. Walter Roe, also dedicated missionaries of the Dutch Reformed church. Mrs. Roe's sister, Elizabeth M. Page, also a missionary, came out from New York each summer with her daughter to work among the Indians at Colony. There she gained the inspiration for her book *In Camp and Tepee*, which traces the work of the Dutch Reformed church.

In spite of the many restrictions imposed on the Arapahoes, Mrs. Roe found them kindly. She had proof of this when she and her husband stopped at an Indian camp at the sign of an approaching storm. After the missionaries had unhitched their horses, something caused the animals to become frightened and run away. Night was approaching and storm clouds were gathering, so the chief led the way to his lodge, where he indicated that she was to sleep in a place of honor. Then he went to join the men who were hunting the horses. The storm came with great fury, though the wives and children of the chief seemed to sleep undisturbed. Mrs. Roe, in the flash of the lightning, saw a woman enter the lodge and go first to one sleeping figure, then to another. When she came to her she was terrified, for she had heard of the cruelty attributed to the Indian women. Carefully the stranger knelt and reached above her head to adjust the dewcloth to keep out the rain. For a moment the two women looked at each other in the flashing light, but neither knew the language of the other. The Indian ran her hand down the missionary's arm and interlocked her little finger with the white woman's in a gesture of lasting friendship. Then she arose and, as quietly as she had entered, disappeared into the storm.

While Wright was studying the Cheyenne language and Roe the Arapaho, they discovered a strange jealousy between the two tribes. When Roe's health failed in 1897, a doctor suggested that he live outside. Consequently, he and Mrs. Roe lived Indian fashion, with the added convenience of a Studebaker hack serving as a chuck wagon. When Roe recovered his health, the missionaries moved into a fine brick house built for them on a hillside overlooking the church at Seger Colony. The Arapahoes taking a prominent part in their work at Colony were Watan (band chief), Washee, Hartley Ridgebear, Joel Little Bird, and Kendall Sore Thumb.

While attending the Lake Mohonk Indian Conference in 1898, Mrs. Roe outlined a plan which she thought might help the Indians socially and industrially and which materialized as the Mohonk Lodge. It started out to be an industrial school, but when the government discontinued issuing rations except to the aged, it proved to be a way of earning money to meet expenses until crops could be harvested.

Mr. and Mrs. Reese Kincaide, who managed the venture until their death, found the Cheyenne and Arapaho Indians to be among the best beadworkers in the world. The Kincaides started with a few articles, and the business grew until they were able to give work to every woman of the two tribes. The Mohonk Lodge still stands (on the spot to which it was eventually moved), beside the highway near Clinton, Oklahoma. It perpetuates the memory of the Dutch Reformed missionaries who tried to give hope and promise to a disheartened people.

Near the end of the nineteenth century lived a blind Arapaho elder, Cheyenne Chief by name, who could not speak a word of English. On her annual visits, Mrs. Page would talk to him through an interpreter. One day when she went to see him, she found him in the depths of despair and asked what was wrong. "Granddaughter," he answered, "my heart is on the ground." Then he explained that Watan, who had never been known to tell a falsehood in his life, had returned from the East with a tale about the white man's having twenty-six tipis stacked on top of each other. "Watan speaks with a forked tongue," he declared.

Mrs. Page could see the picture he conjured by his imagination. How could she explain that the white man's tipi was not conical and that what Watan had said was true? She reached for a box and, taking the old Indian's hand, traced the four sides to show him that the white man's tipi was square sided and that twenty-six tipis could be stacked on top of each other. What Watan had told was true.

"Na," said the old man, shaking his head. That could not be, for the white man, like the Indian, must be near the ground for food and water. Why would people live that far from their needs?

Mrs. Page told him that it was because the land was expensive. If one family lived on a lot, it would cost twenty-six times as much as it would for twenty-six families. He thought this over a moment. Then he asked the cost of a lot in the white man's big city. When Mrs. Page told him, he pondered a moment. Then he picked up a pinch of dirt from his earthen floor. Sifting it through his fingers, he said: "Granddaughter, at that price, the Arapahoes could not afford this much."

With allotments in severalty came the question of tribal lands. In 1891 the Commissioner of Indian Affairs stated that the Northern Arapahoes, who for more than a decade had been considered unwanted guests by the Shoshonis, had equal rights on the reservation. This cleared the way for the allotting agents, but the Northern Arapahoes still had no legal rights. Nevertheless, this did not prevent their taking part in the McLaughlin Agreement of 1896, ceding the Big Springs (at Thermopolis, Wyoming) to the government, and the McLaughlin Relinquishment Agreement of 1904, whereby 1,346,320 acres lying north of Big Wind River were also ceded. The title to Arapaho lands was not legally cleared by the courts until 1938.[23]

23 *82 Ct. Cl. 23*, December 2, 1953; *Sen. Exec. Doc.* No. 247, 54 Cong., 1 sess., 2–4. For details of the Shoshoni case that cleared the titles to Arapaho lands, see Virginia Cole Trenholm and Maurine Carley, *The Shoshonis*, 314–20.

As Cheyenne Chief indicated, the turn of the century found Our People broken in spirit. They had been robbed of their buffalo, dispossessed of their tribal lands, denied their buckskin clothing and their braids, and arbitrarily given meaningless names. But the most drastic regulation of all pertained to their native religion. In an ultimatum designed to put a stop to all ceremonial practices, the commissioner stated: "In many cases these dances and feasts are simply subterfuge to cover degrading acts and to disguise immoral purposes. You [agents] are directed to use your best efforts in the suppression of these evils."[24] Under pressure, the Arapahoes resorted to holding their Sun Dance under other names. In trying to put a stop to this, the agents refused to allow a dance of more than three days' duration, the time required for the preparation alone.

Many letters of protest were exchanged between the agents and the Bureau of Indian Affairs at the time the Sun Dance was seemingly revived, sanctioned, and recorded in 1901 and 1902 among the Southern Arapahoes. The bone of contention, aside from keeping children from school and neglecting crops, was whether or not the old custom of torture was practiced.[25] It was finally agreed that it was, with each Indian suffering the torture being paid fifteen dollars. The incident created a stir at the time, but Dorsey was able to record in full the details of the old ritualistic form of the Sun Dance.

The torture element and the "degrading acts" brought to public notice by Dorsey furnished the excuse for the Indian Regulations of 1904, making the Sun Dance a punishable offense.[26] The act reads: "The 'sun-dance' and other similar dances and so-called religious ceremonies, shall be considered 'Indian offenses,' and any Indian found guilty of being a participant in any one or more of these 'offenses' shall, for the first offense committed, be punished by withholding his rations not less than fifteen

---

[24] W. S. Jones (Commissioner) to U.S. Indian Agents, January 4, 1902, Cheyenne and Arapaho Customs Files, OHS.
[25] Cheyenne and Arapaho Files, The Sun Dance, OHS.
[26] Indian Regulations of 1904, Department of the Interior, IOR, NA.

days or more than thirty days, or by incarceration in the agency prison for a period not exceeding thirty days."

One of the agents who first served at Darlington and later at Fort Washakie maintains that the plan was not a success, even though the Bureau of Indian Affairs tried several years to suppress ceremonial practices.[27] If the Indians disliked their agent, they defied him. If they liked him and did not want to cause him embarrassment, they would "hie themselves away to some remote part of the reservation where unwanted visitors and supervision would both be wanting." Although the Sun Dance was never entirely suppressed, some of the so-called undesirable features were eliminated.

The colorful history of the Arapaho was fast drawing to a close, and he was soon to face new problems as an American citizen. Sharp Nose was the last of the Northern Arapaho chiefs at Fort Washakie to retain his own name—and two wives—until the time of his death in 1900.[28] His wives were Mint and Winnie, and one of his three children was General Crook. He was succeeded by Yellow Calf, a half-brother of Sherman Coolidge. Few knew Yellow Calf as George Caldwell, a name he disliked so much that he used it for legal purposes only. The bands under Black Coal and Sharp Nose had now lost their identity, the former at Lower Arapaho and the latter at Ethete.

In the south, Left Hand, blind and patient, was still chief of the Arapahoes in 1900. His age was given as only fifty-four at the time of his allotment June 30, 1901, but because of his blindness, he was succeeded by Bird Chief in 1908. Left Hand (Nawat, or Niwot, as he was known in Colorado) died June 20, 1911, and was buried on his allotted lands at Left Hand Springs near Geary, Oklahoma.[29] The Southern Arapahoes no longer had bands, but

[27] A. H. Kneale, *Indian Agent*, 156.

[28] Heirship Files, Fort Washakie, Wyoming.

[29] A memorial vesper service honoring Jesse Chisholm (1805–1868) and Left Hand (1840–1911) was held at Left Hand Springs, eight miles northeast of Geary, Oklahoma, on March 3, 1968. Chisholm, of Chisholm Cattle Trail fame, is believed to have died of cholera morbus at Left Hand's camp. The two were friends of long standing. An account of Left Hand's death is given in the *Eufaula Indian Journal*, July 7, 1911. See also the *Sunday Oklahoman*, March 3, 1968.

settlements. Little Raven's Ugly Faces were at Canton, Left Hand's Stubborn People north of Geary, Lump Mouth's Otoes south of Geary, Black Bear's Beef Killers at Calumet, Coyote Robe's (originally Powder Face's) Greasy Leggings south of Calumet, and Watan's Falling-off-Horses at Colony.[30]

Sheridan told the Commissioner of Indian Affairs in 1875 that he had crushed the Indian and it was now up to him to rebuild. He was speaking from the military viewpoint, for it took a quarter of a century longer to subjugate the Arapaho to the will of the white man. The commissioner succeeded in all but one particular. He was unable to suppress the native religion, which survived in the form of the Sun Dance and the Peyote Cult, two of the "many ways to God."

[30] The band names were recalled by May Whiteshirt James and verified by Gus Yellow Hair, Geary, Oklahoma, 1966.

Bibliography

UNPUBLISHED MATERIALS

Allotment Files, 1889–1900. National Archives, Washington, D.C.

Allotment Transcript, June 30, 1891. Oklahoma Historical Society Research Library, Oklahoma City.

Anthony, Scott J. Letters. Colorado State Historical Society, Denver.

"Arapahoes" and "Background on the Cheyenne and Arapaho Agency." Two undated brochures in Cheyenne and Arapaho Agency files, Concho, Oklahoma.

Arapaho Indian Files. Religion and Mythology. Western History Research Center, University of Wyoming, Laramie.

Ashley Papers. Missouri Historical Society, St. Louis.

Bent-Hyde Papers (with map of positions at Sand Creek). Western History Division, University of Colorado, Boulder, Colorado.

Bent–St. Vrain Papers. Missouri Historical Society, St. Louis.

Bretney Collection (including the General Harney pictures). Wyoming State Archives and Historical Department, Cheyenne.

Byers, W. N. "The Centennial State" (photocopy of his original manuscript on "The History of Colorado" in Bancroft Library). Colorado State Historical Society, Denver.

Campbell, Charles E. "Sketches of Early Western Kansas" (including clippings and manuscript materials on microfilm). Manuscript Division, University of Oklahoma, Norman.

Campbell, Governor J. A. Letterbooks, 1869–75. 5 vols. National Archives and Wyoming State Archives and Historical Department, Cheyenne.

Campbell, Walter S. (Stanley Vestal). Collection. Manuscript Division, University of Oklahoma, Norman.

Carter, W. A. (Fort Bridger). Letterbook. Missouri Historical Society, St. Louis.

Census Record Books, 1885, 1890–1900. Wind River Indian Agency, Fort Washakie, Wyoming.

Cheyenne and Arapaho Agency Letterbooks. Indian Archives Division, Oklahoma Historical Society, Oklahoma City.

Cheyenne and Arapaho Files, covering Agents and Agency, Arms and Ammunition, Battles, Captives, Celebrations, Customs, Councils, Dances, Deaths, Depredations, History, Legends, Messiah Craze, Prisoners and Warfare, and Vices (including liquor traffic, the mescal bean, and peyote). Indian Archives Division, Oklahoma Historical Society, Oklahoma City.

Chouteau Collection. Missouri Historical Society, St. Louis.

Chouteau-Papin Collection. Missouri Historical Society, St. Louis.

Clark, William. Papers. Missouri Historical Society, St. Louis.

Collier, Donald. "The Sun Dance of the Plains Indians" and "Indians of the United States." Washington, D.C., 1940. Mimeographed.

Cook, Marshall. Diary. Colorado State Historical Society, Denver.

Cooper, Mrs. Baird S. "White Hawk, Michael, an Arapaho Catechist" (biographical). Wyoming State Archives and Historical Department, Cheyenne.

Cragen, F. W. "Early Far West." 28 notebooks. Pioneer Museum, Colorado Springs, Colorado.

Crawford, Governor S. J. Letterbooks, 1865–68. Kansas State Historical Society, Topeka.

"Custer's Last Stand" (account given by Left Hand, a Northern Arapaho scout with General Crook). Wyoming State Archives and Historical Department, Cheyenne.

Darlington Agency Letterbooks, 1876–1902. Indian Office Records. National Archives, Washington, D.C.

Dawson Scrapbooks (four volumes on "Indians and Indian Wars"; George Bent's "Forty Years with the Cheyennes," is in Vol. I). Colorado State Historical Society, Denver.

Debo, Angie. "Carl Sweezy" (unpublished biographical sketch based on interviews with Sweezy). Personal Files, Marshall, Oklahoma.

Densmore, Frances. "The Peyote Cult and Treatment of the Sick among the Winnebago Indians." MS 3205 (1931) and MS 3261 (1932), Bureau of American Ethnology, Smithsonian Institution.

Drips, Andrew. Papers. Missouri Historical Society, St. Louis.

Evans, John. John Evans Collection. Colorado State Historical Society, Denver.

———. Letterbooks, 1863–64. Colorado State Historical Society, Denver.

Farlow, E. J. "Arapahoes Become Unwelcome Guests of Shoshones." Wyoming State Archives and Historical Department, Cheyenne.

Fidler, Peter. "Chesterfield House Journals" (1801–1802). B. 34/A/3 and B. 39/A/2. Hudson's Bay Company Archives, London, England.

Fort Supply Letterbooks, 1869–78. Manuscript Division, University of Oklahoma, Norman.

Fort Washakie File (letters, papers, clippings, and maps). Western History Research Center, University of Wyoming, Laramie.

Friday, Robert. Statement relating to his grandfather, Chief Friday, dated January 27, 1938. "Arapaho," No. 4445. Bureau of American Ethnology, Smithsonian Institution.

Fritz, Henry E. "The Humanitarian Background of Indian Reform" (Ann Arbor, Michigan, microfilm). University of Wyoming, Laramie.

Gardner, Dorothy, to Stanley Vestal, November 18, 1939. Résumé and Aftermath of Sand Creek. Manuscript Division, University of Oklahoma, Norman.

Goes-in-Lodge. Speech given in Denver at the Wild West Show, Knights Templar Conclave, 1913.

Goertner, Thomas G. "Reflections of a Frontier Soldier (Samuel Tappan) on the Sand Creek Affair." Denver University, 1959.

Greene, A. F. C. "The Arapaho Indians" (February 15, 1941). Wyoming State Archives and Historical Department, Cheyenne.

———. "Fremont County." Wyoming State Archives and Historical Department, Cheyenne.

Hafen, LeRoy, to Clark Wissler, April 16, 1930, concerning the name *Arapaho*. Colorado State Historical Society, Denver.

———. "Historical Background and Development of the Arapaho-Cheyenne Land Area." Colorado State Historical Society, Denver.

Harney, General W. S. Collection. Pictorial History Division, Missouri Historical Society, St. Louis.

Hebard, Grace Raymond. Collection. Western History Research Center, University of Wyoming, Laramie.

Hewes, Gordon. "Early Tribal Migrations in the Northern Great Plains," *Plains Archaeological Conference News Letter*, I, 4 (July 15, 1948). Mimeographed.

Heirship Files. Wind River Indian Agency, Fort Washakie, Wyoming.

"History and Economy of the Indians of the Wind River Reservation." Report No. 106, "Missouri River Basin Investigation." Billings, Montana, July 31, 1950. Mimeographed.

Hoyt, Governor John W. Autobiography (typed by his son, Kepler). Wyoming State Archives and Historical Department, Cheyenne.

Hyde, George E. "Life of George Bent" (transcript). Western History Division, Denver Public Library.

"Indian Pioneer History." Indian Archives Division, Oklahoma Historical Society, Oklahoma City.

"Indian Population and Lands." Department of the Interior, Bureau of Indian Affairs, 1960. Mimeographed.

Kearny, S. W. Manuscript Journal. Missouri Historical Society, St. Louis.

Knoefel, Hugh. "Biography of Captain Alfred Elliott Bates and the Captain Bates Battle" (based on Bates's report). Paper delivered at the annual meeting of the Wyoming State Historical Society. Riverton, Wyoming, 1966.

Left Hand's Autobiography. Indian Archives Division, Oklahoma Historical Society, Oklahoma City.

Little Shield (as symbol of the Plains Hotel, Cheyenne, Wyoming). Wyoming State Archives and Historical Department, Cheyenne.

Lone Man and wife, Phoebe. Interview relating to experiences at Seger Colony. Foreman Collection. Oklahoma Historical Society, Oklahoma City.

Marlatt, Gene R. "Edward Wynkoop: An Investigation of His Role in the Sand Creek Controversy and Other Indian Affairs" (1863–68). Denver University, 1961.

Moore, Joseph G. "A Study of the Episcopal Work among the Indians" (a research unit of the National Council of the Protestant Episcopal Church). Office of the Episcopal Bishop, Laramie, Wyoming.

Moore, J. K., Jr. "Recollections of Early Days at Fort Washakie" (tape recording). Historical Society, Lander, Wyoming.

Newton, L. L. Collection relating to Fort Washakie and the Arapahoes. Western History Research Center, University of Wyoming, Laramie.

Office of Indian Affairs Records. Central, Colorado, and Wyoming

Superintendencies and Upper Arkansas, Upper Platte, and Cheyenne and Arapaho Agencies. National Archives, Washington, D.C. (microfilm files, Wyoming State Archives and Historical Department, Cheyenne).

Post Surgeon's Record Book. Camp Augur, 1869–70; Camp Brown, 1870–78; Fort Washakie, 1878–1909. Wyoming State Archives and Historical Department, Cheyenne.

Ryan, Carmelita. "The Carlisle Indian Industrial School." Georgetown University, Washington, D.C., 1962.

Sage, Sherman. Interview, July, 1940 (by A. F. C. Greene). Wyoming State Archives and Historical Department, Cheyenne.

Schrieber, Charles. Collection. Western History Research Center, University of Wyoming, Laramie.

Searcy, Kate. "Red Moon Boarding School" (Cheyenne school attended by Arapahoes). Searcy Collection. Manuscript Division, University of Oklahoma, Norman.

Seger, John H. "Research and Correspondence" (Hamlin Garland material). Manuscript Division, University of Oklahoma, Norman.

Seger Colony. Photograph Albums. National Archives, Washington, D.C.

Sheridan, Philip H. Papers. Library of Congress, Washington, D.C.

Sherman, William T. Papers. Library of Congress, Washington, D.C.

Sherman-Sheridan Papers (transcript). Manuscript Division, University of Oklahoma, Norman.

Shields, Lillian B. "The Arapaho Indians: Their Association with the White Man." Denver University, 1916.

Sifton, Fr. S. J. "An English-Aáni [Gros Ventre] Dictionary" and "A Grammar of Aáni or Gros Ventre Language" (MSS., 1910, photostatic copies). Department of Anthropology, Catholic University of America, Washington, D.C.

Simpson, M. L. Collection. Western History Research Center, University of Wyoming, Laramie.

Snow, Riley E. "Removal of the Indians from Wyoming." Colorado State College of Education, Greeley, Colorado, 1936.

Stephens, J. A. "Education (report of Reverend Stephens to Bishop M. Marty, President of the Bureau of Catholic Missions, 1891–92, carbon copy). National Archives, Washington, D.C.

Stewart, Omer C. "Ute Indian: Before and After Contact." Paper read at the University of Utah, November 2, 1964. Department of

Anthropology, University of Colorado, Boulder. Mimeographed.
Stone, Forrest R. "Indians at Work and Play." Wind River Indian Agency, Fort Washakie, Wyoming, February, 1937.
Sublette Papers. Missouri Historical Society, St. Louis.
Tappan, Samuel F. Autobiography (dated March 12, 1895). Kansas State Historical Society, Topeka.
Vance, Paul, and Research Committee. "Cheyenne and Arapaho Tribes of Oklahoma." Concho, Oklahoma.
Vasquez Papers. Missouri Historical Society, St. Louis.
Walker, Tacetta. "The Establishment of Ethete." Arapaho Indian Files, Western History Research Center, University of Wyoming, Laramie.
War Department Records. Department of the Missouri. National Archives, Washington, D.C.
Ware, Eugene F. Military Papers, 1859–1870. Abby Nies Collection, Kansas State Historical Society, Topeka.
"Wind River Reservation" (A résumé compiled at Fort Washakie in January, 1966).
Wind River Reservation Files. Religion and Mythology. Western History Research Center, University of Wyoming, Laramie.
Wynkoop, Edward W. "Colorado History" (unfinished manuscript written in 1876, original typed copy). Colorado State Historical Society, Denver.

GOVERNMENT DOCUMENTS

Abert, J. W. "Report of Lieut. J. W. Abert of His Examination of New Mexico," 30 Cong., 1 sess., *Sen. Exec. Doc.* No. 23.
American State Papers, Military Affairs. Vols. II–VI, Washington, 1860–61.
Annual Report of the Commissioner of Indian Affairs, 1850–1906.
Annual Report of the Secretary of War. 1820–77.
"Arapahoes Join Shoshones on Reservation," *House Executive Documents,* Vol. I (1870–71), Pts. 2 and 4, 1870–71.
Bureau of Indian Affairs. "History and Economy of the Indians of the Wind River Reservation, Wyoming." In *Missouri River Basin Investigations,* Department of the Interior, Area Office, Billings, Montana, July 31, 1950.
———. "The Montana-Wyoming Indian." In *Missouri River Basin*

Investigations, Department of the Interior, Billings, Montana, June, 1961.

Chivington, John M., Scott J. Anthony, *et al*. "Engagement with Indians at Sand Creek, Colorado Territory, November 29, 1864." In *The War of the Rebellion*, Series One, Vol. XLI. Washington, 1902.

"Condition of the Indian Tribes," March 3, 1865. *Senate Report No. 156*, 39 Cong., 2 sess.

"Course of Study for Indian Schools" ("Industrial and Literary"). Office of Indian Affairs, 1901.

Department of the Interior and General Land Office. *Cases Relating to the Public Lands*, Vol. XXXIV (July, 1905–June, 1906). Washington, 1906.

Dodge, Henry. "Journal of a March of a Detachment of Dragoons under the Command of Colonel Dodge during the Summer of 1835." *House Exec. Doc*. No. 181, 24 Cong., 1 sess.

"Engagement with Indians at Adobe Fort, November 25, 1864. In *The War of the Rebellion*, Series One, Vol. XLI, 1902.

Jones, William. "Report upon the Reconnaissance of Northwestern Wyoming." Department of the Interior, 1877.

Kappler, Charles J. *Indian Affairs: Laws and Treaties*. 3 vols. Washington, 1903.

Kearny, S. W. "Report of a Summer Campaign to the Rocky Mountains," *House Exec. Doc*. No. 2, 29 Cong., 1 sess.

McLaughlin, James. "Report," *Sen. Doc*. 247, VIII, 54 Cong., 1 sess.

"Massacre of Cheyenne Indians," *Senate Report* No. 142, 38 Cong., 2 sess.

Record of Engagements with Hostile Indians within the Military Division of the Missouri. Washington, 1882.

"Report of Indians Taxed and Not Taxed in the United States," *Misc. Doc*. No. 340, 52 Cong., 1 sess. 28 vols. 1892-97.

Report of Special Commission to Investigate the Affairs at Red Cloud Agency. Washington, G.P.O., 1875.

Richardson, James D. *A Compilation of Messages and Papers of the Presidents*. 10 vols. 1896–99. Supplement 1899–1902.

Royce, Charles C. *Indian Land Cessions in the United States*. Bureau of American Ethnology, *Eighteenth Annual Report*, Pt. 2. Washington, 1899.

"The Sand Creek Massacre," *Sen. Exec. Doc.* No. 26, 39 Cong., 2 sess.

Sawyers, James A. "Report" (encounter with the Araphoes), *House Exec. Doc.* No. 58, 39 Cong., 1 sess.

"Shoshone Tribe of Indians of the Wind River Reservation in Wyoming, Petitioner *vs.* The United States of America, Defendant," *U.S. Court of Claims Report 82* (December 2, 1935) and *U.S. Reports*, Vol. 299 (January 4, 1937).

United States Congress. *House Executive Documents.* No. 41, 30 Cong,. 1 sess.; No. 130, 34 Cong., 1 sess.; No. 97, 40 Cong., 2 sess.; No. 12, 43 Cong., 1, 2, and 3 sess.

———. *Senate Executive Documents.* No. 90, 22 Cong., 1 sess.; No. 23, 30 Cong., 1 sess; No. 1, 31 Cong., 2 sess.; No. 34, 33 Cong., 2 sess.; No. 91, 34 Cong., 1 and 2 sess.; No. 247, 54 Cong., 1 sess.

The War of the Rebellion. Series One. I (1880)–LIII (1902). Washington, 1880.

NEWSPAPERS

Canadian Republican (El Reno, Oklahoma Territory), May 8, 1896.

Central City Register (Central City, Colorado), August 27, October 1 and 22, 1870; June 11, 1871.

Cheyenne Daily Leader. July 14 and 16, 1874; September 18, 1875–June 11, 1876.

Cheyenne Transporter, December 24, 1880.

Daily Denver Times, October 6 and 19, 1883.

Daily Oklahoman, January 7, 1934; July 8, 1951.

Denver Tribune-Republican, September 6, 1885; July 10, 1886.

Eufaula Indian Journal (Eufaula, Oklahoma), July 7, 1911.

Fort Laramie Scout, January 28, 1926.

Goodland News-Republic, February 17, 1927.

Great Falls Tribune, May 19, 1940.

Kansas City Times, November 20, 1890.

Kansas Daily Tribune, August 25, 1865.

Laramie Daily Sentinel, August 4, 1873; December 23, 1938.

Laramie Weekly Boomerang, May 1, 1890.

Laramie Weekly Sentinel, May 3, 1870.

Lawrence Republican, May 22–August 15, 1860.

Leavenworth Daily Conservative, October 29, 1867.
Leavenworth Times, June 4, 1859.
Missouri Democrat, May 25, 1859.
Missouri Republican, October 16, 1832; September 26–November 30, 1851.
Neosho Valley Register (Burlington, Kansas), August 11, 1860.
New York Times, September 26 and 28, 1877.
New York Weekly Tribune, November 13, 1841.
Rocky Mountain News, April 18, 1860; April 5 and July 19, 1862; October 29, 1863; April 27, August 10 and 24, September 21, 24, and 28, and December 17, 1864; June 24 and August 6, 10, and 19, 1865; April 20, 1870; February 29, 1876.
St. Louis Enquirer, July 19, 1824.
Salina Journal, December 26, 1940.
Sunday Oklahoman, March 3, 1968.
Wyoming Churchman (Episcopal Church, Laramie, Wyoming), Centennial Edition, May, 1959; January, 1960.

BOOKS, JOURNALS, AND PAMPHLETS: PRIMARY

Allen, Mary J. *Twentieth Century Pioneering.* Fort Collins, Colorado, B. and M. Printing Company, 1956.
The American Heritage Book of Indians. New York, Simon and Schuster, 1961.
Arthur, Fremont. *Questions and Answers.* Trans. into Arapaho, Laramie, Wyoming, Episcopal Church, n.d.
Baillie-Grohman, William A. *Camps in the Rockies.* New York, Charles Scribner's Sons, 1882.
Beckwourth, James P. *Life and Adventures of James P. Beckwourth.* Ed. by T. D. Bonner. New York, Macmillan, 1892.
Bell, John R. *The Journal of Captain John R. Bell.* Ed. by H. M. Fuller and LeRoy R. Hafen. In LeRoy R. Hafen and Ann W. Hafen (eds.), *The Far West and the Rockies*, Vol. VI. Glendale, The Arthur H. Clark Company, 1957.
Bidwell, John. *Echoes of the Past in California.* Ed. by Milo M. Quaife. Chicago, R. R. Donnelley and Sons, 1928.
Bigelow, John. *Memory of the Life and Public Service of John Charles Frémont.* New York, Derby and Jackson, 1856.

Bourke, John G. *On the Border with Crook.* New York, Charles Scribner's Sons, 1950.

Brackenridge, Henry M. *Journal of a Voyage up the River Missouri in 1811.* Vol. V in Reuben G. Thwaites (ed.), *Early Western Travels.* Cleveland, The Arthur H. Clark Company, 1904.

———. *Views of Louisiana.* Pittsburgh, Cramer, Spear and Eichbaum, 1814.

Bradbury, John. *Travels in the Interior of America.* Vol. V in Reuben G. Thwaites (ed.), *Early Western Travels.* Glendale, California, The Arthur H. Clark Company, 1904–1907.

Burton, Richard F. *The City of the Saints and Across the Rocky Mountains to California.* New York, Harper and Brothers, 1862.

Carrington, Frances C. *My Army Life and the Fort Phil Kearny Massacre.* Philadelphia, J. B. Lippincott, 1910.

Carrington, Margaret I. *Absaraka, Home of the Crows*, Philadelphia, J. B. Lippincott, 1868.

Carson, Christopher (Kit). *Kit Carson's Autobiography.* Ed. by Milo M. Quaife. Chicago, The Lakeside Press, 1935.

Chisholm, James. *Journal in South Pass, 1868.* Ed. by Lola Homsher. Lincoln, University of Nebraska Press, 1960.

Clark, William Philo. *The Indian Sign Language.* Philadelphia, L. R. Hammersly, 1885.

Clyman, James S. *James Clyman, American Frontiersman.* San Francisco, California Historical Society, 1929.

Cohoe. *A Cheyenne Sketchbook.* With commentary by E. Adamson Hoebel and Karen D. Petersen. Norman, University of Oklahoma Press, 1964.

Collins, Hubert E. *Warpath and Cattle Trail.* New York, William Morrow, 1928.

Conrad, H. L. *"Uncle Dick" Wootton.* Chicago, W. E. Dibble and Company, 1950.

Cook, John R. *The Border and the Buffalo.* Ed. by Milo M. Quaife. Chicago, The Lakeside Press, 1938.

Coolidge, Grace. *Teepee Neighbors.* Boston, The Four Seas Company, 1917.

Custer, George A. *My Life on the Plains.* St. Louis, Royal Publishing Co., 1891.

Dale, Harrison C. (ed.). *The Ashley-Smith Explorations and the*

Discovery of a Central Route to the Pacific. Cleveland, The Arthur H. Clark Company, 1941.

Denig, Edwin T. *Five Indian Tribes of the Upper Missouri.* Ed. by John C. Ewers. Norman, University of Oklahoma Press, 1961.

De Smet, Pierre-Jean. *History of Western Missions and Missionaries.* Vols. XXVII and XVIII in Reuben G. Thwaites (ed.), *Early Western Travels.* Cleveland, The Arthur H. Clark Company, 1906.

———. *Letters and Sketches.* Vol. XXIX in Reuben G. Thwaites (ed.), *Early Western Travels.* Cleveland, The Arthur H. Clark Company, 1906.

———. *Life, Letters, and Travels of Father Pierre-Jean De Smet.* Ed. by H. M. Chittenden and A. T. Richardson. 4 vols. New York, Francis P. Harper, 1905.

Dodge, Grenville M. *How We Built the U. P. Railway.* Washington, Government Printing Office, 1910.

Dodge, Richard I. *Our Wild Indians.* Hartford, Connecticut, A. D. Worthington and Company, 1882.

Dyer, Mrs. D. B. *Fort Reno or Picturesque Cheyenne and Arapaho Army Life before the Opening of Oklahoma.* New York, G. W. Dillingham, 1896.

Farnham, Thomas J. *Travels in the Great Western Prairies.* Vols. XXVIII and XXIX in Reuben G. Thwaites (ed.), *Early Western Travels,* Cleveland, The Arthur H. Clark Company, 1904–1905.

Ferris, Warren A. "A Diary of the Wanderings on the Sources of the Rivers Missouri, Columbia, and Colorado, 1835." In Paul C. Phillips (ed.), *Life in the Rocky Mountains.* Denver, Old West Publishing Company, 1940.

Forsyth, George A. *The Story of a Soldier.* New York, D. Appleton and Company, 1905.

Fowler, Jacob. *The Journal of Jacob Fowler.* Ed. by Elliott Coues. New York, Francis P. Harper, 1898.

Franchére, Gabriel. *Narrative of a Voyage to the Northwest Coast.* Vol. VI in Reuben G. Thwaites (ed.), *Early Western Travels.* Cleveland, The Arthur H. Clark Company, 1904.

Frémont, John C. *Memoirs of My Life.* 2 vols. New York, Belford, Clarke, and Company, 1887.

———. *Narratives of Exploration and Adventure.* Ed. by Allan Nevins. New York, Longmans, Green and Company, 1956.

———. *Report of an Exploring Expedition to the Rocky Mountains.* Washington, Blair and Rivers, 1845.

Garrard, Lewis H. *Wah-to-Yah and the Taos Trail.* Ed. by Ralph Bieber. Glendale, The Arthur H. Clark Company, 1938.

Goggles, John. "John Goggles' Story of Peyote." See Stenberg, Mollie P., *infra.*

Greeley, Horace. *An Overland Journey from New York to San Francisco in the Summer of 1859.* New York, C. M. Saxton, Barker, and Company, 1860.

Gregg, Josiah. *Commerce of the Prairies.* Vols. XIX and XX in Reuben G. Thwaites (ed.), *Early Western Travels.* Glendale, The Arthur H. Clark Company, 1904–1907.

———. *Commerce of the Prairies.* Ed. by Max L. Moorhead. Norman, University of Oklahoma Press, 1954.

———. *The Diary and Letters of Josiah Gregg.* Ed. by Maurice G. Fulton. Norman, University of Oklahoma Press, 1941–44.

Gregg, Kate L. (ed.). *The Road to Santa Fé.* Albuquerque, University of New Mexico Press, 1952.

Hafen, LeRoy R. (ed.). *Colorado Gold Rush, and Pike's Peak Gold Rush Guidebooks of 1859.* Glendale, The Arthur H. Clark Company, 1941.

Hafen, LeRoy R., and Ann W. Hafen (eds.). *The Far West and the Rockies.* 15 vols. Glendale, The Arthur H. Clark Company, 1954–61.

———. "The Old Spanish Trail." In *The Far West and the Rockies*, Vol. I. Glendale, The Arthur H. Clark Company, 1954.

———. *Powder River Campaigns and Sawyers Expeditions of 1865.* Vol. XII in *The Far West and the Rockies.* Glendale, The Arthur H. Clark Company, 1961.

———. *Relations with the Indians of the Plains.* Vol. IX in *The Far West and the Rockies.* Glendale, The Arthur H. Clark Company, 1959.

———. *To the Rockies and Oregon.* Vol. III in *The Far West and the Rockies.* Glendale, The Arthur H. Clark Company, 1955.

Hancock, Mrs. A. R. *Reminiscences of Winfield Scott Hancock by His Wife.* New York, Charles L. Webster, 1887.

Hancock, Winfield Scott. *Reports of Major General Hancock upon Indian Affairs and Accompanying Exhibits.* Washington, G.P.O., 1867.

Harmon, D. W. *A Journal of Voyages and Travels in the Interior of North America*. New York, Allerton Book Company, 1922.

Heddist, William. "Experiences of a Missourian, William Heddist." In LeRoy R. Hafen and Ann W. Hafen (eds.), *The Far West and the Rockies*, Vol. I. Glendale, Arthur H. Clark Company, 1954.

Hendry, Anthony. "The Journal of Anthony Hendry, 1754–55," ed. by L. J. Burpee, Royal Society of Canada *Proceedings and Transactions*, Series 3, No. 1. Ottawa, 1907.

Henry, Alexander, and David Thompson. *New Light on the Early History of the Great Northwest*. Ed. by Elliott Coues. 3 vols. New York, Francis P. Harper, 1897.

Holman, Albert M. (ed.). "The Sawyer's Expedition." In LeRoy R. Hafen and Ann W. Hafen (eds.), *The Far West and the Rockies*, Vol. XII. Glendale, The Arthur H. Clark Company, 1961.

Howbert, Irving. *The Indians of the Pike's Peak Region*. New York, The Knickerbocker Press, 1914.

———. *Memories of a Lifetime in the Pike's Peak Region*. New York, G. P. Putnam's Sons, 1925.

Hulbert, A. B. (ed.). *Southwest of the Turquois Trail*. Published by the Stewart Commission of Colorado College, 1933.

Humfreville, J. Lee. *Twenty Years among our Hostile Indians*. New York, Hunter and Company, 1899.

Hyde, George E. (ed.). *Life of George Bent*. Ed. by Savoie Lottinville. Norman, University of Oklahoma Press, 1967.

Irving, Washington. *The Adventures of Captain Bonneville*. New York, J. B. Miller and Company, 1885.

———. *Astoria*. Philadelphia, Carey, Lea, and Blanchard, 1836.

Isham, James. *James Isham's Observations on Hudson's Bay*. Ed. by E. E. Rich. Toronto, Champlain Society, 1949.

James, Edwin. *Account of an Expedition from Pittsburgh to the Rocky Mountains*. Vols. XIV–XVII in Reuben G. Thwaites (ed.), *Early Western Travels*. Glendale, The Arthur H. Clark Company, 1906.

James, Thomas. *Three Years Among the Indians and Mexicans*. Ed. by Walter B. Douglas. St. Louis, Missouri Historical Society, 1916.

Kearny, S. W. *Across the Plains to Bent's Fort*. Ed. by Ralph Bieber. Glendale, The Arthur H. Clark Company, 1937.

Keim, De B. Randolph. *Sheridan's Troopers on the Border: A Winter Campaign on the Plains*. Philadelphia, David McKay, 1891.

322

Kelly, Luther S. *Yellowstone Kelly: The Memoirs of Luther S. Kelly*. Ed. by Milo M. Quaife. New Haven, Yale University Press, 1926.

Kelsey, Henry. *The Kelsey Papers*. Ed. by A. G. Doughty and Chester Martin. Ottawa, Public Archives of Canada, 1929.

Kennedy, Michael. *The Assiniboines*. Norman, University of Oklahoma Press, 1961.

Kern, Richard H. *The Diary of Richard H. Kern*. In *When Old Trails were New*. Ed. by Blanche C. Grant. New York, The Press of the Pioneers, 1934.

Kneale, A. H. *Indian Agent*. Caldwell, Idaho, The Caxton Printers, Ltd., 1950.

La Barre, Weston. *The Peyote Cult*. New Haven, Yale University Press, 1938.

Larocque, François Antoine. *Journal of François Antoine Larocque from the Assiniboine River to the Yellowstone*. Canadian Archives *Publication No. 3*. Ottawa, 1910. Reprint in Sources of Northwest History, No. 20. State University of Montana, Missoula, 1934.

Larpenteur, Charles. *Forty Years a Fur Trader on the Upper Missouri*. Ed. by Elliott Coues. 2 vols. New York, Francis P. Harper, 1898.

La Vérendrye, Chevalier de. "Journal of the Voyage Made by Chevalier de La Vérendrye with One of His Brothers in Search of the Western Sea," in *Margry Papers*, trans. by Anne H. Blegen, *Oregon Historical Quarterly*, XXVI, 2 (June, 1925).

Leonard, Zenas. *The Adventures of Zenas Leonard*. Ed. by John C. Ewers, Norman, University of Oklahoma Press, 1959.

Lewis, Meriwether, and William Clark. *Original Journals of the Lewis and Clark Expedition*. Ed. by Reuben G. Thwaites. 8 vols. New York, Dodd, Mead and Company, 1904–1906.

Lowe, Percival G. *Five Years a Dragoon*. Kansas City, Missouri, Franklin Hudson Publishing Company, 1906.

Luttig, John C. *Journal of a Fur Trading Expedition on the Upper Missouri*. Ed. by Stella M. Drumm. St. Louis, Missouri Historical Society, 1920.

Mackenzie, Alexander. *Voyages from Montreal on the River St. Lawrence through the Continent of North America to the Frozen and Pacific Oceans*. 2 vols. New York, New Amsterdam Book Co., 1862.

McLaughlin, James. *My Friend the Indian*. Boston, Houghton Mifflin Company, 1910.

Marcy, Randolph B. *Marcy and the Gold Seekers: The Journal of Captain R. B. Marcy*. Norman, University of Oklahoma Press, 1939.
————. *The Prairie Traveler*, New York, Harper and Brothers, 1859.
————. *Thirty Years of Army Life on the Border*. New York, Harper and Brothers, 1866.
Maximilian, Alexander Philip (Prince von). *Travels in the Interior of North America*. Illustrations by Carl Bodmer. London, Ackerman and Company, 1843. Vols. XXII–XXIV in Reuben G. Thwaites (ed.), *Early Western Travels*. Cleveland, The Arthur H. Clark Company, 1906.
Mengarini, Gregory. *Mengarini's Narrative of the Rockies*. Ed. by Albert J. Partoll. In *Sources of Northwest History*, No. 25. Missoula, University of Montana, 1938.
Miles, Nelson A. *Personal Recollections and Observations of General Nelson A. Miles*. New York, The Werner Company, 1897.
Miller, Alfred Jacob. *The West of Alfred Jacob Miller*. Ed. by Marvin C. Ross. Norman, University of Oklahoma Press, 1951.
Morse, Jedediah. *A Report to the Secretary of War of the United States on Indian Affairs*. New Haven, S. Converse, 1822.
Nasatir, Abraham P. (ed.), *Before Lewis and Clark*. 2 vols. St. Louis, St. Louis Historical Documents Foundation, 1952.
Nelson, Oliver. *The Cowman's Southwest: Reminiscences of Oliver Nelson*. Ed. by Angie Debo. Glendale, The Arthur H. Clark Company, 1953.
Newell, Robert. *Robert Newell's Memoranda*. Ed. by Dorothy Johansen. Reed College, Portland, Oregon, The Champoeg Press, 1959.
Nidiver, George. *The Life and Adventures of George Nidiver*. Ed. by William H. Ellison. Berkeley, University of California Press, 1937.
North, Luther. *Man of the Plains: The Recollections of Luther North*. Ed. by Donald F. Danker. Lincoln, University of Nebraska Press, 1961.
Nye, W. S. *Carbine and Lance: The Story of Old Fort Sill*. Norman, University of Oklahoma Press, 1937.
Page, Elizabeth M. *In Camp and Tepee*, New York, Fleming H. Revell Co., 1915.
Painter, Charles C. *Cheyenne and Arapaho Revisited*. Philadelphia, Indian Rights Association, 1893.

Palmer, Joel. *Journal of Travels over the Rocky Mountains to the Mouth of the Columbia River.* Vol. XXX in Reuben G. Thwaites (ed.), *Early Western Travels.* Cleveland, The Arthur H. Clark Company, 1906.

Parkman, Francis. *The Journals of Francis Parkman.* Vol. II. New York, Harper and Brothers, 1947.

———. *The Oregon Trail.* New York, Rinehart and Company, Inc., 1931.

———. *The Struggle for a Continent.* Boston, Little, Brown and Company, 1902.

Pattie, James O. *Personal Narrative.* Vol. XVIII in Reuben G. Thwaites (ed.), *Early Western Travels.* Cleveland, The Arthur H. Clark Company, 1906.

Perrin du Lac, M. François. *Travels Through the Two Louisianas and among the Savage Nations of the Missouri.* London, J. G. Barnard, 1807.

Pike, Zebulon M. *The Expeditions of Zebulon Montgomery Pike.* Ed. by Elliott Coues. 3 vols. New York, Francis P. Harper, 1895.

Point, Nicholas. "Letters." In Pierre-Jean De Smet, *Life and Travels among the North American Indians.* New York, Francis P. Harper, 1905.

Preuss, Charles. *Exploring With Frémont.* Trans. and ed. by Erwin G. and Elizabeth K. Gudde. Norman, University of Oklahoma Press, 1958.

Pulsipher, John. "Diary of John Pulsipher." In LeRoy R. Hafen and Ann W. Hafen (eds.), *The Far West and the Rockies*, Vol. III. Glendale, The Arthur H. Clark Company, 1958.

Richardson, Albert D. *Beyond the Mississippi.* Hartford, American Publishing Company, 1869.

Rollins, Philip A. (ed.). *The Discovery of the Oregon Trail.* New York, Charles Scribner's Sons, 1935.

Ruxton, George. *Life in the Far West.* Ed. by LeRoy R. Hafen. Norman, University of Oklahoma Press, 1955.

———. *Ruxton of the Rockies.* Ed. by LeRoy R. Hafen. Norman, University of Oklahoma Press, 1950.

Sage, Rufus. "Rocky Mountain Life." In LeRoy R. Hafen and Ann W. Hafen (eds.), *The Far West and the Rockies*, Vol. III. Glendale, The Arthur H. Clark Company, 1955.

———. *Rufus Sage: His Life and Papers.* Vols. IV and V in LeRoy R.

Hafen and Ann W. Hafen (eds.), *The Far West and the Rockies.* Glendale, The Arthur H. Clark Company, 1956.

Saint-Pierre, Jacques Le Gardeur de. "Memoire ou Journal du Voyage," in *Margry Papers.* Vol. VI. Paris, 1879–88.

Schmitt, Martin F. *General George Crook: His Autobiography.* Norman, University of Oklahoma Press, 1946.

Schultz, James Willard. *Blackfeet and Buffalo.* Ed. by Keith C. Steele. Norman, University of Oklahoma Press, 1962.

Scott, Hugh L. *Some Memories of a Soldier.* New York, The Century Company, 1928.

Seger, John H. *Early Days Among the Cheyenne and Arapaho Indians.* Ed. by Stanley Vestal (Walter S. Campbell). Norman, University of Oklahoma Press, 1956.

Sheridan, Philip H. *Personal Memoirs of P. H. Sheridan.* 2 vols. New York, Webster, 1890.

Shortess, Robert. "The Peoria Party." In LeRoy R. Hafen and Ann W. Hafen (eds.), *The Far West and the Rockies*, Vol. III. Glendale, The Arthur H. Clark Company, 1955.

Simonin, Lewis L. *The Rocky Mountain West in 1867.* Trans. and ed. by Wilson O. Clough. Lincoln, University of Nebraska Press, 1966.

Smith, E. Willard. "Journal." In LeRoy R. Hafen and Ann W. Hafen (eds.), *The Far West and the Rockies*, Vol. III. Glendale, The Arthur H. Clark Company, 1955.

Spotts, David L. *Campaigning with Custer and the 19th Kansas Volunteer Cavalry on the Washita Campaign.* Los Angeles, Wetzel, 1928.

Stuart, Robert. "Journal of Discovery." In Kenneth A. Spaulding (ed.), *On the Oregon Trail.* Norman, University of Oklahoma Press, 1953.

Sweezy, Carl. *The Arapaho Way.* Ed. by Althea Bass. New York, Clarkson N. Potter, Inc., 1966.

Tabeau, Pierre-Antoine. *Tabeau's Narrative of Loisel's Expedition to the Upper Missouri.* Trans. by Rose Abel Wright and ed. by Annie H. Abel. Norman, University of Oklahoma Press, 1939.

Talbot, Ethelbert. *My People of the Plains.* New York, Harper and Brothers, 1906.

Talbot, Theodore. *The Journals of Theodore Talbot.* Ed. by Charles Carey. Portland, Metropolitan Press, 1931.

Thompson, David. *David Thompson's Narrative of His Explorations in Western America*. Ed. by J. B. Tyrrell. Toronto, Champlain Society, 1916.

———. *Journals of David Thompson*. Ed. by M. Catherine White. Missoula, Montana State University, 1950.

Toll, Oliver W. *Arapaho Names and Trails*. Privately published, 1962.

Townsend, John K. *Narrative of a Journey Across the Rocky Mountains to the Columbia River*. Vol. XXI in Reuben G. Thwaites (ed.), *Early Western Travels*. Cleveland, The Arthur H. Clark Company, 1905.

Umfreville, Edward. *The Present State of Hudson's Bay*. London, Charles Stalker, 1790.

Villard, Henry. *The Past and Present of the Pike's Peak Gold Region*. Princeton, New Jersey, Princeton University Press, 1932.

Voorhees, Luke. *Personal Recollections of Pioneer Life on the Mountains and Plains of the Great West*. Cheyenne, Wyoming, privately printed, n.d.

Ware, Eugene F. *The Indian War of 1864*. Topeka, Kansas, Crane and Company, 1911.

Webb, James J. *Adventures in the Santa Fé Trade*. Ed. by Ralph Bieber. Glendale, The Arthur H. Clark Company, 1931.

Williams, Joseph. *Narrative of a Tour from the State of Indiana to the Oregon Territory in the Years 1841–1842. New York*, The Cadmus Book Shop, 1921.

Wyeth, John B. *Oregon: A Short History of a Long Journey*. Vol. XXI in Reuben G. Thwaites (ed.), *Early Western Travels*. Cleveland, The Arthur H. Clark Company, 1905.

Wyeth, Nathaniel J. *The Correspondence and Journals of Captain Nathaniel J. Wyeth*. Ed. by F. G. Young. Eugene, Oregon, University Press, 1899.

BOOKS AND PAMPHLETS: SECONDARY

Arps, Louisa W., and Elinor E. Kingery. *High Country Names*. Denver, The Rocky Mountain Club, 1866.

Arthur, Fremont, and John Roberts. *Book of Common Prayer*. Trans. into Arapaho. Laramie, Wyoming, Episcopal Church, n.d.

Athearn, Robert G. *William Tecumseh Sherman and the Settlement of the West*. Norman, University of Oklahoma Press, 1956.

Bailey, Paul. *Wovoka: The Indian Messiah.* Los Angeles, Westernlore Press, 1957.

Baker, James H., and LeRoy R. Hafen. *History of Colorado.* Vol. I. Denver, Linderman Company, 1927.

Beals, Ralph L. "The Ute and the Arapaho." In *Ethnology of the Rocky Mountain National Park.* Berkeley, California, U.S. Department of the Interior, National Park Service, 1935.

Berthrong, Donald J. *The Southern Cheyennes.* Norman, University of Oklahoma Press, 1963.

Brady, Cyrus T. *Indian Fights and Fighters.* Garden City, New York, Doubleday, Page and Co., 1940.

Brown, Dee. *Fort Phil Kearny.* New York, G. P. Putnam's Sons, 1962.

Brown, Mark H. *The Plainsmen of the Yellowstone.* New York, G. P. Putnam's Sons, 1961.

Burpee, Lawrence J. *The Search for the Western Sea.* Toronto, The Macmillan Company, Ltd., 1935.

Burt, Struthers. *Powder River.* New York. Farrar and Rinehart, 1939.

Butler, Helen. *A Stone on His Shoulder.* Philadelphia, Westminster Press, 1953.

Chittenden, Hiram M. *The American Fur Trade of the Far West.* 2 vols. New York, Barnes and Noble, Inc., 1935.

The Church's Work: A Narrative in Words and Pictures. St. Michael's Mission, Ethete, Wyoming, n.d.

Clark, Ellen E. *Indian Legends from the Northern Rockies.* Norman, University of Oklahoma Press, 1966.

Cooper, Mrs. Baird S. *Wind River Reservation.* Hartford, Connecticut, Church Mission Publishing Company, 1914.

Coutant, C. G. *The History of Wyoming.* Vol. I. Laramie, Spafford and Mathison, 1899.

Coyner, David H. *The Lost Trappers.* New York, Hurst and Company, 1848.

Crossroads of the West. Riverton, Wyoming, Crossroads of the West, Inc., 1965.

Curtis, Edward S. *The North American Indians.* Vols. V and VI. Norwood, Mass., The Plimpton Press, 1911.

Curtis, Natalie. *The Indians' Book.* New York, Harper and Brothers, 1907.

Dale, Edward E. *Indians of the Southwest.* Norman, University of Oklahoma Press, 1949.

David, Robert B. *Finn Burnett, Frontiersman*. Glendale, The Arthur H. Clark Company, 1937.

Davidson, Gordon C. *The North West Company*. University of California *Publications in History*, Vol. VII. Berkeley, 1918.

Dixon, Olive K. *Life of Billy Dixon*. Dallas, P. L. Turner Co., 1914.

Duffus, Robert L. *The Santa Fé Trail*. New York, Longmans, Green and Co., 1930.

Dunn, Jacob P. *Massacres of the Mountains*. New York, Archer House, 1886.

Eastman, Elaine. *Pratt, the Red Man's Moses*. Norman, University of Oklahoma Press, 1935.

Emmitt, Robert. *The Last War Trail: The Utes and the Settlement of Colorado*. Norman, University of Oklahoma Press, 1954.

Ewers, John C. *The Blackfeet*. Norman, University of Oklahoma Press, 1958.

———. *Plains Indian Painting: A Description of Aboriginal Art*. Stanford, California, Stanford University Press, 1939.

Favour, A. H. *Old Bill Williams, Mountain Man*. Chapel Hill, University of North Carolina Press, 1936.

Fletcher, Alice C. *Indian Story and Song from North America*. Boston, Small, Maynard and Company, 1900.

Foreman, Grant. *The Last Trek of the Indians*. Chicago, University of Chicago Press, 1946.

Fritz, Henry E. *The Movement for Indian Assimilation*. Philadelphia, University of Pennsylvania Press, 1963.

Gardner, Dorothy. *The Great Betrayal*. Garden City, New York, Doubleday and Company, Ltd., 1949.

Garland, Hamlin. *The Book of the American Indian*. New York, Harper and Brothers, 1923.

Geffs, Mary L. *Under Ten Flags*. Greeley, Colorado, The McVey Printers, 1938.

Ghent, W. J. *The Early Far West*. New York, Longmans, Green and Co., 1931.

Gittinger, Roy. *The Formation of the State of Oklahoma*. Norman, University of Oklahoma Press, 1939.

The Gospel According to St. Luke. Trans. into Arapaho. New York American Bible Society, 1903.

Grinnell, George B. *The Cheyenne Indians*. 2 vols. New Haven, Yale University Press, 1924.

———. *The Fighting Cheyennes*. New York, Scribner's, 1915.

Hafen, LeRoy R. *Colorado and Its People*. New York, Lewis Historical Publishing Co., 1948.

———. *The Overland Mail*. Cleveland, The Arthur H. Clark Company, 1926.

Hafen, LeRoy R. and W. J. Ghent. *Broken Hand: The Life Story of Thomas Fitzpatrick*. Denver, The Old West Publishing Company, 1931.

Hafen, LeRoy R., and Ann W. Hafen. *The Colorado Story*. Denver, The Old West Publishing Company, 1953.

Hafen, LeRoy R., and Francis M. Young. *Fort Laramie and the Pageant of the West*. Glendale, The Arthur H. Clark Company, 1938.

Hall, Frank. *History of the State of Colorado*. Chicago, Blakely Printing Co., 1889.

Hart, Herbert M. *Old Forts of the Northwest*. Seattle, Superior Publishing Co., 1963.

Hebard, Grace Raymond, and E. A. Brininstool. *The Bozeman Trail*. 2 vols. Cleveland, The Arthur H. Clark Company, 1922.

Hill, Alice Polk. *Tales of the Colorado Pioneers*. Denver, Pierson and Gardiner, 1884.

Hoebel, E. Adamson. *The Cheyennes*. New York, Rinehart and Winston, 1960.

Hoig, Stan. *The Sand Creek Massacre*. Norman, University of Oklahoma Press, 1961.

Hyde, George E. *Indians of the High Plains*, Norman, University of Oklahoma Press, 1959.

———. *The Pawnee Indians*. Denver, J. Van Male, 1934.

———. *Red Cloud's Folk*. Norman, University of Oklahoma Press, 1937.

———. *Spotted Tail's Folk*. Norman, University of Oklahoma Press, 1961.

Inman, Henry. *The Old Santa Fé Trail*. New York, Macmillan, 1897.

Innis, Harold A. *The Fur Trade in Canada*. New Haven, Yale University Press, 1937.

Jackson, Helen Hunt. *A Century of Dishonor*. Boston, Little, Brown and Co., 1917.

Jones, Douglas C. *The Treaty of Medicine Lodge*. Norman, University of Oklahoma Press, 1966.

Kaufman, Edmond G. *The Development of the Missionary and Philanthropic Interest Among the Mennonites of North America.* Berne, Indiana, Mennonite Book Co., 1930.

Knight, Oliver. *Following the Indian Wars.* Norman, University of Oklahoma Press, 1960.

Krehbiel, H. P. *The History of the General Conference of the Mennonites of North America.* St. Louis, A. Wiebusch and Son, 1898.

Lackey, Vinson. *The Forts of Oklahoma.* Ed. by Muriel O. Lackey. Tulsa, Oklahoma, Tulsa Printing Company, 1963.

La Farge, Oliver. *As Long as the Grass Shall Grow.* New York, Longmans, Green and Co., 1940.

Lake Mohonk Conference Proceedings. New York, Lake Mohonk Conference, 1895–1900.

Larson, T. A. *History of Wyoming.* Lincoln, University of Nebraska Press, 1965.

Laubin, Reginald, and Gladys Laubin. *The Indian Tipi: Its History and Construction.* Norman, University of Oklahoma Press, 1957.

Lavender, David. *Bent's Fort.* New York, Doubleday and Company, Inc., 1954.

Leckie, William H. *The Military Conquest of the Southern Plains.* Norman, University of Oklahoma Press, 1963.

Leupp, Francis E. *The Indian and His Problems.* New York, Charles Scribner's Sons, 1910.

Long, Margaret. *The Smoky Hill Trail.* Denver, Kistler, 1943.

Lowie, Robert H. *Indians of the High Plains.* New York, McGraw-Hill Book Company, Inc., 1954.

McGovern, Patrick A. *History of the Diocese of Cheyenne.* Cheyenne, Wyoming Labor Journal, 1941.

McMechen, Edgar C. *Life of Governor Evans.* Denver, The Wahlgreen Publishing Co., 1924.

McNitt, Frank. *The Indian Traders.* Norman, University of Oklahoma Press, 1962.

Manypenny, George W. *Our Indian Wards.* Cincinnati, Robert Clarke and Co., 1880.

Mayhall, Mildred P. *The Kiowas.* Norman, University of Oklahoma Press, 1962.

Mokler, A. J. *Transition of the West.* Chicago, Lakeside Press, 1927.

Morgan, Dale L. *The West of William H. Ashley.* Denver, The Old West Publishing Company, 1964.

Morton, Arthur. *A History of the Canadian West.* London, T. Nelson and Sons, Ltd., 1939.

Mumey, Nolie. *Old Fort and Trading Posts of the West*, Vol. I. Denver, Artcraft Press, 1956.

Nadeau, Remi. *Fort Laramie and the Sioux Indians.* Englewood Cliffs, New Jersey, Prentice-Hall, 1967.

Oglesby, Richard E. *Manuel Lisa and the Opening of the Missouri Fur Trade.* Norman, University of Oklahoma Press, 1963.

Olson, James C. *Red Cloud and the Sioux Problem.* Lincoln, University of Nebraska Press, 1965.

Oklahoma Historic Sites Survey. Oklahoma City, Oklahoma Historical Society, 1958.

Pancoast, Henry S. *The Indian Before the Law.* Philadelphia, Indian Rights Association, 1884.

Paullin, Charles O. *Atlas of the Historical Geography of the United States.* Published by the Carnegie Institution of Washington and the American Geographical Society of New York. Washington, 1937.

Priest, Loring B. *Uncle Sam's Stepchildren: The Reformation of U.S. Indian Policy.* New Brunswick, New Jersey, Rutgers University Press, 1942.

Radin, Paul. *The Story of the American Indian.* Garden City, New York, Garden City Publishing Company, 1937.

Richardson, Rupert N. *The Comanche Barrier to the South Plains Settlement.* Glendale, The Arthur H. Clark Company, 1933. 1933.

Rister, Carl C. *The Southwestern Frontier.* Cleveland, The Arthur H. Clark Company, 1928.

Rogers, Fred B. *Soldiers of the Overland.* San Francisco, The Grabhorn Press, 1938.

Root, Frank A., and William E. Connelley. *The Overland Stage to California.* Topeka, Kansas, W. Y. Morgan, 1901.

Rushmore, Elsie M. *The Indian Policy during Grant's Administration.* Jamaica, Queensbury, New York, The Marion Press, 1914.

Ruth, Kent. *Oklahoma: A Guide to the Sooner State.* Norman, University of Oklahoma Press, 1957.

Sabin, Edwin L. *Kit Carson Days.* 2 vols. New York, The Press of the Pioneers, 1935.

Sandoz, Mari. *Cheyenne Autumn.* New York, McGraw-Hill, 1953.

Schoolcraft, Henry R. *Information Respecting the History, Conditions, and Prospects of the Indian Tribes of the United States.* 6 vols. Philadelphia, Lippincott, Grambo and Company, 1852–60.

Seventy-five Years of General Mission Work among the Cheyenne and Arapaho. Printed by the Mennonite Church, n.d. (Bethel College, North Newton, Kansas).

Seymour, Flora W. *Indian Agents of the Old Frontier.* New York, D. Appleton-Century Company, 1954.

Slattery, Charles L. *Felix Reville Brunot.* New York, Longmans, Green and Co., 1901.

Slotkin, J. S. *The Peyote Religion.* Glencoe, Illinois, The Free Press, 1956.

Smiley, Jerome C. *History of Denver.* Denver, J. H. Williamson and Co., 1913.

———. *Semicentennial History of the State of Colorado.* 2 vols. New York, The Lewis Publishing Co., 1913.

Sprague, Marshall. *Massacre: The Tragedy of White River.* Boston, Little, Brown and Company, 1957.

Spring, Agnes Wright. *Caspar Collins.* New York, Columbia University Press, 1937.

Stewart, Edgar D. *Custer's Luck.* Norman, University of Oklahoma Press, 1955.

Stone, Elizabeth A. *History of Uinta County.* Laramie, Wyoming, The Laramie Printing Company, 1924.

Strahorn, Robert E. *The Handbook of Wyoming.* Chicago, The Western Press, 1877.

Sunder, John E. *Bill Sublette, Mountain Man.* Norman, University of Oklahoma Press, 1959.

Swanton, John R. *The Indian Tribes of North America.* Bureau of American Ethnology *Bulletin 145.* Washington, 1952.

Tatum, Lawrie. *Our Red Brothers and the Peace Policy of President Ulysses S. Grant.* Philadelphia, J. C. Winston Co., 1899.

Taylor, Joseph H. "The Renegade Chief." In *Sketches of Frontier and Indian Life on the Upper Missouri and Great Plains, 1863–1889.* Bismarck, North Dakota, Published by the Author, 1897.

Tebbel, John W., and Keith Jennison. *The American Indian Wars.* New York, Harper and Brothers, 1960.

Trenholm, Virginia Cole, and Maurine Carley. *The Shoshonis.* Norman, University of Oklahoma Press, 1964.

Underhill, Ruth. *Red Man's Religion*. Chicago, University of Chicago Press, 1965.

Vaughn, J. W. *The Battle of Platte Bridge*. Norman, University of Oklahoma Press, 1963.

———. *The Reynolds Campaign on Powder River*. Norman, University of Oklahoma Press, 1961.

Wallace, Ernest, and E. Adamson Hoebel. *The Comanches*. Norman, University of Oklahoma Press, 1952.

Watrous, Ansel. *History of Larimer County* (Colorado). Fort Collins, Colorado, Courier Printing and Publishing Co., 1911.

Webb, Walter Prescott. *The Great Plains*. Boston, Houghton Mifflin, 1936.

Wedel, Waldo. *Prehistoric Man on the Great Plains*. Norman, University of Oklahoma Press, 1961.

Winchell, N. H. *The Aborigines of Minnesota*. St. Paul, The Pioneer Company, 1911.

Wright, Muriel H. *A Guide to the Indian Tribes of Oklahoma*. Norman, University of Oklahoma Press, 1951.

Ziegler, W. H. *Wyoming Indians*. Laramie, Wyoming, n.p., n.d.

ARTICLES, JOURNALS, AND REPORTS
IN PERIODICAL PUBLICATIONS

Anderson, Harry H. "Stand at the Arikaree," *Colorado Magazine*, XLI, 4 (October, 1964).

Andrews, Ralph W. "He Knew the Red Man," *Montana Magazine*, XIV, 2 (Spring, 1964).

Ashley, Susan R. "Reminiscences of Colorado in the Early Sixties," *Colorado Magazine*, XIII, 6 (November, 1936).

Bailey, Adah B. "Monte Blevins, North Park Cattleman," *Colorado Magazine*, XVIII, 1 (January, 1941).

Ball, John. "Across the Continent Seventy Years Ago," *Oregon Historical Quarterly*, III, 4 (Spring, 1902).

Barry, Louise (ed.). "Letters of Pikes Peak Gold Region." Inc. reprint of Albert D. Richardson's "Letters to the Editor," *Lawrence* (Kansas) *Republican*, May 22–August 15, 1860. *Kansas Historical Quarterly*, XII, 1 (February, 1943).

Bass, Althea. "Carl Sweezy, Arapaho Artist," *Chronicles of Oklahoma*, XXXIV, 4 (Winter, 1956–57).

——. "James Mooney in Oklahoma," *Chronicles of Oklahoma*, XXXII, 3 (Autumn, 1954).

"Battles and Skirmishes in Wyoming Territory," *Annals of Wyoming*, XIV, 3 (July, 1942).

Becknell, William. "The Journals of Captain William Becknell," *Missouri Historical Review*, IV, 2 (January, 1910).

Benedict, Ruth F. "The Concept of the Guardian Spirit in North America," American Anthropological Association *Memoirs*, XXIX, 1 (1923).

——. "The Vision in Plains Culture," *American Anthropologist*, XXIV, 1 (1922).

Bent, Charles. "The Charles Bent Papers," *New Mexico Historical Review*, XXX, 2 (April, 1955).

Bent, George. "Forty Years with the Cheyennes," ed. by George E. Hyde, *The Frontier*, IV, 4–9 (October, 1905–March, 1906).

Bidwell, John. "The First Emigrant Train to California," *Century Magazine*, XLI, 1 (1890).

Bieber, Ralph. "The Southwestern Trails to California in 1849," *Mississippi Valley Historical Review*, XII, 3 (December, 1925).

Block, Augusta Hauck. "Lower Boulder and St. Vrain Valley Home Guards and Fort Junction," *Colorado Magazine*, XVI, 5 (September, 1939).

Boggs, William M. "A Short History of Bent's Fort," *Colorado Magazine*, VII, 2 (March, 1930).

Bolton, Henry E. "New Light on Manuel Lisa and the Spanish Trade," *Southwestern Historical Quarterly*, XVII (1913).

Bourke, John G. "Mackenzie's Last Fight with the Cheyennes," *Recruiting News* (1929–30). Army Information Bulletin (reprint of 1890).

Bradley, James M. "Lieutenant Bradley's Journal," *Contributions to the History of Montana*, III (1900).

Bragg, William F. "Feed 'em in the Winter, Fight 'em in the Summer," *The Westerners Brand Book*. Boulder, Johnson Publishing Company, 1945.

Bridger, James. Quoted in *Army and Navy Journal*. IV (June 29, 1867).

Brown, Donald. "The Ghost Dance Religion Among the Oklahoma Cheyennes," *Chronicles of Oklahoma*, XXX, 4 (Winter, 1952–53).

Burkey, E. R. "The Site of the Murder of the Hungate Family by Indians in 1864," *Colorado Magazine*, XII, 4 (July, 1935).

Burnett, Finn. "Account of Tongue River," *Annals of Wyoming*, VIII, 3 (1932).

Cahill, Luke. "An Indian Campaign in 1868," *Colorado Magazine*, IV, 4 (1927).

Caldwell, Martha B. (ed.). "When Horace Greeley Visited Kansas in 1859," *Kansas Historical Quarterly*, IX, 2 (May, 1940).

Campbell, Robert. "Correspondence, 1834–1845," *Glimpses of the Past*, VIII, 1–6 (1941). Missouri Historical Society, St. Louis.

Campbell, Walter S. (Stanley Vestal). "The Cheyenne Dog Soldiers," *Chronicles of Oklahoma*, I, 1 (January, 1923).

Carey, John G. "The Puzzle of Sand Creek," *Colorado Magazine*, XLI, 4 (1964).

Carter, John G. "The Northern Arapaho Flat Pipe and the Ceremony of Covering the Pipe," Bureau of American Ethnology *Bulletin 119*. Washington, 1938.

Cartwright, Willenda D. "The Peyote Cult," Leaflet Nos. 105 and 106, Denver Art Museum, 1950.

Cocking, Mathew. "Journal of Mathew Cocking from York Factory to the Blackfoot Country, 1772–73," ed by L. J. Burpee, Royal Society of Canada *Proceedings and Transactions*, Series 2, Vol. II, Sec. 2. Ottawa, 1908.

Coffin, William H. "Settlements of the Friends in Kansas," *Kansas Historical Collections*, VII (1901–1902).

Collins, Catharine W. "An Army Wife Comes West," ed. by Agnes Wright Spring, *Colorado Magazine*, XXXI, 4 (1954).

Collins, Hubert E. "Ben Williams, Frontier Peace Officer," *Chronicles of Oklahoma*, X, 4 (1932).

Connelley, W. E. "A Journal on the Santa Fé Trail," *Mississippi Valley Historical Review*, XII, 1–2 (1925).

———. "Treaty Held at Medicine Lodge," *Kansas Historical Collections*, XVII (1928).

Cooper, John M. *The Gros Ventres of Montana, II. Religion and Ritual*, Regina Flannery, ed., Catholic University of America *Anthropological Series*, No. 16 (1956).

Dale, Edward Everett. "The Arapaho Country after 1866," *Chronicles of Oklahoma*, XX, 4 (1942).

———. "Ranching on the Cheyenne and Arapaho Reservation," *Chronicles of Oklahoma*, VI, 1, (1928).

"Darlington, the Indian's Friend" (a memorial republished by *The El Reno American* from an old pamphlet). William Sessions, Printer, Low Ausgate, New York, 1873.

Davis, Theodore R. "A Stage Ride to Colorado," *Harper's New Monthly Magazine*, XXXV (July, 1867).

———. "A Summer on the Plains," *Harper's New Monthly Magazine*, XXXVI (February, 1868).

Densmore, Frances. "Cheyenne and Arapaho Music," *Southwest Museum Papers*, No. 10. Los Angeles, 1936.

Dorsey, George A. *The Arapaho Sun Dance.* Publication 75, *Anthropological Series*, IV. Chicago, Field Columbian Museum, 1903.

Dorsey, George A., and Alfred L. Kroeber. *Traditions of the Arapaho.* Publication 81, *Anthropological Series*, V. Chicago, Field Columbian Museum, 1903.

Dusenberry, Verne. "The Montana Cree," *Stockholm Studies in Comparative Religion.* University of Stockholm, 1962.

Ediger, T. A., and Vinnie Hoffman. "Some Reminiscences of the Battle of Washita," *Chronicles of Oklahoma*, XXXIII, 2 (Summer, 1955).

Eggan, Frederick R. "The Cheyenne and Arapaho Kinship System." In *Social Anthropology of North American Tribes.* Chicago, University of Chicago Press, 1937.

Elkin, Henry. "The Northern Arapaho of Wyoming." In Ralph Linton (ed.), *Acculturation in Seven American Indian Tribes.* New York, D. Appleton-Century Company, 1940.

Evans, Hugh. "Journal of Colonel Henry Dodge's Expedition to the Rocky Mountains," ed. by Fred S. Perrine, *Mississippi Valley Historical Review*, XIV, 2 (1927).

Ewers, John C. "The Indian Trade of the Upper Missouri Before Lewis and Clark," *Missouri Historical Society Bulletin*, X, 4 (1954).

Fairchild, S. H. "The Eleventh Kansas Regiment at Platte Bridge," *Kansas Historical Collections*, VIII (1904).

Fitzpatrick, Thomas. "Thomas Fitzpatrick and the First Indian Agency of the Upper Platte and Arkansas," *Mississippi Valley Historical Review*, XV, 3 (December, 1928).

Flannery, Regina. *The Gros Ventres of Montana, I. Social Life.* Catholic University of America *Anthropological Series*, No. 15 (1953).

Ford, Lemuel. "Captain Ford's Journal of an Expedition to the Rocky Mountains," ed. by Louis Pelzer, *Mississippi Valley Historical Review*, XII, 4 (March, 1926).

Foreman, Carolyn T. "Colonel Jesse Henry Leavenworth," *Chronicles of Oklahoma*, XIII, 1 (March, 1935).

Forsyth, George A. "A Frontier Fight," *Harper's New Monthly Magazine*, XCI, (June, 1895).

Freeman, Winfield. "The Battle of the Arikaree," *Transactions of the Kansas State Historical Society*, VI (1897–1900).

Garfield, Marvin H. "Defense of Kansas," *Kansas Historical Quarterly*, I, 1, 2, 4, 5 (1931–32).

Gatchell, T. J. "Fort Phil Kearny and Environs." Gatchell's Drug Store, Fiftieth Anniversary Souvenir. Buffalo, Wyoming, May 22, 1950.

Grinnell, George B. "Bent's Old Fort and Its Builders," *Kansas Historical Collections*, XV (1919–22).

Gross, F. "Nomadism of the Arapaho Indians of Wyoming," *University of Wyoming Publications in Science*, XV, 3 (1950).

Guinn, Jack. "The Red Man's Last Struggle." Reprint from *Empire Magazine*, *Denver Post*, March 27 to May 29, 1966.

Gustin, Marion. "Arapaho Indian Is Distinguished Churchman," *The Spirit of Missions* (Easter, 1931).

Hafen, Ann W. "Efforts to Recover the Stolen Son of Chief Ouray," *Colorado Magazine*, XVI, 2 (1939).

Hafen, LeRoy R. "The Early Fur Trade Posts on the South Platte," *Mississippi Valley Historical Review*, XII, 3 (December, 1925).

———. "Fort Lupton," *Colorado Magazine*, VI, 6 (November, 1929).

———. "Fort St. Vrain," *Colorado Magazine*, XXIV, 2 (October, 1952).

———. "Fraeb's Last Fight and How Battle Mountain Got Its Name," *Colorado Magazine*, VII, 3 (May, 1930).

———. "Mountain Man: Louis Vasquez," *Colorado Magazine*, X, 1 (January, 1933).

———. "Thomas Fitzpatrick and the First Indian Agency in Colorado," *Colorado Magazine*, VI, 2 (March, 1929).

Haines, Francis. "The Northward Spread of the Horse," *American Anthropologist*, N.S., XL, 3 (1938).

Hamilton, William T. "A Trading Expedition Among the Indians in 1858," Montana Historical Society *Contributions*, III (1900).

Harmon, E. M. "The Story of the Indian Fight Near Granby, Colorado," *Colorado Magazine*, XXII, 4 (July, 1945).

Harper, Richard H. "The Missionary Work of the Reformed (Dutch) Church of America in Oklahoma" (Part I, "The Cheyennes and Arapahoes"), *Chronicles of Oklahoma*, XVIII, 3 (1940).

Hayden, F. V. "Contributions to the Ethnology and Philology of the Indian Tribes of the Upper Missouri Valley," American Philological Society *Transactions*, N.S., XII (1862).

Hieb, D. L. "Fort Laramie National Monument," *National Park Service Handbook*, Series No. 20. Washington, 1954.

Hilger, Sister M. Inez. *Arapaho Child Life and Its Cultural Background*. Bureau of American Ethnology *Bulletin 148*. Washington, 1952.

Hodge, Frederick Webb (ed.). *Handbook of American Indians North of Mexico*. Bureau of American Ethnology *Bulletin 30*. 2 vols. Washington, 1907.

Hoopes, A. W. "Thomas S. Twiss, Indian Agent on the Upper Platte," *Mississippi Valley Historical Review*, XX, 3 (1933).

Hornaday, William T. *The Extermination of the American Bison*. Washington, U.S. National Museum, 1887.

Hull, Lewis B. "Soldiering on the High Plains," *Kansas Historical Quarterly*, VII, 1 (1938).

Hultkrantz, Ake. "Some Notes on the Arapaho Sun Dance," *Ethnos*, XVII (1952).

Hunton, John. *John Hunton's Diary*. Ed. by L. G. Flannery. 5 vols. *Lingle* (Wyoming) *Guide Review*, 1956–64.

Hurst, John, and Sigmund Shlesinger. "Battle of the Arikaree," *Kansas Historical Collections*, XV (1919–22).

Indian Rights Association. *Annual Report*, X. Philadelphia (1893).

"Indian Treaties and Councils Affecting Kansas," *Kansas Historical Collections*, XVI (1923–25).

Jablow, Joseph. *The Cheyenne in Plains Indian Trade Relations*. American Ethnological Society Monograph No. 19. New York, J. J. Augustin, 1951.

Jackson, George A. "Diary," *Colorado Magazine*, XII, 6 (November, 1935).

Keeling, H. C. "My Experience with the Cheyenne Indians," *Kansas Historical Collections*, XI (1909–10).

Kingman, Samuel A. "Diary of Samuel Kingman in 1865," *Kansas Historical Quarterly*, I, 5 (November, 1932).

Knopp, T. C. "Rabbit Run," *Chronicles of Oklahoma*, XXIII, 4 (1945).

Kroeber, Alfred L. *The Arapaho*. American Museum of Natural History *Bulletin 18*, Vol. XIII, Pts. 1–4. New York, 1902–1907.

———. "Arapaho Dialects," *Publications in American Archaeology and Ethnology*, XII, 3 (1916). Berkeley, University of California.

———. *Cultural and Natural Areas of Native North America*. Berkeley, University of California, 1939.

———. "Decorative Symbolism of the Arapaho," *American Anthropologist*, N.S., III (1901).

———. "Ethnology of the Gros Ventres," American Museum of Natural History *Anthropological Papers*, Vol. I, Pt. 4. New York, 1908.

———. "Gros Ventre Myths and Tales," American Museum of Natural History *Anthropological Papers*, Vol. I. New York, 1907.

———. *Symbolism of the Arapaho Indians*. American Museum of Natural History *Bulletin 13*. New York, 1900.

La Barre, Weston. "Twenty Years of Peyote Studies," *Current Anthropology*, I, 1 (January, 1960).

Lambert, Julia S. "Plain Tales of the Plains," *The Trail*, VII, 12 (January–September, 1916).

LaRaye, Charles. "The Journal of Charles LaRaye," *South Dakota Historical Collections*, IV (1908).

Le Compte, Janet. "Gantt's Fort and Bent's Picket Post," *Colorado Magazine*, XLI, 2 (Spring, 1964).

———. "Sand Creek," *Colorado Magazine*, XLI, 4 (October, 1964).

Lemley, H. R. "Among the Arapahoes," *Harper's New Monthly Magazine*, XL (March, 1880).

Lockhard, F. M. "A Version of a Famous Battle," *Chronicles of Oklahoma*, V, 13 (September, 1927).

Lowie, Robert H. "Ceremonialism in North America," *American Anthropologist*, N.S., XVI, 4 (October–December, 1914).

———. *The Crow Indian*. New York, Farrar and Rinehart, 1935.

———. "Plains Indians Age Societies." American Museum of Natural History *Anthropological Papers*, Vol. XI, Pt. 13. New York, 1916.

Luebers, H. L. "William Bent's Family and the Indians of the Plains," *Colorado Magazine*, XIII, 1 (January, 1936).

McBratney, Robert. "Exploring the Solomon River Valley, 1869," ed. by Martha B. Caldwell, *Kansas Historical Quarterly*, VI, 1 (1937).

McNeal, T. A. "The Indians Agree to Abandon Kansas," *Kansas Historical Collections*, VI (1897–1900).

Mallery, Garrick. "Sign Language among North American Indians," Bureau of American Ethnology, *First Annual Report*. Washington, 1881.

Mandelbaum, D. "The Plains Cree," American Museum of Natural History *Anthropological Papers*, Vol. XXXVII, Pt. 2. New York, 1940.

Marshall, T. M. (ed.). "The Journals of Jules de Mun," *Missouri Historical Society Collections*, V, 2–3 (1928).

Mason, O. T. "Indian Cradles," *American Anthropologist*, I (1888).

Mead, James R. "The Little Arkansas," *Kansas Historical Collections*, IX (1907).

Merrill, Moses. "Diary of Rev. Moses Merrill," Nebraska Historical Society *Proceedings and Collections*, IV (1892).

Meserve, Charles F. "The First Allotment of Lands in Severalty among the Oklahoma Cheyenne and Arapaho Indians," *Chronicles of Oklahoma*, XI, 4 (1933).

Michelson, Truman. "Narrative of an Arapaho Woman," *American Anthropologist*, N.S., XXXV, 4 (1933).

———. "Preliminary Report on the Linguistic Classification of Algonquian Tribes," Bureau of American Ethnology, *Twenty-eighth Annual Report* (1906–1907), Washington, 1912.

———. "Some Arapaho Kinship Terms and Social Usages," *American Anthropologist*, N.S., XXXVI (1934).

Mishkin, Bernard. "Rank and Warfare among the Plains Indians," American Ethnological Society *Monograph* No. 3 (1940).

Montgomery, Mrs. F. C. "Fort Wallace and Its Relation to the Frontier," *Kansas Historical Collections*, Vol. XVII (1926–28).

Mooney, James. "Arapaho." In Frederick Webb Hodge (ed.), *Handbook of American Indians North of Mexico*. Bureau of American Ethnology *Bulletin 30*. 2 vols. Washington, 1907.

———. *Calendar History of the Kiowa Indians*. Bureau of American Ethnology, *Seventeenth Annual Report*, Pt. 1. Washington, 1898.

———. "The Cheyenne Indians," American Anthropological Association *Memoirs*, I (1905–1907).

———. *The Ghost Dance Religion and the Sioux Outbreak of 1890.*

Bureau of American Ethnology, *Fourteenth Annual Report*, Pt. 2. Washington, 1896.

———. "Little Raven," Bureau of American Ethnology *Bulletin 30*, Vol. II.

———. "Peyote," Bureau of American Ethnology *Bulletin 30*, Vol. II.

———. "Sun Dance," Bureau of American Ethnology *Bulletin 30*, Vol. II.

Moore, Horace C. "The Washita Campaign," *Chronicles of Oklahoma*, II, 4 (1924).

Morris, Robert C. "Wyoming Indians," Wyoming Historical Society *Collections*, I (1897).

Mulloy, William. "A Preliminary Historical Outline for the Northwestern Plains," *University of Wyoming Publications in Science*, XXII, 1 (July, 1958).

Murphy, James C. "The Place of the Northern Arapahoes in the Relations Between the United States and the Indians of the Plains." (1851–79). *Annals of Wyoming*, XLI, 1 and 2 (1969).

Murphy, John. "Reminiscences of the Washita Campaign and of the Darlington Indian Agency," *Chronicles of Oklahoma*, I, 3 (June, 1923).

Murray, E. F. "Mountain Man: George Nidiver." *Colorado Magazine*, X, 3 (May, 1933).

Nesbitt, Paul. "The Battle of the Washita," *Chronicles of Oklahoma*, III, 1 (1925).

Nicholson, William. "A Tour of Indian Agencies in Kansas and Indian Territory," *Kansas Historical Quarterly*, III, 3 (August, 1934).

Nickerson, H. G. "Early History of Fremont County, Wyoming," Wyoming State Historical Society *Bulletins*, II, 1 (1924).

———. "Indian Depredations in Sweetwater County," Wyoming Historical Society *Collections*, I, 1 (1897).

Nunin, Doyce B., Jr. "Milton Sublette: Thunderbolt of the Rockies," *Montana Magazine*, XIII, 3 (Summer, 1963).

Orchard, William C. "The Technique of Porcupine-Quill Decoration among the North American Indians," *American Indian Contributions*, IV, 1. New York, Heye Foundation, 1916.

Palmer, H. E. "History of the Powder River Indian Expedition of 1865," Nebraska State Historical Society *Transactions and Reports*, II (1887).

Patten, James I. "Bates' Famous Battle," *The* (Big Horn) *Rustler* (October, 1899).

Peairs, H. B. "A Visit to Seger (Colony)" *Proceedings*, Thirteenth Annual Meeting, Friends of the Indians. New York, Lake Mohonk Conference, 1895.

Peery, D. W. "The Indian's Friend, John H. Seger," *Chronicles of Oklahoma*, X–XI (1932–33).

Pennock, Jake. "Diary of Jake Pennock, 1865," *Annals of Wyoming*, XXIII, 2 (July, 1951).

Perrigo, Lynn I. "Major Hal Sayr's Diary of the Sand Creek Campaign," *Colorado Magazine*, XV, 2 (March, 1938).

Pike, Zebulon M. "Papers of Zebulon M. Pike, 1806–1807," ed. by H. E. Bolton, *American Historical Review*, XIII (July, 1908).

Powell, J. W. *Linguistic Families of American Indians.* Bureau of American Ethnology, *Seventh Annual Report* (1891).

Pratt, R. H. "The Way out—the Outing System." *Proceedings*, Ninth Conference, Friends of the Indians. New York, Lake Mohonk Conference, 1891.

Prentice, C. A. "Captain Silas S. Soule, a Pioneer Martyr," *Colorado Magazine*, VII, 6 (November, 1935).

Rachlin, Carol. "The Native American Church," *Chronicles of Oklahoma*, XLII, 3 (Autumn, 1964).

Radin, Paul. "Jesse Clay's Account of the Arapaho Manner of Giving the Peyote Ceremony which He Introduced among the Winnebago in 1912," Bureau of American Ethnology, *Thirty-eighth Annual Report* (1923).

Rairdon, J. T. "John Homer Seger: The Practical Indian Educator," *Chronicles of Oklahoma*, XXXIV, 2 (Summer, 1956).

Renaud, E. B. *Archaeological Survey of Eastern Wyoming.* University of Denver *Bulletin* (May, 1932).

Richardson, Albert D. "Leavenworth and Pike's Peak Route," *Southwestern Historical Quarterly*, XI (1942). See also Barry, Louise, *supra.*

Rister, C. C. "Harmful Practices of Indian Traders of the Southwest, 1865–1876," *New Mexico Historical Review*, VI (July, 1931).

Roe, Walter C. "Remarks on Work among the Cheyennes and Arapahoes in Oklahoma." *Proceedings*, Sixteenth Annual Meeting, Friends of the Indians. New York, Lake Mohonk Conference, 1898.

Root, George A. "Extracts from the Diary of Captain Lambert Wolf," *Kansas Historical Quarterly*, IV, 3 (1932).

Ruth, Kent. "The Left Hand House," *The War Chief of the Indian Territory Posse of Oklahoma Westerners*, III, 3 (December, 1969).

Salzmann, Zdenek. "Arapaho," *International Journal of American Linguistics*, XXII (1956), XXVII (1961).

———. "Arapaho Tales," *Hoosier Folklore*, IX, 3 (1950).

Sanford, Albert B. "Life at Camp Weld and Fort Lyon in 1861–1862," *Colorado Magazine*, VII, 4 (July, 1930).

Schreibeis, Charles D. "The Tragedy of Fort Phil Kearny." In *The Westerners Brand Book*. Denver, 1951.

Scott, Hugh L. "The Early History and Names of the Arapaho," *American Anthropologist*, N.S., IX (1907).

She-Wolf. "Account of the Death of Major Joel H. Elliott" (as told to George Bent), *Kansas Historical Collections*, X (1907–1908).

Shields, Lillian B. "Relations with the Cheyenne and Arapaho in Colorado in 1861," *Colorado Magazine*, IV, 4 (August, 1927).

Shirk, George H. "Campaigning with Sheridan," *Chronicles of Oklahoma*, XXXVII, 1 (Spring, 1959).

Small, John. "Trip of Colonel James McLaughlin, Indian Inspector, to the Big Hot Springs, Wyoming," *Annals of Wyoming*, VIII, 1 (July, 1931).

Smith, Maurice G. "Political Organizations of the Plains Indians," *University of Nebraska Studies*, XXIV, 1–2 (1925).

Spier, Leslie. *The Prophet Dance of the Northwest and Its Derivatives.* In American Anthropological Association *Series in Anthropology*, Vol. I. New York, 1935.

———. "The Sun Dance of the Plains Indians," ed. by Clark Wissler, American Museum of Natural History *Anthropological Papers*, Vol. XVI, Pt. 7. New York, 1921.

Spring, Agnes Wright. "Founding of Fort Collins," *Colorado Magazine*, X, 2 (March, 1933).

———. "Rush to the Rockies, 1859," *Colorado Magazine*, XXXVI, 2 (April, 1959).

Steele, Aubrey L. "Beginning of Quaker Administration of Indian Affairs in Oklahoma," *Chronicles of Oklahoma*, XVII, 4 (December, 1939).

Stenberg, Mollie P. "The Peyote Culture among Wyoming Indians," *University of Wyoming Publications in Science*, XII, 4 (1946).

Stobie, Charles S. "With the Indians in Colorado," *Colorado Magazine*, VII, 2 (March, 1930).

Tahan (Joseph K. Griffis). "The Battle of the Washita," *Chronicles of Oklahoma*, VIII, 3 (1930).

Taylor, Alfred A. "Medicine Lodge Peace Council," *Chronicles of Oklahoma*, II, 2 (March, 1924).

Taylor, M. L. "The Western Services of Stephen Watts Kearny, 1815–1848," *New Mexico Historical Review*, XXI, 3 (July, 1946).

Thoburn, Joseph B. "My Experience among the Cheyenne Indians: The Story of Cantonment," *Chronicles of Oklahoma*, III, 1 (1925).

———. "The Peace Council Celebrations at Medicine Lodge," *Chronicles of Oklahoma*, V, 4 (1927).

Thomas, Alfred B. "Spanish Expeditions into Colorado," *Colorado Magazine*, I, 7 (November, 1924).

Tilghman, Zoe A. "A Bed for God," *Oklahoma Today*, XV, 2 (Spring, 1965).

Traux, Allan L. "Manuel Lisa and His North Dakota Trading Post," *North Dakota Historical Quarterly*, II (July, 1928).

Trudeau, Jean Baptiste. "Journal of Jean Baptiste Trudeau among the Arikara Indians in 1795," trans. by Mrs. H. T. Beauregard, *Missouri Historical Society Collections*, IV (1912–13).

———. "Trudeau's Description," ed. by Annie H. Abel, *Mississippi Valley Historical Review*, VIII, 1–2 (1921).

———. "Trudeau's Journal," *South Dakota Historical Collections*, VII (1914).

Underhill, Ruth. "Peyote," International Congress of Americanists *Proceedings*, XXX (1952).

Unrau, William E. "A Prelude to War," *Colorado Magazine*, XLI, 4 (October, 1964).

———. "The Story of Fort Larned," *Kansas Historical Quarterly*, XXIII, 3 (Autumn, 1957).

Voth, H. R. "Arapaho Tales," *Journal of American Folklore*, XXV (1912).

———. "Funeral Customs Among the Cheyenne and Arapaho Indians," *Folklorist*, I (1893).

Weinstein, Robert A., and Russell E. Belous. "Indian Portrait: Fort Sill, 1869," *The American West*, III, 1 (Winter, 1966).

Wheeler, Homer W. "Reminiscences of Old Fort Washakie," *Annals of Wyoming*, I, 4 (1924).

Williams, Ezekiel. "Adventures in Colorado," *Missouri Historical Society Collections*, IV, 2 (1913).

Wilson, H. L. *The Trail of the Arapaho Nation.* Episcopal church leaflet, n.d.

Wilson, R. H. "The Indian Treaty of 1896," *Annals of Wyoming*, VIII, 2 (October, 1922).

Wissler, Clark. "The Influence of the Horse in the Development of Plains Culture," *American Anthropologist*, N.S., XVI, 1 (1914).

———."Population Changes among the Northern Plains Indians," In *Anthropology*, Vol. I. New Haven, Yale University Press, 1936.

———. "Societies of the Plains Indians," American Museum of Natural History *Anthropological Papers*, Vol. XI. New York, 1912–16.

———. "Sun Dance of the Plains Indians," American Museum of National History *Anthropological Papers*, Vol. 16, XVI. New York, 1921.

Woodson, A. E. "The Indians of Oklahoma." *Proceedings*, Fourteenth Annual Meeting, Friends of the Indians. Lake Mohonk Conference, New York, 1896.

Woodward, George A. "The Northern Cheyennes at Fort Fetterman," ed. by John E. Parsons, *Montana Magazine* (Spring, 1959).

Wright, Muriel. "A History of Fort Cobb," *Chronicles of Oklahoma*, XXXIV, 1 (1956).

Wright, Robert M. "Reminiscences of Dodge," *Kansas Historical Collections*, X (1905–1906).

Wynkoop, Edward E. "Edward Wanshier Wynkoop," *Kansas Historical Collections*, XIII (1913–14).

Wyoming Historical Society Collections, I, 1 (1897).

Index

347

Fort Lyon: 169, 170 ff., 181 ff., 190 ff., 228
Fort Mandan: 35
Fort Manuel Lisa: 36
Fort Marion: 65, 253
Fort Morgan: 96
Fort Phil Kearny: 198, 215 f.
Fort Pierre Treaty: 145
Fort Platte: 118
Fort Rankin: 198
Fort Reno, Okla.: 284 f.
Fort Reno, Wyo.: 215, 256
Fort Riley: 161
Fort Robinson: 259
Fort St. Vrain: 102, 128, 152 f.
Fort Sanders: 221
Fort Sedgwick: *see* Fort Rankin
Fort Sill: 228 ff., 284
Fort Stambaugh: 236
Fort Union: 92
Fort Vasquez: 106
Fort Wallace: 217
Fort Washakie: 237 f., 260, 268, 290, 308
Fort William on the Laramie: 94–95
Fort Wise: 164: *see also* Fort Lyon
Fort Wise Treaty: 162 ff., 173, 175
Found-in-Grass (cycle story): 7
Fountain River (in Colorado): 44
Four Old Men (the directions): 56
Fowler, Jacob: 44 ff.
Fox (boys' lodge): *see* Kit Fox Lodge
Fox, The: 221
Fraeb, Henry, killed by Indians: 82, 113
Frémont, John Charles: 115–16, 121, 128
Frémont's Orchard: 177
French: 19, 23, 114
French-Canadians: 17 ff.
Friday ("Friday Fitzpatrick"): 89, 117, 146, 166 ff., 171, 180 f.; trip to Washington, 139; favors Cache la Poudre, 151; at St. Vrain, 151–52; at Deer Creek, 157; signs agreement, 172; at Fort Laramie, 221; at Wind River, 231 f., 260; return to Colorado, 233–34; influence of, 236; as interpreter, 254, 261; death of, 269 & n.; victim of white man's liquor, 277
Friday, Robert: 55
Friday, Zoe: 295–96
Frontier Indians: 140
Funeral customs: 63

Funny Men band: 53
Fur trade: 82, 94

Gantt, John: trader, 96; whiskey peddler, 96; peacemaker, 98; guide, 98
Gantt unofficial peace treaty, with Arapahoes: 98, 119, 133
Garrard, Lewis H., visit with Arapahoes: 124–26
Geary, Okla.: 309
General Allotment Act (Dawes Act): 277, 279
General Council, at Okmulgee, Okla.: 253–54
General Statutes of Oklahoma: 294
Gens de Rapid (Fall Indians): 29
Gens de Vache (Cow or Buffalo People): 17, 21, 23, 29; *see also* Bison Path People
Gens du Serpents (Snake Indians): 15; *see also* Shoshoni Indians
Gerry, Elbridge: 171, 173, 185
Gervais, Jean Baptiste: 82
Ghost Dance: 65, 267, 283 ff., 297–98; origin of, 283; at Wind River, 283; in Indian Territory, 284 ff.; debate concerning, 286 ff.
Ghost Dance music: *see under* songs
Ghost Dance shirts: 289
Gibbon, Colonel John: 256
Gifts: 110
Gilpin, William: 164
Glenn, Captain Hugh: 44, 47
Goggles, Benny: 56n.
Goggles, John: 297
Goggles, Mike, Sr.: 273
Gold: 156, 213; discovery by Indians, 118, 203; Left Hand's tale concerning, 149; in Black Hills, 253, 255
Golden, Colo.: 151
Goldseekers: 132, 148
Good Hearts (Northern Arapahoes): 5
Gordon, Major David: 236
Governor of Massachusetts: 241
Governor of Wyoming: 260
Grand Council (intertribal): 110, 141
Grand Encampment (intertribal): 41
Grandfather (ceremonial): 61, 75
Grandview, Idaho: 37
Grant, President U.S.: 229, 237, 255

355

Hunger, experienced by Arapahoes:
140, 147
Hungry Dance: 278
Hungry Man: 259
Hunt, Wilson Price: 37
Hunting: 7, 12, 65–66, 141
Hunting grounds: 122, 252
Hurons: 13

Ice (bandleader): 243
Immigrant Indians: 141; *see also under
names of tribes*
Independence, Mo.: 47
Indian agencies (Arapaho): *see under
names of agencies*
Indian demands: 239
Indian Peace Commissioners: (1865)
211f.; (1866) 215ff.; (1867) 218ff.;
(1868) 220ff.
Indian Regulations (1904): 307
Indian rights: questioned, 158;
protected, 161
Indian Rights Association: 284
Indian Territory: 221, 223, 233, 248,
254, 260, 264, 276, 297
Industrial School: Mennonite, 271;
Dutch Reformed, 305; *see also*
Mohonk Lodge
Infidelity: 58–59
Interpreters: 22, 44, 124, 142, 168ff.,
213, 251
Intertribal peace council: 109ff., 141ff.
Intertribal warfare: 50ff., 84, 109
Intoxicants: 91, 96, 106, 117–18, 125,
161, 163, 200, 277
Iron-which-Moves (Gros Ventre
chief): 92–93
Iroquois Indians: 13, 27
Irving, Washington: 111
Irwin, Agent James: 251f., 261–62
Isham, James: 17

Jackson, David E.: 82
Jackson, George A.: 149
James, Edwin: 41ff.
James, May Whiteshirt: 309n.
Janice (Janise), Antoine: 171, 173, 208
Jarrot, Agent Vital: 203
Johnston, Colonel Albert Sidney: 146
Jones, Agent Thomas M.: 273, 277
Julesburg, Colo.: first attack upon,
197ff.; second attack upon, 199ff.

Jutson, Collie: 55n.
Jutz, Fr. John: 272

Kananavich (Bison Path People): on
Canadian Plains, 4ff.; south of the
Missouri, 23ff.; allied with Chey-
ennes, 23; war and peace with Sioux,
25; *see* Atsina–Gros Ventre Indians
and Arapaho Indians
Kansas: 33, 161, 178, 195, 214, 216, 219,
220, 224, 249, 255
Kansas Indians: *see* Kaw Indians
Kaw Indians: 110, 219ff., 222f.
Kearny, Colonel Stephen W.: 121ff.
Kelsey, Henry: 14
Ketcham, H. Y.: 176
Kincaide, Mr. and Mrs. Reese: 305
Kingman, Samuel A.: 211
Kinnikinnick: 67
Kiowa-Apache Grand Council: 219
Kiowa-Comanche Reservation: 230
Kiowa country: 197
Kiowa Indians: 34, 41, 45, 48, 50, 103,
109f., 134, 140, 145, 164, 172, 177f.,
182ff., 218ff., 230, 240, 244, 287, 289,
293f.
"Kiowa Road": 287
Kiowa War: 244
Kiowa Way: 297n.; *see also* Peyote
Cult
Kit Fox Lodge: 77
Knock Knees: *see* No-ta-nee
Kohiss: 194
Krehbiel, Christian: 271
Kroeber, Alfred L.: 9–10, 12, 55
Kutenai Indians: 21

La Bonte Creek (in Wyoming): 235
Lake Mohonk Indian Conference:
279, 305
Lander, Wyo.; 232f., 250
Land in Severalty Act: 280
Language, Arapaho: 97
La Porte, Colo.: 151
La Ramie, Jacques: killed by Arapa-
hoes, 46, 82; symbol of fur trade,
46–47
Laramie, Wyo.: 221
Laramie Mountains: 165
Laramie Plains: 111, 115, 165, 202
Laramie River: 82, 94f., 102, 157
Left Hand, Grant: 292

357

of which *The Arapahoes, Our People* is the 105th volume, was inaugurated in 1932 by the University of Oklahoma Press, and has as its purpose the reconstruction of American Indian civilization by presenting aboriginal, historical, and contemporary Indian life. The following list is complete as of the date of publication of this volume.

1. *Forgotten Frontiers:* A Study of the Spanish Indian Policy of Don Juan Bautista de Anza, Governor of New Mexico, 1777–1787. Translated and edited by Alfred Barnaby Thomas.
2. Grant Foreman. *Indian Removal:* The Emigration of the Five Civilized Tribes of Indians.
3. John Joseph Mathews. *Wah'Kon-Tah:* The Osage and the White Man's Road.
4. Grant Foreman. *Advancing the Frontier, 1830–1860.*
5. John H. Seger. *Early Days Among the Cheyenne and Arapahoe Indians.* Edited by Stanley Vestal. Out of print.
6. Angie Debo. *The Rise and Fall of the Choctaw Republic.*
7. Stanley Vestal. *New Sources of Indian History, 1850–1891:* A Miscellany. Out of print.
8. Grant Foreman. *The Five Civilized Tribes.*
9. *After Coronado:* Spanish Exploration Northeast of New Mexico, 1696–1727. Translated and edited by Alfred Barnaby Thomas.
10. Frank G. Speck, *Naskapi:* The Savage Hunters of the Labrador Peninsula. Out of print.
11. Elaine Goodale Eastman. *Pratt:* The Red Man's Moses. Out of print.
12. Althea Bass. *Cherokee Messenger:* A Life of Samuel Austin Worcester.
13. Thomas Wildcat Alford. *Civilization.* As told to Florence Drake. Out of print.
14. Grant Foreman. *Indians and Pioneers:* The Story of the American Southwest Before 1830.
15. George E. Hyde. *Red Cloud's Folk:* A History of the Oglala Sioux Indians.
16. Grant Foreman. *Sequoyah.*
17. Morris L. Wardell. *A Political History of the Cherokee Nation, 1838–1907.* Out of print.
18. John Walton Caughey. *McGillivray of the Creeks.*
19. Edward Everett Dale and Gaston Litton. *Cherokee Cavaliers:*

Forty Years of Cherokee History as Told in the Correspondence of the Ridge-Watie-Boudinot Family.

20. Ralph Henry Gabriel. *Elias Boudinot, Cherokee, and His America*. Out of print.
21. Karl N. Llewellyn and E. Adamson Hoebel. *The Cheyenne Way:* Conflict and Case Law in Primitive Jurisprudence.
22. Angie Debo. *The Road to Disappearance*.
23. Oliver La Farge and others. *The Changing Indian*. Out of print.
24. Carolyn Thomas Foreman. *Indians Abroad*. Out of print.
25. John Adair. *The Navajo and Pueblo Silversmiths*.
26. Alice Marriott. *The Ten Grandmothers*.
27. Alice Marriott. *María:* The Potter of San Ildefonso.
28. Edward Everett Dale. *The Indians of the Southwest:* A Century of Development Under the United States. Out of print.
29. *Popol Vuh:* The Sacred Book of the Ancient Quiché Maya. English version by Delia Goetz and Sylvanus G. Morley from the translation of Adrián Recinos.
30. Walter Collins O'Kane. *Sun in the Sky*.
31. Stanley A. Stubbs. *Bird's-Eye View of the Pueblos*. Out of print.
32. Katharine C. Turner. *Red Men Calling on the Great White Father*.
33. Muriel H. Wright. *A Guide to the Indian Tribes of Oklahoma*.
34. Ernest Wallace and E. Adamson Hoebel. *The Comanches:* Lords of the South Plains.
35. Walter Collins O'Kane. *The Hopis:* Portrait of a Desert People.
36. *The Sacred Pipe:* Black Elk's Account of the Seven Rites of the Oglala Sioux. Edited by Joseph Epes Brown.
37. *The Annals of the Cakchiquels*, translated from the Cakchiquel Maya by Adrián Recinos and Delia Goetz, with *Title of the Lords of Totonicapán*, translated from the Quiché text into Spanish by Dionisio José Chonay, English version by Delia Goetz.
38. R. S. Cotterill. *The Southern Indians:* The Story of the Civilized Tribes Before Removal.
39. J. Eric S. Thompson. *The Rise and Fall of Maya Civilization*. (Revised Edition).
40. Robert Emmitt. *The Last War Trail:* The Utes and the Settlement of Colorado. Out of print.
41. Frank Gilbert Roe. *The Indian and the Horse*.

64. George E. Hyde. *Indians of the Woodlands:* From Prehistoric Times to 1725.
65. Grace Steele Woodward. *The Cherokees.*
66. Donald J. Berthrong. *The Southern Cheyennes.*
67. Miguel León-Portilla. *Aztec Thought and Culture:* A Study of the Ancient Nahuatl Mind. Translated by Jack Emory Davis.
68. T. D. Allen. *Navahos Have Five Fingers.*
69. Burr Cartwright Brundage. *Empire of the Inca.*
70. A. M. Gibson. *The Kickapoos:* Lords of the Middle Border.
71. Hamilton A. Tyler. *Pueblo Gods and Myths.*
72. Royal B. Hassrick. *The Sioux:* Life and Customs of a Warrior Society.
73. Franc Johnson Newcomb. *Hosteen Klah:* Navaho Medicine Man and Sand Painter.
74. Virginia Cole Trenholm and Maurine Carley. *The Shoshonis:* Sentinels of the Rockies.
75. Cohoe. *A Cheyenne Sketchbook.* Commentary by E. Adamson Hoebel and Karen Daniels Petersen.
76. Jack D. Forbes. *Warriors of the Colorado:* The Yumas of the Quechan Nation and Their Neighbors.
77. *Ritual of the Bacabs.* Translated and edited by Ralph L. Roys.
78. Lillian Estelle Fisher. *The Last Inca Revolt, 1780–1783.*
79. Lilly de Jongh Osborne. *Indian Crafts of Guatemala and El Salvador.*
80. Robert H. Ruby and John A. Brown. *Half-Sun on the Columbia:* A Biography of Chief Moses.
81. *The Shadow of Sequoyah:* Social Documents of the Cherokees. Translated and edited by Jack Frederick and Anna Gritts Kilpatrick.
82. Ella E. Clark. *Indian Legends from the Northern Rockies.*
83. *The Indian:* America's Unfinished Business. Compiled by William A. Brophy and Sophie D. Aberle, M.D.
84. M. Inez Hilger, with Margaret A. Mondloch. *Huenun Ñamku:* An Araucanian Indian of the Andes Remembers the Past.
85. Ronald Spores. *The Mixtec Kings and Their People.*
86. David H. Corkran. *The Creek Frontier, 1540–1783.*
87. *The Book of Chilam Balam of Chumayel.* Translated and edited by Ralph L. Roys.

88. Burr Cartwright Brundage. *Lords of Cuzco:* A History and Description of the Inca People in Their Final Days.
89. John C. Ewers. *Indian Life on the Upper Missouri.*
90. Max L. Moorhead. *The Apache Frontier:* Jacobo Ugarte and Spanish-Indian Relations in Northern New Spain, 1769–1791.
91. France Scholes and Ralph L. Roys. *The Maya Chontal Indians of Acalan-Tixchel.*
92. Miguel León-Portilla. *Pre-Columbian Literatures of Mexico.* Translated from the Spanish by Grace Lobanov and the Author.
93. Grace Steele Woodward. *Pocahontas.*
94. Gottfried Hotz. *Eighteenth-Century Skin Paintings.* Translated by Johannes Malthaner.
95. Virgil J. Vogel. *American Indian Medicine.*
96. Bill Vaudrin. *Tanaina Tales from Alaska.* With an introduction by Joan Broom Townsend.
97. Georgiana C. Nammack. *Fraud, Politics, and Dispossession of the Indians:* The Iroquois Land Frontier in the Colonial Period.
98. *The Chronicles of Michoacán.* Translated and edited by Eugene R. Craine and Reginald C. Reindorp.
99. J. Eric S. Thompson. *Maya History and Religion.*
100. Peter J. Powell. *Sweet Medicine:* The Continuing Role of the Sacred Arrows, the Sun Dance, and the Sacred Buffalo Hat in Northern Cheyenne History.
101. Karen Daniels Petersen. *Plains Indian Art from Fort Marion.*
102. Fray Diego Durán. *Book of the Gods and Rites and The Ancient Calendar.* Translated and edited by Fernando Horcasitas and Doris Heyden. Foreword by Miguel León-Portilla.
103. Bert Anson. *The Miami Indians.* Sovereigns of the Wabash.
104. Robert H. Ruby and John A. Brown. *The Spokane Indians:* Children of the Sun. Foreword by Robert L. Bennett.
105. Virginia Cole Trenholm. *The Arapahoes, Our People.*

The paper on which this book is printed bears the watermark of the University of Oklahoma Press and has an effective life of at least three hundred years.